W9-DGY-410

Viva La Mediterranean
A Cultural Feast From HealthMark

by
Jean Oliva-Rasbach, M.S., R.D.
and
Christian W. Schmidt
Executive Chef

DEDICATION

To my husband, Chuck, and son, Eric, who endured an endless array of new foods. Your patience and tastebuds have been greatly appreciated.

And to my mother, who, at an early age, taught me the importance of sound nutrition and instilled the attitude that anyone who can read can cook. So try new things, it can be fun!

© Copyright 1994 by HealthMark Centers, Inc.

All rights reserved. No part of this book may be reproduced or utilized in whole or in part in any form or by any means, electronic or mechanical, including photocopying, recording or information storage and retrieval system, without permission in writing from the author. Exception is granted for brief passages quoted for reviews.

Published by HealthMark Centers, Inc., Englewood, Colorado.
First printing, September, 1994

ISBN # 0-9624784-2-3

FOREWORD

HealthMark was born as a preventive medicine clinic in 1985 with a unique challenge: *How to make healthy food that did not look brown and taste bland, and how to incorporate this into a life-style that was conducive to fun and easy healthful living.* The goal was long-term compliance and not short-term gain.

At that time there was already sufficient evidence to show that severely restrictive diets (8-10% fat) are no better than less restrictive diets (20-25% fat) in lowering cholesterol and triglyceride levels and that diets containing 30% fat do not work. The average intake of fat in the typical American diet is 40% fat.

What matters is long-term compliance and how your life-style looks over a 365-day period and that small indiscretions don't count in the big scheme of things. This led to the famous HealthMark 10% rule, which states, "If you do the right things most of the time (90%), you are allowed 10% indiscretion time. Have fun with it and enjoy without guilt."

Today HealthMark is the leader in the Denver Metroplex providing preventive medicine programs. These include: Comprehensive preventive medical screening and physical examinations; life-style change programs; behavior-based weight-loss programs; worksite health promotion programs that include risk factor screening; and education programs as well as community-based programs that provide labeling of products in supermarkets and of menu items that meet our dietary guidelines in restaurants.

Hot on the heels of our best-selling cookbook *Delitefully HealthMark* comes *Viva La Mediterranean*. This is a feast of wonderful and healthy recipes that are full of color and great taste. So enjoy, be healthy and Bon Appetit.

Robert A. Gleser, M.D.
Founder of HealthMark Centers, Inc.
Denver, Colorado

ACKNOWLEDGMENTS

Many thanks to all the people who have worked to make this book possible:

Rob Gleser for his leadership...

Jill Howell for her business expertise...

Rachael Amos for the superb line drawings and her editing skills...

Kristin Doughty for her creative word processing and page layouts.

Special thanks to Jane Peters, R.D. for her undying efforts in testing and evaluating recipes, analyzing recipes for nutritional content and word processing.

Special thanks to Clarice Oliva and Robin Martin, the primary recipe testers. Their time, effort and reliability have been indispensable.

Jean

To people like Jean Oliva-Rasbach who gave me support in difficult times and kept me going with the project. To Greg Lewis, who is a very special friend and helped me with some of the recipes. Thanks to the Scanticon Denver Culinary Department, Hotel Hershey Culinary Department, Scanticon Princeton Culinary Department, Scanticon Princeton Purchasing Department and the Great American Trading Company, Inc., 320 Victory Drive, VA 22070, Tel. 703-471-4202, fax 703-471-9678 which supplied the Eschenbach porcelain and Singer Equipment Company, 3030 Kutztown Road, Reading, PA 19612, Tel. 215-929-8000, fax 215-929-3060, who supplied the rest of the china and to David Goldberg for his expert photography.

And the people who supported me and this project: Marion Julier, Jorgen Roed, Henry Vergnaud....

And especially my family who gave me the energy to continue and believe in what I'm doing.

And special thanks to Anderson Gibbons, who helped with putting all of the ingredients together and David Goldberg, who did an outstanding job with the food photography.

Christian W. Schmidt

MEDITERRANEAN CUISINE

Does this sound delicious?: A light vegetable soup, made with chicken stock and chopped onions, carrots, celery and garlic, flavored with fresh herbs and a small spoonful of grated Parmigiano-Reggiano cheese; a plate of pasta sauced with small bits of savory ground meat sautéed in olive oil and mixed in with more chopped vegetables and fresh herbs; a loaf of crusty country bread; a piece of fruit, either raw or poached in a light sugar syrup.

That is dinner along the Mediterranean Sea — at a restaurant in Italy's Cinqueterre or in a home in Barcelona; after a day at the souk in Tunis or watching from an Aegean island as the sun goes to bed.

So is this: oven-baked, doughy pizza; risotto and asparagus; pilaf with chicken; Spanish paella. And vegetables with cheeses; bean and lentil soups; grilled fish — and a glass of red wine to help any of this along.

Behold the Mediterranean way of eating, not only good but also good for you.

So have people eaten for centuries, people who sport amazingly low levels of heart disease, diabetes and obesity. To eat this way tastes delicious and is simple to prepare.

Eating in the Mediterranean way emphasizes breads and grains, fresh vegetables and legumes, fish and small amounts of lean meat, and most important, olive oil. The combinations of these foods have been shown, by both anecdotal and scientific history, to be healthfully beneficial.

▼ A LITTLE HISTORY

Perhaps because what is nowadays called "the Mediterranean diet" is so fashionable among cookbook authors, symposia holders and even scientists, we understandably might believe that it is new.

It is not. The distinctive ways of fashioning cooking among the countries that line the Mediterranean Sea is centuries, even millenia, old. It is a style of eating that has perdured because it is healthy — people lived long to recreate it, year after year — and a way of eating that has influenced the cuisines which we consider so familiar.

Without the influence of the Mediterranean and its vast collection of cultures and cooking, we would not have Italian pasta, high French standards for "place of origin" of various foodstuffs or the propagation by Spain of the potato plant and olive tree.

How the Mediterranean way of eating developed is historically fascinating.

Over 6,000 years before the birth of Jesus, Greek traders built up shipping routes throughout the Mediterranean Basin. Greek ships plied the 2,500-mile-long coast of the Mediterranean Sea — what became the coasts of Spain, Egypt, The Maghreb, Turkey, France, Italy, Palestine and other countries.

The constant crossing and recrossing of these shores, by the Phoenicians, Greeks and, later, the Romans, caused much exchange — not only of barter and goods, but of foods as well.

Wild herbs, olives and olive trees, exotic spices, garlic, honey, nuts, oranges, rosewater, wheat and other grains, grapes, rice — all exchanged places, from their native sites to new homes far away.

The "holy trinity" of wheat, olives and grapes (especially in the form of wine) became the hallmark of what became the Mediterranean way of eating. It was not a "Roman" way of eating or a "Greek" manner of cooking or even an Northern African or Turkish way. It was the Mediterranean way.

That manner of cooking and eating continues today.

▼ A WAY OF LIFE

But eating in the Mediterranean manner is not just about food: it is about a way of life, where meals tend to be long and relaxed and where physical activity — walking to work, for instance, or using stairs instead of elevators — is routine.

The Mediterranean way is also an attitude about eating. There is a mindfulness about food.

Thinking about food, frankly, may be the most important facet about life in the Mediterranean. Italians, it is said, talk only about three things: what they ate for their last meal; what they are eating at present; and what they will eat next.

But far from an obsession about food, the consensus along the Mediterranean is that eating is one of the most important things we do, that meals are social activity, that they express communion and community and that they educate the young.

Finally, Mediterranean cooking isn't so much about recipes as it is about ingredients: the freshest, truly ripe tomatoes; dew-new vegetables; naturally-raised meats and fowl; sweet, firm potatoes; fish with the scent of the sea; fresh milk and dairy products, without added stabilizers and preservatives.

Along the Mediterranean, recipes follow the seasons and the markets. Foods are eaten at their proper time in season and only the best possible provenance finds its way to the kitchen. An Italian friend says that, even when the family was poor, the food budget was the last to be shaved.

▼ THE FOUR KEY ELEMENTS OF THE MEDITERRANEAN WAY OF EATING

Four key tenets characterize the Mediterranean way of eating. Let's take a look at them in turn, contrasting them with the somewhat less healthy, common American way of eating and living.

1. Energy from grains, fruits and vegetables.

Many of the best known Mediterranean foods are based in grains (corn, wheat and rice): polenta, bread, pita, couscous, pasta, pilaf and risotto. Very often, these grains are paired with vegetables, as in recipes calling for steamed vegetables in a pilaf or tomato sauces for polenta.

The Mediterranean basin raises many fruits and vegetables which are also favorites of Americans as well: tomatoes, eggplant, zucchini, onions, carrots, peppers, apples, oranges, peaches and apricots. Think of all the Mediterranean recipes calling for mixtures of vegetables: ratatouille, gazpacho, salads and salsas.

Mediterraneans are far ahead of North Americans in the consumption of fruits, vegetables and grains. Fewer than 10% of us eat the recommended minimum of five servings a day. Almost all Mediterraneans daily eat twice as many fruits and vegetables and five times as many grains as we do.

2. Meat occasionally.

In Mediterranean countries, meat is used in sauces or mixed in with vegetables or eaten only on, say, Sundays or special days. The idea of sitting down to attack a large slab of beef doesn't occur to those along the Mediterranean. Red meat is simply not the main source for protein.

That's good news about the consumption of saturated fats — a big help to the heart. Think of how meat is consumed in Mediterranean countries: in Italy, as see-through thin slices of prosciutto wrapped around fresh figs; in France, as stews of vegetables and starches merely flavored with meat; or in Greece, as only one part of deep-dish pies.

3. Fat from plant oils and olive oil over all.

In the war against fats, olive oil has the edge on causing the least harm. It seems to do good things to cholesterol, especially in the relationship between "good" cholesterol (HDL) and "bad" cholesterol (LDL). Reducing overall fat intake lowers both sorts of cholesterol, but using olive oil is effective in lowering LDL while maintaining levels of HDL.

In Greece, olive oil is practically a beverage. It is used to flavor foods, much the way we used to slather ketchup on meats, potatoes and eggs: as a condiment. It is the universal choice for dressing vegetables in Greece — never butter.

Even with the ubiquitous use of olive oil, the Mediterranean diet is lower in total fat consumption than our typical American diet. One study, for example, showed that fat provided about 25% of the total diet in southern Italy.

4. Moderate consumption of wine.

The value of two glasses of wine per day has been argued for years, and today there may be some evidence linking it to the prevention of heart disease! While we would never prescribe alcohol for medicinal purposes, if the occasion is right, enjoy it. With great Mediterranean food, the occasion almost always seems right.

It is inconceivable that a lunch in Corfu or a dinner in Barcelona would occur without wine. (Of course, in the several Moslem countries along the Mediterranean, alcohol is forbidden — though wine production in Algeria, Tunisia and Palestine is at an all-time high.)

— *Bill St. John*

TABLE OF CONTENTS

CONTRIBUTORS

In addition to the authors, the following people have contributed recipes:

Ann-Marie Dow

Nuria Fabrellas

Robin Martin

Mary Medici

Paul's Place Restaurant

Clarice Oliva

Sadie Oliva

Rosemarie Schutte

Joan Wilson

TESTERS

All of the recipes contained in this book were tested in typical American households. Many thanks to the testers named below. They gave generously of their time to prepare and evaluate numerous recipes.

PRIMARY TESTERS

Robin Martin
Clarice Oliva
Jane Peters

OTHER TESTERS

Foy Bailey
Marilyn Bernstein
Dian Boberick
Carol Brezczek
Beth Brown
Pat Carlson
Joan E. Carter
Samantha Cerney
Susan Cervey
Judy Coffee
Pattie Dore
Janet Fethke
Kathy Handley
Linda Harris
Lorrie Heinson
Ray Herr
Donna Hoffbuhr
Eileen Horn
Trudy Kuzava
Phyllis Manning
Dave Martin
Antoinette Martinez

Anne Mason
Karen Muir
Melanie Neal
Linda Osmundson
Don Paul
Wayne Peters
Troy A. Pickett
Julie Reagan
Shannan Sawyer
Eileen Schoen
Roey Schmidt
Rosemarie Schutte
Kirk Schlueter
Sherma Sloan
Cindy Suiter
Marti Stebbins
Linda Twenhofel
Laurie Vaggalis
Tammy VanOpdorp
Patty Wagner
Steven Yannicelli

NUTRITION ANALYSIS

All recipes were analyzed using the Food Processor PLUS computer-based nutritional analysis program from ESHA Research Salem, OR. Nutrients reported are calories, protein, carbohydrate, total fat, cholesterol, dietary fiber and sodium. A further breakdown of the types of fats is included (saturated fat, monounsaturated fat and polyunsaturated fat). The total value of the types of fat will be slightly less than the value reported for total fat because of rounding and the omission of small fractions of other fatty acids.

Also reported is the percent of calories derived from protein, carbohydrate, fat and alcohol.

Nutrition information is reported per serving unless otherwise stated. The number of servings is indicated directly under the recipe name.

The recipes were adjusted to be as low in total fat, saturated fat, cholesterol and sodium as possible, while retaining optimum flavor. The fat content goal was 30% calories as fat, or less than 5 grams of fat per serving. Some very low-calorie recipes such as salad dressings and salads are higher than 30% calories as fat, but the total fat content is 5 grams or less per serving. (See HealthMark dietary guidelines *(p. 3)* for assistance in determining your recommended daily fat intake.)

The maximum allowable cholesterol level was set at 150 mg per serving. You will find some items containing shellfish to be slightly higher in cholesterol.

The target sodium level was 800 mg per serving. All recipes that state "salt to taste" were calculated without added salt. To learn more about sodium, see HealthMark dietary guidelines. There are a few shellfish recipes that exceed this limit. If you are following a sodium-restricted diet, you are advised to avoid these items.

HEALTHMARK DIETARY GOALS

The recipes in this book are based on the dietary principles of HealthMark listed below. At HealthMark, we teach the art of balance and moderation, but do not expect perfection. If you can follow the dietary guidelines 90% of the time, your health risks due to your diet are greatly diminished. In this book, you will find some desserts that are "HealthMark" and some that are "almost HealthMark." "Almost HealthMark" items are to be used in your food plan no more than 10% of the time. That is a time when you choose not to follow the guidelines but are careful not to "throw caution to the wind." The 10% time rule allows for greater flexibility without the all-or-nothing rules.

▼ *Dietary Goal #1:* The primary dietary goal at HealthMark is to reduce the total amount of fat people eat. The recommended upper limit is 20% of total calories from fat. That translates to 45 grams of fat per day for a 2000-calorie food plan.

Individuals who are following a calorie-restricted food plan, trying to lose weight, or have high serum cholesterol, will find that 20% of calories will translate to 30-35 grams of fat per day.

Although HealthMark's dietary goals state 20% calories as fat, each individual food is not required to be only 20% calories as fat. There are many foods we hope you are eating that are fat free: such as fruits, vegetables, breads and grains. The target fat content for the recipes in this book was 30% calories as fat, with a total fat content below 12 grams per serving. In most cases the total fat is considerably below 12 grams per serving. When you are determining how much fat you should be eating, it is better to rely on the actual fat grams eaten instead of using percentages.

We do not eliminate fat from the diet completely because it has a few important functions, such as aiding in proper growth, maintaining healthy skin, carrying fat-soluble vitamins in the body and aiding satiety (the feeling of satisfaction after eating).

Eating too much fat and cholesterol can increase your risk of heart disease, atherosclerosis, obesity and cancer. Reducing total fat consumption is the first step, but balancing the different types of fat is also important.

▼ *Dietary Goal #2:* Saturated fat intake should be no more than 15 grams (1 tablespoon) daily.

Saturated fat is found mostly in animal protein, with the exception of two plant sources: coconut and palm oil. It is solid at room temperature. The most important thing to remember about saturated fat is that eating saturated fat raises your blood cholesterol about three times more than does eating cholesterol.

Common sources of saturated fat include:
- ▼ red meat (T-Bone, ribs, ham, pork chops, rib-eye)
- ▼ whole-milk dairy products (whole milk, cheeses, whole-milk yogurt)
- ▼ chicken and turkey skin
- ▼ coconut and palm oil
- ▼ hydrogenated oils (solid shortening) and partially hydrogenated oils (found in many processed foods)
- ▼ cocoa butter
- ▼ lard
- ▼ butter

Monounsaturated fat is the best fat choice. It helps lower the LDL portion of your cholesterol (the bad stuff) without lowering the HDL portion (the good stuff). Limit yourself to 15 grams per day. Sources are:
- ▼ olive oil and olives
- ▼ canola oil
- ▼ peanut oil, peanuts and peanut butter

Polyunsaturated fat is the third type of fat. It helps lower the LDL, but also lowers HDL (we want HDL to be high). It is found in:
- ▼ vegetable oils (corn, safflower, soy, sunflower and cottonseed)
- ▼ fish oils (omega-3 fatty acids)
- ▼ margarine
- ▼ salad dressings
- ▼ mayonnaise

Remember, unsaturated fats are better for your heart than saturated fat, BUT **all fat is still 9 calories per gram** and is stored in the body as fat if not used.

▼ *Dietary Goal #3:* Cholesterol intake should be kept at 150 mg per day on average. Cholesterol is a wax-like substance produced in the body. It is necessary for the release of adrenaline and transportation of hormones in the body. The liver produces almost all the cholesterol we need; therefore, you do not need to eat cholesterol to stay alive.

Food cholesterol is found **only** in animal products:
- ▼ meats, poultry, fish, seafood, dairy products and egg yolks

Saturated fat and cholesterol are found together in many foods, such as meats and dairy products. Since studies show that eating saturated fat has a more profound affect on blood cholesterol than does dietary cholesterol, we know that the issue is fat, not cholesterol. However, if you keep your saturated fat intake at the recommended levels, your dietary cholesterol intake will most likely take care of itself.

▼ *Dietary Goal #4:* Eat more complex carbohydrates and fiber. The main role of complex carbohydrates is to provide your body with energy. Complex carbohydrates include breads, grains, pasta, vegetables and fruits. Your diet should consist of 60% of calories derived from these carbohydrates.

Fiber provides bulk. HealthMark recommends that you eat 25-35 grams of fiber daily. The average American consumes only 10-15 grams of fiber daily. Fiber is found in whole grains, oats, vegetables and fruits. Eating more fiber can help to decrease your risk for colon cancer and will also help to fill you up!

▼ *Dietary Goal #5:* Limit consumption of sodium. Excess sodium is not the problem we used to think it was. Those individuals with hypertension (high blood pressure) should still restrict their sodium intake. HealthMark recommends limiting sodium intake to 2400 mg daily. That is equivalent to 1 teaspoon of salt. If you don't have hypertension, you should still limit your sodium intake to a reasonable level. When people begin to decrease the salt in their foods, they need to do it slowly. You are trying to achieve a taste change, and taste changes come slowly. Most of the recipes in this book state "salt to taste" to account for individual preferences in salt intake and desire for salt taste. Let your better judgment and your tastebuds be your guide. Taste before salting. Expand your flavors by using fresh herbs and lemon in place of salt.

▼ *Dietary Goal #6:* Limit your consumption of refined sugars and alcohol. Although sugar is a carbohydrate it is a simple carbohydrate, which is not the same as a complex carbohydrate. They are recommended in smaller quantities, especially if you are diabetic. Other health reasons for limiting sugar intake include: 1) reducing dental cavities: (the number-one health risk for eating sugar); 2) reducing the risk of elevated triglyceride levels which are related to your body weight, alcohol intake and sugar intake. Elevated triglycerides are a risk factor for coronary artery disease; and 3) body weight, which is a personal issue. If you are trying to lose weight, refined sugar should be restricted simply for reasons of caloric content. For sugar intake, you make the decision as to how much is too much. The desserts in this book were primarily designed to be low in fat. Some alterations have been made for sugar content, but that was not the primary goal.

Use the dietary goals to guide your food choices throughout the day. Each food or meal does not have to equal 20% of calories as fat. Your average for the day, which includes fat-free fruits, breads and cereals, should be 20% calories as fat. It seems to be more helpful if you just count your grams of fat rather than dealing with percentages. By keeping track of your total fat grams, you can incorporate some higher-fat treats and still come out just fine. Strive for balance and variety — eating is much more enjoyable that way.

Recipe Modification Suggestions

As we become more aware of the relationship between lifestyle choices and diseases such as heart disease, stroke, diabetes, certain cancers and obesity, eating habits are changing. The health-conscious cook reads recipes with an eye toward reducing or eliminating some of the ingredients that play havoc with our health. With a bit of modification most recipes can be "lightened" without sacrificing taste or visual appeal.

Read every recipe with an eye toward eliminating as much fat, cholesterol, sodium and sugar as possible without sacrificing flavor or quality. Don't hesitate to experiment with recipes to find out what works best. Fat, salt and sugar can usually be reduced without significantly altering flavor or texture.

Use the following tips and techniques to guide you as you modify favorite recipes and develop new dishes destined to become family — and company — favorites.

Reducing Fat

1. Use lean cuts of meat *(see table p. 16)* and trim all visible fat before cooking.

2. Cook poultry without the skin; reduce cooking time slightly to keep it moist. You may grill frozen, skinless chicken breasts without thawing. They will retain more moisture.

3. Substitute skinless chicken and turkey for red meat. Turkey works well in recipes that call for pork or veal.

4. Use cooking methods and utensils that minimize or eliminate using fat to cook. Broil, bake, roast, poach or stir-fry instead of pan frying or deep-fat frying. Be sure to use non-stick cookware; coat lightly with cooking spray or brush lightly with oil, if necessary, to keep food from sticking.

6. Sauté in non-stick cookware using minimal amounts of olive oil or sauté with broth, wine or water (cover the pan if necessary to prevent liquid from evaporating). Microwave mushrooms, onions, zucchini and other vegetables in a covered container in place of sautéeing.

7. Prepare stocks, soups, sauces and stews ahead of time; chill, then remove all hardened fat. If there is not time to do this, skim off as much fat as possible, then add several ice cubes. Fat will congeal and cling to the ice cubes, which can then be discarded.

8. Reduce the amount of fat in baked goods by one-third to one-half. Use canola oil whenever possible. Quick breads and muffins are just as good when made with canola oil rather than a more saturated fat such as butter, shortening or stick margarine.

   To add moisture to baked goods (such as muffins) when reducing oil, add any of the following in place of the eliminated oil: applesauce, mashed bananas, crushed pineapple, cranberries, pumpkin, grated zucchini, grated carrots.

   Substitute soft margarine for butter or stick margarine when a recipe calls for creaming butter and sugar together. This will give better results than using oil. Experiment with recipes to see what works best; soft (tub) margarines contain more air and water than stick margarine and will not work in all circumstances.

   Certain recipes, such as cakes, are too difficult to adjust; enjoy these as an occasional treat or use a lowfat recipe.

9. Use nonfat or 1% dairy products (milk, yogurt or cottage cheese). Use evaporated skim milk in soups, sauces and baking.

10. Purchase lowfat or part-skim cheese (no more than 5 grams of fat per ounce) and use less than called for in the recipe, because even lowfat cheese is high in fat. Look for skim-milk ricotta cheese.

11. To make rich sauces without cream, add ¼ to ⅓ cup nonfat dry milk into one cup of liquid nonfat milk. Stir well before using to dissolve powdered milk. Use this "HealthMark cream" in place of the cream or whole milk called for in a recipe. Use this same technique to create creamy sauces with a chicken or beef flavor. Substitute salt-free, defatted chicken or beef stock for liquid nonfat milk. Add a touch of dry white or red wine or sherry for an elegant flavor.

12. Replace sour cream with either nonfat drained yogurt or nonfat sour cream depending on the consistency and flavor desired in the recipe. Nonfat yogurt is tart and thinner than nonfat sour cream. To use in cooking, blend 1 to 2 tablespoons of flour or one tablespoon of cornstarch into the yogurt before adding it to the recipe. Heat gently to prevent curdling.

   For a thicker consistency, drain yogurt overnight in the refrigerator. Place yogurt in a strainer lined with cheesecloth or several coffee filters. Cover and suspend over a bowl to catch the liquid that will drain off. This is called yogurt cheese and may be eaten plain or with herbs added. It is good for dips and salad dressings.

13. Substitute 3 tablespoons unsweetened cocoa powder and 1 tablespoon oil for 1 ounce baking chocolate.

14. Eliminate nuts from a recipe or use only ¼ to ⅓ cup.

REDUCING CHOLESTEROL

1. Reduce the amount of meat, fish or poultry in a recipe — 3 to 4 ounces per serving is ample.

2. Avoid organ meats, which are very high in cholesterol. Also, use seafoods such as shrimp, crab, lobster and calamari (squid) sparingly because they are high in cholesterol.

3. Use fewer egg yolks and whole eggs. In baking, substitute 1-2 egg whites for each whole egg. As the number of eggs in a recipe increases, decrease the whites. For example, in place of 2 eggs use 4 whites, but in place of 4 eggs, use 1 whole egg plus 6 whites.

4. Use eggless pasta in place of pasta made with egg yolks (most is eggless unless specified on the label).

5. Use nonfat or 1% dairy products to reduce cholesterol, fat and calories. Replace whole-milk cheese with cheeses made from skim or part-skim milk, such as part-skim mozzarella.

REDUCING SALT AND SODIUM

1. Your taste for salt will diminish as you gradually reduce the amount you use. If salt is necessary in a recipe, use sparingly.

2. Even though nothing else tastes exactly like salt, other seasonings will enhance the flavor of foods and compensate for the salt you have eliminated. Use the following seasonings to add zest to foods: fresh lemon or lime juice; lemon or lime zest; flavored vinegars (e.g. tarragon, raspberry, wine); dried onion flakes; onion or garlic powder; pepper; hot pepper sauce; mustard and herb blends.

3. Condiments such as soy sauce, Worcestershire™ sauce, hot pepper sauce and mustard are relatively high in sodium, but if used sparingly can enliven foods without overdoing the sodium.

4. Eliminate or reduce salt in all recipes except yeast breads, where salt is necessary to control growth of the yeast. Even in yeast breads salt can usually be reduced.

5. Crush dried herbs before using to release more flavor.

6. Buy salt-free or low-sodium canned vegetables, beans, tomato sauce and tomato paste.

7. Use wines and liqueurs — sparingly — to flavor foods. If cooked at or above boiling temperature, the alcohol evaporates, eliminating most of the calories while the flavor remains.

8. Rinse canned seafood (such as tuna, salmon, shrimp, crab, clams), vegetables and beans to reduce salt content.

REDUCING SUGAR

1. In most recipes, sugar can be reduced by one-third to one-half. In cookies, bars and cakes, replace the sugar you have eliminated with nonfat dry milk.

2. Brown sugar or honey may be substituted for white sugar; both are slightly sweeter than white sugar, therefore less can be used (as above). Nutritionally, they are all similar; there is no nutritional advantage to brown sugar or honey.

3. When sugar is decreased, enhance flavor with spices (cinnamon, nutmeg or cloves) and extracts (vanilla, almond, orange or lemon). Doubling the amount of vanilla called for increases the sweetness without adding calories.

   The amount of spice may also be increased to boost flavor when sugar is decreased, but be careful of strong spices, such as cloves and ginger, as they can easily overpower the recipe. The safest spices to increase are cinnamon, nutmeg and allspice.

4. When reducing sugar in quick breads, cakes and cookies, use fruits which add sweetness naturally such as raisins, dried apricots, dates or bananas.

5. For added sweetness, soak raisins and other dried fruit in hot water (or a liqueur) for 10 to 15 minutes then add to the batter along with the soaking liquid.

6. When using canned fruits, choose juice- or water-packed fruits.

ADDING FIBER

1. Use whole-wheat flour whenever possible. It is heavier than white flour, so use less: $7/8$ cup whole-wheat flour to 1 cup white flour. Experiment to find out what works best in a recipe. Some recipes will turn out well with all whole-wheat flour, others are better when half whole-wheat and half white (unbleached) flour is used.

    Also, try whole-wheat pastry flour. It can be substituted for all of the white flour in a recipe as it has a lighter texture than whole-wheat flour, but has the same fiber content.

2. Add wheat bran, oat bran or oatmeal to baked goods, cereals, casseroles, soups and pancakes. Start with one or two tablespoons and increase gradually. Substitute up to ½ cup oatmeal or oat bran for part of the flour in baked goods.

3. Use more vegetables, whole grains (bulgur, brown rice, corn, barley and oatmeal), dried beans, split peas and lentils.

COOK'S TIPS

▼ Add flavor to baked goods, sauces and other dishes by adding zest, the thin outer layer of an orange, lemon or other citrus peel. Use a zester (a tool available in cookware stores) or a grater to remove the zest.

▼ Fresh herbs have the best flavor, but if not available, substitute ½ to 1 teaspoon dried herb per tablespoon of fresh herb. Give dried herbs a fresh taste by mixing with an equal amount of chopped fresh parsley, then let stand 10 to 15 minutes before using.

▼ Olive oil and canola oil are the best choices for cooking oils. Use olive oil for sautéeing and salad dressings; choose canola for baking.

▼ Bake in non-stick pans coated with cooking spray or brush pan lightly with oil.

▼ A ¼ cup measure is just the right size for scooping muffin batter into a muffin cup.

▼ Muffins and other baked goods can easily be prepared in the food processor: measure dry ingredients into work bowl first and pulse until just blended; add nuts and/or dried fruit and pulse until chopped. Add liquid ingredients and pulse until batter is just blended.

▼ Microwave lemons and limes for 10-15 seconds before juicing. It makes juicing easier and you get a larger yield.

▼ Honey is easier to measure when warmed.

▼ To substitute honey for sugar, decrease liquid in the recipe by ¼ cup. If recipe has no liquid added, add 4 tablespoons flour. Decrease baking temperature by 25° to prevent overbrowning.

▼ Measure oil first, then honey will slide out of the cup easily.

▼ If unsalted nuts are not available, rinse salted nuts then toast briefly before using.

▼ Eggs are easiest to separate when cold; the whites beat up to greatest volume at room temperature.

▼ If fresh orange juice is not available, substitute frozen orange concentrate — one tablespoon equals about ¼ cup fresh juice.

▼ For best results, preheat oven before baking.

▼ Prick meat all over with a fork to allow marinade to penetrate thoroughly.

▼ To prevent skinless chicken from drying out, reduce cooking time by a few minutes.

▼ Wash poultry with warm water before using to decrease bacteria and minimize chance of illness. Be sure to wash hands, utensils, cutting board, sink and anything else that comes in contact with raw poultry.

▼ Cook beef and buffalo to 180° F internal tenperature to avoid contamination with E. coli. We advise against eating rare beef.

Substitutes for Healthy Cooking

Use:	In Place Of:
Skim milk	Whole or 2% milk
Nonfat dry milk	Cream; non-dairy creamer
Evaporated skim milk	Evaporated whole milk
Nonfat yogurt	Lowfat or regular yogurt
1% cottage cheese	2% or 4% cottage cheese
Part-skim, lowfat, or fat-free cheese	Regular cheese
Nonfat yogurt or drained nonfat yogurt, fat-free sour cream	Sour cream
Nonfat frozen yogurt, fruit ice, sorbet, ice milk, or fat-free ice cream	Ice cream
Liquid margarine, canola oil or olive oil	Butter, stick margarine
Egg whites, egg substitute	Whole eggs or egg yolks
Eggless pasta	Egg noodles or pasta
Marinara sauce or commercial fat-free sauces	Cheese or cream sauce for pasta
Lowfat dressing or fat-free dressing	Blue cheese or creamy dressing

COOKING TECHNIQUES

Al dente:

A term used to define the degree of tenderness of cooked pasta. The pasta should be just cooked, not hard, but not mushy. It should still have some body.

Blanch:

Drop the food into boiling water for a minimal amount of time, remove quickly and chill. Blanching is used to set the color, and partially cook, but it also keeps the greatest amount of nutrients and flavor content.

Cleaning and Cooking Live Mussels and Clams:

Scrub the mussels and pull off their "beards" (that black fuzzy stuff hanging out of the shell). Discard any mussels which are broken or open. You can keep live mussels for a day in the refrigerator in a bucket of cold salted water. To cook, place mussels in a saucepan with ¼-inch water. Cover and boil. The shells will open in 3-10 minutes. Remove from heat immediately and discard any which remain closed. Clams can also be prepared in the same way.

Julienne:

Cut the vegetables into thin strips similar to match sticks.

Parboil:

Cook vegetables in boiling water until just tender when pricked with a fork.

Reduction:

Created with a combination of different flavors, i.e. wines, liqueurs, herbs, etc., and finished with your desired stock. You then reduce the sauce to the desired consistency.

To roast peppers, garlic and shallots:

Heat grill to hottest setting, or heat broiler. Place whole washed vegetables on the grill. Sear until all sides are black. Remove the vegetables to a large pan and cover with a lid. (May also place in a paper bag.) Let sit 15 minutes, then remove skin.

Roux:

A binding material that can be made with 1½ tablespoons of liquid margarine and 2 tablespoons of flour. (Yields approximately 3 cups.) To prepare: preheat margarine over medium heat, then sift flour into the margarine. Stir constantly with wooden spoon for a few minutes. Do not allow the sauce to turn brown.

Salmon rose:
> To prepare the rose, fold thin slices of smoked or raw salmon into a rose or flower shape.

Toasting seeds, nuts and bread crumbs:
> Use a non-stick frying pan. Place item in cool pan. Heat over medium heat shaking from time to time. May also use a toaster oven. Place item on the tray, turn on to toast. Use low setting and repeat until you have obtained the desired color.

Tomatoes, peel and seed:
> Bring a pan of water to boiling. Drop the whole tomato into the boiling water for 1-2 minutes. Remove tomato and gently peel off the skin. Cut the tomato in half and gently squeeze out the seeds.

Whisk:
> Beat rapidly using a whisk. A whisk is a cooking utensil that consists of many curved wires. It helps to keep sauces smooth.

Zest:
> Using a tool called a zester, remove the outer colored portion of a lemon, lime or orange. Avoid using the white portion because it is bitter. If you do not have a zester you may use a grater.

DEFINITIONS OF FOOD ITEMS

FOOD ITEMS

▼ **Beans:**

Garbanzo (chick-peas) is the Spanish name for chick-peas. They are found in Spain and Greece and have a whitish-yellow color. They are used in a variety of salads, soups, stews and purées.

Kidney beans (red) originated in France. They are used in many vegetable dishes, stews and salads.

Lima beans are a native of South America that are now grown extensively in California and Florida. They are prepared just like navy beans.

Navy beans (white) have a round and white appearance with a starchy texture. They are a member of the kidney-bean family and are very popular in France.

When using dry beans, sort through them carefully. Remove any shrivelled beans and small stones. Rinse beans thoroughly and soak overnight. Discard the soaking water before cooking to decrease the gas that beans cause. If using canned beans, look for the low-sodium type, and drain and rinse well. The recipes were calculated using dry beans, unless canned beans were specifically called for in the recipe.

▼ **Bouquet garni:** This is a vegetable and herb bundle. It usually consists of washed, cleaned carrots, celery, leeks, onions, cabbage and fresh herbs, such as a bay leaf, thyme and oregano, and tied with a string or rolled in cheese cloth. This is an item you must assemble yourself. You may make it as simple or elaborate as you wish.

▼ **Croutons:** There is a fat-free version located in the specialty or diet section of a full-service grocery store. We have also included a recipe for croutons in the book *(see p. 536)*.

▼ **Defatted beef stock:** If you made your own beef/veal stock using our recipe, there is no need to de-fat the broth. If you purchased your beef stock in a can, make sure you choose a low-sodium version. It will still contain fat. The simplest way to remove this fat is to place the unopened can in the refrigerator for a few hours. When you open the can, the fat will have hardened and be floating on top of the broth. Simply scoop it out and discard it.

▼ **Egg substitutes:** Egg substitutes are simply egg whites that have been homogenized and then colored. When choosing an egg substitute, look for ones that are colored with carotene instead of yellow dye #5. Some frozen egg products contain egg yolks (read your labels). Other egg substitutes contain oil. You must consider the oil in your final fat count. Use egg whites whenever possible to save money.

▼ **Fat content of meats:**
   3.5 ounces of cooked meat

Type of meat	Fat (grams)	% calories as fat
Beef (select grade)		
Eye of round	6	30
Top round	6	28
Chuck	9	36
Top loin	8	38
Sirloin	9	38
Tenderloin	10	43
Chicken		
Breast, no skin	4	21
Breast, with skin	8	36
Drum, no skin	6	31
Thigh, no skin	11	47
Wing, with skin	19	59
Lamb		
Leg	8	38
Loin chop	10	45
Shoulder	11	48
Pork		
Tenderloin	5	27
Center Loin	8	45
Fresh Ham (leg)	11	45
Turkey		
Breast, no skin	1	7
Breast, with skin	3	18
Leg, no skin	2	17
Wing, no skin	10	43
Veal		
Leg	3	18
Sirloin	6	32
Loin chop	7	36
Shoulder roast	7	37

▼ **Fennel:** A vegetable found in regular grocery stores during the spring and summer. Many specialty stores will carry it year round. It looks something like celery, but the base is a very round white bulb. It has stalks and fern-like leaves. To use, clean carefully and chop only the white portions. It has a mild anise flavor.

▼ **Flour:**

Bread flour — A high-gluten flour used for breads. It is found in regular grocery stores.

Gluten — Pure gluten flour. This is found in specialty stores. Use this when making breads if you do not have bread flour. Use only 1 tablespoon per loaf of bread.

Semolina — It is yellow and coarse and used primarily for making pasta. It is usually found is specialty stores or natural food stores. Buy it in bulk.

Whole-wheat pastry flour — A whole-wheat flour that has been ground finer that regular whole-wheat flour. It makes a smoother product. Usually found in specialty stores or natural food stores. Save money and buy it in bulk.

▼ **Greens: (flavor and uses)**

Belgian endive looks like a small cone with a yellow top. It is wonderful with all kinds of salads but also may be used as a vegetable. If not properly handled or stored it easily gets bitter. It has a crunchy, light-bitter taste.

Bibb lettuce is light green with a yellow heart. It has a mild flavor and is used primarily for salads and garnishes.

Escarole is known as the European iceberg lettuce because it has a similar flavor and is used the same way.

Kale is a member of the cabbage family but used mostly as a decorative food item. It can be used just like cabbage, but the leaves are tougher.

Leaf lettuce, green and red is similar to bibb lettuce and has a mild flavor. It is widely used for garnishes, sandwiches and variety of different salads.

Radiccio is in the endive family. It is a small head of red lettuce with a bitter taste. It is used mostly in combination salads and as a garnish, especially in Italian cuisine.

Romaine is a leaf lettuce that is green on the outside with light yellow leaves inside. It has a mild flavor and can be used as salad or as vegetable to be steamed, braised, etc.

Savoy cabbage is similar to white cabbage but milder in flavor and softer in texture. It can be used just like cabbage.

Spinach — Use tender young leaves. Remove the stems by tearing them out.

▼ **Herbs:** All herbs can be dried by hanging them upside down, just like sun-dried tomatoes. Dried herbs should be used in smaller quantities because their flavors are more concentrated. Overuse causes bitterness and a foul taste.

Basil has many different species (opal basil, mint basil, shortleaf basil, etc.). The traditional one comes from Eastern Asia and Central Europe. The leaves have one of the most desired aromatic flavors. They are used in many dishes such as tomato recipes, Italian dishes, ratatouille, salads, roasts, ragouts, soups, dressings and vinegars.

Oregano comes from Italy and Mexico. It originated from the Marjoram family and it has a similar aromatic flavor. It is used in soups, vegetables, ragouts, pizzas, egg dishes, lamb, veal, Greek salads and mushrooms.

Parsley grows all over the Mediterranean countries (almost like a weed) and can be harvested many times throughout the year. The roots have been used in different dishes for seasoning since they have a stronger flavor than the leaf itself. The leaves are mainly used for garnishing, and in salads, soups and sauces. Parsley is used mainly to accompany other dishes; don't cook with it, but rather season with it.

Rosemary is grown in small and large-leaved bunches. The smaller-leaved variety is not as overpowering in flavor. Rosemary has wonderful aromatic flavors and may be used in stews, roasts, marinades, vegetables (especially eggplants), mushrooms, sauces and ratatouille.

Sage originated in Europe. It grows almost 4 feet high and has grayish-looking leaves. The flavor is distinctive and very aromatic. Sage should be used in small quantities in items such as poultry, sauces, meats, game, seafood, rice, egg dishes, tomato dishes and stuffing.

Thyme originated in France, Spain and Yugoslavia. It is a small-leaved herb that is grown in small bushes. It has a strong aromatic flavor and is used usually in small quantities for ragouts, sauces, soups, stuffings, seafoods, game, patés, terrines and marinades.

▼ **Italian seasoning:** This can be found in a jar in the dry-spice section of your grocery store. If you do not have this, you may substitute parsley, oregano, basil and thyme in your recipes.

▼ **Leeks:** They look like a giant scallion, usually 1-inch in diameter with a white bulb at the bottom. The stalks are stiff, flat and long. When using a leek, remove the roots. Begin slicing from the white portion. You will begin to find dirt the farther up you go — so keep rinsing the dirt out. Cut until the stalks seem to be too tough.

▼ **Lentils:** Light brown, light red and olive green are very popular throughout Europe and are used in soups, vegetable dishes, purées, salads and stews.

▼ **Marsala:** A wine used in Italian cooking. It has a sherry-like flavor. You may substitute dry sherry for Marsala if you wish.

▼ **Mushrooms, dried:** Found in packages in your grocery store. Check in the produce section as well as the specialty-food section. The mushrooms will have to be reconstituted by soaking them in warm water.

▼ **Oils:** Featured in this book are monounsaturated fats, such as olive oil. It is recommended that you choose a darker olive oil because it will have the most flavor. The light versions are only lighter in color and flavor (because of a different processing method). They still contain the same amount of fat and calories. (Refer to the dietary goals section *(see p. 3)* for more information.) The other monounsaturated oil used throughout the book is canola oil.

All oils should be stored in the refrigerator to prevent oxidation. Use a small bottle for your olive oil. When refrigerated, it will solidify. The smaller volume will warm up to room temperature more quickly than a large bottle.

▼ **Pesto:** Is made from basil, olive oil, parmesan cheese and pine nuts. It is very high in fat. You can make your own or purchase it in your grocery store. Buy only a small jar and use sparingly. You can eliminate the oil for a "mock pesto."

▼ **Scallions:** Also called green onions. They have a white bulb at the bottom and long, thin green stalks. When using scallions, remove the roots and then chop the entire bulb and stalk.

▼ **Spices:**
Cinnamon is from the Far East, but is used throughout Greece, Spain and France. It has a delicate flavor.

Cloves are a dried flower. Cloves have both a strong flavor and a strong fragrance. They are used in desserts, marinades, stews and seafood dishes.

Cumin is a very stong spice and is used in many Spanish and Moroccan dishes.

Paprika is a Hungarian pepper. It has a strong red-orange color and is used in stews, risottos, soups and meats. Be careful not to roast paprika because it will become bitter.

Saffron is from a specific variety of crocus. It has both a strong flavor and strong color, and is used in many Spanish dishes. Saffron is very expensive, so use it sparingly, but don't avoid it, the flavor is wonderful.

Turmeric is from the ground root of a tropical plant. It has a powerful yellow color, but a mild flavor, and is used in many Spanish dishes.

▼ **Stock, chicken or beef:** May be purchased in the spice section of your grocery store. Some stores also carry soup bases. These make a reasonable substitute. In general, most of these products contain MSG. If you have reactions to MSG, you should avoid commercial stocks.

The best suggestion is to make an entire stock recipe one day and freeze it in 1-cup portions. Put the frozen product in a freezer bag for future use. The stock will maintain its quality for 3-6 months.

▼ **Vegetable brunoise:** Very finely diced assortment of vegetables.

▼ **Yogurt, drained:** Also known as yogurt cheese. To prepare, place a colander or strainer in a bowl. Place a coffee filter or cheesecloth in the strainer. Pour the nonfat plain yogurt into the filter paper and cover it with plastic wrap. Place the entire apparatus in the refrigerator. Let the yogurt drain for 4-24 hours. The longer it drains, the thicker it will be. When finished, discard the yellow liquid that has accumulated in the bowl. Transfer the drained yogurt back into the yogurt carton. (Some brands of yogurt will not drain due to the binders they contain.)

Useful Kitchen Supplies

BLENDER
BROILER PAN
COFFEE GRINDER
DOUBLE BOILER
FOOD MILL
FOOD PROCESSOR
GARLIC PRESS
GRILL: charcoal or gas
LEMON JUICER
MEAT POUNDER
MORTAR AND PESTLE
NON-STICK PANS: frying pans / saucepans / soup pots / baking sheets
STEAMER
WHISKS
ZESTER

Conversions

1 teaspoon	=	5 grams
1 tablespoon	=	3 teaspoons
1 tablespoon	=	½ fluid ounce
1 cup	=	16 tablespoons
1 cup	=	8 fluid ounces
1 pound	=	16 weighed ounces
1 ounce	=	29 grams
1 tablespoon fresh herbs	=	½-1 teaspoon dried herbs
1 ounce chocolate	=	3 tablespoons cocoa plus 1 tablespoon canola oil
1 tablespoon cornstarch	=	2 tablespoons flour (used for thickening)
⅛ teaspoon garlic powder	=	1 small clove garlic
1 cup yogurt	=	1 cup buttermilk

JEAN OLIVA-RASBACH: PRIMARY AUTHOR

Jean Oliva-Rasbach is a Registered Dietitian and the Director of Nutrition at HealthMark in Denver, Colorado. She holds a Bachelor's Degree in Food Science and Nutrition from Colorado State University and a Master's Degree in Human Nutrition from Virginia Polytechnic Institute and State University.

Jean's love for food and cooking has been part of her entire life. Her mother is an excellent cook and taught her a variety of cooking techniques and flavor combinations. Throughout her life she has always been interested in trying new recipes and then improving upon those recipes. She enjoys experimenting with food for guests, as entertaining is another one of her loves.

As a dietitian, she has used her skills to modify recipes to accommodate the changing field of nutition. Her primary goal in modifying a recipe is to make it tasty. As a working mother she is very aware of time limitations. So, in order to blend her love for cooking and feeding her family healthy meals with short-order cooking, she has adopted a few time-saving techniques. Some of those include preparing stocks ahead, making enough to serve as leftovers, utilizing the relishes and sauces for more than one item and most importantly, planning ahead.

Jean believes that eating and cooking should be fun and rewarding. One only needs to read a recipe to prepare it. The next step is to enjoy!

DARRELL ANDERSON: COVER ARTIST

Darrell Anderson is a Denver fine artist whose talent is rapidly becoming recognized not only on the local level, but nationally and internationally. He enhances spirit in his art through the use of rich colors as seen in his New Orleans jazz musicians, Paris street scenes or captivating children's faces.

Capable of expressing his art through several mediums, Anderson has taken on the new challenge of mosaic tiles to accomplish two commissioned projects awarded him. At the new Denver International Airport each eight-foot-square figure, containing over 9,000 tiles, represents the various cultural and ethnic travelers that will be coming through this new international center. His diversity is shown in the array of commissions he has done in addition to the above, such as the serigraph of Colorado Rockies Manager, Don Baylor, "Baylor Ball," for their inaugural year. His involvement in juried and invitational exhibits such as the Cherry Creek Arts Festival and Artist in Residence for the syndicated television show, Jazz Alley, shows his acceptance within the art community.

Anderson's ability to envision the likeness of various people of the world for these projects comes naturally. After traveling and living in Europe as a child, being stationed in Thailand and serving all over the Orient, as a race relations instructor during the Vietnam war and working for 12 years as Frontier Airlines' first male flight attendant, he has become a keen observer.

In the summer of 1992, Anderson was invited to represent Denver at "Brest 92," a maritime celebration in Brest/Brittany France, Denver's sister-city. He was so well received and was such an effective ambassador on this artistic and cultural exchange, he was extended an invitation to Burkina Faso's Film Festival 1993 by Alfred Gouba, Mayor of Supone, Burkina Faso, West Africa. He was able to use this opportunity to further expand global cultural appreciation through person-to-person contact with members of their film-making and artistic societies.

RACHAEL AMOS: LINE DRAWING ARTIST

Rachael Amos is a fine artist who spent many of her formative years working in an obsessively realistic style. Although she no longer takes that approach, she still loves the appearances of things and has enjoyed presenting the appearance of many basic foodstuffs for this cookbook.

ABOUT THE CHEF AND SCANTICON: EXECUTIVE CHEF CHRISTIAN SCHMIDT

The Scanticon® began in 1969 in Denmark where the first Scanticon Conference Center Hotel was developed and built. Today Scanticon is an international company, headquartered in Princeton, New Jersey, USA, which specializes in the management and development of first-class Conference Center Hotels and Resorts.

The Scanticon Princeton Conference Center Hotel is an AAA Four Diamond property, located on 25 secluded wooded acres. The facility features 301 deluxe guest rooms, 36 dedicated conference rooms, recreational amenities, banquet facilities and three restaurants, including The Black Swan — the hotel's gourmet restaurant and central New Jersey's only AAA Four Diamond restaurant. The Scanticon Princeton has gained international recognition as a property with award-winning conference, hotel and food and beverage facilities.

The growth of The Scanticon continued with The Scanticon Denver Conference Center Hotel and Resort, which opened in 1989. The Scanticon Denver is a AAA Four Diamond property featuring 302 guest rooms, 33 dedicated conference rooms, recreational amenities including the championship Inverness Golf Course, indoor and outdoor banquet facilities, and four restaurants including The Black Swan — also boasting an AAA Four Diamond rating. The Scanticon Denver has established a reputation throughout metropolitan Denver for its award-winning cuisine and fabulous buffets.

Executive Chef Christian Schmidt was responsible for establishing many of the culinary standards that are in place today at The Scanticon Princeton and Denver. Chef Schmidt, born in West Germany and trained at Landesberufsschule für das Hotel und Gaststatengewerbe, has worked for a variety of first-class hotels and resorts throughout the U.S. Chef Schmidt's creativity is carried out through exciting menus, wonderful food presentations and plate artistry. "Chef Schmidt is an artist in the kitchen," states Marion Julier, General Manager at The Scanticon Denver. He brought a wealth of culinary expertise to The Scanticon Denver when he opened the property in 1989.

Henry Vergnaud, General Manager at The Scanticon Princeton, indicated "Chef Schmidt exemplifies the role, the style and the depth of the younger generation of hotel executive chefs, but above all it is Christian's commitment to pleasing the customer's palate that has spurred his desire to excel in his craft."

Scanticon Hotel – Denver, CO
Scanticon Hotel – Princeton, NJ

Vegetarian Lasagne *(page 352)*
Ricotta CheeseTortellini
with Sun-Dried Tomato Sauce *(page 350)*

Fresh Vegetables Are Essential
for Mediterranean Cooking

Fresh Herbs Will Enhance Your Dishes

Dried Herbs and Spices

Grains and Pasta

Mediterranean Breads

Cioppino *(page 378)*

Stuffed Eggplant *(page 153)*
Pineapple Boat *(page 180)*

Peppers and Tomatoes *(page 398)*
Trout with Mushrooms *(page 384)*

Salmon Terrine *(page 159)*
Ratatouille *(page 256)*

Tequila Prawns *(page 96)*
Peaches and Cod *(page 225)*

SPAIN

In Barcelona, along La Rambla, the broad, wild, people-packed, eccentric, tree-shaded avenue that leads from the city's port to its center, is La Boqueria, the largest and most active of Mediterranean Spain's open markets. It is a magnificent place. Where better to find a region's stomach than where it buys its food?

La Boqueria is a riot of colors and aromas. There are stalls devoted to selling the meat from only the outsides of animals — and others solely for what comes from inside. There are vendors for mushrooms and others for tropical fruits. A huge section of La Boqueria is set aside for fans of fin and gill: stalls for smoked and kippered eels, herring and salmon, others for shellfish only, still more for flat fish and sea fish and fresh fish.

Smells swirl in the open air like nose fairies: mushrooms heady with the aroma of newly-turned earth and just-picked fruit as fresh as the smell of the morning.

It is difficult to encapsulate the key elements of Spanish Mediterranean cuisine in short order. Two things, however, stand out. One is a rich use of sauces such as romesco, a spicy sauce that uses pulverized nuts to thicken and flavor it or alioli, heady with garlic and olive oil. Another interesting element is the combination in one plate of both meat and fish ("mountain and sea") so that, for instance, we have recipes for pork tenderloin with clams or paella.

And everywhere in Mediterranean Spain there is pa amb tomaquet — dry bread rubbed with fresh tomato pulp and seasoned with salt and garlic — and an abundant use of vegetables and greens like parsley, as in escalibada.

The present-day cooking of Spain, however, is no more than the accumulation of its past. It is a history of trade and conquest.

The trade routes of Spain, especially Mediterranean Spain and the area we call Catalonia, were the trade routes of Rome, Greece, Phoenecia, the Visigoths and, most important, Arabia. Spanish Mediterranean cooking looks less in toward the Iberian peninsula than outward, to Europe and the Mediterranean Basin.

Spanish cooking also is a result of its conquests, most especially the New World.

The Americas gave to Spain foodstuffs that have become quintessentially important to the whole of the Mediterranean way of eating: the potato; the tomato; chiles of every stripe; and, of course, the naughty chocolate.

What Spanish cooking does with these ingredients is especially kind on the American palate. Spain's twists on onions, peppers, eggplant, tomatoes, garlic, olive oil, herbs (especially parsley), fresh fish and shellfish, rice, pasta, chicken, veal and pork — all have familiar rings with New World tastes.

Bill St. John
Food and Wine Editor
Rocky Mountain News

TABLE OF CONTENTS

TABLE OF CONTENTS

— MOST COMMONLY USED ITEMS FOR SPANISH RECIPES —

▼ FRESH SUPPLIES
Cilantro
Egg substitute
Garlic
Lemons
Onions
Parsley
Peppers, all types
Tomatoes
Wine, dry white

▼ PANTRY SUPPLIES
Cinnamon stick
Coriander seed
Olive oil
Paprika
Red pepper flakes
Rice
Saffron
Turmeric
Vinegar, white wine

— MENU SUGGESTIONS —

▼ CASUAL
Gazpacho
Codfish Cakes with Spinach and Rice
Lemon Sorbet

▼ FORMAL
Tomato Garlic Prawns
Cold Stufed Vegetables
Peppery Lobster Soup with Saffron
Exotic Garden Salad
Beef with Plums and Peppered Potatoes
Caramel Custard

▼ SUMMER
Roasted Pepper, Tomato and Eggplant Dip
Cream of Pea Soup with Shrimp
Chicken with Saffron Rice
Compote of Melon

▼ WINTER
Clams in a Garlic Vegetable Broth
Roasted Vegetable Salad
Fricando
Rice with Sherry
Almond Crusted Custard Pie

▼ QUICK BUT AUTHENTIC
Mixed Greens
Omelette with Potatoes and Onions
Crema Catalana

CLAMS IN A GARLIC VEGETABLE BROTH
Serves 6

4 lbs.	cherrystone clams, in shell, scrubbed
1 Tbl.	olive oil
2 cloves	garlic, minced
¾ cup	leeks, diced, white portion only
1 tsp.	fennel seeds
½	red onion, diced
⅓ cup	celery, diced
⅔ cup	carrots, diced
1 cup	sweet white wine
2 cups	fish stock *(see p. 540)*
pinch	saffron
to taste	salt and freshly ground pepper

In a large saucepan, heat the olive oil. Sauté the garlic, leeks, fennel seeds, onion, celery and carrots until soft. Add the white wine, fish stock and saffron. Season to taste with salt and pepper. Bring to a boil. Add the clams, cover and cook until clams open. Discard the clams that do not open. Arrange the open clams in a large bowl and serve with garlic bread.

Alcohol Note: The alcohol content was computed prior to cooking. Once the alcohol is heated to the boiling point, the alcohol disappears along with most of the calories from the alcohol.

Nutrient Content Per Serving

Calories	312.0
Protein	43.1 g
Carbohydrates	13.5 g
Fat – Total	5.5 g
Cholesterol	138.0 mg
Dietary Fiber	1.4 g
Sodium	230.0 mg

Percent of Calories

57%	Protein
18%	Carbohydrate
17%	Fat
8%	Alcohol

Fat Breakdown

Saturated Fat	0.7 g
Monounsaturated Fat	2.0 g
Polyunsaturated Fat	1.2 g

ESCARGOT WITH HERBED PLUM TOMATOES
Serves 6

36	snails, rinsed, drained
1	shallot, chopped
3 cloves	garlic, minced
1 oz.	sun-dried tomatoes
1 tsp.	rosemary, chopped
½ tsp.	fennel seeds
2 tsp.	olive oil
½ cup	dry white wine
½ cup	veal stock *(see p. 536)*
15 oz.	canned plum tomatoes, drained, chopped, reserve juice
¼ cup	sweet white wine
to taste	salt and pepper

Rehydrate sun-dried tomatoes with warm water. Chop.

In a non-stick skillet, heat oil over medium heat. Sauté the shallots, garlic, sun-dried tomatoes and herbs. Add the snails and dry white wine. Simmer 3 minutes. Remove the snails. Add the veal stock and tomato juice. Reduce to a thick ragout-like consistency. Add the plum tomatoes and sweet white wine and return snails to the pan. Cook for 2-5 minutes. Season with salt and pepper to taste. Serve immediately.

Cook's Note: Easy to prepare. Serve with crackers or small rounds of bread. Is also good with mussels in place of snails.

Alcohol Note: The alcohol content was computed prior to cooking. Once the alcohol is heated to the boiling point, the alcohol disappears along with most of the calories from the alcohol.

Nutrient Content Per Serving

Calories	100.0
Protein	10.7 g
Carbohydrates	5.4 g
Fat – Total	2.6 g
Cholesterol	30.0 mg
Dietary Fiber	1.1 g
Sodium	250.0 mg

Percent of Calories

42% Protein
21% Carbohydrate
24% Fat
13% Alcohol

Fat Breakdown

Saturated Fat	0.5 g
Monounsaturated Fat	1.4 g
Polyunsaturated Fat	0.4 g

Mushrooms with Parsley and Garlic
Serves 8

1 lb.	mushrooms
2 tsp.	olive oil
4 lg. cloves	garlic, minced
4 Tbl.	parsley, chopped
to taste	salt and pepper
¼ cup	dry white wine
1 Tbl.	lemon juice

Cut mushrooms into quarters. In a non-stick frying pan, sauté garlic in the olive oil for 1 minute. Add mushrooms, parsley, salt and pepper and continue to cook until the mushrooms are soft. Add wine. Cook down until the liquid has almost evaporated. Arrange in a serving dish and drizzle with lemon juice.

Cook's Note: May use wild mushrooms or any combination you choose.

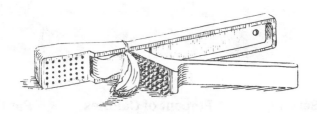

Nutrient Content Per Serving

Calories	21.1
Protein	1.3 g
Carbohydrates	3.1 g
Fat – Total	0.8 g
Cholesterol	0.0 mg
Dietary Fiber	0.8 g
Sodium	2.9 mg

Percent of Calories

20% Protein	
50% Carbohydrate	
29% Fat	

Fat Breakdown

Saturated Fat	0.1 g
Monounsaturated Fat	0.4 g
Polyunsaturated Fat	0.2 g

BROILED MUSHROOMS
Serves 4

2 cups	mushrooms
1 tsp.	olive oil
to taste	salt

Sauce:

1 Tbl.	powdered butter replacement
2 Tbl.	white wine
2 Tbl.	fresh parsley, chopped
1 tsp.	garlic, minced

Clean mushrooms. Arrange on a plate and drizzle olive oil over top. Season with salt to taste. Broil for 10 minutes.

To prepare sauce:

Dissolve powdered butter replacement in the white wine. Add parsley and garlic. Pour sauce over top and serve.

Nutrient Content Per Serving		Percent of Calories	Fat Breakdown	
Calories	43.6	18% Protein	Saturated Fat	0.2 g
Protein	2.2 g	56% Carbohydrate	Monounsaturated Fat	0.8 g
Carbohydrates	7.1 g	26% Fat	Polyunsaturated Fat	0.2 g
Fat – Total	1.5 g			
Cholesterol	0.0 mg			
Dietary Fiber	2.5 g			
Sodium	497.0 mg			

STEAMED MUSSELS WITH BALSAMIC-GINGER VINAIGRETTE
Serves 6

3 lbs.	mussels in shells, cleaned *(see p. 13)*
1 cup	fish stock *(see p. 540)*
3 cloves	garlic, minced
¼ cup	balsamic-ginger vinaigrette *(see p. 559)*

In a large cooking pot, bring the fish stock and garlic to a boil over medium heat. Add the mussels and cover. Simmer until the mussels open. Discard the mussels that did not open. Chill the remaining mussels in a bowl with the liquid.

Prepare the balsamic-ginger vinaigrette according to the recipe. Discard cooking liquid from the mussels. Toss the chilled mussels with the balsamic vinaigrette. Serve immediately.

Alcohol Note: The alcohol content was computed prior to cooking. Once the alcohol is heated to the boiling point, the alcohol disappears along with most of the calories from the alcohol.

Nutrient Content Per Serving

Calories	211.0
Protein	27.2 g
Carbohydrates	9.4 g
Fat – Total	6.2 g
Cholesterol	63.5 mg
Dietary Fiber	0.2 g
Sodium	649.0 mg

Percent of Calories

53%	Protein
18%	Carbohydrate
27%	Fat
2%	Alcohol

Fat Breakdown

Saturated Fat	1.1 g
Monounsaturated Fat	1.8 g
Polyunsaturated Fat	1.6 g

ROASTED PEPPER, TOMATO AND EGGPLANT DIP
Serves 8

1	eggplant, cut in half lengthwise
½ tsp.	olive oil
to taste	salt and pepper
dash	garlic powder
½	lemon, juice of
1	sweet red pepper roasted, diced fine
1	tomato, peeled, seeded, chopped
2 Tbl.	V-8 juice, low-sodium
3 Tbl.	red wine vinegar
2 tsp.	olive oil
3 leaves	basil, chopped

Preheat oven to 400° F. Measure olive oil into a small bowl. Apply to cut side of eggplant with a pastry brush. Season the inside of the eggplant with salt, pepper, dash of garlic powder and the lemon juice. Cover the eggplant with foil and cook on a baking sheet for 25 minutes. Cool, scoop out the eggplant and chill.

Roast the red pepper *(see p. 13)*, then skin, seed and dice fine. Purée the chilled eggplant until smooth. In a bowl, combine the eggplant and remaining ingredients. Season with salt and pepper to taste.

Cook's Note: Goes well with belgian endive leaves or onion crackers.

% Calories as Fat — Above the HM✔ guidelines: Although this recipe has a high percentage of calories as fat (>30%), the total fat is less than 5 grams per serving. This will easily fit within your allotment of 45 grams per day. This happens most often in low-calorie recipes.

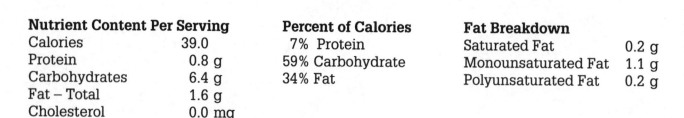

Nutrient Content Per Serving	
Calories	39.0
Protein	0.8 g
Carbohydrates	6.4 g
Fat – Total	1.6 g
Cholesterol	0.0 mg
Dietary Fiber	2.5 g
Sodium	16.6 mg

Percent of Calories	
7%	Protein
59%	Carbohydrate
34%	Fat

Fat Breakdown	
Saturated Fat	0.2 g
Monounsaturated Fat	1.1 g
Polyunsaturated Fat	0.2 g

SPANISH PRAWN COCKTAIL
Serves 6

18 lg.	prawns, cleaned and deveined
1 cup	fish stock *(see p. 540)*
1 tsp.	fennel seeds

Cocktail sauce:

¼ cup	fat-free mayonnaise
2	tomatoes, peeled, seeded, diced fine
1	anchovy, rinsed, drained, chopped
½ tsp.	capers, drained, minced
1 Tbl.	cognac
3 Tbl.	cooking liquid from prawns
to taste	freshly ground pepper

Garnish:

lemon wedges

Bring the fish stock and fennel seeds to a boil. Add the prawns and cook approximately 5 minutes until done. Remove the prawns, drain and chill. Save the liquid for the sauce.

To prepare the cocktail sauce:
Whisk all ingredients together in a bowl. Season with pepper to taste.

To Serve:
Arrange the chilled prawns on a platter. Serve the sauce on the side or in a bowl placed in the center of the platter. Garnish with lemon wedges, if desired.

Cook's Note: If you can't find prawns you may substitute jumbo shrimp. The serving size is small due to the high cholesterol content of prawns.

Alcohol Note: The alcohol content was computed prior to cooking. Once the alcohol is heated to the boiling point, the alcohol disappears along with most of the calories from the alcohol.

Nutrient Content Per Serving

Calories	45.9
Protein	4.85 g
Carbohydrates	4.0 g
Fat – Total	0.6 g
Cholesterol	32.5 mg
Dietary Fiber	0.6 g
Sodium	172.0 mg

Percent of Calories

42% Protein
35% Carbohydrate
12% Fat
11% Alcohol

Fat Breakdown

Saturated Fat	0.1 g
Monounsaturated Fat	0.1 g
Polyunsaturated Fat	0.2 g

SAUTÉED PRAWNS WITH A SPICED TOMATO MARMALADE

Serves 6

18 lg.	prawns, cleaned, peeled, deveined
1 cup	fish stock *(see p. 540)*
1 tsp.	fennel seeds
to taste	salt and pepper
½ tsp.	red pepper flakes
6 Tbl.	tomato marmalade *(see p. 549)*

In a medium non-stick frying pan over medium heat, combine all ingredients except marmalade. Heat quickly until prawns are pink, then chill.

Prepare tomato marmalade according to directions. Add chilled marmalade to prawns. Let marinate at least 2 hours. Serve chilled with marmalade.

Alcohol Note: The alcohol content was computed prior to cooking. Once the alcohol is heated to the boiling point, the alcohol disappears along with most of the calories from the alcohol.

Nutrient Content Per Serving		Percent of Calories	Fat Breakdown	
Calories	32.7	49% Protein	Saturated Fat	0.1 g
Protein	3.9 g	17% Carbohydrate	Monounsaturated Fat	0.4 g
Carbohydrates	1.4 g	26% Fat	Polyunsaturated Fat	0.3 g
Fat – Total	0.9 g	8% Alcohol		
Cholesterol	35.1 mg			
Dietary Fiber	0.3 g			
Sodium	40.5 mg			

TOMATO GARLIC PRAWNS
Serves 6

18 lg.	prawns, peeled, deveined
2 tsp.	olive oil
3 Tbl.	onions, chopped
6 cloves	garlic, minced
1 tsp.	red pepper flakes
2	tomatoes, peeled, seeded, diced
to taste	salt and pepper
1	lemon, juice of

In a non-stick skillet, sauté the onions, garlic and flaked red peppers in olive oil. Add the prawns and tomatoes. Heat, stirring constantly until prawns are cooked through, approximately 3 minutes. Season with salt and pepper to taste. Sprinkle with lemon juice and serve immediately.

% Calories as Fat — Above the HM guidelines: Although this recipe has a high percentage of calories as fat (>30%), the total fat is less than 5 grams per serving. This will easily fit within your allotment of 45 grams per day. This happens most often in low-calorie recipes.

Nutrient Content Per Serving

Calories	47.3
Protein	4.4 g
Carbohydrates	3.8 g
Fat – Total	1.9 g
Cholesterol	35.1 mg
Dietary Fiber	0.9 g
Sodium	44.6 mg

Percent of Calories

35% Protein
31% Carbohydrate
34% Fat

Fat Breakdown

Saturated Fat	0.3 g
Monounsaturated Fat	1.2 g
Polyunsaturated Fat	0.3 g

COLD STUFFED VEGETABLES
Serves 6

6	artichoke bottoms (fresh or canned)
3 lg.	tomatoes
¼ cup	onion, chopped
½ cup	canned beets, drained, chopped
¼ cup	parsley, chopped
¼ cup	cilantro, chopped
3	lemons, juice of
to taste	salt and freshly ground black pepper
½ cup	mayonnaise, fat-free

Garnish:

6 tsp.	black olives
6 tsp.	parsley

Cut the tomatoes in half and remove the seeds by squeezing them out. Using a tablespoon carefully hollow out the tomatoes. Reserve the pulp. Chop the pulp and add onions, beets, parsley, cilantro and lemon juice. Season to taste with salt and black pepper. Blend in the mayonnaise.

Hollow out the artichoke bottoms. Fill the tomatoes and artichokes with the pulp mixture. Arrange on an attractive plate. Garnish with chopped black olives and parsley leaves.

Nutrient Content Per Serving

Calories	104.0
Protein	5.3 g
Carbohydrates	24.1 g
Fat – Total	0.6 g
Cholesterol	0.0 mg
Dietary Fiber	7.9 g
Sodium	388.0 mg

Percent of Calories

17% Protein
79% Carbohydrate
4% Fat

Fat Breakdown

Saturated Fat	0.1 g
Monounsaturated Fat	0.1 g
Polyunsaturated Fat	0.2 g

ROASTED VEGETABLES
(ESCALIBADA)
Serves 4

1	sweet red pepper
1	green bell pepper
1 med.	eggplant
1 med.	onion
1 Tbl.	white wine vinegar
1 tsp.	olive oil
1 clove	garlic, minced
to taste	salt and pepper

Roast the peppers, eggplant and onion and remove skin *(see p. 13)*. Arrange on a platter and cover with vinegar, oil, garlic and salt and pepper to taste. May serve cold or hot.

To serve cold, refrigerate for 2 hours. To serve hot, add a clove of garlic and heat for a few minutes.

Nutrient Content Per Serving

Calories	65.8
Protein	1.7 g
Carbohydrates	13.3 g
Fat – Total	1.5 g
Cholesterol	0.0 mg
Dietary Fiber	5.2 g
Sodium	5.4 mg

Percent of Calories

9% Protein
72% Carbohydrate
19% Fat

Fat Breakdown

Saturated Fat	0.2 g
Monounsaturated Fat	0.9 g
Polyunsaturated Fat	0.3 g

BROCHETTE OF VEGETABLES

Serves 8

2	tomatoes, sliced thin
1	sweet red pepper, sliced in strips (optional to roast, *see p. 13*))
1	onion, sliced thin
16	mushrooms, sliced
1 cup	pineapple, diced
1	eggplant or zucchini, peeled and diced
1 loaf	french bread
1 tsp.	olive oil
3 cloves	garlic, minced

Combine all vegetables in a large shallow baking dish prepared with cooking spray. Bake, covered at 350° F for 40 minutes or until vegetables are tender. Drain juices.

To serve:
Slice bread into 16 slices. Mix together garlic and olive oil. Lightly brush olive oil onto slices. Toast under the broiler until slightly brown. Arrange vegetables on bread slices. Place under the broiler for 1-2 minutes or until vegetables begin to brown.

Cook's Note: May also purée the vegetables and use as a spread on the bread. May cook in the microwave if pressed for time.

Nutrient Content Per Serving

Calories	155.0
Protein	5.1 g
Carbohydrates	30.6 g
Fat – Total	2.2 g
Cholesterol	0.0 mg
Dietary Fiber	4.7 mg
Sodium	220.0 mg

Percent of Calories

13% Protein
76% Carbohydrate
12% Fat

Fat Breakdown

Saturated Fat	0.4 g
Monounsaturated Fat	0.9 g
Polyunsaturated Fat	0.5 g

BUTTERNUT SQUASH SOUP WITH APPLES

Serves 6

2 med.	butternut squash
1 tsp.	olive oil
½ med.	onion, diced fine
2	apples, peeled, diced fine
4 cups	chicken stock *(see p. 538)*
1½ cups	skim milk
½ cup	nonfat dry milk
½ tsp.	powdered butter replacement
¼ tsp.	lemon juice
pinch	ground mace
to taste	salt and pepper

Garnish:

2 tsp.	pine nuts, toasted

Cut squash in half and remove seeds. Place squash in a baking dish cut side down with a little water. Bake at 375° F for 20-30 minutes until flesh is soft. Scoop the meat from the squash and purée.

Heat the oil in a large non-stick frying pan, add the onion and apples. Sauté for 5 minutes over low heat until lightly browned. Add the squash purée, and the chicken stock, simmer for 10 minutes, stirring constantly.

In a measuring cup, combine the skim milk with the nonfat dry milk and the powdered butter replacement. Stir until powdered milk dissolves.

Stir the milk mixture into the soup and reduce by one-third. Add lemon juice, mace, salt and pepper to taste. Strain before serving to achieve a smooth texture. Garnish with toasted pine nuts.

Cook's Note: To toast pine nuts, place them in a dry non-stick frying pan and heat over medium-low. Watch closely to prevent burning.

Nutrient Content Per Serving

Calories	147.0
Protein	7.2 g
Carbohydrates	28.1 g
Fat – Total	1.8 g
Cholesterol	3.1 mg
Dietary Fiber	4.3 g
Sodium	91.8 mg

Percent of Calories

18% Protein
72% Carbohydrate
10% Fat

Fat Breakdown

Saturated Fat	0.4 g
Monounsaturated Fat	0.9 g
Polyunsaturated Fat	0.4 g

SPINACH GARBANZO SOUP
Serves 8

2 cups	canned garbanzo beans, rinsed, drained
½ lb.	cod fillets
1½ lbs.	fresh spinach, deveined
4 whole	blanched almonds, toasted
1 tsp.	garlic, minced
2 tsp.	olive oil
1 slice	french bread, crusts trimmed, cubed
1 cup	onions, chopped
2 Tbl.	flour
1 tsp.	paprika

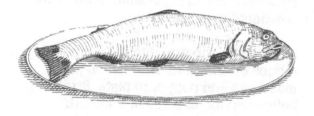

In a shallow pan, cover fish with 1 inch of water. Bring to a boil. Poach fish until it flakes easily. Drain, remove any bones and skin. Separate into large bite-size pieces.

Steam or microwave spinach. Squeeze all moisture from it. Save liquid.

Using a food processor or mortar and pestle, make a paste of almonds and garlic. Add 1 teaspoon oil and continue to mash.

In a non-stick pan prepared with cooking spray, toast the bread cubes to make croutons. Remove from pan and mash croutons into garlic and almond paste.

Add 1 teaspoon olive oil to skillet. Sauté ½ cup of the onions until transparent. Sprinkle flour over the onions. Sauté until browned. Add spinach. Cook.

Add paprika, cod, garbanzos and 2 cups of spinach juice. Cover and simmer 20 minutes.

Cook's Note: May substitute frozen chopped spinach.

Nutrient Content Per Serving

Calories	152.0
Protein	12.9 g
Carbohydrates	19.6 g
Fat – Total	3.2 g
Cholesterol	12.2 mg
Dietary Fiber	5.3 g
Sodium	126.0 mg

Percent of Calories

32% Protein
49% Carbohydrate
18% Fat

Fat Breakdown

Saturated Fat	0.4 g
Monounsaturated Fat	1.4 g
Polyunsaturated Fat	0.9 g

GARLIC SOUP
Serves 4

8 cloves	garlic, minced
1 tsp.	olive oil
3 cups	bread, crusts removed, cubed
1 Tbl.	paprika
6 cups	chicken stock *(see p. 538)*
½ tsp.	salt
¼ tsp.	cayenne pepper
½ tsp.	cumin
4	egg whites, slightly beaten with pinch of tumeric
2 Tbl.	fresh parsley, chopped

Heat oil in a non-stick skillet. Sauté garlic over medium heat until soft but not brown. Add bread cubes and cook until golden. Add paprika, stock, salt, cayenne pepper and cumin. Bring to a boil. Simmer uncovered for 30 minutes. Using a whisk, beat soup until bread is pulverized. While stiring, slowly add egg whites. Heat 1-2 minutes. Do not boil. Serve at once, garnished with parsley.

Cook's Note: May substitute ½ cup egg substitute for the egg whites.

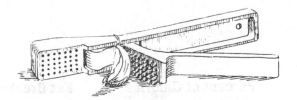

Nutrient Content Per Serving

Calories	96.2
Protein	5.9 g
Carbohydrates	13.6 g
Fat – Total	2.0 g
Cholesterol	0.7 mg
Dietary Fiber	1.1 g
Sodium	436.0 mg

Percent of Calories

25% Protein
57% Carbohydrate
19% Fat

Fat Breakdown

Saturated Fat	0.3 g
Monounsaturated Fat	1.2 g
Polyunsaturated Fat	0.4 g

GAZPACHO
Serves 4

4 cups	tomatoes, chopped,seeded
1 lg.	cucumber, peeled, seeded and chopped
3	scallions, chopped
1	bell pepper, chopped
1 clove	garlic, minced
¼	avocado, chopped
1 tsp.	olive oil
¼ cup	white wine vinegar

Garnish:

½ cup	plain nonfat yogurt

Purée two-thirds of the vegetables. Add oil and vinegar. Add remainder of vegetables. Chill. Serve very cold with a dollop of plain yogurt, accompanied by crusty bread.

Cook's Note: Very refreshing!

Nutrient Content Per Serving

Calories	104.0
Protein	4.3 g
Carbohydrates	16.2 g
Fat – Total	3.8 g
Cholesterol	0.6 mg
Dietary Fiber	3.8 g
Sodium	43.2 mg

Percent of Calories

15% Protein
56% Carbohydrate
30% Fat

Fat Breakdown

Saturated Fat	0.6 g
Monounsaturated Fat	2.2 g
Polyunsaturated Fat	0.6 g

PEPPERY LOBSTER SOUP WITH SAFFRON
Serves 6

2 1¼-lb.	live lobsters
4 cups	chablis
dash	saffron
1½	carrots, chopped coarse
¼ stalk	celery, chopped coarse
1 cup	onion, sliced thin
1	sweet red pepper, chopped
1 tsp.	olive oil
1 cup	plum tomatoes, chopped
½ lb.	potatoes, peeled, sliced thin
1 Tbl.	fresh lemon juice
dash	cayenne pepper
to taste	white pepper

Garnish:

3 Tbl.	watercress, chopped
6 slices	french bread

Cook's Note: Has a smooth, rich texture. May use roasted red pepper for a richer flavor.

In a large pot, bring 3 cups of the wine and saffron to a boil. Add lobster, cover and simmer for 10 minutes. Remove lobster and immediately immerse in cold water. Separate the meat from the shells. Chop meat and set aside. Add the shells, legs and claws back to the lobster liquid and simmer 15 minutes. Skim the froth. Add carrots, celery and ½ cup of the onion and simmer for 2 hours. Strain the stock through a large sieve, pressing hard on the solids. Add water and remaining cup of wine to make the stock up to 3 cups.

In a non-stick frying pan, sauté remaining ½ cup onions and peppers in oil until soft. Add tomatoes, potatoes and drained stock. Boil until potatoes are tender.

Using a food processor, purée the mixture until smooth. Simmer. Add chopped lobster meat, lemon juice, cayenne pepper and white pepper to taste. Heat through. Garnish with chopped watercress. Serve hot with french bread.

Alcohol Note: The alcohol content was computed prior to cooking. Once the alcohol is heated to the boiling point, the alcohol disappears along with most of the calories from the alcohol.

Nutrient Content Per Serving		Percent of Calories		Fat Breakdown	
Calories	365.0	45% Protein		Saturated Fat	0.3 g
Protein	40.5 g	21% Carbohydrate		Monounsaturated Fat	0.9 g
Carbohydrates	19.1 g	5% Fat		Polyunsaturated Fat	0.3 g
Fat – Total	2.1 g	29% Alcohol			
Cholesterol	136.0 mg				
Dietary Fiber	2.2 g				
Sodium	739.0 mg				

MUSSEL SOUP
Serves 6

1 lb.	mussels, out of shells
1 lg.	onion, diced
1 tsp.	canola oil
2 cloves	garlic, minced
2 med.	tomatoes, diced
2 cups	fish stock *(see p. 540)*
1 Tbl.	almonds, chopped
1 Tbl.	parsley, dry
1 tsp.	thyme, dry
1	bay leaf

In a non-stick frying pan, sauté onions in oil. Add garlic and cook 1 minute. Add tomatoes and fish stock. Simmer for 5-10 minutes. Add remaining ingredients. Cook for 20 minutes.

Cook's Note: May add rice or pasta for a complete meal. To remove mussels from shells, steam them until they open *(see p. 13)*.

Alcohol Note: The alcohol content was computed prior to cooking. Once the alcohol is heated to the boiling point, the alcohol disappears along with most of the calories from the alcohol.

% Calories as Fat — Above the HM✔ guidelines:
Although this recipe has a high percentage of calories as fat (>30%), the total fat is less than 5 grams per serving. This will easily fit within your allotment of 45 grams per day. This happens most often in low-calorie recipes.

Nutrient Content Per Serving		**Percent of Calories**	**Fat Breakdown**	
Calories	113.0	36% Protein	Saturated Fat	0.5 g
Protein	10.2 g	29% Carbohydrate	Monounsaturated Fat	1.5 g
Carbohydrate	8.3 g	31% Fat	Polyunsaturated Fat	1.2 g
Fat – Total	3.9 g	4% Alcohol		
Cholesterol	21.2 mg			
Dietary Fiber	1.4 g			
Sodium	222.0 mg			

Onion Soup España
Serves 6

6 med.	onions, sliced thin
1 Tbl.	olive oil
5 cups	chicken stock *(see p. 538)*
to taste	pepper
6 slices	white bread, crusts removed
3 oz.	lowfat swiss cheese, grated

In a non-stick frying pan over medium heat, sauté onions in oil until light brown. Add stock and season with pepper to taste. Simmer for 45 minutes.

Toast bread. Transfer soup to individual ovenproof bowls. Arrange cheese and toast on top of soup. Place soup bowls in the oven and bake at 375° F for 5 minutes. Remove when cheese is melted and slightly brown.

Cook's Note: Do not use fat-free swiss cheese. It will not melt completely.

Nutrient Content Per Serving

Calories	157.0
Protein	7.6 g
Carbohydrates	22.8 g
Fat – Total	4.0 g
Cholesterol	5.8 mg
Dietary Fiber	2.1 g
Sodium	182.0 mg

Percent of Calories

19% Protein	
58% Carbohydrate	
23% Fat	

Fat Breakdown

Saturated Fat	1.0 g
Monounsaturated Fat	2.3 g
Polyunsaturated Fat	0.5 g

CREAM OF PEA SOUP WITH SHRIMP
Serves 6

2 lbs.	peas, fresh or frozen
½ lb.	bay shrimp, peeled
2 tsp.	olive oil
½ med.	onion, chopped
4 cups	chicken stock *(see p. 538)*
2 pinches	turmeric
1 tsp.	sugar
2 cups	skim milk
½ cup	nonfat dry milk
1 tsp.	fresh mint
to taste	salt and pepper

In a non-stick pan, heat the olive oil. Sauté the onions and peas. Add chicken stock, turmeric, sugar, skim milk, nonfat dry milk, mint and salt and pepper to taste. Bring to a boil, then reduce heat and simmer for 10 minutes.

Using a slotted spoon, remove peas and onions to a blender or food processor. Add enough liquid to make a smooth purée. Return purée to the pot. Add the shrimp. Heat until shrimp are pink.

Nutrient Content Per Serving

Calories	246.0
Protein	22.2 g
Carbohydrates	33.0 g
Fat – Total	3.0 g
Cholesterol	60.9 mg
Dietary Fiber	8.0 g
Sodium	321.0 mg

Percent of Calories

36% Protein
53% Carbohydrate
11% Fat

Fat Breakdown

Saturated Fat	0.6 g
Monounsaturated Fat	1.3 g
Polyunsaturated Fat	0.7 g

RADISH SOUP
Serves 8

1½ lbs.	red radishes, washed, trimmed, sliced thin
¼ cup	red wine vinegar
5½ cups	potatoes, peeled, cubed
5 cups	chicken stock *(see p. 538)*
6	scallions, sliced julienne
to taste	salt and pepper

In a soup pot, combine radishes (reserve ½ cup for garnish), vinegar, potatoes and chicken stock. Bring to a boil and simmer until potatoes are very tender. Cool slightly. Transfer to a blender or food processor and purée until smooth. Chill. Garnish with scallions and reserved radishes.

Cook's Note: This has a pungent odor when it is cooking, but will mellow when served.

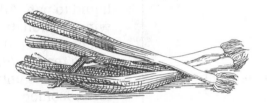

Nutrient Content Per Serving

Calories	108.0
Protein	2.5 g
Carbohydrates	25.1 g
Fat – Total	0.6 g
Cholesterol	0.0 mg
Dietary Fiber	2.9 g
Sodium	26.3 mg

Percent of Calories

8% Protein
87% Carbohydrate
5% Fat

Fat Breakdown

Saturated Fat	0.1 g
Monounsaturated Fat	0.0 g
Polyunsaturated Fat	0.1 g

RICE AND SHELLFISH SOUP
Serves 4

1 qt.	water
8 sm.	clams in shells, scrubbed *(see p. 13)*
2 tsp.	olive oil
½ cup	onions, finely chopped
1 tsp.	garlic, minced
1	bay leaf
1 lg.	tomato, peeled, seeded, chopped fine
2 Tbl.	fresh parsley, chopped
¼ cup	rice
¼ cup	dry white wine
⅛ tsp.	saffron
⅛ tsp.	turmeric
1 tsp.	fresh lemon juice
8 med.	shrimp, peeled, drained, cut into ½-inch pieces

Bring water to a boil. Boil clams for 5-10 minutes until they open. Discard clams that do not open. Set clams aside. Reserve liquid.

In a non-stick pan, sauté onions, garlic and bay leaf in olive oil until soft. Add tomatoes and parsley. Cook until moisture evaporates. Remove from heat.

Strain clam liquid through a sieve. Return liquid to pan. Add tomato mixture, rice, wine, saffron, turmeric and lemon juice. Simmer covered for 15-20 minutes or until rice is tender. Add shrimp and clams. Cook 3 minutes or until shrimp turn pink. Taste for seasoning.

Cook's Note: May be cooked ahead of time.

Alcohol Note: The alcohol content was computed prior to cooking. Once the alcohol is heated to the boiling point, the alcohol disappears along with most of the calories from the alcohol.

Nutrient Content Per Serving		**Percent of Calories**	**Fat Breakdown**	
Calories	132.0	27% Protein	Saturated Fat	0.5 g
Protein	8.9 g	42% Carbohydrate	Monounsaturated Fat	1.9 g
Carbohydrates	13.7 g	23% Fat	Polyunsaturated Fat	0.6 g
Fat – Total	3.4 g	8% Alcohol		
Cholesterol	31.9 mg			
Dietary Fiber	0.8 g			
Sodium	76.8 mg			

RICE AND VEGETABLE SOUP
Serves 6

1 sm.	onion, chopped
1 tsp.	olive oil
1 lg.	potato, diced
½ cup	carrots, diced
5 cups	chicken stock *(see p. 538)*
4 cups	peas, cooked (if frozen, just thaw)
½ cup	rice, cooked
to taste	salt and pepper

In a non-stick frying pan, sauté the onion in olive oil until golden brown. Parboil the potatoes in the microwave. In a soup pot, add the onions and carrots, potatoes and stock. Cook for 20 minutes. Add peas, rice, salt and pepper to taste.

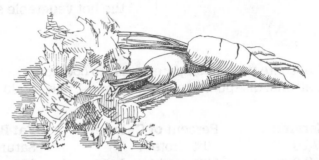

Nutrient Content Per Serving

Calories	171.0
Protein	7.4 g
Carbohydrates	33.6 g
Fat – Total	1.1 g
Cholesterol	0.0 mg
Dietary Fiber	6.8 g
Sodium	15.1 mg

Percent of Calories

17% Protein
77% Carbohydrate
 6% Fat

Fat Breakdown

Saturated Fat	0.2 g
Monounsaturated Fat	0.6 g
Polyunsaturated Fat	0.2 g

THYME SOUP
Serves 4

2 Tbl.	sun-dried tomatoes
1 Tbl.	roasted garlic, minced
8 sprigs	thyme, chopped
4 slices	french bread, toasted
4 cups	vegetable stock *(see p. 542)*
to taste	salt and pepper

Place dried tomatoes in 1 cup boiling water and cover. Let sit off the heat for 5 minutes. Chop tomatoes.

Using a food processor, mix the sun-dried tomatoes, garlic and thyme into a paste and spread lightly on each piece of bread. Toast under the broiler until golden brown. Arrange in individual bowls. Pour the hot vegetable stock over bread.

Alcohol Note: The alcohol content was computed prior to cooking. Once the alcohol is heated to the boiling point, the alcohol disappears along with most of the calories from the alcohol.

Nutrient Content Per Serving

Calories	176.0
Protein	3.8 g
Carbohydrates	22.2 g
Fat – Total	4.8 g
Cholesterol	0.0 mg
Dietary Fiber	2.0 g
Sodium	248.0 mg

Percent of Calories

9% Protein
50% Carbohydrate
24% Fat
17% Alcohol

Fat Breakdown

Saturated Fat	0.7 g
Monounsaturated Fat	1.3 g
Polyunsaturated Fat	2.4 g

WHITE BEAN SOUP
Serves 6

1 cup	dry white beans
1 qt.	water
2 qts.	chicken stock *(see p. 538)*
	(or water)
1½ lb.	turkey ham
1 cup	onions, chopped
½ tsp.	salt
½ lb.	turkey sausage, sliced thin
½ lb.	turnip greens, washed and
	shredded
2 sm.	potatoes, peeled, cubed

Either soak beans overnight or boil briskly for 2 minutes and soak 1 hour. Drain water and rinse beans.

Add 2 quarts stock or water, turkey ham, onions and salt. Simmer 1½ hours. Then add sausage, turnip greens and potatoes. Simmer 30 minutes. Serve hot with fresh bread.

Cook's Note: May use any dark green that you choose. Makes a great one-dish meal. May substitute canned beans. Must rinse well. Beans are then added during the last 30 minutes of cooking so they will not disintegrate.

Nutrient Content Per Serving

Calories	354.0
Protein	25.5 g
Carbohydrates	44.8 g
Fat – Total	8.8 g
Cholesterol	51.8 mg
Dietary Fiber	9.8 g
Sodium	833.0 mg

Percent of Calories

28% Protein
50% Carbohydrate
22% Fat

Fat Breakdown

Saturated Fat	2.9 g
Monounsaturated Fat	2.9 g
Polyunsaturated Fat	2.5 g

VEGETABLE SOUP
Serves 8

¼ lb.	green cabbage, cored, shredded
2	carrots, cut julienne
1	turnip, cut julienne
1	bay leaf
1 Tbl.	salt
2 qts.	chicken stock *(see p. 538)*
1 tsp.	olive oil
1 cup	onions, diced
1 tsp.	garlic, minced
2	tomatoes, peeled, seeded, chopped
1 Tbl.	fresh parsley
1	potato, cut julienne
½ cup	peas, frozen

In a large soup pot, combine cabbage, carrots, turnips, bay leaf and salt. Cover with chicken stock. Bring to a boil. Simmer 30 minutes.

In a separate pan, sauté onions and garlic in oil. Add tomatoes and parsley and cook down. Add to soup. Add potato and cook 20 minutes. Add peas, cook 10 minutes or until all vegetables are tender. Taste for seasoning. Serve hot.

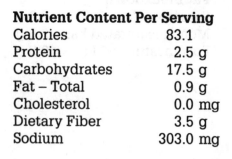

Nutrient Content Per Serving		Percent of Calories	Fat Breakdown	
Calories	83.1	11% Protein	Saturated Fat	0.1 g
Protein	2.5 g	79% Carbohydrate	Monounsaturated Fat	0.5 g
Carbohydrates	17.5 g	9% Fat	Polyunsaturated Fat	0.2 g
Fat – Total	0.9 g			
Cholesterol	0.0 mg			
Dietary Fiber	3.5 g			
Sodium	303.0 mg			

ZUCCHINI SOUP
Serves 6

2 lg.	zucchini
1 med.	onion
2 tsp.	olive oil
to taste	salt and pepper
5 cups	chicken stock *(see p. 538)*

In a saucepan, sauté the zucchini and onions in the oil for 10 minutes. Season with salt and pepper to taste. Add stock. Simmer for 15 minutes. Transfer soup to a blender and purée until smooth. Serve hot or cold.

Cook's Note: May add nonfat cream cheese when blending for a smoother texture.

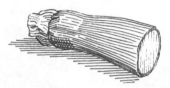 

Nutrient Content Per Serving

Calories	23.7
Protein	0.7 g
Carbohydrates	3.7 g
Fat – Total	0.9 g
Cholesterol	0.0 mg
Dietary Fiber	0.8 g
Sodium	1.1 mg

Percent of Calories

12% Protein
58% Carbohydrate
30% Fat

Fat Breakdown

Saturated Fat	0.1 g
Monounsaturated Fat	0.6 g
Polyunsaturated Fat	0.1 g

NAVY BEAN SALAD
Serves 4

2 cups	navy beans, canned, drained and rinsed
½ cup	cilantro-shallot vinaigrette *(see p. 126)*
1 lg.	onion, chopped fine
2	tomatoes, chopped
¼ cup	olives, chopped

In a bowl, mix beans with vinaigrette. Add onions, tomatoes and olives. Cover and refrigerate for 1-2 hours to allow beans to marinate.

Nutrient Content Per Serving

Calories	185.0
Protein	9.4 g
Carbohydrates	32.6 g
Fat – Total	3.0 g
Cholesterol	0.9 mg
Dietary Fiber	9.9 g
Sodium	66.1 mg

Percent of Calories

19% Protein
67% Carbohydrate
14% Fat

Fat Breakdown

Saturated Fat	0.5 g
Monounsaturated Fat	1.7 g
Polyunsaturated Fat	0.6 g

Exotic Garden Salad
Serves 4

Choose a variety of strong-flavored greens from this list:

Romaine
Arugula
Escarole
Spinach
Bibb (for contrast)

Topping:
¼ head   radiccio
1 med.   red pepper
½ head   belgian endive

Garnish:
sliced starfruit
Asian pear fans
strawberry halves
marigolds

Dressing:
Mango Vanilla *(see p. 129)*

Rinse lettuce well, but without damaging the leaves. Place lettuce in a spinner and spin gently to remove any excess water. Refrigerate, covered with a moist towel.

Arrange the lettuce in the center of a plate and top with a very fine julienne of: radicchio, red peppers and belgian endive.

Garnish around the lettuce with starfruit, pears, strawberries and marigolds. Serve with Mango Vanilla Dressing.

Serve the dressing on the side.

Nutrient Content Per Serving
(including 2 tablespoons of Mango Vanilla Dressing per serving)

Calories	56.9
Protein	2.0 g
Carbohydrates	9.8 g
Fat – Total	1.5 g
Cholesterol	0.0 mg
Dietary Fiber	1.8 g
Sodium	29.5 mg

Percent of Calories
13% Protein
65% Carbohydrate
22% Fat

Fat Breakdown

Saturated Fat	0.2 g
Monounsaturated Fat	0.8 g
Polyunsaturated Fat	0.2 g

MIXED GREENS
Serves 2

½ head   romaine lettuce
½ bunch   watercress
1   tomato, sliced thin
½   red onion, sliced in thin rings
8   black olives

Dressing
1 tsp.   olive oil
½ cup   fresh lemon juice
to taste   salt

Tear lettuce into pieces. Add remaining ingredients. Combine dressing ingredients. Toss salad with dressing.

% Calories as Fat — Above the HM✔ guidelines:
Although this recipe has a high percentage of calories as fat (>30%), the total fat is less than 5 grams per serving. This will easily fit within your allotment of 45 grams per day. This happens most often in low-calorie recipes.

Nutrient Content Per Serving

Calories	102.0
Protein	3.6 g
Carbohydrates	15.1 g
Fat – Total	4.8 g
Cholesterol	0.0 mg
Dietary Fiber	3.6 g
Sodium	140.0 mg

Percent of Calories

12% Protein
51% Carbohydrate
37% Fat

Fat Breakdown

Saturated Fat	0.7 g
Monounsaturated Fat	3.1 g
Polyunsaturated Fat	0.7 g

LIMA BEAN SALAD
Serves 4

1 lb.	lima beans, frozen
1 sm.	scallion, left whole
2 sprigs	mint
1	bay leaf
to taste	salt and pepper

Dressing:

1 Tbl.	olive oil
1 clove	garlic, minced
2 tsp.	mint, chopped
1 Tbl.	parsley, chopped
1 Tbl.	thyme, chopped
to taste	salt and pepper
1 tsp.	dijon mustard
¼ cup	white wine vinegar

Place lima beans in a medium saucepan. Cover with water. Add scallion, mint, bay leaf and salt and pepper to taste. Cover and simmer 15-20 minutes or until limas are tender. Drain and discard herbs.

To prepare the dressing:
Whisk together all dressing ingredients. Toss limas with dressing. May serve hot or cold.

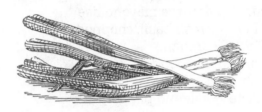

Nutrient Content Per Serving

Calories	154.0
Protein	7.7 g
Carbohydrates	23.4 g
Fat – Total	3.8 g
Cholesterol	0.0 mg
Dietary Fiber	7.8 g
Sodium	50.2 mg

Percent of Calories

19% Protein
59% Carbohydrate
21% Fat

Fat Breakdown

Saturated Fat	0.5 g
Monounsaturated Fat	2.6 g
Polyunsaturated Fat	0.5 g

LOBSTER AND ASPARAGUS SALAD
Serves 6

3 1¼-lb.	live lobsters
1 lb.	fresh asparagus, left whole
1 head	bibb lettuce
1 head	radicchio
¼ cup	sweet red pepper, cut julienne
½ cup	carrots, cut julienne
¼ cup	leeks, cut julienne
¼ cup	celery, cut julienne

Dressing:

2	lemons, juice of
1 cup	fat-free mayonnaise
1 Tbl.	fresh basil, chopped
1 Tbl.	oregano
¼ cup	rice vinegar
pinch	saffron
to taste	salt and pepper

Dressing:
In a small blender container, combine all ingredients. Set aside.

Lobster:
Bring 2 inches of water to a boil in a large pot. Put live lobster into pot and close the lid tight. Steam for 10-15 minutes or until lobster turns pink. Remove and chill. Crack the shell away from the meat.

Asparagus:
Place asparagus in the top of a steamer. Steam until barely tender (5-10 minutes). Chill.

Arrange the lettuces and asparagus on a dinner plate. Slice the lobster meat on top of lettuce. Sprinkle with dressing and top with julienne of vegetables.

Cholesterol — Above the HM✔ guidelines: Occasionally a lowfat recipe is high in cholesterol. In this case the cholesterol stems from the shellfish. The level is moderately high (>150 mg per serving) but may fit into your weekly average of 150 mg per day.

Sodium — Above the HM✔ guidelines: This recipe exceeds the HealthMark limits for sodium (800 mg per serving). The excess sodium is coming from the shellfish. If you have hypertension (high blood pressure) and must restrict your sodium intake, this recipe may push your total sodium intake above your desired level for that day. *(Refer to HealthMark Dietary Goals p. 3.)*

Nutrient Content Per Serving		**Percent of Calories**	**Fat Breakdown**	
Calories	318.0	71% Protein	Saturated Fat	0.6 g
Protein	55.6 g	21% Carbohydrate	Monounsaturated Fat	0.7 g
Carbohydrates	16.4 g	8% Fat	Polyunsaturated Fat	0.5 g
Fat – Total	2.8 g			
Cholesterol	270.0 mg			
Dietary Fiber	2.1 g			
Sodium	1308.0 mg			

MUSHROOM SALAD
Serves 6

1 lb.	mushrooms, sliced
¾ cup	white wine vinegar
1 Tbl.	olive oil
to taste	salt and pepper

Garnish:
basil

In a saucepan, heat the mushrooms until the moisture has evaporated and mushrooms are dry. Chill. Place in a jar. Fill jar with white wine vinegar. Add olive oil, and salt and pepper to taste. Marinate mushrooms covered for 8 days.

Cook's Note: May serve as a salad or an appetizer. May use any type of fresh mushrooms.

% Calories as Fat — Above the HM✔ guidelines: Although this recipe has a high percentage of calories as fat (>30%), the total fat is less than 5 grams per serving. This will easily fit within your allotment of 45 grams per day. This happens most often in low-calorie recipes.

Nutrient Content Per Serving		Percent of Calories	Fat Breakdown	
Calories	43.0	12% Protein	Saturated Fat	0.3 g
Protein	1.6 g	42% Carbohydrate	Monounsaturated Fat	1.7 g
Carbohydrates	5.3 g	46% Fat	Polyunsaturated Fat	0.3 g
Fat – Total	2.6 g			
Cholesterol	0.0 mg			
Dietary Fiber	1.0 g			
Sodium	3.3 mg			

Potato Salad with a Spanish Flair
Serves 4

3 med.	potatoes, unpeeled, cubed
1	onion, diced
3	tomatoes, cubed
1	green bell pepper, diced
2 cloves	garlic, minced
2 stalks	celery, diced
½ cup	cilantro-shallot vinaigrette *(see p. 126)*
	lettuce

Boil potatoes until tender. Rinse and drain. In a bowl, combine all vegetables except lettuce. Add vinaigrette. Chill. Line a serving bowl with lettuce leaves. Serve cold.

Nutrient Content Per Serving

Calories	224.0
Protein	5.5 g
Carbohydrates	49.3 g
Fat – Total	1.8 g
Cholesterol	0.9 mg
Dietary Fiber	5.7 g
Sodium	39.4 mg

Percent of Calories

9% Protein
84% Carbohydrate
7% Fat

Fat Breakdown

Saturated Fat	0.3 g
Monounsaturated Fat	0.9 g
Polyunsaturated Fat	0.4 g

RICE SALAD
Serves 4

1¼ cups	rice, cooked
3 cups	water
3 cups	mushrooms
1	apple, cubed
	lettuce
	parsley
½ cup	cilantro-shallot vinaigrette
	(see p. 126)

Bring water to a boil. Add rice, cover and simmer 20 minutes. Chill. Stir in mushrooms and apple cubes. Toss with vinaigrette. Arrange lettuce on platter and top with rice mixture.

Cook's Note: May add other vegetables as desired.

Nutrient Content Per Serving

Calories	153.0
Protein	3.8 g
Carbohydrates	31.4 g
Fat – Total	1.8 g
Cholesterol	0.9 mg
Dietary Fiber	2.0 g
Sodium	3.0 mg

Percent of Calories

10%	Protein
80%	Carbohydrate
10%	Fat

Fat Breakdown

Saturated Fat	0.3 g
Monounsaturated Fat	0.9 g
Polyunsaturated Fat	0.3 g

GRILLED TUNA SALAD
Serves 6

6 4-oz.	tuna or swordfish steaks
2 Tbl.	fish marinade *(see p. 555 or 556)*
1 head	bibb lettuce, torn
¼ head	radicchio, torn
¼ head	belgian endive, torn
3 cups	carrots, celery, leeks, onions, cut julienne
1 Tbl.	cilantro-shallot vinaigrette *(see p. 126)*

Garnish:

2	orange sections
dash	fresh chives
	fresh ground black pepper
	lemon wedges

Marinate the fish for 5 minutes. Grill and cut into strips. Arrange lettuces on individual plates. Top with julienne of vegetables. Arrange the fish attractively on top of vegetables. Sprinkle with the vinaigrette. Garnish, right before serving, with orange segments, chives, fresh ground black pepper and squeeze of lemon.

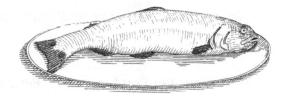

Cook's Note: Serve with fresh bread for a light meal!

Although the % of calories from fat is above 30, the total fat content is low. Of the 6.2 grams of fat, 5.6 grams are from the fish (a good-fat source).

Nutrient Content Per Serving

Calories	189.0
Protein	27.0 g
Carbohydrates	2.9 g
Fat – Total	6.2 g
Cholesterol	43.1 mg
Dietary Fiber	0.7 g
Sodium	52.1 mg

Percent of Calories

62%	Protein
7%	Carbohydrate
32%	Fat

Fat Breakdown

Saturated Fat	1.5 g
Monounsaturated Fat	3.5 g
Polyunsaturated Fat	2.0 g

ROASTED VEGETABLE SALAD
Serves 6

1 med.	zucchini
1 lg.	onion
2	green peppers
2	red peppers
1	eggplant
1 Tbl.	olive oil
to taste	salt
2 Tbl.	rice vinegar

Preheat grill to hottest setting. Leave vegetables whole and unpeeled. Grill all the vegetables until they are very soft and the skins are brown. Put the peppers in a plastic bag and close it tight for 10 minutes to loosen the skins. When the vegetables are cool enough to handle, peel them and cut into long thin strips. Toss with oil and vinegar. Chill. Serve cold.

% Calories as Fat — Above the HM✔ guidelines: Although this recipe has a high percentage of calories as fat (>30%), the total fat is less than 5 grams per serving. This will easily fit within your allotment of 45 grams per day. This happens most often in low-calorie recipes.

Nutrient Content Per Serving		**Percent of Calories**	**Fat Breakdown**	
Calories	69.7	8% Protein	Saturated Fat	0.4 g
Protein	1.6 g	61% Carbohydrate	Monounsaturated Fat	1.7 g
Carbohydrates	11.7 g	31% Fat	Polyunsaturated Fat	0.4 g
Fat – Total	2.6 g			
Cholesterol	0.0 mg			
Dietary Fiber	4.1 g			
Sodium	4.6 mg			

CORNBREAD
Serves 12

1 cup	yellow cornmeal
1½ tsp.	salt
1 cup	boiling water
1 Tbl.	olive oil
1 pkg	active dry yeast
1 tsp.	sugar
¼ cup	lukewarm water
2 cups	flour

In a large mixing bowl combine the cornmeal, salt and boiling water. Mix until smooth. Add the olive oil. Let cool to lukewarm.

In a separate small bowl, combine the yeast, sugar and lukewarm water. Let rest in a warm, draft-free place approximately 10 minutes.

Incorporate the yeast into the cornmeal. Add 1½ cups of the flour. Knead for 5 minutes adding the remaining flour as necessary to make a firm dough. Pat dough into a round, flat loaf and place in a 9-inch round baking pan that has been prepared with cooking spray. Cover with plastic wrap. Let rise until double in bulk approximately 30 minutes. Bake at 350° F for 25-30 minutes or until the top is golden brown. Transfer to a rack to cool.

Nutrient Content Per Serving

Calories	144.0
Protein	3.6 g
Carbohydrates	28.2 g
Fat – Total	1.9 g
Cholesterol	0.0 mg
Dietary Fiber	2.4 g
Sodium	272.0 mg

Percent of Calories

10% Protein
78% Carbohydrate
12% Fat

Fat Breakdown

Saturated Fat	0.3 g
Monounsaturated Fat	1.0 g
Polyunsaturated Fat	0.4 g

GARBANZOS A LA CATALANA
Serves 4

2 cups	garbanzo beans, dry
1 tsp.	tomato paste
⅔ cup	raisins
4⅓ cups	chicken stock *(see p. 538)* or vegetable stock *(see p. 542)*
2 cloves	garlic, cut in half
2 Tbl.	parsley, chopped
1 oz.	almonds, toasted, chopped

Soak garbanzos overnight. Drain. Add fresh water.

In a saucepan, cook garbanzo beans until tender. Drain water. Add tomato paste and enough water to simmer. Add raisins, stock, garlic, parsley, almonds. Simmer for 10-15 minutes.

Cook's Note: May use canned garbanzos, rinsed and drained. Add to the stock. May add sautéed onions to tomato paste. May add potatoes to garbanzos.

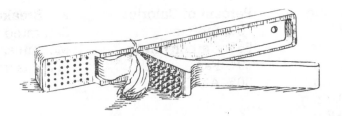

Nutrient Content Per Serving

Calories	267.0
Protein	9.7 g
Carbohydrates	47.9 g
Fat – Total	6.0 g
Cholesterol	0.0 mg
Dietary Fiber	8.1 g
Sodium	76.4 mg

Percent of Calories

14% Protein
67% Carbohydrate
19% Fat

Fat Breakdown

Saturated Fat	0.6 g
Monounsaturated Fat	2.9 g
Polyunsaturated Fat	1.8 g

RICE WITH SHERRY
Serves 4

1 tsp.	olive oil
1 med.	onion, chopped fine
1 cup	rice, short-grain
1 cup	sherry
1½ cups	chicken stock *(see p. 538)*
to taste	salt and pepper

In a non-stick frying pan, sauté the onion in the olive oil until soft. Add the rice and cook 2 minutes. Add sherry, cover and simmer until the sherry has been absorbed. Add the chicken stock, cover and simmer 20 minutes or until all stock is absorbed and the rice is tender. Add salt and pepper to taste if desired.

Alcohol Note: The alcohol content was computed prior to cooking. Once the alcohol is heated to the boiling point, the alcohol disappears along with most of the calories from the alcohol.

Nutrient Content Per Serving

Calories	127.0
Protein	1.8 g
Carbohydrates	17.5 g
Fat – Total	1.3 g
Cholesterol	0.0 mg
Dietary Fiber	0.7 g
Sodium	5.8 mg

Percent of Calories
6% Protein
55% Carbohydrate
9% Fat
30% Alcohol

Fat Breakdown

Saturated Fat	0.2 g
Monounsaturated Fat	0.9 g
Polyunsaturated Fat	0.2 g

SPINACH WITH RICE
Serves 4

1 lb.	spinach, washed, deveined, cut in strips
1 lg.	onion, chopped fine
1 tsp.	olive oil
1 cup	chicken stock *(see p. 538)*
pinch	saffron
1 Tbl.	fresh parsley, chopped
¼ cup	rice
to taste	salt and pepper

In a non-stick pan over medium heat, sauté onion in olive oil until golden. Add spinach, chicken stock and saffron. Bring to a boil. Add parsley and rice. Cover, simmer 20 minutes or until rice is cooked and water is absorbed. Add salt and pepper to taste.

Cook's Note: Serve with chicken, lamb or fish that is not too spicy.

Nutrient Content Per Serving

Calories	94.0
Protein	4.6 g
Carbohydrates	17.0 g
Fat – Total	1.7 g
Cholesterol	0.0 mg
Dietary Fiber	3.8 g
Sodium	91.8 mg

Percent of Calories

18% Protein
67% Carbohydrate
15% Fat

Fat Breakdown

Saturated Fat	0.2 g
Monounsaturated Fat	0.9 g
Polyunsaturated Fat	0.3 g

Simple Saffron Rice
Serves 4

1 tsp.	olive oil
1 med.	onion, chopped fine
1½ cups	rice
¼ tsp.	salt
3 cups	water
pinch	saffron

Sauté onions in olive oil until translucent. Add rice and sauté 2 minutes stirring constantly. Add salt, water and saffron. Bring to a boil. Cover and simmer 20 minutes. Fluff rice with a fork. Taste for seasoning.

Cook's Note: May add more saffron to your taste (up to ¼ teaspoon). Good with chicken, fish or vegetables.

Nutrient Content Per Serving

Calories	266.0
Protein	5.0 g
Carbohydrates	55.8 g
Fat – Total	1.6 g
Cholesterol	0.0 mg
Dietary Fiber	0.8 g
Sodium	137.0 mg

Percent of Calories

8% Protein
87% Carbohydrate
6% Fat

Fat Breakdown

Saturated Fat	0.3 g
Monounsaturated Fat	1.0 g
Polyunsaturated Fat	0.2 g

SAFFRON RICE WITH ALL THE TRIMMINGS
Serves 8

1 tsp.	olive oil
2 cups	rice, uncooked
1	sweet bell pepper, diced
½ tsp.	saffron
1 tsp.	turmeric
to taste	salt
6	cardamon pods
1 tsp.	paprika
⅛ tsp.	cayenne pepper
4 cups	chicken stock *(see p. 538)*

In a large non-stick frying pan, heat olive oil. Gently brown the rice and peppers (15 minutes). Add saffron, turmeric, salt (if desired), cardamon pods, paprika, cayenne pepper and cold stock. Cover and simmer 20 minutes or until rice is cooked and all liquid is absorbed.

Remove cardamon pods. Fluff rice with a fork before serving.

Nutrient Content Per Serving

Calories	181.0
Protein	3.5 g
Carbohydrates	38.4 g
Fat – Total	1.0 g
Cholesterol	0.0 mg
Dietary Fiber	1.0 g
Sodium	2.8 g

Percent of Calories
- 8% Protein
- 87% Carbohydrate
- 5% Fat

Fat Breakdown

Saturated Fat	0.2 g
Monounsaturated Fat	0.5 g
Polyunsaturated Fat	0.2 g

BLACK BEANS
Serves 16

3 lbs.	black turtle beans, presoaked in water overnight
1 med.	yellow onion, chopped
2 Tbl.	garlic, minced
2 cups	celery, chopped
2 Tbl.	olive oil
8 oz.	lean turkey ham, diced
2 Tbl.	tomato purée
1 cup	white wine
1 gal.	chicken stock *(see p. 538)*
1 tsp.	ground cumin
dash	cayenne pepper
to taste	salt and pepper

Garnish:

sour cream, fat-free
red onion, chopped

In a large non-stick frying pan, sauté the onion, garlic and celery in the olive oil until lightly browned. Add the turkey ham and tomato purée. Heat through. Add the drained black beans, white wine and chicken stock. Bring to a boil, then reduce heat to low. Simmer, uncovered, for 30 minutes.

Add the cumin, cayenne pepper and salt and pepper to taste. Simmer 10-15 minutes longer or until it thickens.

Garnish with a dollop of fat-free sour cream and chopped red onion.

Cook's Note: After beans are soaked overnight, discard water and rinse well under running water to decrease gassiness.

Alcohol Note: The alcohol content was computed prior to cooking. Once the alcohol is heated to the boiling point, the alcohol disappears along with most of the calories from the alcohol.

Nutrient Content Per Serving

Calories	171.0
Protein	10.6 g
Carbohydrates	23.3 g
Fat – Total	3.3 g
Cholesterol	5.4 mg
Dietary Fiber	5.7 g
Sodium	203.0 mg

Percent of Calories

24% Protein
53% Carbohydrate
17% Fat
6% Alcohol

Fat Breakdown

Saturated Fat	0.7 g
Monounsaturated Fat	1.8 g
Polyunsaturated Fat	0.5 g

SPANISH OMELETTE
Serves 4

1	potato, peeled, cubed
2	carrots, cubed
4 oz.	turkey sausage, loose
1 med.	onion, chopped
2 Tbl.	white wine
8	egg whites (or 1 cup egg substitute)
1 tsp.	canola oil
pinch	turmeric
½ cup	peas, frozen, thawed
1	tomato, chopped

Boil potatoes and carrots until tender. Drain. In a non-stick frying pan, brown sausage and onion. Add wine. Combine potatoes and sausage.

Break the egg whites into a separate bowl and beat with canola oil and turmeric. Pour over potato and sausage mixture. Add peas and tomatoes. Bake at 350° F until egg sets. Serve hot.

Alcohol Note: The alcohol content was computed prior to cooking. Once the alcohol is heated to the boiling point, the alcohol disappears along with most of the calories from the alcohol.

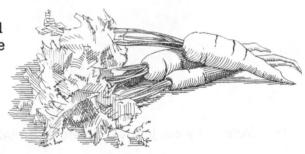

Nutrient Content Per Serving

Calories	221.0
Protein	16.5 g
Carbohydrates	24.8 g
Fat – Total	6.1 g
Cholesterol	23.0 mg
Dietary Fiber	4.1 g
Sodium	339.0 mg

Percent of Calories

29% Protein
44% Carbohydrate
24% Fat
 3% Alcohol

Fat Breakdown

Saturated Fat	1.7 g
Monounsaturated Fat	2.5 g
Polyunsaturated Fat	1.7 g

OMELETTE OF POTATOES AND ONIONS
Serves 4

3	potatoes, peeled, sliced in ⅛-inch-thick rounds
2 tsp.	olive oil
½ cup	onions, chopped
1 cup	egg substitute

Brush 1 teaspoon oil on a non-stick baking sheet. Rub potatoes in the oil to coat sparsely. Bake potatoes at 400° F until browned. (Approximately 40 minutes.)

In a non-stick pan, sauté onions in remaining teaspoon of oil until translucent. Beat egg substitute until frothy. Stir in cooked potatoes and onions.

Heat a non-stick skillet. Coat with cooking spray. Pour egg mixture into pan. Cover and cook over medium heat until firm. To flip omelette, slide onto a dish and invert back into the pan. Cook second side for 3 minutes or until it begins to brown. Serve immediately.

Cook's Note: May use leftover potatoes. It makes a nice Sunday morning brunch entrée!

Nutrient Content Per Serving

Calories	189.0
Protein	10.1 g
Carbohydrates	27.3 g
Fat – Total	4.5 g
Cholesterol	0.6 mg
Dietary Fiber	2.1 g
Sodium	117.0 mg

Percent of Calories

21% Protein
58% Carbohydrate
21% Fat

Fat Breakdown

Saturated Fat	0.8 g
Monounsaturated Fat	2.2 g
Polyunsaturated Fat	1.3 g

VEGETABLE CANALON
Serves 6

14	manicotti shells
2 lbs.	fresh spinach, chopped
3½ oz.	fresh tuna steaks, cubed
1 med.	onion, chopped
1½ cups	mushrooms, sliced thin
½ tsp.	olive oil
2 cups	bechamel sauce *(see p. 554)*
1 oz.	parmesan cheese, grated

Cook manicotti shells al dente. Drain. Cool.

Microwave spinach until completely wilted.

In a large non-stick frying pan, sauté onions and mushrooms in olive oil. Add tuna steaks and cook until done. Break tuna into small pieces as it cooks.

Combine drained spinach, tuna, onion and mushrooms. Fill manicotti with this mixture. Arrange manicotti in a baking dish prepared with cooking spray.

Prepare the bechamel sauce and pour over manicotti. Sprinkle grated parmesan cheese over top. Cover and bake at 350° F for 20-30 minutes or until heated through and cheese is melted.

Cook's Note: May substitute any tomato sauce for the bechamel sauce.

Nutrient Content Per Serving

Calories	356.0
Protein	21.6 g
Carbohydrates	53.5 g
Fat – Total	7.1 g
Cholesterol	13.7 mg
Dietary Fiber	7.0 g
Sodium	330.0 mg

Percent of Calories

24% Protein
59% Carbohydrate
18% Fat

Fat Breakdown

Saturated Fat	2.3 g
Monounsaturated Fat	2.0 g
Polyunsaturated Fat	1.9 g

CANALON WITH SEAFOOD
Serves 4

1 lb.	manicotti shells
½ lb.	shrimp
½ lb.	monkfish (may substitute cod, scallops or halibut)
1 lb.	mussels in shells
2	tomatoes, diced
2 Tbl.	parmesan cheese, grated

Poaching liquid:

1	lemon, juice of
½ cup	white wine
1 cup	water
1½ cups	bechamel sauce *(see p. 554)*

Cook manicotti shells al dente. Drain. Cool.

Poach fish in poaching liquid. Steam mussels and shrimp and remove shells. Chop all fish and seafood and combine with tomatoes.

Prepare one recipe of bechamel sauce.

Stuff manicotti with fish mixture. Arrange in a baking dish prepared with cooking spray. Pour bechamel sauce over manicotti. Sprinkle parmesan cheese on top. Cover and bake at 350° F for 30 minutes or until heated through.

Cook's Note: May serve with your choice of tomato-based sauce instead of bechamel sauce.

Nutrient Content Per Serving

Calories	475.0
Protein	47.0 g
Carbohydrates	47.1 g
Fat – Total	9.1 g
Cholesterol	149.0 g
Dietary Fiber	2.7 g
Sodium	630.0 mg

Percent of Calories

41% Protein
42% Carbohydrate
18% Fat

Fat Breakdown

Saturated Fat	2.5 g
Monounsaturated Fat	2.2 g
Polyunsaturated Fat	2.6 g

CODFISH CAKES
Serves 4

1 lb.	whole cod
1 cup	bread crumbs
¼ cup	fresh cilantro, chopped
1 Tbl.	fresh parsley, chopped
½ tsp.	fresh mint, chopped
2 Tbl.	paprika
2 cloves	garlic, minced
1 tsp.	salt
⅛ tsp.	black pepper
3	egg whites

Poach cod in water until cooked enough to crumble. Drain well. When cool enough to handle, discard bones and crumble. Mix cod with remaining ingredients. Form into patties. Spray a non-stick baking sheet with cooking spray and bake at 350° F for 20 minutes or until golden brown. Serve garnished with parsley sprigs.

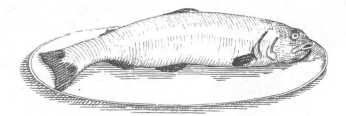

Nutrient Content Per Serving

Calories	217.0
Protein	26.6 g
Carbohydrates	20.9 g
Fat – Total	2.6 g
Cholesterol	48.7 mg
Dietary Fiber	2.7 g
Sodium	853.0 mg

Percent of Calories

50% Protein
39% Carbohydrate
11% Fat

Fat Breakdown

Saturated Fat	0.5 g
Monounsaturated Fat	0.7 g
Polyunsaturated Fat	0.9 g

COD AND POTATO CASSEROLE
Serves 4

1 lb.	cod
6 med.	potatoes, peeled, sliced in ¼-inch rounds
4	onions, sliced in thin rings
1 tsp.	olive oil
1 tsp.	garlic, minced
16	black olives, sliced thin
2 Tbl.	parsley, chopped

Parboil or microwave potatoes until just tender. Prepare a non-stick baking dish with cooking spray.

In a small frying pan, sauté onions in the olive oil until translucent. Add garlic and sauté 1 minute longer.

Wash the cod and pat dry.

Assemble the casserole as follows: potatoes on the bottom, cod next, then onions. Cover and bake at 300° F for 30-45 minutes until cod is cooked and potatoes are tender. Sprinkle olives and parsley on top before serving.

Nutrient Content Per Serving

Calories	300.0
Protein	25.2 g
Carbohydrates	41.1 g
Fat – Total	4.2 g
Cholesterol	48.7 mg
Dietary Fiber	5.1 g
Sodium	193.0 mg

Percent of Calories

33% Protein
54% Carbohydrate
12% Fat

Fat Breakdown

Saturated Fat	0.6 g
Monounsaturated Fat	2.4 g
Polyunsaturated Fat	0.7 g

CRAB IN A SHERRY AND BRANDY SAUCE
Serves 4

1 lb.	crabmeat, steamed and removed from shell
1 clove	garlic, minced
1 tsp.	olive oil
1	leek, white portion, chopped
1 med.	tomato, peeled, seeded, chopped
¼ cup	sherry
¼ cup	brandy
1 tsp.	powdered butter replacement
¼ cup	chicken stock *(see p. 538)*
2 Tbl.	parsley, chopped
pinch	cayenne pepper
to taste	salt
to taste	freshly ground black pepper
½ cup	bread crumbs

In a non-stick frying pan sauté the garlic in olive oil. Add the leeks and cook for 5 minutes or until soft. Add the tomato, sherry, brandy and powdered butter replacement. Simmer 1 minute.

Stir in the crab, chicken stock, parsley, cayenne pepper, salt and freshly ground black pepper. Leave uncovered and simmer for 3 minutes.

In a toaster oven or dry non-stick frying pan, brown the bread crumbs. Arrange crab mixture in individual gratin dishes. Sprinkle bread crumbs on top. Bake at 350° F for 15 minutes or until the top is golden and crisp.

Cook's Note: Makes 4 hearty servings. Could also make 6 moderate servings.

Alcohol Note: The alcohol content was computed prior to cooking. Once the alcohol is heated to the boiling point, the alcohol disappears along with most of the calories from the alcohol.

Nutrient Content Per Serving

Calories	245.0
Protein	25.3 g
Carbohydrates	15.8 g
Fat – Total	4.0 g
Cholesterol	113.0 mg
Dietary Fiber	1.7 g
Sodium	439.0 mg

Percent of Calories

42% Protein
26% Carbohydrate
15% Fat
17% Alcohol

Fat Breakdown

Saturated Fat	0.6 g
Monounsaturated Fat	1.4 g
Polyunsaturated Fat	1.2 g

Stuffed Fish
Serves 4

Stuffing:

¼	onion, minced
2 cloves	garlic, minced
1 tsp.	olive oil
1 cup	bread crumbs
2 Tbl.	fresh lemon juice
2 Tbl.	fresh parsley
to taste	salt and pepper (optional)
1 lb.	rockfish or cod
½ cup	dry white wine
1 clove	garlic, whole
1	bay leaf
½ tsp.	cumin
½ tsp.	paprika
2	plum tomatoes, seeded and chopped
½	onion, sliced thick
2 Tbl.	white wine vinegar

To prepare stuffing:

Sauté onions and garlic in oil. Add remaining stuffing ingredients. Roll fish fillets around stuffing or simply layer stuffing between fillets like a sandwich.

Arrange fish in a baking dish prepared with cooking spray. Add remaining ingredients. Cover and bake 40 minutes at 350° F or until fish flakes easily when poked with a fork.

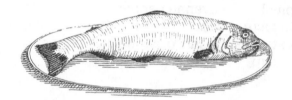

Cook's Note: Stuffing can be made in a more traditional manner by using 4 slices of bread soaked in water in place of bread crumbs. Using this substitution, the stuffing will be gummy.

Alcohol Note: The alcohol content was computed prior to cooking. Once the alcohol is heated to the boiling point, the alcohol disappears along with most of the calories from the alcohol.

Nutrient Content Per Serving

Calories	164.0
Protein	21.5 g
Carbohydrates	9.1 g
Fat – Total	2.3 g
Cholesterol	49.0 mg
Dietary Fiber	1.1 g
Sodium	105.0 mg

Percent of Calories

53% Protein
22% Carbohydrate
13% Fat
12% Alcohol

Fat Breakdown

Saturated Fat	0.4 g
Monounsaturated Fat	1.1 g
Polyunsaturated Fat	0.5 g

Halibut with a Green Sauce
Serves 6

3 lbs.	halibut
2 Tbl.	peas, cooked or defrosted

Sauce:

½ cup	onions, diced
2 Tbl.	olive oil
½ cup	flour
1½ cups	water
1 cup	white wine
2 tsp.	garlic, minced
½ cup	fresh parsley, chopped
1 tsp.	salt

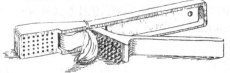

To prepare sauce:

Sauté onions in olive oil until soft but not brown. Add flour, mix well. Whisk in water and wine, whisking constantly. Whisk until sauce thickens. Simmer 3 minutes.

Separately, mash garlic, parsley and salt into a smooth paste. Whisk into sauce.

Meanwhile, prepare fish by grilling or baking. (Bake fish 20 minutes per inch of thickness.) When fish is cooked, arrange on a baking platter, pour green sauce over fish, arrange peas on top. Bake 5 minutes or until peas are warmed.

Alcohol Note: The alcohol content was computed prior to cooking. Once the alcohol is heated to the boiling point, the alcohol disappears along with most of the calories from the alcohol.

Nutrient Content Per Serving

Calories	364.0
Protein	48.8 g
Carbohydrates	10.4 g
Fat – Total	9.9 g
Cholesterol	72.6 mg
Dietary Fiber	0.9 g
Sodium	486.0 mg

Percent of Calories

56% Protein
12% Carbohydrate
25% Fat
 7% Alcohol

Fat Breakdown

Saturated Fat	1.4 g
Monounsaturated Fat	5.0 g
Polyunsaturated Fat	2.3 g

BAKED RED SNAPPER
Serves 4

2 lbs.	red snapper fillets
1	lemon, cut in wedges
½ cup	bread crumbs
¼ cup	dijon mustard
2 Tbl.	fresh parsley, chopped
2 tsp.	garlic, minced
2 Tbl.	paprika
1 Tbl.	lemon juice
2	potatoes, sliced in ¼-inch rounds
to taste	salt and black pepper

Parboil the potatoes. Peeling is optional.

Score the fish deeply. Place a lemon wedge in each slit. Combine mustard, parsley, garlic, paprika and lemon juice. Spread over fish.

In a baking dish prepared with cooking spray, arrange the potatoes. Sprinkle with salt and pepper to taste. Place fish on top and cover with bread-crumb mixture. Bake, uncovered at 350° F for 15-20 minutes or until fish and potatoes are cooked.

Cook's Note: A simple baked fish.

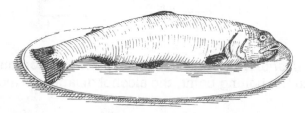

Nutrient Content Per Serving

Calories	416.0
Protein	52.0 g
Carbohydrates	39.7 g
Fat – Total	5.1 g
Cholesterol	84.0 mg
Dietary Fiber	5.0 g
Sodium	460.0 mg

Percent of Calories

50% Protein
39% Carbohydrate
11% Fat

Fat Breakdown

Saturated Fat	0.9 g
Monounsaturated Fat	1.5 g
Polyunsaturated Fat	1.7 g

GRILLED SHRIMP WITH SPICED TOMATO SAUCE
Serves 6

36   jumbo shrimp, peeled and
            deveined

Marinade:
2   lemons, juice of
2   limes, juice of
1 Tbl.   olive oil
1 tsp.   paprika
to taste   salt and pepper

Spiced Tomato Sauce:
1 cup   tomato ragout *(see p. 552)*
dash   cayenne pepper

Combine all marinade ingredients. Marinate shrimp for 10 minutes. Skewer and grill quickly over hot coals.

To prepare the spiced tomato sauce:
In a saucepan, combine all sauce ingredients. Bring to a boil. Serve hot.

To serve:
Line a plate with ½ cup spiced tomato sauce. Arrange shrimp on top.

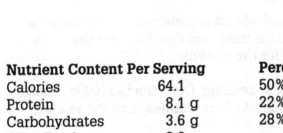

Nutrient Content Per Serving		**Percent of Calories**	**Fat Breakdown**	
Calories	64.1	50% Protein	Saturated Fat	0.3 g
Protein	8.1 g	22% Carbohydrate	Monounsaturated Fat	1.2 g
Carbohydrates	3.6 g	28% Fat	Polyunsaturated Fat	0.3 g
Fat – Total	2.0 g			
Cholesterol	70.2 mg			
Dietary Fiber	0.7 g			
Sodium	113.0 mg			

TEQUILA PRAWNS
Serves 6

2 lbs.	jumbo prawns, peeled and deveined

Marinade:

¼ cup	tequila
¼ cup	lime juice
1 Tbl.	anise seeds
1 Tbl.	coriander seeds
¼ bunch	cilantro, chopped
2 oz.	candied ginger
to taste	salt and pepper

Sauce:

1 cup	sweet white wine
1 Tbl.	turmeric
1 tsp.	paprika
1 cup	chicken stock *(see p. 538)*
2 cloves	garlic, minced
dash	cayenne pepper

Combine all marinade ingredients. Marinate prawns for 10 minutes. Season with salt and pepper if desired. Grill quickly over hot coals.

In a saucepan, combine all sauce ingredients. Reduce until it starts to thicken. Season with salt and pepper if desired. Use as a sauce for dipping the prawns.

Cook's Note: This dish is higher in cholesterol than HealthMark recommends. Make sure the rest of your week is low cholesterol and enjoy this special treat. You can decrease the cholesterol content by substituting some sea scallops for the prawns.

Alcohol Note: The alcohol content was computed prior to cooking. Once the alcohol is heated to the boiling point, the alcohol disappears along with most of the calories from the alcohol.

Nutrient Content Per Serving		Percent of Calories	Fat Breakdown	
Calories	234.0	55% Protein	Saturated Fat	0.5 g
Protein	31.4 g	12% Carbohydrate	Monounsaturated Fat	0.6 g
Carbohydrates	7.1 g	12% Fat	Polyunsaturated Fat	1.1 g
Fat – Total	3.2 g	21% Alcohol		
Cholesterol	230.0 mg			
Dietary Fiber	1.1 g			
Sodium	228.0 mg			

GRILLED SWORDFISH STEAK
Serves 4

4 6-oz.	swordfish steaks
1 8-oz. can	V-8 juice, low-sodium
1 sm.	hot red pepper
1 Tbl.	powdered butter replacement
½ lb.	angel-hair pasta, uncooked

Garnish: (optional)
cucumber swirl
tomato relish *(see p. 550)*

In a saucepan, reduce the V-8 juice slowly to half its amount. Add the hot pepper and powdered butter replacement.

Grill the swordfish steak over hot coals (5 minutes each side) or until done. Cook the pasta al dente.

To serve:
Ladle some sauce on a dinner plate along with a roll of angel-hair pasta. Arrange the swordfish on the pasta. Top it with tomato relish and garnish with cucumber swirl and seasonal vegetables.

Nutrient Content Per Serving

Calories	441.0
Protein	41.7 g
Carbohydrates	47.0 g
Fat – Total	8.4 g
Cholesterol	66.3 mg
Dietary Fiber	4.4 g
Sodium	202.0 mg

Percent of Calories
39% Protein
44% Carbohydrate
17% Fat

Fat Breakdown

Saturated Fat	2.1 g
Monounsaturated Fat	3.2 g
Polyunsaturated Fat	2.0 g

SWORDFISH WITH TOMATILLO SAUCE
Serves 4

4 7-oz.	swordfish steaks
2 Tbl.	lemon juice
to taste	salt and pepper
¼ cup	yellow onion, chopped fine
1 clove	garlic, minced
2 tsp.	canola oil

Sauce:

8	tomatillo, peeled, chopped
1	jalapeno, seeded, chopped
¼ cup	cilantro
½ cup	chicken stock *(see p. 538)* or fish stock *(see p. 540)*

To prepare sauce:

Sprinkle swordfish with lemon juice and salt and pepper to taste. Combine tomatillo, jalapeno, cilantro and stock in a food processor. Process until smooth.

In a non-stick frying pan, sauté onions and garlic in oil for 4 minutes. Add tomatillo mixture to onions and garlic. Simmer and reduce 5-10 minutes. Add salt and pepper to taste.

Grill or broil swordfish for 4 minutes per side. Serve sauce over swordfish.

Cook's Note: Tomatillos look like green tomatoes and are used in Mexican cooking. They are always eaten cooked, and have a faintly apple-like flavor. This sauce can be used on other fish steaks, such as halibut or shark.

Although the % of calories from fat is above 30, the majority of the fat is from the swordfish. Of the 11.1 grams of fat, 8 grams are from the swordfish (a good-fat source).

Nutrient Content Per Serving		Percent of Calories	Fat Breakdown	
Calories	293.0	56% Protein	Saturated Fat	2.4 g
Protein	40.3 g	9% Carbohydrate	Monounsaturated Fat	4.5 g
Carbohydrates	6.2 g	35% Fat	Polyunsaturated Fat	2.6 g
Fat – Total	11.1 g			
Cholesterol	77.4 mg			
Dietary Fiber	0.3 g			
Sodium	334.0 mg			

FRESH TUNA-POTATO STEW
Serves 4

1 tsp.	olive oil
1 cup	onions, chopped fine
2 cloves	garlic, minced
4 lg.	tomatoes, peeled, seeded and chopped
4	potatoes, peeled, cut into medium chunks
½ tsp.	paprika
2 cups	boiling water
1 cup	fish stock *(see p. 540)*
¼ tsp.	salt
¼ tsp.	black pepper
1½ lbs.	fresh tuna, cut in thick strips
1	lemon, juice of

In a non-stick pan, sauté onions and garlic in oil until onions begin to brown. Add tomatoes and cook until most of the liquid evaporates. Add potatoes, paprika, boiling water, fish stock and salt and pepper to taste. (Liquid should completely cover the potatoes.) Cover and simmer 15 minutes or until potatoes are just tender.

Add tuna. Cover and cook 5 minutes or until fish is done. Squeeze lemon over top. Serve at once.

Cook's Note: May substitute swordfish, mahi mahi or halibut for the tuna.

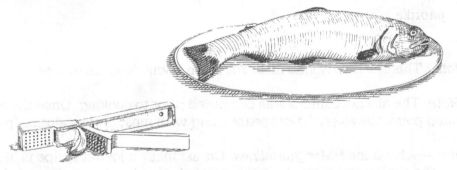

Nutrient Content Per Serving

Calories	529.0
Protein	46.0 g
Carbohydrates	61.6 g
Fat – Total	10.5 g
Cholesterol	64.6 mg
Dietary Fiber	6.7 g
Sodium	228.0 mg

Percent of Calories

35% Protein
47% Carbohydrate
18% Fat

Fat Breakdown

Saturated Fat	2.5 g
Monounsaturated Fat	3.7 g
Polyunsaturated Fat	3.4 g

VELVET SEAFOOD PLATTER
Serves 4

10 oz.	monkfish (may substitute cod)
4 med.	shrimp, peeled and deveined
6 oz.	squid
½ lb.	mussels in shells
1 recipe	bechamel sauce *(see p. 554)* (with substitutes stated in recipe)
1½ cups	rice, cooked

Poaching liquid:

1	lemon, juice of
1	onion, chopped
¼ cup	parsley, chopped
½ cup	white wine
1 cup	water

Garnish:

paprika

Poach monkfish, shrimp and squid in poaching liquid. Steam mussels. Remove from shells.

Prepare bechamel sauce substituting poaching water for half of the milk. Arrange rice on a serving platter.

Arrange monkfish, squid and mussels on top. Cover with bechamel sauce. Top with shrimp. Garnish with paprika.

Cook's Note: This is a hearty side dish. For some it will do as an entrée.

Alcohol Note: The alcohol content was computed prior to cooking. Once the alcohol is heated to the boiling point, the alcohol disappears along with most of the calories from the alcohol.

Cholesterol — Above the HM✔ guidelines: Occasionally a lowfat recipe is high in cholesterol. In this case the cholesterol stems from the shellfish. The level is moderately high (>150 mg per serving) but may fit into your weekly average of 150 mg per day.

Nutrient Content Per Serving		Percent of Calories	Fat Breakdown	
Calories	311.0	42% Protein	Saturated Fat	0.9 g
Protein	31.5 g	40% Carbohydrate	Monounsaturated Fat	1.1 g
Carbohydrates	30.0 g	12% Fat	Polyunsaturated Fat	1.3 g
Fat – Total	4.2 g	6% Alcohol		
Cholesterol	176.0 mg			
Dietary Fiber	1.2 g			
Sodium	374.0 mg			

Clams in Garlic/Vegetable Broth *(page 41)*
Stuffed Fish *(page 92)*
Brochette of Vegetables *(page 52)*

Grilled Tuna Salad *(page 76)*
Gazpacho *(page 56)*

Charred Buffalo Carpaccio *(page 113)*
with Whole-Grain Mustard Sauce *(page 553)*

Prawn Cocktail *(page 47)*
Paella *(page 106)*

ZARZUELA
Serves 6

1	onion, chopped fine
3 cloves	garlic, minced
2 tsp.	olive oil
2 lbs.	monkfish (or 2 lbs. lobster)
6 lg.	shrimp
1 med.	sweet red pepper, chopped
3	tomatoes, chopped fine
¼ tsp.	saffron
2 Tbl.	parsley, chopped
1	bay leaf
½ tsp.	thyme
¼ tsp.	crushed red pepper flakes
¾ cup	white wine
¼ cup	lemon juice
to taste	salt and pepper
12	mussels in shells

Garnish:

	parsley
1	lemon, cut in wedges

In a non-stick frying pan, sauté onion and garlic in oil. Add monkfish and shrimp and cook for 5 minutes. Add sweet red pepper, tomatoes, saffron, parsley, bay leaf, thyme, crushed red pepper, wine, lemon juice and salt and pepper to taste. Simmer uncovered for 10 minutes.

Steam the mussels until they open, and set aside. Cut the fish into chunks. Arrange zarzuela in a serving dish and place mussels decoratively on top.

To serve, garnish with parsley and lemon wedges.

Cook's Note: Can use any fish you desire. If you choose to use lobster in place of monkfish, steam the lobster until pink, cut meat in chunks and set aside. Return the lobster to the pan with the wine and simmer for the 10 minutes.

Alcohol Note: The alcohol content was computed prior to cooking. Once the alcohol is heated to the boiling point, the alcohol disappears along with most of the calories from the alcohol.

Nutrient Content Per Serving		**Percent of Calories**	**Fat Breakdown**	
Calories	199.0	61% Protein	Saturated Fat	0.5 g
Protein	30.1 g	15% Carbohydrate	Monounsaturated Fat	1.4 g
Carbohydrates	7.3 g	14% Fat	Polyunsaturated Fat	0.7 g
Fat – Total	3.1 g	10% Alcohol		
Cholesterol	77.4 mg			
Dietary Fiber	1.5 g			
Sodium	119.0 mg			

PAELLA
Serves 8

4	chicken breasts, boneless, skinless, cut into medium chunks
1 Tbl.	olive oil
1 lg.	sweet red pepper, seeded, cut into medium-size chunks
1 lg.	green pepper, seeded, cut into medium-size chunks
1 med.	onion, minced
2 lbs.	tomatoes, peeled, seeded, chopped
4 cloves	garlic, minced
3 cups	rice
8	jumbo scallops
8 lg.	cherrystone clams, in shells, scrubbed
6 cups	fish stock *(see p. 540)*
2½ tsp.	salt
to taste	pepper
1 tsp.	saffron
1	bay leaf
8	prawns, peeled, deveined
1 lb.	mussels, in shells, scrubbed *(see p. 13)*

In a large skillet, heat oil over medium heat. Sear chicken quickly and remove from pan. Add peppers, onions and tomatoes and sauté for 5-10 minutes or until light golden brown. Add the garlic, rice, scallops, clams and fish stock. Bring to a boil. Return the chicken to pan and season with salt, pepper, saffron and bay leaf. Mix well, cover and bake at 375° F for 20-30 minutes.

Add the shrimp and mussels, stir and bake for another 5-10 minutes. Serve immediately. May be served with lemon wedges.

Cook's Note: A variety of vegetables may be added to the paella before baking. Those that are especially good are asparagus, fresh peas or artichoke hearts. Let your taste buds be your guide! If you like more zing, add some chile carbé or hot pepper!

Alcohol Note: The alcohol content was computed prior to cooking. Once the alcohol is heated to the boiling point, the alcohol disappears along with most of the calories from the alcohol.

Sodium — Above the HM✔ guidelines This recipe exceeds the HealthMark limits for sodium (800 mg per serving). The excess sodium is coming from the shellfish. If you have hypertension (high blood pressure) and must restrict your sodium intake, this recipe may push your total sodium intake above your desired level for that day. *(Refer to HealthMark Dietary Goals p. 3.)*

Nutrient Content Per Serving		**Percent of Calories**	**Fat Breakdown**	
Calories	475.0	28% Protein	Saturated Fat	1.0 g
Protein	32.8 g	58% Carbohydrate	Monounsaturated Fat	2.2 g
Carbohydrates	67.4 g	12% Fat	Polyunsaturated Fat	1.7 g
Fat – Total	6.0 g	2% Alcohol		
Cholesterol	72.5 mg			
Dietary Fiber	3.1 g			
Sodium	925.0 mg			

BRAISED CHICKEN WITH ALMONDS

Serves 4

4	chicken breasts, boneless, skinless
	salt and pepper (optional)
	flour
1½ tsp.	olive oil
1 cup	onions, chopped fine
1½ cups	dry white wine
1 cup	chicken stock *(see p. 538)*
2 Tbl.	fresh parsley, chopped
1	bay leaf
1 Tbl.	garlic, minced
¼ cup	blanched almonds
pinch	saffron

Pound chicken breasts flat. Coat with flour. Shake to remove excess. Sprinkle with salt and pepper if desired. Brown in a non-stick pan, using 1 teaspoon of the olive oil. Set aside.

Sauté onions in same pan using remaining ½ teaspoon of oil until soft. Return chicken to pan. Spread onions over chicken. Add wine, stock, parsley and bay leaf. Cover tightly and simmer 20 minutes.

Combine garlic, almonds, and saffron. Mash with a mortar and pestle until smooth. Add to pan and cook uncovered for 10 minutes. Remove chicken to a heated platter. Reduce liquid to strengthen the flavor. Serve hot over rice.

Alcohol Note: The alcohol content was computed prior to cooking. Once the alcohol is heated to the boiling point, the alcohol disappears along with most of the calories from the alcohol.

Nutrient Content Per Serving

Calories	279.0
Protein	30.1 g
Carbohydrates	7.3 g
Fat – Total	8.1 g
Cholesterol	68.4 mg
Dietary Fiber	1.9 g
Sodium	148.0 mg

Percent of Calories

43% Protein
10% Carbohydrate
26% Fat
20% Alcohol

Fat Breakdown

Saturated Fat	1.1 g
Monounsaturated Fat	4.7 g
Polyunsaturated Fat	1.5 g

CHICKEN WITH GARLIC
Serves 4

4	chicken breasts, boneless, skinless
4 Tbl.	flour
2 tsp.	olive oil
2 cloves	garlic, minced
1 cup	white wine
½ cup	chicken stock *(see p. 538)*
1	lemon, juice of

Garnish:
  parsley

Pound chicken breasts until flat.

Coat with flour. In a non-stick frying pan, brown chicken in oil over medium heat. Remove chicken from pan. Brown the garlic in frying pan. Return chicken to pan. Add wine and stock. Simmer until chicken is done. Add lemon juice. Garnish with parsley and serve.

Alcohol Note: The alcohol content was computed prior to cooking. Once the alcohol is heated to the boiling point, the alcohol disappears along with most of the calories from the alcohol.

Nutrient Content Per Serving		Percent of Calories	Fat Breakdown	
Calories	220.0	53% Protein	Saturated Fat	0.7 g
Protein	28.3 g	13% Carbohydrate	Monounsaturated Fat	2.0 g
Carbohydrates	7.2 g	16% Fat	Polyunsaturated Fat	0.6 g
Fat – Total	3.8 g	18% Alcohol		
Cholesterol	68.4 mg			
Dietary Fiber	0.3 g			
Sodium	79.7 mg			

CHICKEN WITH SAFFRON RICE
Serves 4

4	chicken breasts, skinless and boneless
	garlic powder
	fresh ground black pepper
1 tsp.	olive oil
1 cup	onions, minced
1 Tbl.	paprika
2 cups	tomatoes, chopped
2 cloves	garlic, minced
a few drops	Tabasco™
2 tsp.	oregano, dry
1 cup	rice
1 cup	peas, fresh or frozen
2 cups	chicken stock *(see p. 538)*
⅛ tsp.	saffron
to taste	salt
2 Tbl.	fresh parsley, chopped

Wash chicken breasts and pat dry. Sprinkle with garlic powder and black pepper. Heat olive oil in a non-stick pan. Gently brown the chicken. Remove chicken to a heated platter. Add onions to pan and cook until translucent. Add paprika, tomatoes, garlic, Tabasco™ and oregano. Cook down.

Return chicken to pan. Add rice, peas, chicken stock, saffron and salt to taste. Bring to a boil. Cover and simmer 20-30 minutes or until chicken is tender and rice has absorbed all the water. Stir in parsley. Serve hot.

Nutrient Content Per Serving

Calories	393.0
Protein	36.4 g
Carbohydrates	50.6 g
Fat – Total	4.1 g
Cholesterol	68.4 mg
Dietary Fiber	4.2 g
Sodium	478.0 mg

Percent of Calories

38% Protein
53% Carbohydrate
10% Fat

Fat Breakdown

Saturated Fat	0.7 g
Monounsaturated Fat	1.4
Polyunsaturated Fat	0.7 g

CHICKEN WITH VEGETABLES
Serves 4

4	chicken breasts, boneless, skinless
1	onion, diced fine
1 tsp.	olive oil
3	tomatoes, chopped
1	green pepper, chopped fine
1	eggplant, peeled, chopped fine

In a medium, non-stick frying pan, sauté the onion in the oil. Add the tomatoes, green pepper and eggplant. Cook until vegetables are halfway cooked.

Arrange chicken in a baking dish prepared with cooking spray. Spread vegetables over the top. Bake, covered, at 350° F for 30-40 minutes or until chicken is done.

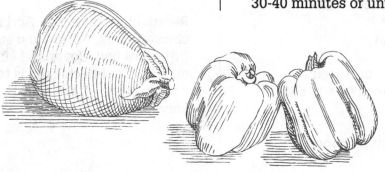

Nutrient Content Per Serving

Calories	216.0
Protein	29.8 g
Carbohydrates	17.9 g
Fat – Total	3.3 g
Cholesterol	68.4 mg
Dietary Fiber	6.4 g
Sodium	90.6 mg

Percent of Calories

54% Protein
32% Carbohydrate
13% Fat

Fat Breakdown

Saturated Fat	0.7 g
Monounsaturated Fat	1.3 g
Polyunsaturated Fat	0.7 g

GRILLED CHICKEN WITH VEGETABLE TOMATO RAGOUT
Serves 6

6	chicken breasts, boneless, skinless
2 Tbl.	olive oil
1	eggplant, peeled, diced
1	zucchini, diced
1	green pepper, diced
1	red onion, diced
2 lg.	tomatoes, peeled, seeded, diced
2 cloves	garlic, minced
2	shallots, chopped fine
to taste	salt
¼ cup	red wine
12 oz.	tomato juice, low-sodium
¼ bunch	fresh basil, chopped
¼ bunch	chives, chopped

In a large non-stick skillet, sear the chicken breasts in the olive oil until golden brown on both sides. Remove the chicken and keep warm. To the skillet add the vegetables, garlic and shallots. Sear until slightly brown. Season with salt to taste. Add red wine, tomato juice and chicken. Let simmer 20-30 minutes. Arrange chicken breasts on a platter. Pour the sauce over top and garnish with fresh basil and chives.

Cook's Note: This dish goes great with risotto or pasta.

Alcohol Note: The alcohol content was computed prior to cooking. Once the alcohol is heated to the boiling point, the alcohol disappears along with most of the calories from the alcohol.

Nutrient Content Per Serving		**Percent of Calories**	**Fat Breakdown**	
Calories	229.0	51% Protein	Saturated Fat	1.1 g
Protein	29.2 g	22% Carbohydrates	Monounsaturated Fat	3.7 g
Carbohydrates	12.6 g	25% Fat	Polyunsaturated Fat	0.9 g
Fat – Total	6.4 g	2% Alcohol		
Cholesterol	68.4 mg			
Dietary Fiber	4.2 g			
Sodium	88.7 mg			

BEEF WITH PLUMS
Serves 4

1 lb.	top round, sliced thin
1	carrot, sliced
2	onions, diced
2 cloves	garlic, minced
1 tsp.	tomato paste
¼ cup	red wine
3	plums, chopped
1	bay leaf
½ tsp.	thyme, chopped

Garnish:
2 Tbl.	fresh parsley, chopped

Pound sliced beef with a meat tenderizer. Coat a large frying pan with cooking spray. Sauté meat with carrot, onions, garlic and tomato paste until tender. Remove vegetables from pan and purée with red wine in a blender. Meanwhile, allow meat to brown. Add vegetable purée, plums, bay leaf and thyme. Cover and simmer 30 minutes. Remove bay leaf before serving. Garnish with parsley.

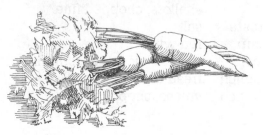

Variation:
- Ingredients as above plus 2 cups veal stock *(see p. 536)* and 1 cup burgundy wine or merlot. Prepare as above. At end add 2 cups veal stock and 1 cup wine to meat. Cook for 30 minutes.

Cook's Note: May use mushrooms, vegetables or raisins instead of plums. May serve over rice or with noodles.

Alcohol Note: The alcohol content was computed prior to cooking. Once the alcohol is heated to the boiling point, the alcohol disappears along with most of the calories from the alcohol.

Nutrient Content Per Serving		**Percent of Calories**	**Fat Breakdown**	
Calories	268.0	57% Protein	Saturated Fat	2.0 g
Protein	37.1 g	19% Carbohydrate	Monounsaturated Fat	2.4 g
Carbohydrates	12.7 g	20% Fat	Polyunsaturated Fat	0.4 g
Fat – Total	6.0 g	4% Alcohol		
Cholesterol	95.2 mg			
Dietary Fiber	2.1 g			
Sodium	88.5 mg			

CHARRED BUFFALO CARPACCIO
Serves 4

16 oz.	buffalo steak
1 tsp.	anise seed
1 tsp.	coriander
1 tsp.	black pepper
to taste	salt
2 tsp.	Basil Mustard-Seed Oil (see p. 562)

1 sm.	eggplant
2 tsp.	olive oil
pinch	white pepper
pinch	salt
⅛ tsp.	garlic powder
dash	lemon juice, fresh

Garnish:

2 Tbl.	Grenadine Onions (see p. 533)

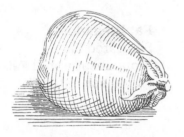

Grind together anise seeds, coriander, black pepper and salt until smooth. Season the buffalo with the basil mustard seed oil and ground spices. Using almost a blackening technique, sear the buffalo almost dark brown over hot coals. Remove, chill and then freeze it (for better cutting and portion control). Don't slice it until it is frozen semi-solid. Trim it, then slice thinly with a sharp knife and arrange on a dinner plate.

To prepare roasted eggplant:
Slice eggplant lengthwise, cut off the edges on both ends and slice into ¼-inch-thick slices. Brush with mixture of olive oil, white pepper, salt, garlic powder and lemon juice. Grill quickly.

To serve:
Arrange cold buffalo on a dinner plate with hot grilled eggplant. Garnish dish with grenadine onions.

Cook's Note: May grind spices in a coffee grinder — it goes quicker. Boiled new potatoes make a nice finishing touch. May serve the meat hot or cold.

Nutrient Content Per Serving

Calories	251.0
Protein	33.8 g
Carbohydrates	14.0 g
Fat – Total	6.6 g
Cholesterol	93.0 mg
Dietary Fiber	4.6 g
Sodium	103.0 mg

Percent of Calories

54% Protein	
22% Carbohydrate	
24% Fat	

Fat Breakdown

Saturated Fat	1.6 g
Monounsaturated Fat	3.7 g
Polyunsaturated Fat	0.7 g

FRICANDO
Serves 4

1 lb.	veal scallops
12	dried mushrooms
2 Tbl.	flour
½ tsp.	olive oil
1 med.	onion, sliced thin
2	tomatoes, chopped
½ cup	chicken stock *(see p. 538)*
1 tsp.	cornstarch

Soak dried mushrooms in warm water for 2-3 hours. Drain. Rinse mushrooms. Cut the large ones into small pieces.

Coat the veal with flour. In a non-stick frying pan, gently brown the veal in ½ teaspoon olive oil. Remove veal from pan and keep warm.

In the same pan, sauté the onions and tomatoes. Add stock to pan and bring to a boil. Reduce heat and whisk in the cornstarch until the sauce thickens. Add mushrooms and simmer 8 minutes. Return veal to the pan. Heat through. Serve immediately.

Nutrient Content Per Serving

Calories	278.0
Protein	32.4 g
Carbohydrates	18.1 g
Fat – Total	8.4 g
Cholesterol	118.0 mg
Dietary Fiber	2.8 g
Sodium	105.0 mg

Percent of Calories

46% Protein
26% Carbohydrate
27% Fat

Fat Breakdown

Saturated Fat	2.9 g
Monounsaturated Fat	3.2 g
Polyunsaturated Fat	0.9 g

PORK TENDERLOIN
WITH CLAMS, TOMATOES AND CORIANDER
Serve 4

Marinade:

1½ cups	dry white wine
1 Tbl.	paprika
¼ tsp.	salt
¼ tsp.	fresh ground black pepper
2 cloves	garlic, minced
1	bay leaf
1 lb.	pork tenderloin
2 med.	onions, sliced thin
1	sweet red pepper, sliced in strips
2 cloves	garlic, minced
2	tomatoes, chopped
¼ tsp.	crushed red pepper flakes
to taste	salt and pepper
24	clams in shell, scrubbed (*see p. 13*)
¼ cup	fresh coriander (cilantro), chopped

Garnish:

1	lemon, cut in wedges

Trim pork of all visible fat. Cut in cubes. Combine all marinade ingredients. Add pork to marinade. Refrigerate for 3-6 hours. Drain meat, but reserve marinade. Discard bay leaf. In a non-stick pan prepared with cooking spray, gently brown pork cubes. Remove and set aside. Add marinade to pan. Bring to a boil. Cook, uncovered, until liquid is reduced to 1 cup. Return pork to pan. Set aside (off the heat). In a separate non-stick pan prepared with cooking spray, gently sauté onions and red peppers until onions are translucent. Add garlic, tomatoes, crushed red pepper and salt and pepper if desired. Simmer 3-4 minutes. Arrange clams over sauce. Cover and cook over high heat for 5-10 minutes or until clams open. Discard any unopened clams. Combine pork with clams and all the juices. Heat through for 5 minutes. Sprinkle top with coriander and garnish with lemon wedges.

Cook's Note: Serve with French bread. May be cooked ahead of time, and it makes a good potluck meal or as a leftover.

Alcohol Note: The alcohol content was computed prior to cooking. Once the alcohol is heated to the boiling point, the alcohol disappears along with most of the calories from the alcohol.

Nutrient Content Per Serving

Calories	379.0
Protein	48.9 g
Carbohydrates	13.9 g
Fat – Total	7.0 g
Cholesterol	130.0 mg
Dietary Fiber	2.3 g
Sodium	276.0 mg

Percent of Calories

53% Protein
15% Carbohydrate
17% Fat
15% Alcohol

Fat Breakdown

Saturated Fat	2.1 g
Monounsaturated Fat	2.3 g
Polyunsaturated Fat	1.0 g

APPLESAUCE
Serves 4

3	tart apples
½	lemon, juice of
pinch	nutmeg
1 tsp.	powdered butter replacement

Peel apples and slice thin. Sprinkle with lemon juice. Place in a saucepan with ½ cup water and nutmeg. Boil for 10 minutes. Add powdered butter replacement. Serve hot.

Cook's Note: If prepared the day before, just heat up.

Nutrient Content Per Serving

Calories	63.6
Protein	0.2 g
Carbohydrates	16.5 g
Fat – Total	0.4 g
Cholesterol	0.0 mg
Dietary Fiber	2.2 g
Sodium	5.0 mg

Percent of Calories

1%	Protein
94%	Carbohydrate
5%	Fat

Fat Breakdown

Saturated Fat	0.1 g
Monounsaturated Fat	0.0 g
Polyunsaturated Fat	0.1 g

BROCCOLI WITH BECHAMEL SAUCE
Serves 4

1 head	broccoli flowerettes
1 cup	bechamel sauce *(see p. 554)*

Steam the broccoli. Prepare the bechamel sauce. Pour bechamel sauce over broccoli. Serve hot.

Nutrient Content Per Serving

Calories	68.3
Protein	4.4 g
Carbohydrates	8.2 g
Fat – Total	2.3 g
Cholesterol	2.7 mg
Dietary Fiber	1.3 g
Sodium	96.1 mg

Percent of Calories

25% Protein
46% Carbohydrate
29% Fat

Fat Breakdown

Saturated Fat	0.7 g
Monounsaturated Fat	0.7 g
Polyunsaturated Fat	0.7 g

CORN ON THE COB WITH A HINT OF ANISE
Serves 4

4 lg.   ears of fresh corn
1 Tbl.   sugar
1 tsp.   anise seed

Shuck corn. Place all ingredients in a pan of water. Boil 10 minutes or until corn is tender.

Cook's Note: Even if you don't like anise, you might like this. It has a nice twist to it.

Nutrient Content Per Serving
Calories   75.6
Protein   2.4 g
Carbohydrates   18.2 g
Fat – Total   0.6 g
Cholesterol   0.0 mg
Dietary Fiber   2.5 g
Sodium   3.1 mg

Percent of Calories
11% Protein
83% Carbohydrate
 6% Fat

Fat Breakdown
Saturated Fat   0.1 g
Monounsaturated Fat   0.2 g
Polyunsaturated Fat   0.3 g

PARSLEY POTATOES
Serves 4

6 sm.	boiling potatoes
1 Tbl.	olive oil
½ cup	onions, chopped
2 tsp.	garlic, minced
½ cup	fresh parsley, chopped
1½ cups	boiling water
to taste	salt and pepper

Wash potatoes. Slice into ½-inch-thick rounds. Rub oil on a non-stick baking sheet. Rub potatoes on both sides to get some oil on them. Lay potatoes flat in a single layer. Bake at 400° F until they start to brown (approx. 30 minutes). Flip potatoes and repeat.

Arrange potatoes in a baking dish. Cover with onions, garlic, parsley, boiling water and salt and pepper to taste. Bake 20 minutes uncovered or until potatoes are tender. Remove potatoes to a serving dish. Pass the cooking liquid as a sauce.

Cook's Note: Takes approximately 1 hour to prepare.

Nutrient Content Per Serving

Calories	107.0
Protein	2.4 g
Carbohydrates	17.3 g
Fat – Total	3.6 g
Cholesterol	0.0 mg
Dietary Fiber	1.6 g
Sodium	21.7 mg

Percent of Calories
9% Protein
63% Carbohydrate
29% Fat

Fat Breakdown

Saturated Fat	0.5 g
Monounsaturated Fat	2.5 g
Polyunsaturated Fat	0.4 g

PEPPERED POTATOES
Serves 4

2 lbs.	new potatoes
1 Tbl.	olive oil
to taste	salt

Sauce:

1 tsp.	olive oil
2 Tbl.	tomato paste
3 Tbl.	wine vinegar
2 tsp.	paprika
pinch	cayenne pepper

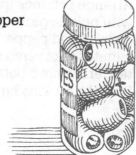

Boil the potatoes in their skins until they are almost tender. Drain. When they are cool enough to handle, peel and cut them into bite-sized pieces.

Spray a non-stick baking sheet with cooking spray. Coat potatoes with oil and salt to taste. Arrange potatoes in a single layer on the prepared baking sheet. Bake at 400° F until golden, turning once to brown the underside (approximately 45 minutes). Transfer to a serving dish.

Mix all the sauce ingredients together, pour over the potatoes and mix well. Serve hot or warm.

Nutrient Content Per Serving

Calories	231.0
Protein	5.2 g
Carbohydrates	43.6 g
Fat – Total	5.0 g
Cholesterol	0.0 mg
Dietary Fiber	4.5 g
Sodium	78.8 mg

Percent of Calories

9%	Protein
73%	Carbohydrate
19%	Fat

Fat Breakdown

Saturated Fat	0.7 g
Monounsaturated Fat	3.3 g
Polyunsaturated Fat	0.6 g

SPINACH WITH ALMONDS
Serves 4

1 clove	garlic, cut in half
1 Tbl.	pine nuts
1 Tbl.	almonds, slivered
1 lb.	cooked spinach or 2 10-oz. pkgs. frozen spinach
to taste	salt

Heat a non-stick frying pan. Rub with garlic. Discard garlic. Toast pine nuts and almonds in this pan over low heat. Remove nuts and set aside. Add spinach. Heat through. Add nuts and salt to taste; serve.

% Calories as Fat — Above the HM✓ guidelines: Although this recipe has a high percentage of calories as fat (>30%), the total fat is less than 5 grams per serving. This will easily fit within your allotment of 45 grams per day. This happens most often in low-calorie recipes.

Nutrient Content Per Serving

Calories	64.4
Protein	4.9 g
Carbohydrates	6.3 g
Fat – Total	3.7 g
Cholesterol	0.0 mg
Dietary Fiber	4.2 g
Sodium	115.0 mg

Percent of Calories

25% Protein
32% Carbohydrate
43% Fat

Fat Breakdown

Saturated Fat	0.5 g
Monounsaturated Fat	1.5 g
Polyunsaturated Fat	1.3 g

String Beans with Tomatoes
Serves 4

1 lb.	green beans, cut in 2-inch lengths
¼ cup	onions, chopped
2 cloves	garlic, minced
1 tsp.	olive oil
4	tomatoes, peeled, seeded and chopped
1 Tbl.	fresh parsley, chopped
to taste	black pepper

Steam beans until just tender. (May microwave with added water or use thawed frozen beans.) Sauté onions and garlic in olive oil. When onions are translucent, add tomatoes, parsley and pepper to taste. Simmer until liquid thickens. Add green beans and heat through.

Nutrient Content Per Serving

Calories	76.9
Protein	3.3 g
Carbohydrates	15.2 g
Fat – Total	1.7 g
Cholesterol	0.0 mg
Dietary Fiber	5.4 g
Sodium	18.5 mg

Percent of Calories

15% Protein
68% Carbohydrate
17% Fat

Fat Breakdown

Saturated Fat	0.2 g
Monounsaturated Fat	0.9 g
Polyunsaturated Fat	0.3 g

STEWED VEGETABLES
Serves 6

1 Tbl.	olive oil
1 med.	onion, sliced thin
4 sm.	zucchini, sliced
3	tomatoes, peeled and chopped
¼ cup	fresh parsley, chopped
1 clove	garlic, minced
¼ tsp.	salt
1 8-oz pkg.	frozen lima beans

In a large non-stick skillet, heat oil. Sauté onion in oil until soft. Add remaining ingredients. Cover and simmer until vegetables are tender.

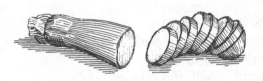

Cook's Note: May substitute potatoes for limas. Has a more subtle flavor when potatoes are used in place of limas. May wish to add bell pepper or black pepper.

Nutrient Content Per Serving

Calories	83.3
Protein	3.7 g
Carbohydrates	12.4 g
Fat – Total	2.7 g
Cholesterol	0.0 mg
Dietary Fiber	3.9 g
Sodium	104.0 mg

Percent of Calories

17% Protein
56% Carbohydrate
27% Fat

Fat Breakdown

Saturated Fat	0.4 g
Monounsaturated Fat	1.7 g
Polyunsaturated Fat	0.4 g

VEGETABLE FLAN
Serves 4

3	carrots, cubed
2	potatoes, cubed
1 cup	green beans
¾ cup	brussels sprouts
5 cups	spinach, torn in bite-sized pieces
1 Tbl.	olive oil
1 cup	egg substitute
2 cups	skim milk
to taste	salt and pepper

Steam all vegetables. Drain and pat dry or flan will be runny. Heat oil in a non-stick frying pan. Sauté the vegetables 5 minutes. In a baking dish prepared with cooking spray, whisk together the egg substitute, milk and salt and pepper if desired. Add the vegetables.

Place egg substitute and vegetable pan in a pan of water. The water should come half-way up the sides of the baking dish. Place both pans in the oven and bake at 350° F for 40 minutes or until eggs are set. Chill. Unmold. Serve cold.

Cook's Note: Best to make the day before. May serve with tomatoes, steamed asparagus or tomato sauce. Choose any combination of green vegetables that you like.

Nutrient Content Per Serving

Calories	167.0
Protein	8.4 g
Carbohydrates	22.4 g
Fat – Total	5.4 g
Cholesterol	1.7 mg
Dietary Fiber	3.7 g
Sodium	136.0 mg

Percent of Calories

20% Protein
52% Carbohydrate
28% Fat

Fat Breakdown

Saturated Fat	0.7 g
Monounsaturated Fat	2.6 g
Polyunsaturated Fat	0.5 g

VEGETABLE PISTO
Serves 6

1 clove	garlic, minced
3 cups	onions, chopped
2	zucchini, cubed
2	green peppers, seeded and chopped
1 Tbl.	olive oil
pinch	salt
4	tomatoes, peeled, seeded and chopped
2	egg whites
to taste	salt and pepper

In a non-stick skillet, gently sauté garlic, onions, zucchini and peppers in olive oil. Add salt. Cover and simmer for 40 minutes.

In a separate pan bring tomatoes to a boil. Mash them with a potato masher as they cook. Evaporate all of the liquid until mixture becomes thick. Stir tomatoes into the vegetables. Add the egg whites, stirring constantly. Bring to a simmer. Remove from heat immediately. Taste for seasoning.

% Calories as Fat — Above the HM✔ guidelines. Although this recipe has a high percentage of calories as fat (>30%), the total fat is less than 5 grams per serving. This will easily fit within your allotment of 45 grams per day. This happens most often in low-calorie recipes.

Nutrient Content Per Serving

Calories	72.8
Protein	3.0 g
Carbohydrates	10.7 g
Fat – Total	2.7 g
Cholesterol	0.0 mg
Dietary Fiber	2.5 g
Sodium	72.5 mg

Percent of Calories

15% Protein
54% Carbohydrate
31% Fat

Fat Breakdown

Saturated Fat	0.4 g
Monounsaturated Fat	1.7 g
Polyunsaturated Fat	0.4 g

CILANTRO-SHALLOT VINAIGRETTE
Serves 4
Yield: ½ cup

Combine all ingredients and mix well.

2 Tbl.	shallots, minced
1 Tbl.	olive oil
¼ cup	red wine vinegar
¼ cup	fresh cilantro, chopped fine

Cook's Note: May add roasted red peppers for variety.
Use the vinaigrette as a marinade for fish or chicken.

% Calories as Fat — Above the HM✔ guidelines: Although this recipe has a high percentage
of calories as fat (>30%), the total fat is less than 5 grams per serving. This will easily fit within
your allotment of 45 grams per day. This happens most often in low-calorie recipes.

Nutrient Content Per Serving

Calories	35.7
Protein	0.1 g
Carbohydrates	1.8 g
Fat – Total	3.4 g
Cholesterol	0.0 mg
Dietary Fiber	0.1 g
Sodium	1.0 mg

Percent of Calories

2%	Protein
18%	Carbohydrate
80%	Fat

Fat Breakdown

Saturated Fat	0.5 g
Monounsaturated Fat	2.5 g
Polyunsaturated Fat	0.3 g

SPICED TOMATO SAUCE
Serves 6

2 cups	tomatoes, chopped
1 tsp.	garlic, chopped
1 Tbl.	shallots, chopped
1 Tbl.	serrano pepper, chopped
1 Tbl.	olive oil
¼ cup	chicken stock *(see p. 538)*
to taste	salt and pepper

In a non-stick frying pan, sauté garlic, shallots and peppers in olive oil until tender. Add tomatoes and chicken stock. Bring to a boil. Season with salt and pepper to taste. Purée in food processor until smooth.

% Calories as Fat — Above the HM✔ guidelines: Although this recipe has a high percentage of calories as fat (>30%), the total fat is less than 5 grams per serving. This will easily fit within your allotment of 45 grams per day. This happens most often in low-calorie recipes.

Nutrient Content Per Serving

Calories	31.0
Protein	0.4 g
Carbohydrates	2.5 g
Fat – Total	2.4 g
Cholesterol	0.0 mg
Dietary Fiber	0.6 g
Sodium	24.7 mg

Percent of Calories

5% Protein	
30% Carbohydrate	
65% Fat	

Fat Breakdown

Saturated Fat	0.3 g
Monounsaturated Fat	1.7 g
Polyunsaturated Fat	0.3 g

GREEN SAUCE

Serves 8
Yield: 2 cups

1½ cups	spinach
2 Tbl.	parsley, chopped
1 Tbl.	thyme, chopped
½ tsp.	mustard
½ cup	mayonnaise, fat-free

Steam spinach until completely wilted. Drain. Add remaining ingredients and mix well.

Cook's Note: Serve with fish or meat.

Nutrient Content Per Serving

Calories	13.6
Protein	0.3 g
Carbohydrates	3.1 g
Fat – Total	0.1 g
Cholesterol	0.0 mg
Dietary Fiber	0.3 g
Sodium	182.0 mg

Percent of Calories

10% Protein
87% Carbohydrate
 4% Fat

Fat Breakdown

Saturated Fat	0.0 g
Monounsaturated Fat	0.0 g
Polyunsaturated Fat	0.0 g

MANGO VANILLA DRESSING
Serves 48

1 lb.	mango meat, fresh or canned
¼ cup	vanilla oil *(see p. 563)*
2 qts.	apple juice
1 Tbl.	fresh chervil, chopped
½ cup	gewurztraminer wine
½	vanilla bean
to taste	salt and pepper

Heat apple juice in a pan. Reduce to 1 quart. Let cool. Place all ingredients, except the oil and vanilla bean, in a blender. Blend with the gewurztraminer wine until smooth. Slowly add the oil and blend. Add vanilla bean. Thin it out with some wine if it gets too thick. Season with salt and pepper to taste. Store in refrigerator. Keeps 1 week.

Alcohol Note: The alcohol content was computed prior to cooking. Once the alcohol is heated to the boiling point, the alcohol disappears along with most of the calories from the alcohol.

Nutrient Content Per 2 Tablespoons		Percent of Calories	Fat Breakdown	
Calories	37.3	1% Protein	Saturated Fat	0.2 g
Protein	0.1 g	67% Carbohydrate	Monounsaturated Fat	0.8 g
Carbohydrates	6.5 g	28% Fat	Polyunsaturated Fat	0.1 g
Fat – Total	1.2 g	4% Alcohol		
Cholesterol	0.0 mg			
Dietary Fiber	0.2 g			
Sodium	1.5 mg			

ROMESCO SAUCE
(Makes 1 cup)

1 clove	garlic, minced
8	almonds, toasted, chopped
3	roasted red peppers, cooked, chopped
⅛ sm.	chili pepper
2 med.	tomatoes
4 Tbl.	vinegar
1 Tbl.	olive oil

Grind together garlic and almonds. Add remaining ingredients. Mix in food processor until smooth. Strain the sauce through a sieve.

Serve with fish or roasted vegetables.

Cook's Note: May increase the spiciness by adding more chili pepper.

% Calories as Fat — Above the HM✔ guidelines: Although this recipe has a high percentage of calories as fat (>30%), the total fat is less than 5 grams per serving. This will easily fit within your allotment of 45 grams per day. This happens most often in low-calorie recipes.

Nutrient Content Per Recipe		**Percent of Calories**	**Fat Breakdown**	
Calories	37.6	7% Protein	Saturated Fat	0.3 g
Protein	0.8 g	39% Carbohydrate	Monounsaturated Fat	1.7 g
Carbohydrates	4.1 g	53% Fat	Polyunsaturated Fat	0.3 g
Fat – Total	2.5			
Cholesterol	0.0 mg			
Dietary Fiber	1.0 g			
Sodium	3.6 mg			

BROILED APPLES
Serves 5

5	apples
½ cup	brown sugar
1 Tbl.	powdered butter replacement
2 Tbl.	rum
2 Tbl.	jam (any flavor)

Remove core, but do not peel apples. Be sure the hole from removing the core does not puncture the bottom of the apple.

Combine brown sugar, powdered butter replacement and rum. Fill center of apple. Arrange apples in a baking dish. Add 1 inch of water to the baking pan. Bake at 325° F for 40-60 minutes or until apples are tender. Drain and reserve the baking water. Add jam to the baking water. Pour over apples. Serve hot.

Nutrient Content Per Serving

Calories	161.0
Protein	0.3 g
Carbohydrates	41.6 g
Fat – Total	0.5 g
Cholesterol	0.0 mg
Dietary Fiber	2.9 g
Sodium	18.6 mg

Percent of Calories

1%	Protein
97%	Carbohydrate
3%	Fat

Fat Breakdown

Saturated Fat	0.1 g
Monounsaturated Fat	0.0 g
Polyunsaturated Fat	0.1 g

CARAMEL APPLES
Serves 4

3 lg.	green delicious apples, peeled, cored and sliced in wedges
¼ cup	sugar
½ cup	water
¼ cup	golden raisins
¼ cup	rum

In a saucepan, melt the sugar until it starts to brown. Carefully add the water, apples and raisins. The sugar will crystallize immediately. Cook slowly over low heat until apples are tender.

Add the rum. Chill or serve hot with nonfat frozen yogurt.

Cook's Note: If served alone, may want 4 apples. When served over yogurt, 3 apples are sufficient.

Nutrient Content Per Serving

Calories	173.0
Protein	0.5 g
Carbohydrates	36.3 g
Fat – Total	0.4 g
Cholesterol	0.0 mg
Dietary Fiber	2.7 g
Sodium	1.5 mg

Percent of Calories

1%	Protein
79%	Carbohydrate
2%	Fat
18%	Alcohol

Fat Breakdown

Saturated Fat	0.1 g
Monounsaturated Fat	0.0 g
Polyunsaturated Fat	0.1 g

CREMA CATALANA
Serves 4

¾ cup	egg substitute
½ cup	sugar
2 cups	skim milk
1	cinnamon stick
1	lemon, peel of
2½ Tbl.	cornstarch

Combine egg substitute and sugar in a small bowl. In a medium saucepan, scald skim milk with cinnamon stick and lemon peel. Carefully add the milk mixture to egg substitute and sugar, beating constantly so as not to curdle the eggs.

Combine cold milk and cornstarch. Add to hot milk. Return to the saucepan. Heat over medium-low, stirring constantly until milk boils. Remove pan from stove. Pour into individual serving bowls. Chill.

Cook's Note: It is supposed to be a little runny.

Nutrient Content Per Serving		**Percent of Calories**	**Fat Breakdown**	
Calories	231.0	16% Protein	Saturated Fat	1.0 g
Protein	9.3 g	64% Carbohydrate	Monounsaturated Fat	1.2 g
Carbohydrates	36.8 g	20% Fat	Polyunsaturated Fat	2.8 g
Fat – Total	5.2 g			
Cholesterol	3.1 mg			
Dietary Fiber	0.1 g			
Sodium	153.0 mg			

CARAMEL CUSTARD
(FLAN)
Serves 8

Custard:

2 cups	skim milk
¾ cup	egg substitute
¼ cup	sugar
½ tsp.	vanilla extract

Sauce:

6 Tbl.	egg substitute
¾ cup	skim milk
¼ cup	nonfat dry milk
¾ tsp.	salt
½ cup	brown sugar
1 Tbl.	powdered butter replacement
1 Tbl.	lemon juice

Pre-heat oven to 325° F.

Custard:
In a medium saucepan scald milk over medium heat, stirring constantly. Set aside to cool. In a large mixing bowl beat egg substitute, sugar and vanilla. Add warm milk a little at a time so as not to cook the egg. Pour egg mixture into a 1-quart baking dish. Set dish in a pan of water. Water should come halfway up the side of the baking pan. Bake for 1 hour at 325° F. Custard is done when a knife inserted into custard comes out clean.

Sauce:
In the top of a double boiler, combine all sauce ingredients except lemon juice. Heat until mixture thickens, whisking constantly. Add lemon juice a little at a time so as not to curdle the eggs.

Remove custard from oven. Pour sauce over custard.

Cook's Note: Flan may be served hot or cold. May be served with fresh strawberries.

Nutrient Content Per Serving		**Percent of Calories**	**Fat Breakdown**	
Calories	153.0	19% Protein	Saturated Fat	0.8 g
Protein	7.5 g	58% Carbohydrate	Monounsaturated Fat	0.9 g
Carbohydrates	22.1 g	23% Fat	Polyunsaturated Fat	2.1 g
Fat – Total	3.9 g			
Cholesterol	2.6 mg			
Dietary Fiber	0.0 g			
Sodium	333.0 mg			

ORANGE CARAMEL CUSTARD
Serves 8

Caramel Sauce:

1 cup	sugar
¼ cup	water

Custard:

3	oranges
	peel of the oranges
4 cups	skim milk
½ cup	nonfat dry milk
2	cinnamon sticks
1 tsp.	vanilla
1½ cups	egg substitute
1½ cups	sugar

Caramel Sauce:

In a small, heavy skillet heat sugar and water. Stir until clear. Cook over medium heat until syrup turns light brown. Quickly pour syrup into custard cups and swirl to coat the bottoms. Set aside.

Custard:

Peel oranges. Save peel. Separate oranges into sections. Set aside.

In a saucepan combine orange peel (make sure all white portion has been removed), milk, powdered milk and cinnamon sticks. Scald milk. Let stand for 15 minutes. Discard orange peel and cinnamon sticks. Stir in vanilla extract.

Using a mixer, beat egg substitute and sugar. While mixing add milk, straining through a sieve to remove any particles. Place 2-3 orange segments into each custard bowl. Pour in the milk. Fill to the top. Place custard cups in a baking pan. Fill pan with enough water to come halfway up the sides of the custard cups. Bake at 325° F for 40 minutes. Remove cups from water. Refrigerate 3 hours until custard is set.

To unmold custards, run a knife around the edge. Briefly dip bowl into hot water. Place a chilled serving dish over top of custard bowl. Invert and rap bottom of custard cup. Serve cold.

Cook's Note: May use vanilla bean in place of vanilla extract for a smoother vanilla flavor. The white portion of the orange peel tastes bitter.

Nutrient Content Per Serving		**Percent of Calories**	**Fat Breakdown**	
Calories	362.0	13% Protein	Saturated Fat	0.5 g
Protein	11.8 g	83% Carbohydrate	Monounsaturated Fat	0.5 g
Carbohydrates	76.5 g	5% Fat	Polyunsaturated Fat	0.8 g
Fat – Total	1.9 g			
Cholesterol	3.5 mg			
Dietary Fiber	1.2 g			
Sodium	170.0 mg			

LEMON SORBET
Serves 6

4	egg whites
2 Tbl.	sugar
1 cup	sugar
6	lemons, juice of and peel
1	orange

To prepare a meringue:
Beat egg whites until foamy. Add 2 tablespoons of sugar continue beating until soft peaks form.

To prepare syrup:
Combine 1 cup of sugar with ¼ cup of water. Heat and stir until sugar is dissolved. Add peel of 3 lemons. Cook for 2-3 minutes. Remove peel. When syrup is done, add juice of lemons and orange. Place in the freezer.

When sorbet is half-way frozen, fold in half of the meringue. Continue to freeze. When almost solid, fold in remaining meringue. Return to freezer.

Cook's Note: Incredibly refreshing! Serve with biscotti. More difficult to make than ice cream. The syrup is very important. May use different flavors, such as strawberry or other fruits.

Nutrient Content Per Serving		Percent of Calories	Fat Breakdown	
Calories	185.0	6% Protein	Saturated Fat	0.0 g
Protein	3.2 g	93% Carbohydrate	Monounsaturated Fat	0.0 g
Carbohydrates	46.2 g	1% Fat	Polyunsaturated Fat	0.0 g
Fat – Total	0.2 g			
Cholesterol	0.0 mg			
Dietary Fiber	1.9 g			
Sodium	38.3 mg			

ALMOND-CRUSTED CUSTARD PIE
Serves 12

Crust:

½ cup	almond paste
2	egg whites
¼ cup	sugar
1 cup	flour

Custard:

1 cup	skim milk
½ cup	egg substitute
2 Tbl.	cornstarch
½ cup	sugar
1	vanilla bean
2 cups	fresh fruit
¼ cup	jelly

To prepare crust:
Beat almond paste with egg whites until smooth. (A food processor works great.) Beat in sugar and flour. Prepare a 9-inch pie tin with cooking spray. Press dough into pie tin to form a crust. Bake at 350° F for 10 minutes. Let cool.

To prepare custard:
Place all ingredients in a double boiler. Whisk constantly until the custard thickens. Pour into crust.

Bake at 350° F for 10 minutes. Remove from oven. Layer sliced fresh fruit in a single decorative layer. Spread with a thin layer of jelly.

Cook's Note: For the fruit topping, choose from fresh strawberries, raspberries, kiwi fruit or grapes. The jelly should compliment the fruit.

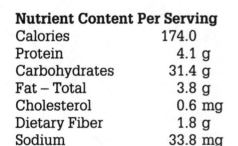

Nutrient Content Per Serving

Calories	174.0
Protein	4.1 g
Carbohydrates	31.4 g
Fat – Total	3.8 g
Cholesterol	0.6 mg
Dietary Fiber	1.8 g
Sodium	33.8 mg

Percent of Calories

9% Protein
71% Carbohydrate
20% Fat

Fat Breakdown

Saturated Fat	0.5 g
Monounsaturated Fat	1.9 g
Polyunsaturated Fat	1.2 g

Compote of Melon
Serves 4

1½ cups	honeydew, peeled, seeded, cubed
1½ cups	cantaloupe, peeled, seeded, cubed
½ cup	jicama, chopped
2 sm.	plums, diced
1 Tbl.	cilantro, chopped
2 Tbl.	honey

Garnish:

1	lemon, juice of
	fresh mint sprigs

Combine all ingredients and chill for 10 minutes. Serve in a glass bowl garnished with fresh mint sprigs.

Cook's Note: If compote is allowed to sit longer than 10 minutes before being served, jicama may begin to brown. To avoid browning, coat jicama with the lemon juice and serve after chilling.

Nutrient Content Per Serving		Percent of Calories		Fat Breakdown	
Calories	91.4	5% Protein		Saturated Fat	0.1 g
Protein	1.2 g	92% Carbohydrate		Monounsaturated Fat	0.1 g
Carbohydrates	23.4 g	3% Fat		Polyunsaturated Fat	0.1 g
Fat – Total	0.4 g				
Cholesterol	0.0 mg				
Dietary Fiber	1.7 g				
Sodium	13.2 mg				

RICE PUDDING
Serves 4

1½ cups	skim milk
2-inch piece	vanilla bean
2-inch piece	cinnamon stick
6 pieces	lemon peel
	(1½ inches x ½ inch)
6 cups	water
½ cup	rice, short-grain
¼ tsp.	salt
6 Tbl.	egg substitute
⅓ cup	sugar
½ tsp.	ground nutmeg

Garnish:

1 tsp.	ground cinnamon

In a medium saucepan combine the milk, vanilla bean, cinnamon stick and lemon peel. Scald milk. Cover and remove from heat and let sit for 20-30 minutes. Remove vanilla bean and cinnamon stick.

In a separate pan, bring water to a boil. Add rice, stirring constantly. Add salt. Reduce heat. Simmer the rice for 15-20 minutes uncovered. Drain liquid from rice. Spread rice onto paper towels to dry slightly.

In a mixing bowl beat together the egg substitute and sugar. Pour this into the milk mixture. Cook over low heat, stirring constantly until the custard thickens. Add the rice and nutmeg. Pour custard into a dish to cool.

To serve:
Spoon into dishes and garnish with ground cinnamon.

Cook's Note: May add ¼ cup of raisins, currants or candied fruit. Must use short-grain rice to obtain the desired consistency.

Nutrient Content Per Serving		**Percent of Calories**	**Fat Breakdown**	
Calories	170.0	15% Protein	Saturated Fat	0.6 g
Protein	6.4 g	70% Carbohydrate	Monounsaturated Fat	0.6 g
Carbohydrates	29.6 g	15% Fat	Polyunsaturated Fat	1.4 g
Fat – Total	2.8 g			
Cholesterol	2.1 mg			
Dietary Fiber	0.4 g			
Sodium	226.0 mg			

SPONGE CAKE ROLL
Serves 8

Filling:

2 cups	skim milk
2 sticks	cinnamon
1 4-inch piece	vanilla bean
¼ cup	egg substitute
¼ cup	sugar
¼ cup	flour
2 Tbl.	dark rum

Sponge Cake:

2	egg yolks
1 cup	sugar
¼ cup	boiling water
1 tsp.	vanilla
1 cup	flour
1½ tsp.	baking powder
¼ tsp.	salt
9	egg whites
	powdered sugar

To prepare filling:

Prepare ahead and let cool to room temperature. Chilled is fine too. In the top of a double boiler combine milk, cinnamon and vanilla bean. Scald milk. Continue cooking 10 minutes. Cover and set aside.

Beat together egg substitute and sugar until thick. Beat in flour. Discard cinnamon stick and vanilla bean. Slowly add milk to eggs, beating constantly. Return mixture to top of double boiler. Whisk constantly until thick. Stir in rum. Let cool. Stir occasionally to keep from forming crust on the surface of the cream. (May be refrigerated for up to 2 days.)

To prepare sponge cake:

Prepare a jelly-roll pan with cooking spray. Cover with wax paper. Spray again. Sprinkle wax-paper surface with flour. Invert pan and tap bottom to rid of excess flour. Preheat oven to 350° F. Beat egg yolks until very light. Beat in sugar a little at a time. Drizzle in the water while beating. Cool. Beat in vanilla. In a separate bowl sift together flour, baking powder and salt. Add flour to egg yolks. Beat well. Fold in stiffly beaten egg whites. Spread onto prepared jelly-roll pan. Bake for 25 minutes. Turn oven off and let cake cool for 10 minutes. Unmold cake and let cool shaped in a loose roll.

To Assemble:

Gently unfold jelly roll. Spread with an even layer of rum cream. Roll again. Sprinkle with powdered sugar just before serving.

Cook's Note: You must add the egg yolks for the cake or it will be too dry.

Nutrient Content Per Serving		Percent of Calories		Fat Breakdown	
Calories	271.0	14% Protein		Saturated Fat	0.6 g
Protein	9.6 g	75% Carbohydrate		Monounsaturated Fat	0.7 g
Carbohydrates	50.8 g	8% Fat		Polyunsaturated Fat	0.7 g
Fat – Total	2.4 g				
Cholesterol	54.3 mg				
Dietary Fiber	0.5 g				
Sodium	179.0 mg				

FRANCE

The most important guest at a table in Mediterranean France is the food.

In all of France, food is theater and, despite the encroachments of bigger super-markets and microwave ovens, it is craft.

Food is a market street on any Saturday morning: The butcher, the baker and the fish monger who unshutter the long windows of their shops to begin another day with food at the center of life.

Food in Mediterranean France is a small and very old bistro a few steps from the sea wall. A waiter with his long white apron tied tightly at the waist moves with those liquid limbs that deliver plates in the swirls and arcs of a magician. He carries three small wine bottles by their necks between the forefinger and middle finger of his right hand and along the length of his left forearm three plates sit as on a buffet.

Food here is to sit for an hour or two or three at table, to smell the freshness of yeast and flour in a warm baguette just birthed from its wood-burning ovens and to linger over meals as if they were served in bed.

Though many consider French cooking the world's pre-eminent cuisine, its beginnings along the Mediterranean were humble (and remain, especially at the Mediterranean Sea, particularly simple to this day).

The French rue to admit this, but they owe much of their cooking prowess to another Mediterranean: Catherine de Medici, a Floren-tine, who ascended to French royalty by her marriage in 1533 to Henry II. She brought with her many of the culinary skills of the Italian court, which had already perfected such things that the French knew nothing about at the time: the use of the fork; sauce-making; cake-making. She also introduced such vegetables to France as the Savoy cabbage, the artichoke and broccoli.

Perhaps the greatness of French cooking, however, owes less to Italian influence than to an inbred French awe of the law. The French codify everything, not the least their foodstuffs.

Under elaborate systems of appellation controlée ("the provenance or name of the product is guaranteed and controlled as to its place of origin"), known mostly for French wines, French laws guarantee that products coming from a specific region do, in fact, originate there.

This means a great deal when, for example, special soils, growing conditions and climate not duplicable elsewhere in France lend to a particular foodstuff its unique character.

Too, French law stipulates strict controls on weights, fat content, claims of nutritional value and so on for a myriad of products. In this, the French influence has been strongly felt on the production of other foodstuffs in the Mediterranean Basin (and, indeed, throughout Europe itself to this day).

Bill St. John
Food and Wine Editor
Rocky Mountain News

TABLE OF CONTENTS

Table of Contents

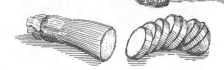

— Most Commonly Used Items for French Recipes —

▼ FRESH SUPPLIES
anchovy paste
basil
carrots
chives
egg substitute
garlic
lemons
mushrooms
mustard, dijon
parsley
peppers, sweet, all colors
rosemary

scallions
shallots
sour cream, nonfat
swiss cheese, lowfat
tomatoes
yogurt, plain nonfat

▼ PANTRY SUPPLIES
powdered butter
   replacement
canola oil
nonfat dry milk

mustard, dry
nutmeg
olive oil
pepper, white
pepper sauce, hot
rice
tarragon
thyme
vanilla
vermouth, dry
vinegar, red wine
vinegar, rice
vinegar, white wine

— Menu Suggestions —

▼ CASUAL
Vegetable Pesto Salad
Beef Bourguignon with Risi Bisi Rice
Peach Crepes

▼ FORMAL
Canapés with Cottage Cheese Spread
Vegetable Sticks with Anchovy Dip
Salmon Terrine with Tomato Slices and
   Belgian Endive
Butternut Squash Soup
Sautéed Elk Medallions with Chateau
   Potatoes
Red Cabbage with Apples
Crepes Grand Marnier

▼ SUMMER
BBQ Prawns with Whole-Grain Mustard
   Sauce
Orange Salad
Chicken with Creamy Pepper Sauce
Rustic Vegetables, Lemon Herbed Rice
Melon Basket

▼ WINTER
Creamy Mussel Soup
Lentil Salad
Grilled Veal Chop
Potatoes au Gratin, Rustic Vegetables
Black Forest Crepes

▼ QUICK BUT AUTHENTIC
Fresh Vegetable Salad
Grilled Swordfish Steak Sandwich
Caramel Banana Parfait

COTTAGE CHEESE CANAPÉS
Serves 6

Basic Information:
Canapés are small finger-sized open-faced sandwiches. Use ¼-½ slice of bread per canapé. Use bread that is day-old white, firm wheat or pumpernickel. You may cut the breads into shapes. Toast the breads before topping. Choose one or more toppings and arrange decoratively on a serving platter.

COTTAGE CHEESE SPREAD:

½ cup	1% cottage cheese
½ tsp.	caraway seeds, ground
1 tsp.	chives, chopped
1 Tbl.	lemon juice
to taste	salt
to taste	paprika
6 slices	white bread, toasted

Garnish:
fresh parsley, chopped

Place cottage cheese in a food processor. Process until smooth. Add remaining ingredients. Blend well. Spread on breads. Garnish with parsley.

Nutrient Content Per Serving

Calories	106.0
Protein	5.4 g
Carbohydrates	17.5 g
Fat – Total	1.5 g
Cholesterol	2.1 mg
Dietary Fiber	0.8 g
Sodium	240.0 mg

Percent of Calories

21% Protein
67% Carbohydrate
13% Fat

Fat Breakdown

Saturated Fat	0.4 g
Monounsaturated Fat	0.6 g
Polyunsaturated Fat	0.3 g

CREAM CHEESE CANAPÉS
Serves 6

CREAM CHEESE SPREAD:

2 oz.	fat-free cream cheese
1 oz.	regular cream cheese
2 tsp.	powdered butter replacement

6 slices   white bread, toasted

Garnish:

paprika
fresh parsley, chopped

Cream together. Spread on breads. Sprinkle one-half of each canapé with paprika and other half with chopped parsley.

Cook's Note: See basic information for canapés on page 145.

Nutrient Content Per Serving

Calories	118.0
Protein	4.7 g
Carbohydrates	17.6 g
Fat – Total	2.9 g
Cholesterol	8.3 mg
Dietary Fiber	0.7 g
Sodium	240.0 mg

Percent of Calories

16% Protein
61% Carbohydrate
23% Fat

Fat Breakdown

Saturated Fat	1.3 g
Monounsaturated Fat	0.9 g
Polyunsaturated Fat	0.4 g

LOBSTER CANAPÉS
Serves 6

LOBSTER SALAD:

1 6-oz.	lobster tail
3 tsp.	fat-free mayonnaise
	julienne of lettuce
6 slices	white bread, toasted

Garnish:

thin lemon wedges

Cook's Note: See basic information for canapés on page 145.

Steam lobster tail 8 minutes per pound. Chill. Slice in thin pieces.

Spread toast with a thin coating of mayonnaise. Top with a layer of lettuce. Lay lobster on top. Garnish with lemon wedges.

Nutrient Content Per Serving

Calories	125.0
Protein	8.6 g
Carbohydrates	17.4 g
Fat – Total	2.1 g
Cholesterol	22.8 mg
Dietary Fiber	0.7 g
Sodium	367.0 mg

Percent of Calories

28% Protein
57% Carbohydrate
15% Fat

Fat Breakdown

Saturated Fat	0.8 g
Monounsaturated Fat	0.7 g
Polyunsaturated Fat	0.4 g

SHRIMP CANAPÉS
Serves 6

SHRIMP:

12 med.	shrimp
1 tsp.	powdered butter replacement
2 tsp.	lemon juice
¼ cup	parsley, chopped
6 slices	white bread, toasted

Steam shrimp until pink and chill. Peel. Place shrimp, powdered butter replacement and lemon juice in food processor. Process until smooth. Spread on toast. Top with parsley.

Cook's Note: See basic information for canapés on page 145.

Nutrient Content Per Serving

Calories	108.0
Protein	5.9 g
Carbohydrates	17.3 g
Fat – Total	1.5 g
Cholesterol	22.6 mg
Dietary Fiber	0.8 g
Sodium	188.0 mg

Percent of Calories

22% Protein
65% Carbohydrate
13% Fat

Fat Breakdown

Saturated Fat	0.4 g
Monounsaturated Fat	0.5 g
Polyunsaturated Fat	0.4 g

TOMATO CANAPÉS
Serves 6

TOMATO:

2 Tbl.	horseradish
2 Tbl.	fat-free mayonnaise
3	ripe tomatoes, sliced in rounds
to taste	salt and pepper

6 slices	white bread, toasted

Garnish:

2 Tbl.	parsley, chopped

Mix together horseradish and mayonnaise. Spread on toast. Lay tomatoes on top. Sprinkle with salt and pepper to taste. Garnish with chopped parsley.

Cook's Note: See basic information for canapés on page 145. When buying prepared horseradish, look for nitrate and sulfite free.

Nutrient Content Per Serving

Calories	110.0
Protein	3.6 g
Carbohydrates	20.9 g
Fat – Total	1.5 g
Cholesterol	1.3 mg
Dietary Fiber	1.6 g
Sodium	230.0 mg

Percent of Calories

13% Protein
75% Carbohydrate
12% Fat

Fat Breakdown

Saturated Fat	0.3 g
Monounsaturated Fat	0.5 g
Polyunsaturated Fat	0.4 g

ANCHOVY DIP
Serves 8

1 can	anchovies, drained and patted dry
2 cups	skim milk
15 oz.	1% cottage cheese
2 Tbl.	sour cream, nonfat

Garnish:
      chives, chopped

Rinse anchovies and pat dry. Soak anchovies in milk for 30 minutes to leech salt. Discard the milk. Whip cottage cheese in food processor until smooth. Chop anchovies in food processor. Add remaining ingredients. Chill.

Cook's Note: Serve with french bread, melba rounds, crackers or raw vegetables. It has a subtle flavor of anchovies that will get stronger as the dish ages.

Nutrient Content Per Serving

Calories	55.5
Protein	8.9 g
Carbohydrates	1.8 g
Fat – Total	1.2 g
Cholesterol	8.4 mg
Dietary Fiber	0.0 g
Sodium	478.0 mg

Percent of Calories

66% Protein
14% Carbohydrate
21% Fat

Fat Breakdown

Saturated Fat	0.5 g
Monounsaturated Fat	0.4 g
Polyunsaturated Fat	0.2 g

DEVIL DIP
Serves 8

16 oz.	1% cottage cheese, dry-curd
3 Tbl.	mayonnaise, fat-free
¼ cup	walnuts, chopped
¾ cup	raisins, chopped
1	bell pepper, roasted, *peeled,* seeded, chopped *(see p. 13)*
1	sweet red pepper, chopped
2 tsp.	Tabasco™
pinch	cayenne pepper
to taste	salt and pepper

Purée cottage cheese in a food processor until smooth. Combine with remaining ingredients. You may process again for a smoother texture. Chill.

Cook's Note: Serve with raw vegetables, bread and crackers. It's spicy!

Nutrient Content Per Serving

Calories	127.0
Protein	11.4 g
Carbohydrates	15.9 g
Fat – Total	2.6 g
Cholesterol	3.8 mg
Dietary Fiber	1.3 g
Sodium	81.5 mg

Percent of Calories

34% Protein
48% Carbohydrate
17% Fat

Fat Breakdown

Saturated Fat	0.3 g
Monounsaturated Fat	0.6 g
Polyunsaturated Fat	1.5 g

ROQUEFORT DIP
Serves 8

2 oz.	roquefort cheese
1½ cup	sour cream, nonfat
to taste	salt and pepper
1 Tbl.	Worcestershire sauce™
dash	Tabasco™

Combine all ingredients and chill. Serve with raw vegetables and lowfat crackers.

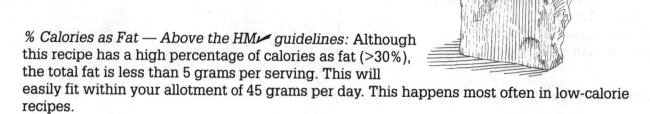

% Calories as Fat — Above the HM✔ guidelines: Although this recipe has a high percentage of calories as fat (>30%), the total fat is less than 5 grams per serving. This will easily fit within your allotment of 45 grams per day. This happens most often in low-calorie recipes.

Nutrient Content Per Serving

Calories	54.4
Protein	4.5 g
Carbohydrates	5.0 g
Fat – Total	2.2 g
Cholesterol	6.4 mg
Dietary Fiber	0.0 g
Sodium	179.0 mg

Percent of Calories

31% Protein	
35% Carbohydrate	
34% Fat	

Fat Breakdown

Saturated Fat	1.4 g
Monounsaturated Fat	0.6 g
Polyunsaturated Fat	0.1 g

STUFFED EGGPLANT
Serves 4

2 sm.	eggplant
2 sm.	zucchini, sliced in rounds
3	tomatoes, remove pulp and cube
2 cloves	garlic, minced
1	onion, diced
1 tsp.	olive oil
1 oz.	swiss cheese, grated fine
to taste	salt and pepper

Cut eggplant in half lengthwise. Remove pulp leaving a shell. Chop pulp into small cubes. Coat a non-stick frying pan with cooking spray and sauté pulp and zucchini. When browned, remove from pan. Sauté garlic and onions in olive oil. When onions are brown return eggplant and zucchini. Add tomatoes, salt and pepper to taste. Heat through. Stuff eggplant shells. Sprinkle cheese on top. Bake 25 minutes at 450° F. Serve hot.

Cook's Note: Serve with bread rounds, plain crackers or melba toast.

Nutrient Content Per Serving

Calories	143.0
Protein	5.6 g
Carbohydrates	24.8 g
Fat – Total	4.1 g
Cholesterol	6.5 mg
Dietary Fiber	10.2 g
Sodium	35.9 mg

Percent of Calories

14% Protein
63% Carbohydrate
23% Fat

Fat Breakdown

Saturated Fat	1.6 g
Monounsaturated Fat	1.5 g
Polyunsaturated Fat	0.6 g

PEPPERS AND ANCHOVIES
Serves 4

4	yellow bell peppers
1	green bell pepper
6	anchovies
1 clove	garlic, minced
2 tsp.	olive oil
to taste	salt and pepper

Rinse anchovies several times, pat dry and slice in very thin lengths. Roast peppers *(see p. 13)*. Cut in 1-inch wide strips. Chill peppers.

Whisk together garlic and olive oil. Arrange peppers on a serving platter, in a pattern like spokes of a wheel. Lay 1 slice of anchovy on each pepper. Drizzle oil mixture over top. Serve at room temperature.

Cook's Note: May use yellow, green and red peppers for a prettier presentation.

% Calories as Fat — Above the HM✔ guidelines: Although this recipe has a high percentage of calories as fat (>30%), the total fat is less than 5 grams per serving. This will easily fit within your allotment of 45 grams per day. This happens most often in low-calorie recipes.

Nutrient Content Per Serving

Calories	58.6				
Protein	2.6 g				
Carbohydrates	6.2 g				
Fat – Total	3.0 g				
Cholesterol	5.1 mg				
Dietary Fiber	1.5 g				
Sodium	222.0 mg				

Percent of Calories

17% Protein
40% Carbohydrate
43% Fat

Fat Breakdown

Saturated Fat	0.5 g
Monounsaturated Fat	1.9 g
Polyunsaturated Fat	0.4 g

TOMATOES STUFFED WITH RICE
Serves 6

6	tomatoes
½ cup	white rice, uncooked
1 cup	chicken stock *(see p. 538)*
3 oz.	swiss cheese, fat-free, grated
2	chicken breasts, boneless, skinless
12	black olives, chopped
6	anchovies, chopped
½ tsp.	tarragon
to taste	salt and pepper
1 clove	garlic, minced

Cook rice in 1 cup chicken stock for 20 minutes. Poach chicken breast in water. Cut into small pieces.

Slice tops off tomatoes. Scoop out inside. Cube tomato pulp. Combine all ingredients except tomato. Stuff into tomato. Place tomatoes in steamer rack. Steam 10 minutes.

Cook's Note: May be served with a green salad as a lunch. It makes a great leftover.

Nutrient Content Per Serving

Calories	176.0
Protein	16.5 g
Carbohydrates	17.9 g
Fat – Total	4.4 g
Cholesterol	33.4 mg
Dietary Fiber	1.9 g
Sodium	452.0 mg

Percent of Calories

37% Protein
40% Carbohydrate
22% Fat

Fat Breakdown

Saturated Fat	1.0 g
Monounsaturated Fat	1.9 g
Polyunsaturated Fat	0.9 g

CHICKEN AND SHRIMP COCKTAIL
Serves 6

1 lb.	chicken breast, boneless, skinless
24 sm.	shrimp, boiled, peeled and deveined
½ lb.	pineapple, fresh, cored and cubed
2	belgian endives
2 Tbl.	fresh chives, chopped

Sauce:

8 oz.	yogurt, plain, nonfat
3 Tbl.	mayonnaise, fat-free
1 tsp.	dijon mustard
1 tsp.	ketchup
1 tsp.	lemon juice
pinch	paprika
pinch	cayenne pepper

Roast or grill chicken breasts. Cut into cubes. Chop shrimp. Whisk together all sauce ingredients. In a bowl, combine pineapple, chicken, shrimp and chives. Add sauce and marinate 1 hour in refrigerator.

Arrange chicken mixture in six small serving bowls. Clean endive and garnish bowl with leaves sticking up around the edges.

Cook's Note: May purchase fresh pineapple already cubed.

Nutrient Content Per Serving

Calories	145.0
Protein	23.2 g
Carbohydrates	9.3 g
Fat – Total	1.4 g
Cholesterol	75.7 mg
Dietary Fiber	0.5 g
Sodium	220.0 mg

Percent of Calories

65% Protein
26% Carbohydrate
9% Fat

Fat Breakdown

Saturated Fat	0.4 g
Monounsaturated Fat	0.3 g
Polyunsaturated Fat	0.3 g

CHILLED BARBECUED PRAWNS WITH WHOLE-GRAIN MUSTARD SAUCE

Serves 6

18	prawns, peeled, deveined
¼ cup	fish marinade *(see p. 555 or 556)*
1	sweet red pepper, cut julienne
2 bunches	watercress
¼ cup	whole grain mustard sauce *(see p. 553)*

Marinate prawns in fish marinade for 10 minutes. Grill prawns 3-4 minutes or until pink. Chill. Decoratively arrange pepper strips and watercress on serving plates. Top with hot prawns. Pass mustard sauce on the side for dipping.

% Calories as Fat — Above the HM✔ guidelines: Although this recipe has a high percentage of calories as fat (>30%), the total fat is less than 5 grams per serving. This will easily fit within your allotment of 45 grams per day. This happens most often in low-calorie recipes.

Nutrient Content Per Serving

Calories	51.1
Protein	4.3 g
Carbohydrates	2.8 g
Fat – Total	2.6 g
Cholesterol	35.1 mg
Dietary Fiber	0.5 g
Sodium	104.0 mg

Percent of Calories

33% Protein
22% Carbohydrate
45% Fat

Fat Breakdown

Saturated Fat	0.4 g
Monounsaturated Fat	1.8 g
Polyunsaturated Fat	0.3 g

CRAB ROLLS
Serves 4

1 bunch	spinach, fresh, washed and deveined
1 cup	bean sprouts, chopped
2 Tbl.	teriyaki sauce
16 lg.	shrimp, boiled, peeled, deveined and chopped
4 oz.	imitation krab, chopped
1	lemon, juice of
4	plum tomatoes, diced
3	scallions, sliced thin
1 Tbl.	fresh cilantro, chopped
1 clove	garlic, minced
2 tsp.	olive oil

Combine all ingredients except spinach leaves. Roll 2 tablespoons of mixture tightly into each spinach leaf. Chill. Arrange on a plate and garnish with fresh cilantro.

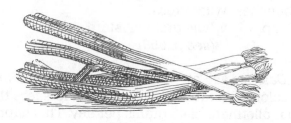

% Calories as Fat — Above the HM guidelines: Although this recipe has a high percentage of calories as fat (>30%), the total fat is less than 5 grams per serving. This will easily fit within your allotment of 45 grams per day. This happens most often in low-calorie recipes.

Nutrient Content Per Serving

Calories	115.0
Protein	12.4 g
Carbohydrates	10.3 g
Fat – Total	3.3 g
Cholesterol	51.1 mg
Dietary Fiber	2.1 g
Sodium	445.0 mg

Percent of Calories

41% Protein
27% Carbohydrate
32% Fat

Fat Breakdown

Saturated Fat	0.5 g
Monounsaturated Fat	1.8 g
Polyunsaturated Fat	0.6 g

SALMON TERRINE
Serves 16

2½ lbs.	salmon, fresh or canned
4 slices	white bread, crusts removed
1 cup	skim milk
6 sprigs	fresh chervil, chopped
6 branches	fresh chives, chopped
4	egg whites
12 oz.	sour cream, nonfat
to taste	salt and pepper
1 lb.	marlin fillets
1	lime, zest of

Garnish:

¼ lb.	smoked salmon slices
	lime slices
	salmon eggs
	tomato slices

Soak white bread in the milk. Add chopped herbs. Set aside. In a food processor, combine salmon, 3 egg whites, ⅔ of the sour cream, ⅔ of the bread mixture, salt and pepper if desired. Process until smooth. Refrigerate.

In the food processor, combine marlin with remaining sour cream, bread mixture and egg white. Process until smooth. Refrigerate.

Pre-heat oven to 400° F. Prepare a bread pan with cooking spray. Spread one-half of the salmon mixture in the bottom, then spread a layer of the marlin, top with one-half of the lime zest. Add a layer of the remaining salmon mixture. Top with slices of smoked salmon. Add more lime zest. Place bread pan in a larger baking pan and fill baking pan half full with water. Cover with aluminum foil. Cook 1 hour. Make sure water does not evaporate from baking pan. Chill 6 hours in refrigerator before unmolding. Garnish with lime slices and salmon eggs (optional) or tomato slices.

Cook's Note: If using canned salmon, drain liquid, remove skin and bones and rinse.

% Calories as Fat — Above the HM✓ guidelines: Although this recipe has a high percentage of calories as fat (>30%), the total fat is less than 10 grams per serving. This will easily fit within your allotment of 45 grams per day. This happens most often in low-calorie recipes. The majority of the fat is from the salmon. This is considered a good fat.

Nutrient Content Per Serving		Percent of Calories	Fat Breakdown	
Calories	218.0	50% Protein	Saturated Fat	1.5 g
Protein	26.9 g	13% Carbohydrate	Monounsaturated Fat	3.9 g
Carbohydrates	6.7 g	37% Fat	Polyunsaturated Fat	2.3 g
Fat – Total	8.8 g			
Cholesterol	68.1 mg			
Dietary Fiber	0.1 g			
Sodium	180.0 mg			

Chestnut Soup
Serves 6

1 lb.	chestnuts
1 sm.	onion, chopped fine
1 tsp.	sugar
1 Tbl.	lemon zest
¼ tsp.	nutmeg
2½ cups	chicken stock *(see p. 538)*
to taste	salt and pepper
5 cups	skim milk
1 cup	fat-free sour cream
¼ cup	cornstarch
½ cup	chicken breast, cooked, chopped (optional)

To prepare chestnuts: Score an "X" onto the flat side of the chestnut. Place in a pan and cover with water. Cover and simmer 15 minutes. Let cool, then peel.

In a soup pot, combine the chestnuts, onion, sugar, lemon zest, nutmeg, stock and salt and pepper to taste. Cover and simmer 30 minutes or until chestnuts are tender.

Transfer soup to a food processor and purée until smooth. Add milk and sour cream. In a small bowl, combine cornstarch with a little of the soup. Whisk the cornstarch into the soup and allow to thicken a bit. Stir in the cooked chicken, heat through and serve.

Nutrient Content Per Serving

Calories	346.0
Protein	17.2 g
Carbohydrates	61.8 g
Fat – Total	3.4 g
Cholesterol	17.4 mg
Dietary Fiber	10.3 g
Sodium	146.0 mg

Percent of Calories

20% Protein
71% Carbohydrate
9% Fat

Fat Breakdown

Saturated Fat	0.9 g
Monounsaturated Fat	1.2 g
Polyunsaturated Fat	1.0 g

COLD BEET SOUP
Serves 8

6 cups	beets, sliced
2 qts.	water
1 cup	potatoes, peeled, cubed, boiled
1 cup	scallions, minced
1 cup	radishes, sliced thin
1 cup	cucumber, seeds removed, sliced thin
3 Tbl.	fresh lemon juice
to taste	salt and pepper

Garnish:

8 tsp.	nonfat sour cream
1 cup	dill pickles, minced
1 cup	potatoes, cooked, peeled, diced

In a medium saucepan, heat beets, water and salt. Bring to a boil. Reduce heat and simmer 20-30 minutes, until beets are tender. Drain, reserving liquid. Cool beets, trim, discard top and peel.

Chop beets, add to reserved liquid, cool. Stir in potatoes, scallions, radishes, cucumber and lemon juice. Season to taste with salt and pepper. Chill overnight.

To serve, garnish with sour cream, dill pickles and potatoes.

Cook's Note: If using canned beets, drain canning liquid and replace with water. Begin with chopping.

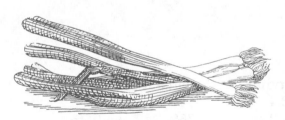

Nutrient Content Per Serving

Calories	72.7
Protein	2.4 g
Carbohydrates	16.7 g
Fat – Total	0.4 g
Cholesterol	0.0 mg
Dietary Fiber	3.4 g
Sodium	607.0 mg

Percent of Calories

12% Protein
84% Carbohydrate
4% Fat

Fat Breakdown

Saturated Fat	0.1 g
Monounsaturated Fat	0.0 g
Polyunsaturated Fat	0.1 g

CREAMY CARROT SOUP

Serves 6

1 med.	onion, chopped fine
1 tsp.	olive oil
1 lg.	potato, peeled, cut in cubes
1 lb. (6)	carrots, cut in chunks
3½ cups	chicken stock *(see p. 538)*
1 cup	skim milk
to taste	salt and white pepper

In a large soup pot, sauté the onion in olive oil. Add potatoes, carrots, and chicken stock. Cover and simmer 30 minutes or until vegetables are tender.

Transfer soup to a food processor and purée. Return to the pot and stir in the milk. Heat through and season with salt and white pepper.

Cook's Note: May also be served chilled.

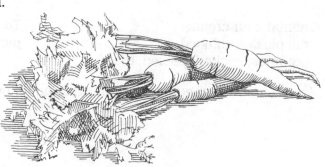

Nutrient Content Per Serving

Calories	78.4
Protein	2.9 g
Carbohydrates	15.3 g
Fat – Total	1.0 g
Cholesterol	0.8 mg
Dietary Fiber	3.2 g
Sodium	49.1 mg

Percent of Calories

14% Protein
75% Carbohydrate
11% Fat

Fat Breakdown

Saturated Fat	0.2 g
Monounsaturated Fat	0.6 g
Polyunsaturated Fat	0.2 g

CREAMY MUSSEL SOUP
Serves 10

5 lbs.	mussels in shells
1 med.	onion, chopped fine
3 ribs	celery, chopped coarse
2	leeks, white and part of greens, chopped coarse
2 cloves	garlic, minced
2 sprigs	parsley, whole
1 Tbl.	olive oil
¼ tsp.	anise seed, ground
1	bay leaf
pinch	saffron
2 cups	white wine
2 cups	fish stock *(see p. 540)*
2 cups	water
pinch	cayenne pepper
to taste	salt
¼ cup	arrowroot
5 Tbl.	water
½ cup	fat-free sour cream

In a large non-stick pot, sauté onions, celery, leeks, garlic and parsley in olive oil. Cook until just wilted. Add anise seed, bay leaf, saffron, white wine, stock, water, cayenne and salt to taste. Cover and simmer for 1 hour.

Steam mussels and remove from shells. Place mussels and solid portions of soup in a food processor. Purée until smooth. Return to the pot. Mix together the arrowroot and water. Add the arrowroot mixture to the soup. Heat until soup thickens. Whisk sour cream into soup. Add mussels. Heat through, but do not boil. Serve with bread rounds.

Cook's Note: Add some hot french bread *(see p. 206)* for a nice meal.

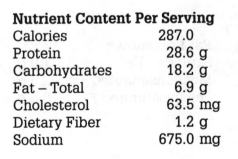

Nutrient Content Per Serving

Calories	287.0
Protein	28.6 g
Carbohydrates	18.2 g
Fat – Total	6.9 g
Cholesterol	63.5 mg
Dietary Fiber	1.2 g
Sodium	675.0 mg

Percent of Calories

41% Protein
26% Carbohydrate
22% Fat

Fat Breakdown

Saturated Fat	1.2 g
Monounsaturated Fat	2.2 g
Polyunsaturated Fat	1.7 g

ALSATIAN ONION SOUP
Serves 8

2 Tbl.	olive oil
3 lbs.	yellow onions, peeled, sliced thin
6 cloves	garlic, minced
¼ cup	brandy
2 cups	chablis
1 qt.	chicken stock *(see p. 538)*
1 Tbl.	fresh marjoram, chopped
¼ Tbl.	fresh thyme, chopped
1	bay leaf, crushed
⅛ tsp.	ground allspice
to taste	salt and black ground pepper

Garnish:

8 lg.	paprika croutons *(see p. 534)*
8 tsp.	parmesan cheese, grated

In a large soup pot, heat the oil over medium heat. Sauté onions and garlic. Glaze them without browning (keep them blonde). Heat brandy in a separate pan. Flame the brandy for just a moment. Add the brandy and white wine to the pot. Reduce a little. Add chicken stock and all remaining ingredients. Simmer, uncovered 30 minutes. Season with salt and pepper to taste.

Garnish each serving with a paprika crouton and 1 teaspoon freshly grated parmesan cheese. May also garnish with fresh sliced olives.

Cook's Note: This is not a French Onion soup. The seasonings are different.

Alcohol Note: The alcohol content was computed prior to cooking. Once the alcohol is heated to the boiling point, the alcohol disappears along with most of the calories from the alcohol.

Nutrient Content Per Serving

Calories	177.0
Protein	3.4 g
Carbohydrates	18.4 g
Fat – Total	4.6 g
Cholesterol	1.7 mg
Dietary Fiber	3.2 g
Sodium	63.3 mg

Percent of Calories

7% Protein
40% Carbohydrate
23% Fat
30% Alcohol

Fat Breakdown

Saturated Fat	1.0 g
Monounsaturated Fat	2.9 g
Polyunsaturated Fat	0.5 g

SPLIT PEA SOUP
Serves 8

3 cups	split green peas, dry
2 qts.	chicken stock *(see p. 538)*
4 cloves	garlic, minced
1 sprig	parsley, whole
2	bay leaves
½ tsp.	dried thyme
½ tsp.	dried marjoram
2 med	onions, halved
4	cloves
¼ tsp.	smoke flavor
to taste	salt and pepper

In a large pot combine split peas, stock, garlic and herbs. Poke a clove into each onion half and add to soup. Bring to a boil, cover and simmer 2 hours or until peas are soft. Add water if necessary. Add smoke flavor and salt and pepper to taste. Remove parsley, bay leaf, onions and cloves.

Cook's Note: May serve as is, purée entire soup or purée only half. You choose the texture you desire. Smoke flavor is a liquid found in the supermarket.

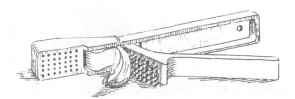

Nutrient Content Per Serving

Calories	65.5
Protein	3.6 g
Carbohydrates	12.7 g
Fat – Total	0.5 g
Cholesterol	0.0 mg
Dietary Fiber	3.8 g
Sodium	6.0 mg

Percent of Calories

21% Protein
73% Carbohydrate
 6% Fat

Fat Breakdown

Saturated Fat	0.1 g
Monounsaturated Fat	0.1 g
Polyunsaturated Fat	0.2 g

VEGETABLE PESTO SOUP
Serves 6

2 lg.	carrots, peeled, cut in small cubes
4 med.	potatoes, peeled, cut in small cubes
2	leeks, white portion only, sliced thin
2 sm.	zucchini, cut in cubes
to taste	salt and pepper
⅔ cup	pasta, any small noodle, uncooked
½ lb.	green beans, cut in 1-inch pieces
½ lb.	navy beans, canned, drained and rinsed
2	tomatoes, peeled, seeded, mashed
6 cloves	garlic, minced
1 bunch	fresh basil, chopped
⅔ cup	parmesan cheese, grated
1 tsp.	olive oil

In 10 cups of water, combine carrots, potatoes, leeks, zucchini, salt and pepper to taste. Cook 45 minutes. Add pasta and beans. Cook 15 minutes. Combine tomato, garlic and basil in food processor and process until smooth. Add parmesan. Continue to process until well mixed. Add oil and mix, then add to soup. Serve immediately.

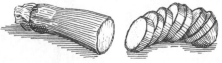

Cook's Note: May want to sprinkle grated parmesan on top.

Nutrient Content Per Serving

Calories	243.0
Protein	11.3 g
Carbohydrates	41.9 g
Fat – Total	4.3 g
Cholesterol	7.4 mg
Dietary Fiber	8.1 g
Sodium	200.0 mg

Percent of Calories

18% Protein
67% Carbohydrate
15% Fat

Fat Breakdown

Saturated Fat	2.0 g
Monounsaturated Fat	1.4 g
Polyunsaturated Fat	0.4 g

SHRIMP BISQUE
Serves 4

1 lb.	shrimp, peeled and deveined
1 tsp.	olive oil
1 med.	onion, chopped fine
1 med.	carrot, chopped fine
¼ cup	cognac
1 Tbl.	rice
2 lg.	tomatoes, chopped fine
1 tsp.	tomato paste
2 cups	fish stock (see p. 540)
1 cup	water
2 cups	white wine
1	bouquet garni (see p. 15)
to taste	salt and pepper
2 Tbl.	fat-free sour cream

In a non-stick pan, sauté shrimp, onions and carrots in the oil. Add one-half of the cognac and flame to remove alcohol. Add rice, tomatoes, tomato paste, stock, water, wine, bouquet garni, salt and pepper to taste. Simmer 5 minutes. Remove shrimp and chop. Cover and continue to simmer another 15 minutes.

Transfer soup to a food processor. Process one-third of the shrimp with the soup to obtain a smooth texture. Return to pot with remaining shrimp. Add remaining cognac and stir in the sour cream. Heat through, but do not boil.

Cholesterol — Above the HM✔ guidelines: Occasionally a lowfat recipe is high in cholesterol. In this case the cholesterol stems from the shellfish. The level is moderately high (>150 mg per serving) but may fit into your weekly average of 150 mg per day.

Alcohol Note: The alcohol content was computed prior to cooking. Once the alcohol is heated to the boiling point, the alcohol disappears along with most of the calories from the alcohol.

Nutrient Content Per Serving

Calories	309.0
Protein	25.1 g
Carbohydrates	17.4 g
Fat – Total	4.2 g
Cholesterol	173.0 mg
Dietary Fiber	2.1 g
Sodium	202.0 mg

Percent of Calories

32% Protein
22% Carbohydrate
12% Fat
34% Alcohol

Fat Breakdown

Saturated Fat	0.7 g
Monounsaturated Fat	1.3 g
Polyunsaturated Fat	1.4 g

SNOW PEA ZUCCHINI SOUP
Serves 8

½ lb.	snow peas
¼ lb.	zucchini, cut in small cubes
1	onion, chopped fine
1 tsp.	olive oil
3 cups	chicken stock *(see p. 538)*
½ cup	rice, uncooked
1 Tbl.	chives, chopped
3 cups	hot water
¾ cup	fresh spinach, cut julienne
¼ tsp.	nutmeg
to taste	salt and pepper

Sauté onions in olive oil until translucent. In a soup pan, heat stock. Add rice and onions. Cover and simmer for 15 minutes. Add zucchini and cook 10 minutes. Add snow peas, chives and water. Simmer 15 minutes. Add spinach, nutmeg, salt and pepper to taste. Cook only until spinach wilts. Serve hot.

Cook's Note: This is a clear broth with beautiful green vegetables floating around.

Nutrient Content Per Serving		Percent of Calories	Fat Breakdown	
Calories	74.3	14% Protein	Saturated Fat	0.2 g
Protein	2.6 g	72% Carbohydrate	Monounsaturated Fat	0.6 g
Carbohydrates	13.3 g	14% Fat	Polyunsaturated Fat	0.3 g
Fat – Total	1.2 g			
Cholesterol	0.0 mg			
Dietary Fiber	1.3 g			
Sodium	563.0 mg			

TOMATO CONSOMME
Serves 8

1¾ cups	celery, diced fine
1½ cups	carrot, diced fine
2 med.	onions, diced fine
8	egg whites
4 cups	tomato juice, low-sodium
4 cups	chicken stock *(see p. 538)*
2	bay leaves
1 tsp.	dry tarragon
½ Tbl.	peppercorns, crushed
½ tsp.	dry thyme
to taste	salt and pepper

In a food processor, purée celery, carrots and onions. In a large pot, add celery mixture and the remaining ingredients. Quickly bring to a boil. Reduce heat and simmer, partially covered for 1 hour. When consomme is clear and flavorful, strain through cheesecloth.

Nutrient Content Per Serving

Calories	65.3
Protein	4.8 g
Carbohydrates	12.4 g
Fat – Total	0.2 g
Cholesterol	0.0 mg
Dietary Fiber	2.9 g
Sodium	94.2 mg

Percent of Calories

27% Protein
70% Carbohydrate
3% Fat

Fat Breakdown

Saturated Fat	0.0 g
Monounsaturated Fat	0.0 g
Polyunsaturated Fat	0.1 g

CREAM OF WATERCRESS SOUP
Serves 6

2 bunches	watercress, washed and dried, stems removed
2 tsp.	olive oil
1 Tbl.	onion, minced
3 cups	chicken stock *(see p. 538)*
4 med.	potatoes, peeled and quartered
1 cup	skim milk
¼ cup	nonfat dry milk powder
to taste	salt and freshly ground pepper
to taste	hot pepper sauce (optional)

In a large non-stick pan, sauté onions in olive oil until clear. Add 1 cup of water and chicken stock. Bring to a boil. Add potatoes and cook partially covered until tender (add more water if necessary). Add watercress, (reserving some for garnish), cook 5 minutes. Transfer soup to a food processor or blender and purée. Return purée to the pot and bring back to a simmer. Remove from heat. Add skim milk and powdered milk. Season with salt, pepper and hot pepper sauce to taste. Garnish with fresh watercress tops.

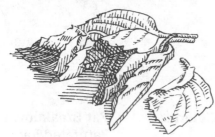

Nutrient Content Per Serving

Calories	115.0
Protein	4.9 g
Carbohydrates	20.6 g
Fat – Total	1.7 g
Cholesterol	1.7 mg
Dietary Fiber	1.5 g
Sodium	56.2 mg

Percent of Calories
17% Protein
70% Carbohydrate
13% Fat

Fat Breakdown

Saturated Fat	0.3 g
Monounsaturated Fat	1.1 g
Polyunsaturated Fat	0.2 g

ASPARAGUS WITH SHERRY DIJON DRESSING
Serves 4

1 lb.   asparagus spears

Dressing:
2 Tbl.   white wine vinegar
1 Tbl.   dijon-style mustard
2 oz.   fat-free tofu, soft
1 tsp.   sesame oil
to taste   salt and pepper
2 Tbl.   sherry

Garnish:
2 Tbl.   chives, chopped

Remove bottom 1½ inches of stem. Steam or microwave asparagus until just tender.

To prepare the dressing, process all ingredients in a food processor until smooth. Add sherry to thin to desired consistency.

Spoon dressing over asparagus. Serve at room temperature. Garnish with chives.

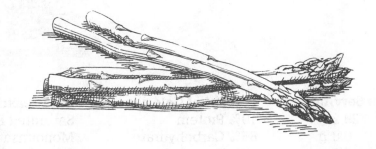

Nutrient Content Per Serving

Calories	51.4
Protein	3.3 g
Carbohydrates	7.7 g
Fat – Total	1.8 g
Cholesterol	0.0 mg
Dietary Fiber	2.7 g
Sodium	52.6 mg

Percent of Calories
22% Protein
51% Carbohydrate
27% Fat

Fat Breakdown

Saturated Fat	0.3 g
Monounsaturated Fat	0.7 g
Polyunsaturated Fat	0.7 g

RED CABBAGE SLAW WITH RASPBERRY VINAIGRETTE
Serves 8

1 sm. head	red cabbage (6 cups)	Shred cabbage.

Dressing:

½ cup	raspberry vinegar	To prepare the dressing, combine all dressing ingredients. Pour over cabbage. Let marinate at least 4 hours.
2 Tbl.	lemon juice	
2 Tbl.	sugar	
1 tsp.	caraway seeds, ground	
to taste	salt and pepper	

Cook's Note: Caraway flavor is rather strong. Adjust to your taste.

Nutrient Content Per Serving

Calories	29.2
Protein	0.8 g
Carbohydrates	7.3 g
Fat – Total	0.2 g
Cholesterol	0.0 mg
Dietary Fiber	1.0 g
Sodium	9.7 mg

Percent of Calories

10% Protein
85% Carbohydrate
5% Fat

Fat Breakdown

Saturated Fat	0.0 g
Monounsaturated Fat	0.0 g
Polyunsaturated Fat	0.1 g

CARROTS AND GREENS
Serves 6

½ lb.	spinach or other strong green
2 lg.	carrots, grated rough
2	apples, grated rough
1 Tbl.	hazelnuts

Dressing:

2	lemons, zested fine and juiced
2 tsp.	olive oil
to taste	salt and pepper
1 Tbl.	honey
2 tsp.	rice vinegar

Bake hazelnuts at 200° F for 10 minutes. Remove skins and crush a little.

Clean and de-stem the spinach. In a large bowl, combine all dressing ingredients. Add carrots, apples, greens and nuts to the dressing. Mix and serve.

Cook's Note: Add a chilled, grilled, cold chicken breast for a complete meal.

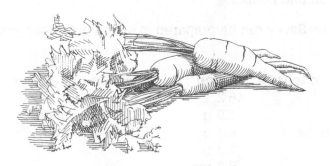

Nutrient Content Per Serving		Percent of Calories	Fat Breakdown	
Calories	78.8	7% Protein	Saturated Fat	0.3 g
Protein	1.6 g	66% Carbohydrate	Monounsaturated Fat	1.7 g
Carbohydrates	14.4 g	27% Fat	Polyunsaturated Fat	0.3 g
Fat – Total	2.6 g			
Cholesterol	0.0 mg			
Dietary Fiber	2.8 g			
Sodium	38.5 mg			

CAULIFLOWER SALAD
Serves 6

1 head	cauliflower

Sauce:

1 tsp.	olive oil
2 Tbl.	dijon mustard
¼ cup	white wine vinegar
1 med.	onion, chopped fine
½ cup	fresh chives, chopped
½ tsp.	tarragon
1 tsp.	thyme or 1 sprig fresh thyme
2	tomatoes, chopped
1	cucumber, chopped
5	radishes, chopped
to taste	salt and pepper

Break the cauliflower into small flowerets. Steam until just barely tender. Combine remaining ingredients. Pour over hot cauliflower. Serve hot.

Cook's Note: Sauce can be prepared in a food processor, pulse only to chop. Has a refreshing flavor.

Nutrient Content Per Serving

Calories	46.2
Protein	1.9 g
Carbohydrates	8.4 g
Fat – Total	1.3 g
Cholesterol	0.0 mg
Dietary Fiber	2.4 g
Sodium	81.7 mg

Percent of Calories

15% Protein	
63% Carbohydrate	
22% Fat	

Fat Breakdown

Saturated Fat	0.2 g
Monounsaturated Fat	0.8 g
Polyunsaturated Fat	0.2 g

KIWI FRUIT, ORANGE AND PEPPERS
Serves 6

½ lb.	yellow pepper, sliced thin
½ lb.	sweet red pepper, sliced thin
½ med.	onion, sliced in thin rounds, separate rings
2	oranges, peeled, cut in bite-size pieces
1	apple, tart, peeled, cut in bite-size pieces
4	kiwi fruit, peeled, cut in rounds

Dressing:

2 Tbl.	vinegar
1 Tbl.	lite soy sauce
1 tsp.	sugar
to taste	pepper

Arrange fruits and vegetables decoratively in a bowl. Combine dressing ingredients. Drizzle dressing over salad. Serve immediately.

Cook's Note: A flavored vinegar will enhance flavor. Try raspberry vinegar for a twist. May use roasted peppers for a milder pepper flavor.

Nutrient Content Per Serving

Calories	93.6
Protein	1.9 g
Carbohydrates	23.1 g
Fat – Total	0.5 g
Cholesterol	0.0 mg
Dietary Fiber	4.6 g
Sodium	124.0 mg

Percent of Calories

7% Protein
88% Carbohydrate
4% Fat

Fat Breakdown

Saturated Fat	0.1 g
Monounsaturated Fat	0.1 g
Polyunsaturated Fat	0.2 g

LENTIL SALAD
Serves 8

2½ cups	green lentils, uncooked
1 med.	onion, halved
1 clove	garlic, whole
1	bay leaf
1 cup	chicken stock *(see p. 538)*

Dressing:

⅓ cup	red wine vinegar
1 Tbl.	olive oil
to taste	salt
to taste	fresh ground black pepper

Rinse lentils. In a large saucepan, combine lentils, onion, garlic and bay leaf. Cover with chicken stock and water. Bring to a boil, then simmer, covered for 30-40 minutes or until lentils are tender. Add water if necessary. Do not overcook so that lentils breakdown. All liquid should be absorbed.

Remove from heat. Discard garlic, onion and bay leaf.

To prepare dressing, whisk together dressing ingredients. Pour over warm lentils. Serve warm.

Nutrient Content Per Serving

Calories	226.0
Protein	17.1 g
Carbohydrates	36.1 g
Fat – Total	2.3 g
Cholesterol	0.0 mg
Dietary Fiber	7.5 g
Sodium	6.6 mg

Percent of Calories

29% Protein
62% Carbohydrate
9% Fat

Fat Breakdown

Saturated Fat	0.3 g
Monounsaturated Fat	1.3 g
Polyunsaturated Fat	0.4 g

Mussel Salad
Serves 6

½ lb.   mussels, in shell
½ lb.   mussels, out of shell *(see p. 13)*
4   potatoes, cubed
3   tomatoes, sliced
2 Tbl.   fresh parsley, chopped
to taste   salt and pepper

Marinade:
2 cloves   garlic, minced
1 tsp.   olive oil
3 Tbl.   red wine vinegar

Clean mussels. Steam only enough to open (2 minutes). Put in a bowl with marinade. Let marinate one hour.

Parboil potatoes. Arrange tomatoes and potatoes in a serving dish. Add mussels including marinade and parsley. Chill. Serve cold.

Cook's Note: May be made ahead. A good potluck or leftover. Very colorful and appealing to the eye.

Nutrient Content Per Serving	
Calories	234.0
Protein	20.4 g
Carbohydrates	28.2 g
Fat – Total	4.4 g
Cholesterol	42.4 mg
Dietary Fiber	2.3 g
Sodium	288.0 mg

Percent of Calories	
35% Protein	
48% Carbohydrate	
17% Fat	

Fat Breakdown	
Saturated Fat	0.8 g
Monounsaturated Fat	1.4 g
Polyunsaturated Fat	1.1 g

OCTOPUS SALAD
Serves 4

1 lb.	octopus
6 cups	chicken stock *(see p. 538)*
1	eggplant, cubed
1	zucchini, cubed
6 cups	mixed greens, washed and torn
½	sweet red pepper, cubed

Dressing:

2 Tbl.	white wine vinegar
2 tsp.	olive oil
2 tsp.	dijon mustard
to taste	salt and pepper

Rinse octopus for 15 minutes. Boil for 20 minutes. Cut in thick slices. Place in a pan with chicken stock, cover and simmer for 50 minutes. Drain and chill.

Steam eggplant and zucchini until soft. Chill. Arrange greens and pepper on plate. Decoratively arrange eggplant, zucchini on the bed of greens.

Whisk together all dressing ingredients and pour over salad.

Cook's Note: Octopus can be purchased at specialty seafood markets.

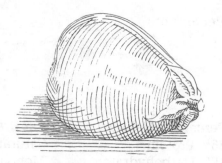

Nutrient Content Per Serving

Calories	193.0
Protein	20.7 g
Carbohydrates	19.9 g
Fat – Total	4.3 g
Cholesterol	54.4 mg
Dietary Fiber	7.3 g
Sodium	342.0 mg

Percent of Calories

41% Protein
40% Carbohydrate
19% Fat

Fat Breakdown

Saturated Fat	0.7 g
Monounsaturated Fat	2.0 g
Polyunsaturated Fat	0.8 g

ORANGE SALAD

Serves 6

4	Belgian endives, core removed
4 lg.	oranges, peeled, sliced in rounds
2 Tbl.	walnuts, chopped

Vinaigrette:

⅓ cup	raspberry vinegar
1 tsp.	olive oil
to taste	salt and pepper

Toast walnuts in oven for 10 minutes at 350° F. Arrange endive leaves decoratively around the perimeter of a glass bowl. Arrange oranges in the bowl. Sprinkle with walnuts. Add vinaigrette. Chill.

Nutrient Content Per Serving

Calories	83.4
Protein	1.9 g
Carbohydrates	15.8 g
Fat – Total	2.4 g
Cholesterol	0.0 mg
Dietary Fiber	3.2 g
Sodium	2.0 mg

Percent of Calories

8% Protein	
69% Carbohydrate	
23% Fat	

Fat Breakdown

Saturated Fat	0.2 g
Monounsaturated Fat	0.9 g
Polyunsaturated Fat	1.1 g

PINEAPPLE BOAT SALAD
Serves 6

3	fresh pineapples
2	oranges, peeled, sliced thin
½	honeydew, peeled, sliced thin
½	cantaloupe, peeled, sliced thin
3	kiwi, peeled, sliced thin
6 sm. bunches	red seedless grapes
6 sprigs	fresh mint
2 cups	fresh berries
3 cups	1% lowfat cottage cheese

Cut the pineapples in half. Remove the meat from the inside to create a boat. Cut the pineapple meat into chunks. Arrange fruit and cottage cheese nicely in the pineapple boats and serve.

Nutrient Content Per Serving

Calories	341.0
Protein	17.0 g
Carbohydrates	68.4 g
Fat – Total	3.1 g
Cholesterol	5.0 mg
Dietary Fiber	7.9 g
Sodium	477.0 mg

Percent of Calories

18% Protein
74% Carbohydrate
  7% Fat

Fat Breakdown

Saturated Fat	1.0 g
Monounsaturated Fat	0.6 g
Polyunsaturated Fat	0.7 g

POTATO SALAD
Serves 6

1 lb.   new potatoes, sliced ¼-inch thick (skin on)
1 bunch   watercress
1 bunch   radishes, sliced thin
12 leaves   fresh basil

Dressing:
1 Tbl.   olive oil
6 Tbl.   lemon juice
2 cloves   garlic, sliced thin
½ tsp.   rosemary
½ tsp.   thyme
pinch   cumin
to taste   salt and pepper

Boil sliced potatoes until barely tender, 15-20 minutes. Drain potatoes, cool slightly.

To prepare dressing:
Combine all ingredients.

Add most of dressing to potatoes and mix. Arrange watercress and radishes decoratively on one side of plate and the potatoes on the other side. Drizzle the remaining dressing over the watercress and radishes. Chill 2 hours before serving.

Nutrient Content Per Serving

Calories	110.0
Protein	2.1 g
Carbohydrates	21.2 g
Fat – Total	2.4 g
Cholesterol	0.0 mg
Dietary Fiber	1.9 g
Sodium	11.4 mg

Percent of Calories

7% Protein
74% Carbohydrate
19% Fat

Fat Breakdown

Saturated Fat	0.3 g
Monounsaturated Fat	1.7 g
Polyunsaturated Fat	0.3 g

POTATO AND MUSHROOM SALAD
Serves 8

1½ lb.   potatoes, peeled, sliced thin
¼ cup   white wine
½ head   lettuce
½ lb.   mushrooms, sliced

Dressing:
¾ cup   mayonnaise, fat-free
2 Tbl.   dijon mustard
1 Tbl.   fresh basil, chopped
¼ cup   skim milk
to taste salt and pepper

Boil potatoes for 15 minutes until just tender.

To prepare dressing:
In a small saucepan, combine mayonnaise, mustard and basil. Whisk in skim milk until dressing is somewhat runny.

Add wine to the potatoes and toss with dressing. Arrange lettuce in a bowl and add potatoes. Arrange mushrooms on top. Serve immediately.

Cook's Note: This is a warm potato salad. Peeling the potatoes is optional. Leaving the peel on increases the fiber from 2.0 grams to 2.5 grams per serving.

Alcohol Note: The alcohol content was computed prior to cooking. Once the alcohol is heated to the boiling point, the alcohol disappears along with most of the calories from the alcohol.

Nutrient Content Per Serving

Calories	131.0
Protein	3.4 g
Carbohydrates	28.2 g
Fat – Total	0.5 g
Cholesterol	0.1 mg
Dietary Fiber	2.0 g
Sodium	318.0 mg

Percent of Calories

10% Protein
83% Carbohydrate
3% Fat
4% Alcohol

Fat Breakdown

Saturated Fat	0.1 g
Monounsaturated Fat	0.2 g
Polyunsaturated Fat	0.1 g

RATATOUILLE SALAD
Serves 8

2	zucchini, sliced in rounds
1	eggplant, cut in wedges
2	bell peppers, sliced in rounds
1	onion, sliced in rounds
2 cloves	garlic, minced
2 tsp.	olive oil
3	tomatoes, sliced lengthwise
1	hot pepper, diced
½ cup	wine vinegar
to taste	salt and pepper

In a non-stick pan, sauté zucchini, eggplant, peppers, onions and garlic in oil for 5 minutes. Add tomatoes and hot pepper. Cook covered over low heat for 20 minutes. Drain off excess water. Add vinegar and salt and pepper to taste. Serve at room temperature.

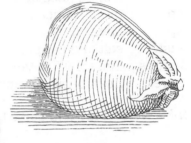

Nutrient Content Per Serving

Calories	53.6
Protein	1.5 g
Carbohydrates	10.5 g
Fat – Total	1.5 g
Cholesterol	0.0 mg
Dietary Fiber	3.4 g
Sodium	7.6 mg

Percent of Calories

10% Protein
68% Carbohydrate
22% Fat

Fat Breakdown

Saturated Fat	0.2 g
Monounsaturated Fat	0.9 g
Polyunsaturated Fat	0.3 g

MIXED SEAFOOD SALAD
Serves 4

1 lb.	mixed seafood: mussels, scallops, calamari, shrimp
4 leaves	lettuce, whole
½ lb.	cherry tomatoes, cut in half
12	black olives, sliced

Dressing:

1	lemon, juice of
1 tsp.	garlic, minced
2 tsp.	olive oil
to taste	salt and pepper
2-3 drops	Tabasco™ to taste (optional)
4 leaves	fresh basil, chopped

Steam seafood in a small amount of water for 8-10 minutes.

To prepare dressing:
Combine lemon juice, garlic, olive oil, salt and pepper.

Add Tabasco™ and basil. Add seafood to salad dressing and mix well, being careful not to break up the seafood. Let marinate 30 minutes. Arrange on plate with lettuce leaves, tomatoes and olives. Serve chilled.

Cook's Note: May add anise to the dressing for a change of flavor.

% Calories as Fat — Above the HM✔ guidelines: Although this recipe has a high percentage of calories as fat (>30%), the total fat is less than 5 grams per serving. This will easily fit within your allotment of 45 grams per day. This happens most often in low-calorie recipes.

Cholesterol — Above the HM✔ guidelines: Occasionally a lowfat recipe is high in cholesterol. In this case the cholesterol stems from the shellfish. The level is moderately high (>150 mg per serving) but may fit into your weekly average of 150 mg per day.

Nutrient Content Per Serving

Calories	172.0
Protein	23.8 g
Carbohydrates	5.8 g
Fat – Total	5.9 g
Cholesterol	173.0 mg
Dietary Fiber	1.4 g
Sodium	261.0 mg

Percent of Calories

56% Protein
13% Carbohydrate
31% Fat

Fat Breakdown

Saturated Fat	0.9 g
Monounsaturated Fat	3.0 g
Polyunsaturated Fat	1.2 g

SHELLFISH SALAD
Serves 6

6 leaves	lettuce, whole
1	leek, sliced thin
6	cherry tomatoes, cut in half
6 stalks	celery, cut in sticks
¼ lb.	salad shrimp, peeled, steamed
½ lb.	medium shrimp, peeled, steamed
1 lb.	mussels, in shells, cleaned and steamed *(see p. 13)*
1 lb.	clams, in shells, cleaned and steamed
1	shallot, minced

Dressing:

1 Tbl.	olive oil
¼ cup	white wine vinegar
pinch	saffron
to taste	salt and pepper

Arrange seafood and vegetables on a platter. Leave mussels and clams in their shells and place on top. Whisk together salad dressing ingredients. Pour over salad. Serve immediately.

Cholesterol — Above the HM✓ guidelines: Occasionally a lowfat recipe is high in cholesterol. In this case the cholesterol stems from the shellfish. The level is moderately high (>150 mg per serving) but may fit into your weekly average of 150 mg per day.

Nutrient Content Per Serving

Calories	365.0
Protein	51.5 g
Carbohydrates	16.2 g
Fat – Total	7.3 g
Cholesterol	199.0 mg
Dietary Fiber	2.4 g
Sodium	634.0 mg

Percent of Calories

56% Protein
27% Carbohydrate
17% Fat

Fat Breakdown

Saturated Fat	1.6 g
Monounsaturated Fat	3.2 g
Polyunsaturated Fat	2.4 g

TOMATO SALAD
Serves 4

4 lg.	ripe tomatoes, sliced in thin rounds
1 Tbl.	onion, chopped

Dressing:

1 tsp.	olive oil
3 Tbl.	lemon juice
1 clove	garlic, pressed
1 tsp.	fresh basil, chopped
1 tsp.	sugar
1 Tbl.	dijon mustard
to taste	salt and pepper

Whisk together dressing ingredients. Arrange tomatoes and onions on a plate. Add dressing. Chill.

Cook's Note: May add 1 ounce of provolone to the salad. Each ounce will increase the fat by 5 grams.

Nutrient Content Per Serving

Calories	60.0
Protein	1.9 g
Carbohydrates	11.2 g
Fat – Total	1.9 g
Cholesterol	0.0 mg
Dietary Fiber	2.6 g
Sodium	65.6 mg

Percent of Calories

11% Protein
64% Carbohydrate
25% Fat

Fat Breakdown

Saturated Fat	0.3 g
Monounsaturated Fat	1.1 g
Polyunsaturated Fat	0.4 g

Fresh Vegetable Salad
Serves 6

8 spears	asparagus, cut in 1-inch wedges
2 cups	corn, frozen or fresh
3	scallions, cut in ¼-inch slices
1 clove	garlic, minced
4	plum tomatoes, cubed
1	sweet red pepper, sliced thin
8	olives, sliced

Dressing:

1	lemon, juice of
½ cup	red wine vinegar
to taste	salt and pepper

Cook's Note: Best when served immediately. Do not allow it to marinate.

Steam asparagus and corn. Chill. Add cooled asparagus and corn to cut vegetables.

To prepare dressing:
Combine all dressing ingredients. Chill.

Pour dressing over vegetables and serve.

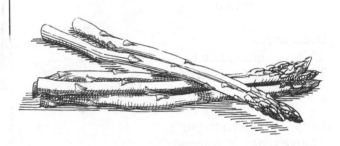

Nutrient Content Per Serving

Calories	82.3
Protein	2.9 g
Carbohydrates	19.4 g
Fat – Total	0.9 g
Cholesterol	0.0 mg
Dietary Fiber	4.0 g
Sodium	16.6 mg

Percent of Calories
12% Protein
79% Carbohydrate
9% Fat

Fat Breakdown

Saturated Fat	0.1 g
Monounsaturated Fat	0.2 g
Polyunsaturated Fat	0.4 g

VEGETABLES WITH ROASTED PEPPER, MUSHROOM AND BASIL VINAIGRETTE

Serves 8

1 cup	artichoke bottoms, diced
2	green peppers and 1 red pepper, roasted and cut into strips *(see p. 13)*
1	red onion, sliced thinly buttercrunch lettuce leaves for serving
1 lb.	fresh mushrooms, stemmed, sliced

Dressing:

2 Tbl.	lime juice
2 Tbl.	red wine vinegar
2 Tbl.	rice vinegar or brown rice vinegar
1 tsp.	brown sugar
2 cloves	garlic, minced
to taste	freshly ground pepper
1 Tbl.	fresh basil, chopped
1 tsp.	fresh mint, chopped
⅔ cup	chicken stock *(see p. 538)*

Garnish:

fresh mint, chopped or fresh basil, chopped for garnish

To prepare dressing:
Combine all dressing ingredients in a screw-top jar and shake thoroughly. Adjust flavors to your taste.

Roast peppers. Cut into strips.

Combine sliced peppers, red onion and artichokes with vinaigrette dressing and chill several hours. An hour before serving, add mushrooms. Mix lightly and refrigerate.

To serve:
Line salad plates with buttercrunch lettuce and mound with salad mixture. Sprinkle with chopped herbs of your choice.

Nutrient Content Per Serving		**Percent of Calories**	**Fat Breakdown**	
Calories	48.3	17% Protein	Saturated Fat	0.1 g
Protein	2.4 g	76% Carbohydrate	Monounsaturated Fat	0.0 g
Carbohydrates	10.9 g	7% Fat	Polyunsaturated Fat	0.2 g
Fat – Total	0.4 g			
Cholesterol	0.0 mg			
Dietary Fiber	3.2 g			
Sodium	17.8 mg			

CREPE BATTER
Makes 16

½ cup	egg substitute
1	egg, whole
⅛ tsp.	salt
1 cup	flour
¼ cup	nonfat dry milk
1 tsp.	powdered butter replacement
1½ cup	water

In a mixing bowl, combine egg substitute, egg and salt. Turn mixer to low setting. Gradually add flour and dry milk. Mix until smooth. Batter should be runny. Let stand at least 1 hour in refrigerator.

Stir batter if it has separated. Spoon a few tablespoons of batter into a pre-heated non-stick crepe pan or use a crepe maker.

Heat a non-stick 6-inch skillet or crepe pan over medium heat until hot. Pour ¼ cup batter into hot pan, tilting pan to coat it evenly with batter. Cook 1-2 minutes until batter bubbles and edges turn light brown. Do not turn. Remove with spatula to wax paper. Crepes should be very thin.

Cook's Note: May need to spray the pan with non-stick cooking spray. You can store crepes in an air-tight container by placing a layer of wax paper between the crepes. Store in the refrigerator for up to 1 week.

▼ This recipe is used for the following items:
Seafood Thermador Crepes (see p. 222)
Broccoli au Gratin Crepes (see p. 242)

Nutrient Content Per Crepe

Calories	46.8
Protein	2.8 g
Carbohydrates	7.1 g
Fat – Total	0.7 g
Cholesterol	13.7 mg
Dietary Fiber	0.2 g
Sodium	45.9 mg

Percent of Calories

25% Protein	
62% Carbohydrate	
13% Fat	

Fat Breakdown

Saturated Fat	0.2 g
Monounsaturated Fat	0.2 g
Polyunsaturated Fat	0.2 g

DESSERT CREPES
Makes 8

½ cup	egg substitute
⅛ tsp.	salt
½ cup	flour
1 Tbl.	white sugar
½ cup	skim milk
2 Tbl.	nonfat dry milk
⅛ cup	water
1 tsp.	powdered butter replacement

In a mixing bowl, combine egg substitute and salt. Turn mixer to low setting. Gradually add remaining ingredients. Mix until smooth. Let stand at least 1 hour in refrigerator.

Stir batter if it has separated. Spoon a few tablespoons of batter into a pre-heated non-stick crepe pan or use a crepe maker. Crepes should be very thin.

Heat a non-stick 6-inch skillet or crepe pan over medium heat until hot. Pour ¼ cup batter into hot pan, tilting pan to coat it evenly with batter. Cook 1-2 minutes until batter bubbles and edges turn light brown. Do not turn. Remove with spatula to wax paper.

Cook's Note: May need to spray the pan with non-stick cooking spray. You can store crepes in an air-tight container by placing a layer of wax paper between the crepes. Store in the refrigerator for up to 1 week.

▼ This recipe is used for the following items:
Black Forest Crepes (see p. 264)
Crepes Grand Marnier (see p. 265)
French Cream Crepes with Raspberry Sauce (see p. 266)
Peach Crepes (see p. 267)

Nutrient Content Per Serving		Percent of Calories	Fat Breakdown	
Calories	60.5	26% Protein	Saturated Fat	0.1 g
Protein	3.9 g	64% Carbohydrate	Monounsaturated Fat	0.2 g
Carbohydrates	9.5 g	10% Fat	Polyunsaturated Fat	0.3 g
Fat – Total	0.6 g			
Cholesterol	0.8 mg			
Dietary Fiber	0.2 g			
Sodium	48.3 mg			

ALL-PURPOSE CREPE BATTER
Makes 16

½ cup	egg substitute
¼ tsp.	salt
2 cups	flour
2½ cups	skim milk
¼ cup	nonfat dry milk
1 Tbl.	canola oil

In a mixing bowl, combine egg substitute and salt. Turn mixer to low setting. Gradually add flour, alternating with milk and dry milk. Mix until smooth. Mix in oil. Let stand at least 1 hour in refrigerator.

Heat a non-stick 6-inch skillet or crepe pan over medium heat until hot. Pour ¼ cup batter into hot pan, tilting pan to coat it evenly with batter. Cook 1-2 minutes until batter bubbles and edges turn light brown. Do not turn. Remove with spatula to wax paper. Crepes should be very thin.

Cook's Note: May need to spray the pan with a non-stick cooking spray. You can store crepes in an air-tight container by placing a layer of wax paper between the crepes. Store in the refrigerator for up to 1 week. These crepes are slightly higher in fat than the basic crepes or dessert crepes.

▼ This recipe is used for the following items:
Crepes with Mushrooms (see p. 192)
Crepes Florentine (see p. 402)

Nutrient Content Per Crepe

Calories	77.8
Protein	3.2 g
Carbohydrates	13.0 g
Fat – Total	1.3 g
Cholesterol	0.4 mg
Dietary Fiber	0.4 g
Sodium	57.5 mg

Percent of Calories

17% Protein	
68% Carbohydrate	
15% Fat	

Fat Breakdown

Saturated Fat	0.1 g
Monounsaturated Fat	0.6 g
Polyunsaturated Fat	0.4 g

CREPES WITH MUSHROOMS
Serves 6

1 recipe	all-purpose crepes *(see p. 191)*

Sauce:

1 Tbl.	shallots, minced
10 oz.	fresh mushrooms, sliced
2½ tsp.	olive oil
2½ tsp.	flour
½ cup	skim milk
2 oz.	gruyere cheese, grated fine
to taste	salt and freshly ground pepper

Garnish:

lemon wedges
fresh parsley

Prepare crepes according to recipe.

In a non-stick frying pan, sauté shallots and mushrooms in 1 teaspoon olive oil over medium heat until soft. In a saucepan, combine the remaining 1½ teaspoons of oil and flour. Stir constantly over medium heat for 3 minutes until mixture starts to loosen from the bottom of the pan. Do not allow to brown. Add milk and whisk constantly until smooth and silky. Add the cheese and melt slowly into the sauce. Season with salt and pepper to taste. Combine the sauce and mushrooms. Arrange on a hot platter. Fold the crepes in triangles and place nicely on top. Garnish with lemon wedges and parsley.

Cook's Note: Gruyere cheese makes it really tasty.

Nutrient Content Per Serving		**Percent of Calories**	**Fat Breakdown**	
Calories	288.0	19% Protein	Saturated Fat	2.5 g
Protein	13.3 g	55% Carbohydrate	Monounsaturated Fat	3.9 g
Carbohydrates	39.2 g	27% Fat	Polyunsaturated Fat	1.6 g
Fat – Total	8.6 g			
Cholesterol	11.9 mg			
Dietary Fiber	1.8 g			
Sodium	44.4 mg			

SPAGHETTI WITH GREEN BEANS
Serves 6

1 lb.	spaghetti, uncooked, break to length of green beans
1 lb.	green beans, fresh
to taste	salt and pepper
3 oz.	swiss, lowfat, grated

Sauce:

1 bunch	basil, chopped
2 cloves	garlic, minced
1 tsp.	olive oil
1 tsp.	anchovy paste
3 Tbl.	white wine

Bring 4-8 cups of water to a boil and add green beans. Cook 5 minutes. Add spaghetti, cook 10 minutes. Pasta should be cooked al dente.

To prepare sauce:
Blend basil, garlic, oil, anchovy paste and wine in a food processor until smooth. Drain spaghetti and green beans, mix with sauce. Add salt and pepper to taste. Sprinkle with swiss cheese. Serve immediately.

Nutrient Content Per Serving

Calories	339.0
Protein	15.6 g
Carbohydrates	62.8 g
Fat – Total	2.8 g
Cholesterol	5.2 mg
Dietary Fiber	7.6 g
Sodium	81.0 mg

Percent of Calories

18% Protein
74% Carbohydrate
7% Fat

Fat Breakdown

Saturated Fat	0.8 g
Monounsaturated Fat	0.9 g
Polyunsaturated Fat	0.6 g

TABOULE DE VERDURE
Serves 4

1½ cups bulgur wheat, cooked
2 cloves garlic, minced
3 scallions, diced
½ tsp. olive oil
4 tomatoes, cut in bite-size pieces
½ cup chervil, washed and stemmed
½ cup parsley, washed and stemmed
10 leaves mint

Dressing:
1 Tbl. olive oil
1 lemon, juice of
¼ cup white wine vinegar
1 Tbl. dijon mustard
to taste salt and pepper

Sauté garlic and onions in oil. In a bowl combine tomatoes, garlic, onions, cooked bulgur wheat, chervil, parsley and mint.

To prepare dressing:
Combine all ingredients. Pour dressing over taboule. Chill thoroughly before serving.

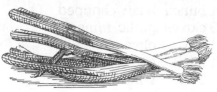

Cook's Note: To cook bulgur wheat bring 1½ cups of water to a boil. Add ¾ cup dry bulgur wheat. Cook until all water is absorbed. May be served over a bed of lettuce garnished with tomatoes around the taboule salad.

Nutrient Content Per Serving
Calories 131.0
Protein 3.8 g
Carbohydrates 21.6 g
Fat Total 4.8 g
Cholesterol 0.0 mg
Dietary Fiber 5.4 g
Sodium 69.0 mg

Percent of Calories
11% Protein
60% Carbohydrate
30% Fat

Fat Breakdown
Saturated Fat 0.6 g
Monounsaturated Fat 3.2 g
Polyunsaturated Fat 0.6 g

RICE TIMBALE WITH ARTICHOKES
Serves 6

6 sm.	fresh artichokes
1	lemon, sliced
1 med.	onion, minced
1 tsp.	olive oil
1¼ cups	white rice, uncooked
3 cups	chicken stock *(see p. 538)*
¼ tsp.	nutmeg
to taste	salt and pepper
1 oz.	lowfat swiss cheese, grated
1 tsp.	powdered butter replacement
4	egg whites
½ cup	bechamel sauce *(see p. 554)*

In a non-stick frying pan, sauté onion in oil over medium heat. Add rice, chicken stock, nutmeg, salt and pepper to taste. Cover and cook 20 minutes.

Remove cover and cook until all of the liquid is absorbed. Remove from heat and cool slightly. Add cheese, powdered butter replacement and egg whites. Mix well.

Prepare a round mold with cooking spray. Press in rice mixture until firm. Bake at 350° F for 30 minutes or until browned.

Clean artichokes. Remove choke and outer leaves. Trim off the sharp points. Steam with lemon in the water for a few minutes.

To serve:
Unmold rice ring onto a large serving platter. Arrange hot artichokes around edge. Pour warm bechamel sauce over rice and artichokes.

Cook's Note: May use mushrooms in place of artichokes.

Nutrient Content Per Serving		**Percent of Calories**	**Fat Breakdown**	
Calories	265.0	18% Protein	Saturated Fat	0.7 g
Protein	12.5 g	73% Carbohydrate	Monounsaturated Fat	1.1 g
Carbohydrates	49.7 g	9% Fat	Polyunsaturated Fat	0.6 g
Fat – Total	2.6 g			
Cholesterol	3.0 mg			
Dietary Fiber	7.2 g			
Sodium	754.0 mg			

RICE CONFETTI
Serves 8

2 cups	rice, uncooked
1	onion, diced fine
1 tsp.	canola oil
2 sm.	zucchini, diced
1	sweet red pepper, diced
1	yellow pepper, diced
to taste	salt and pepper
½ cup	white wine
1 cup	chicken stock *(see p. 538)*
1 tsp.	powdered butter replacement
3 oz.	swiss cheese, lowfat, grated

Sauté onion in oil for 3 minutes. Add vegetables, salt and pepper to taste. Cover and cook for 10 minutes. Add rice and wine. Cook uncovered until wine evaporates. Add stock and powdered butter replacement. Cover and cook 20 minutes over low heat, stirring occasionally. Serve with grated swiss cheese on top.

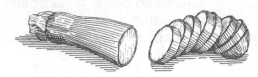

Cook's Note: Makes a great potluck item.

Alcohol Note: The alcohol content was computed prior to cooking. Once the alcohol is heated to the boiling point, the alcohol disappears along with most of the calories from the alcohol.

Nutrient Content Per Serving

Calories	218.0
Protein	7.4 g
Carbohydrates	39.7 g
Fat – Total	1.7 g
Cholesterol	3.7 mg
Dietary Fiber	1.0 g
Sodium	131.0 mg

Percent of Calories

14% Protein
75% Carbohydrate
 7% Fat
 4% Alcohol

Fat Breakdown

Saturated Fat	0.5 g
Monounsaturated Fat	0.7 g
Polyunsaturated Fat	0.3 g

LEMON HERBED RICE
Serves 4

¾ cup   rice, uncooked
1½ cups   chicken stock *(see p. 538)*

Sauce:
2 tsp.   olive oil
2 Tbl.   lemon juice
½ tsp.   lemon zest
¼ cup   herbs, chopped (parsley, basil, mint)
to taste   salt and freshly ground black pepper

Bring stock to a boil. Add rice, cover and simmer 20 minutes or until all liquid is absorbed.

Whisk together sauce ingredients. Pour over cooked rice.

Nutrient Content Per Serving

Calories	158.0
Protein	3.0 g
Carbohydrates	30.5 g
Fat – Total	2.6 g
Cholesterol	0.0 mg
Dietary Fiber	1.5 g
Sodium	5.5 mg

Percent of Calories

8% Protein
77% Carbohydrate
15% Fat

Fat Breakdown

Saturated Fat	0.4 g
Monounsaturated Fat	1.7 g
Polyunsaturated Fat	0.3 g

RISI BISI RICE
Serves 6

2 cups	long grain white rice, uncooked
½ Tbl.	canola oil
½	yellow onion, diced fine
1 cup	green peas, fresh or frozen
4 cups	chicken stock *(see p. 538)*
to taste	salt and pepper

Rinse the rice. Add oil to a casserole dish which can be used on the stove top. Sauté onion over medium heat until translucent. Do not let onion get brown. Preheat oven to 350° F. In the casserole dish mix together peas, rice and chicken stock. Cover and cook for 30 minutes or until all liquid is absorbed. Serve immediately.

Cook's Note: Serve with poultry and stews.

Nutrient Content Per Serving
Calories	267.0
Protein	6.4 g
Carbohydrates	53.9 g
Fat – Total	2.1 g
Cholesterol	0.4 mg
Dietary Fiber	2.0 g
Sodium	623.0 mg

Percent of Calories
10%	Protein
83%	Carbohydrate
7%	Fat

Fat Breakdown
Saturated Fat	0.4 g
Monounsaturated Fat	0.6 g
Polyunsaturated Fat	1.0 g

TOMATO AND RICE GRATIN
Serves 4

2 cups	white rice, cooked
6 lg.	tomatoes
1 clove	garlic, minced
1 med.	onion, chopped
½ tsp.	olive oil
1 tsp.	thyme, dry
⅓ cup	parmesan cheese, grated
to taste	salt and pepper
2 oz.	mozzarella, lowfat, sliced thin
1 tsp.	fresh oregano

Garnish:

6-8 leaves	fresh basil

Peel 2 of the tomatoes and mash with garlic and onion. (May gently pulse in food processor.) Sauté in olive oil for 5 minutes. Add rice, thyme, parmesan and salt and pepper to taste. Cover and cook for 5 minutes.

Slice remaining 4 tomatoes. Coat a casserole dish with cooking spray. Add rice. On top of the rice, layer tomatoes alternating with mozzarella. Top with oregano. Cover and bake 15 minutes at 350° F. Garnish with basil.

Nutrient Content Per Serving

Calories	286.0
Protein	13.1 g
Carbohydrates	44.3 g
Fat – Total	7.0 g
Cholesterol	14.8 mg
Dietary Fiber	4.4 g
Sodium	271.0 mg

Percent of Calories

18% Protein	
61% Carbohydrate	
21% Fat	

Fat Breakdown

Saturated Fat	3.6 g
Monounsaturated Fat	2.1 g
Polyunsaturated Fat	0.6 g

RICE AND VEGETABLE SALAD
Serves 8

4 cups	long grain rice, cooked
2 cups	corn, frozen, thawed
1 cup	green beans
2 stalks	celery, chopped
1	sweet red pepper, diced
4	tomatoes, diced

Dressing:

2 Tbl.	dijon mustard
¼ cup	white wine vinegar
1 Tbl.	olive oil
to taste	salt and pepper

Bring 4 cups of water to a boil. Add 2 cups of rice. Cover and simmer 20 minutes.

Whisk together dressing ingredients. Microwave corn and green beans on high setting for 4-5 minutes. Cool. Combine all ingredients. Add dressing. Chill before serving.

Cook's Note: Add skinless chicken or shrimp and serve with a baguette for a complete meal. (May need to add one-half more dressing.)

Nutrient Content Per Serving

Calories	207.0
Protein	5.1 g
Carbohydrates	42.8 g
Fat – Total	2.4 g
Cholesterol	0.0 mg
Dietary Fiber	3.4 g
Sodium	67.3 mg

Percent of Calories

10% Protein
80% Carbohydrate
10% Fat

Fat Breakdown

Saturated Fat	0.4 g
Monounsaturated Fat	1.5 g
Polyunsaturated Fat	0.4 g

Asparagus with Dijon Dressing *(page 171)*
Sautéed Elk Medallions *(page 237)*
Chilled BBQ Prawns
with Whole-Grain Mustard Sauce *(page 157)*

Orange Salad *(page 179)*
Grilled Swordfish Steak Sandwich *(page 218)*

Seafood Thermador Crepes *(page 222)*
Chateau Potatoes *(page 253)*
Red Cabbage and Apples *(page 243)*

Zucchini Omelette *(page 207)*
Creamy Mussel Soup *(page 163)*

FENNEL AND SAFFRON BREAD
Serves 8

1 pkg.	active dry yeast
1¼ cup	luke warm water
1 Tbl.	sugar
2 cups	all-purpose flour
1½ tsp.	salt
1 Tbl.	fennel seed, ground
⅛ tsp.	saffron
1 cup	semolina flour
2 Tbl.	cornmeal, coarse ground

Mix yeast with warm water. Let stand 10 minutes. Add sugar and 1 cup of flour. Mix together and let stand 5 minutes in a warm spot.

Once this mixture is foamy, add salt, fennel seed and saffron. In a separate bowl, combine semolina with remaining flour. Blend into yeast mixture. Knead 10 minutes. Place dough in a bowl and cover with a damp cloth. Allow to rise in a warm, draft-free place 1 hour or until doubled in bulk.

Punch down and shape into a ball. Knead for 5 minutes. Place on a baking sheet that has been sprinkled with cornmeal. Spray a warm, damp cloth with cooking spray and cover dough. Allow to rise 1 hour. Bake at 375° F for 40 minutes or until crust is brown.

Cook's Note: A beautiful sunshine yellow bread.

Nutrient Content Per Serving		**Percent of Calories**	**Fat Breakdown**	
Calories	200.0	13% Protein	Saturated Fat	0.1 g
Protein	6.3 g	84% Carbohydrate	Monounsaturated Fat	0.1 g
Carbohydrates	41.2 g	3% Fat	Polyunsaturated Fat	0.2 g
Fat – Total	0.7 g			
Cholesterol	0.0 mg			
Dietary Fiber	1.9 g			
Sodium	402.0 mg			

FRENCH BREAD
Makes 2 loaves (16 slices per loaf)

½ cup   skim milk
1 cup   hot water
1 Tbl.   active dry yeast
2 tsp.   salt
1 Tbl.   sugar
1½ Tbl.   canola oil
2 cups   bread flour
2 cups   white flour

Scald the skim milk. Add the hot water to it. Let cool to 85° F. Separately dissolve the yeast in another ¼ cup of lukewarm tap water. Let yeast rest 10 minutes. Combine salt, sugar, canola oil, yeast and milk mixture. In a large bowl sift together both flours. Slowly incorporate the yeast mixture into flour, working the mass into a smooth dough. Add more flour as necessary. Knead

10 minutes. Cover dough with a moist towel and set aside in a draft-free place to rise approximately 30 minutes.

Punch down the dough. Divide into two equal balls. Knead each for 5 minutes. Shape into two long rolls. Cut ¼-inch deep diagonal slits across top. Place dough onto a baking pan dusted with cornmeal. Let the dough sit covered with a moist towel (sprayed with cooking spray) until almost doubled in size (approximately 30 minutes).

Preheat oven to 400° F. Set an ovenproof bowl of water in the bottom of oven to create steam. Bake the bread for 15 minutes then reduce heat to 350° F and bake 30 minutes longer or until golden brown and crispy.

Variations:

■ **Rosemary Rolls** – *Makes 4 dozen*
2 Tbl.   fresh rosemary, chopped
2 Tbl.   garlic, roasted, chopped
           (see p. 13)

Add these ingredients before dough rises. Follow the rest of instructions for the French Bread dough. Set the rolls 2 inches apart.

■ **Onion rolls** – *Makes 4 dozen*
1   yellow onion, peeled, diced fine
1 Tbl.   olive oil

In a skillet, sauté the onions in the olive oil. Make sure you don't brown the onions, just glaze them until done. Add half of the onions to the dough before rising. Cut a crisscross into each roll and top with onions. Set the rolls 2 inches apart.

Cook's Note: Can be done in a bread machine. May use all white flour and ¼ cup gluten flour instead of bread flour. May also add one-half whole wheat flour for more fiber.

Nutrient Content Per Slice		**Percent of Calories**	**Fat Breakdown**	
Calories	66.1	11% Protein	Saturated Fat	0.1 g
Protein	1.8 g	77% Carbohydrate	Monounsaturated Fat	0.2 g
Carbohydrates	12.6 g	11% Fat	Polyunsaturated Fat	0.4 g
Fat – Total	0.8 g			
Cholesterol	0.1 mg			
Dietary Fiber	0.5 g			
Sodium	136.0 mg			

ZUCCHINI OMELETTE
Serves 4

2 sm.	zucchini, sliced thin
1	scallion, sliced thin
¾ cup	green beans, cut in 1-inch pieces
2	tomatoes, peeled and chopped
1 tsp.	olive oil
2 cups	egg substitute
1 branch	fresh basil, chopped fine
to taste	salt and pepper

In a non-stick pan, sauté vegetables in 1 teaspoon olive oil until soft. Divide vegetables onto 4 individual oven proof gratin dishes prepared with cooking spray.

In a bowl, beat egg substitute, basil, salt and pepper to taste. Pour egg mixture into each of the four gratin dishes. Bake for 10-15 minutes at 400° F until set.

% Calories as Fat — Above the HM✔ guidelines: Although this recipe has a high percentage of calories as fat (>30%), the total fat is less than 5.5 grams per serving. This will easily fit within your allotment of 45 grams per day. This happens most often in low-calorie recipes.

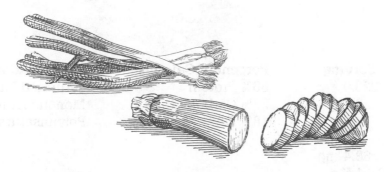

Nutrient Content Per Serving

Calories	136.0
Protein	16.2 g
Carbohydrates	5.5 g
Fat – Total	5.5 g
Cholesterol	1.3 mg
Dietary Fiber	1.6 g
Sodium	229.0 mg

Percent of Calories

47% Protein
16% Carbohydrate
37% Fat

Fat Breakdown

Saturated Fat	1.0 g
Monounsaturated Fat	2.0 g
Polyunsaturated Fat	2.2 g

CHICKEN WITH APRICOT CHUTNEY
Serves 6

6	chicken breasts, skinless, boneless
4 Tbl.	flour
1 tsp.	olive oil
¼ cup	Sage wine reduction *(see p. 543)*
¼ cup	Apricot chutney *(see p. 545)*

Pound chicken breasts flat. Coat with flour. In a non-stick pan, sauté in olive oil until browned on both sides. Spread apricot chutney on serving plate. Arrange chicken on top of apricot chutney. Top with the sage wine reduction.

Nutrient Content Per Serving

Calories	226.0
Protein	28.7 g
Carbohydrates	13.7 g
Fat – Total	4.0 g
Cholesterol	68.4 mg
Dietary Fiber	1.6 g
Sodium	84.5 mg

Percent of Calories

56% Protein
27% Carbohydrate
18% Fat

Fat Breakdown

Saturated Fat	0.7 g
Monounsaturated Fat	1.6 g
Polyunsaturated Fat	1.2 g

CHICKEN BRAISED IN BEER
Serves 4

4	chicken breasts, boneless, skinless
2 tsp.	olive oil
1 sm	onion, chopped fine
1 clove	garlic, minced
¼ cup	gin
12 oz.	dark beer or ale
1	bouquet garni *(see p. 15)*
to taste	salt and pepper
5 cups	mushrooms, sliced thick
2 Tbl.	cornstarch
¼ cup	fat-free sour cream

Garnish:

2 Tbl.	parsley, chopped

In a large non-stick frying pan, brown chicken breasts in 1 teaspoon of the olive oil. Add the onion, garlic and remaining 1 teaspoon of olive oil and cook until onion is browned. Add the gin and flame. Add the beer, bouquet garni and salt and pepper to taste. Bring to a boil, then simmer uncovered for 15 minutes. Add mushrooms. Cover and simmer 30-45 minutes.

Remove chicken and mushrooms to a serving platter and keep warm. Discard bouquet garni. Whisk together cornstarch and sour cream. Stir into the sauce until it thickens. Pour over the chicken. Garnish with parsley.

Alcohol Note: The alcohol content was computed prior to cooking. Once the alcohol is heated to the boiling point, the alcohol disappears along with most of the calories from the alcohol.

Nutrient Content Per Serving

Calories	301.0
Protein	30.3 g
Carbohydrates	23.3 g
Fat – Total	4.0 g
Cholesterol	68.4 mg
Dietary Fiber	4.5 g
Sodium	97.1 mg

Percent of Calories

40% Protein
31% Carbohydrate
12% Fat
17% Alcohol

Fat Breakdown

Saturated Fat	0.8 g
Monounsaturated Fat	2.1 g
Polyunsaturated Fat	0.6 g

COQ AU VIN
Serves 4

4	chicken breasts, boneless, skinless
1 tsp.	olive oil
1 med.	onion, chopped
½ lb.	mushrooms, quartered
2 tsp.	thyme, chopped
1	bay leaf
pinch	nutmeg
1 cup	Riesling wine
½ cup	fat-free sour cream
1 Tbl.	cornstarch
2 Tbl.	skim milk
1 tsp.	powdered butter replacement

Pound chicken breasts flat. In a large non-stick frying pan, over medium heat, sauté chicken breasts in olive oil until browned and cooked through. Add onions and mushrooms, cook until tender. Add thyme, bay leaf, nutmeg and wine. Cover and simmer 5 minutes.

Remove chicken, onions and mushrooms to a heated serving platter. Reduce liquid to ½ cup. Whisk together sour cream, cornstarch, milk and powdered butter replacement. Whisk into liquid and thicken. Pour sauce over chicken.

Cook's Note: A beautiful lowfat meal for company.

Alcohol Note: The alcohol content was computed prior to cooking. Once the alcohol is heated to the boiling point, the alcohol disappears along with most of the calories from the alcohol.

Nutrient Content Per Serving

Calories	234.0
Protein	31.2 g
Carbohydrates	11.2 g
Fat – Total	2.9 g
Cholesterol	68.5 mg
Dietary Fiber	1.3 g
Sodium	112.0 mg

Percent of Calories

53% Protein
19% Carbohydrate
11% Fat
17% Alcohol

Fat Breakdown

Saturated Fat	0.6 g
Monounsaturated Fat	1.2 g
Polyunsaturated Fat	0.6 g

GRILLED CHICKEN BREAST WITH RATATOUILLE
Serves 4

4	chicken breasts, boneless, skinless
1	lemon, juice of
2 tsp.	olive oil
to taste	salt
2 tsp.	coriander, ground
2 tsp.	black pepper, ground
1 recipe	ratatouille *(see p. 256)*

Garnish:
lemon slices

Cook's Note: This has a fresh and light flavor.

Combine lemon juice, olive oil and salt to taste. Add coriander and black pepper. Sprinkle the mixture on top of chicken and press onto meat. Grill. Heat the ratatouille and top with the chicken breast. Garnish with lemon.

Nutrient Content Per Serving

Calories	151.0
Protein	27.3 g
Carbohydrates	0.7 g
Fat – Total	3.7 g
Cholesterol	68.4 mg
Dietary Fiber	0.0 g
Sodium	76.8 mg

Percent of Calories

75% Protein
2% Carbohydrate
23% Fat

Fat Breakdown

Saturated Fat	0.7 g
Monounsaturated Fat	2.0 g
Polyunsaturated Fat	0.5 g

CHICKEN WITH CREAMY HERBS
Serves 6

6	chicken breasts, boneless, skinless
4 sm.	zucchini, grated
2	shallots, minced
1 tsp.	canola oil
⅓ cup	sour cream, nonfat
4 Tbl.	herbs (parsley, tarragon and chives)
1 sm.	carrot, cubed
2 cloves	garlic, minced
1 Tbl.	powdered butter replacement
1 Tbl.	pine nuts
to taste	salt and pepper

Sauté zucchini and shallots in canola oil until dry. Set aside and cool. Add sour cream, herbs, carrots, garlic, powdered butter replacement, pine nuts, salt and pepper to taste.

Preheat oven to 400° F. Spray a non-stick baking pan with cooking spray. Lay chicken breasts in a single layer. Spread vegetable mixture over top. Bake 30-45 minutes.

Cook's Note: Serve over pasta.

Nutrient Content Per Serving
Calories	163.0
Protein	28.8 g
Carbohydrates	4.4 g
Fat – Total	3.0 g
Cholesterol	68.4 mg
Dietary Fiber	0.6 g
Sodium	101.0 mg

Percent of Calories
72% Protein
11% Carbohydrate
17% Fat

Fat Breakdown
Saturated Fat	0.6 g
Monounsaturated Fat	1.1 g
Polyunsaturated Fat	0.9 g

CHICKEN FRICASSÉE
Serves 4

4	chicken breasts, boneless, skinless
4 Tbl.	flour
1 tsp.	olive oil
½ cup	dry white wine
2 cups	chicken stock *(see p. 538)*
12	pearl onions
2 sprigs	parsley
1	bay leaf
2 cups	mushrooms, sliced
1 Tbl.	fresh thyme (or ½ tsp. dry)
2 Tbl.	skim milk
⅓ cup	sour cream, nonfat
1 Tbl.	cornstarch

Garnish:

    parsley, chopped

Pound chicken breasts until flat. Coat with flour. In a non-stick frying pan, brown chicken breasts in olive oil. Add wine, stock, onions, parsley and bay leaf. Cover and simmer 30 minutes.

Add mushrooms and thyme. Simmer 10 minutes. Whisk together skim milk, sour cream and cornstarch. Remove chicken and keep warm. Carefully whisk milk mixture into sauce and heat through. Do not boil. Serve sauce over chicken breasts. Garnish with parsley.

Alcohol Note: The alcohol content was computed prior to cooking. Once the alcohol is heated to the boiling point, the alcohol disappears along with most of the calories from the alcohol.

Nutrient Content Per Serving

Calories	232.0
Protein	30.8 g
Carbohydrates	15.3 g
Fat – Total	2.9 g
Cholesterol	68.5 mg
Dietary Fiber	1.6 g
Sodium	205.0 mg

Percent of Calories

54% Protein
27% Carbohydrate
11% Fat
 8% Alcohol

Fat Breakdown

Saturated Fat	0.6 g
Monounsaturated Fat	1.2 g
Polyunsaturated Fat	0.5 g

CHICKEN WITH CREAMY PEPPER SAUCE
Serves 4

4	chicken breasts, boneless, skinless
1 tsp.	olive oil
2 Tbl.	onions, puréed in food processor
1 tsp.	powdered butter replacement
1 lb.	peppers (yellows and reds), sliced
pinch	sugar
to taste	salt and pepper
3 Tbl.	dry vermouth
⅓ cup	sour cream, nonfat

In a non-stick frying pan, sauté chicken in olive oil. Remove to a heated platter. In a non-stick frying pan, sauté puréed onion. Add powdered butter replacement, peppers, sugar and salt and pepper to taste. Cook 5 minutes over low heat.

Return chicken to the pan. Cook 10 minutes covered and 5 minutes uncovered. Add vermouth. Remove chicken to the serving platter. Put sauce in a food processor and blend until smooth. Add sour cream. Serve chicken over pasta. Pour sauce on top.

Cook's Note: May use white wine in place of vermouth. May use roasted peppers for a smoother flavor.

Alcohol Note: The alcohol content was computed prior to cooking. Once the alcohol is heated to the boiling point, the alcohol disappears along with most of the calories from the alcohol.

Nutrient Content Per Serving

Calories	218.0
Protein	29.7 g
Carbohydrates	10.7 g
Fat – Total	5.1 g
Cholesterol	68.4 mg
Dietary Fiber	1.9 g
Sodium	99.2 mg

Percent of Calories

55% Protein
20% Carbohydrate
21% Fat
 4% Alcohol

Fat Breakdown

Saturated Fat	0.9 g
Monounsaturated Fat	2.9 g
Polyunsaturated Fat	0.7 g

CHICKEN WITH SPRING VEGETABLES
Serves 4

4	chicken breasts, boneless, skinless
1	onion, chopped
1 tsp.	olive oil
1 Tbl.	white wine
2 cups	chicken stock *(see p. 538)*
1	bouquet garni *(see p. 15)*
½ cup	sour cream, nonfat
1 Tbl.	powdered butter replacement
to taste	salt and pepper
1 bunch	baby carrots
1 bunch	scallions
12 oz.	lima beans, frozen
12 oz.	peas, frozen

In non-stick pan coated with cooking spray, brown chicken. Remove chicken. Sauté onion in olive oil. Add wine and evaporate. Return chicken to pan, add stock and bouquet garni. Simmer uncovered for 30 minutes. Remove chicken and reduce liquid to ¼ cup. Add sour cream, powdered butter replacement, salt and pepper to taste. Heat through, then return chicken to the pan. Heat 5 minutes.

Steam vegetables in separate pan. Arrange chicken on a platter surrounded by vegetables for a beautiful presentation.

Cook's Note: May cook all vegetables in the microwave. Serve with rice.

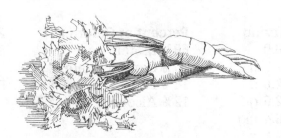

Nutrient Content Per Serving

Calories	427.0
Protein	47.4 g
Carbohydrates	51.0 g
Fat – Total	4.1 g
Cholesterol	68.4 mg
Dietary Fiber	13.6 g
Sodium	695.0 mg

Percent of Calories

44% Protein
47% Carbohydrate
 9% Fat

Fat Breakdown

Saturated Fat	1.0 g
Monounsaturated Fat	1.5 g
Polyunsaturated Fat	0.9 g

TARRAGON CHICKEN
Serves 4

4	chicken breasts, boneless, skinless, pounded flat
1 tsp.	olive oil
½ cup	dry white wine
4	shallots, minced
½ cup	white wine tarragon vinegar
1 bunch	tarragon leaves, chopped

In a large non-stick frying pan, brown the chicken in the olive oil. Remove chicken, keep warm.

To the pan, add the wine and shallots. Bring to a rapid simmer. Add vinegar. Return chicken to the pan. Reduce heat, cover and simmer 10 minutes until chicken absorbs some of the sauce. Add tarragon. Serve with colorful vegetables.

Alcohol Note: The alcohol content was computed prior to cooking. Once the alcohol is heated to the boiling point, the alcohol disappears along with most of the calories from the alcohol.

Nutrient Content Per Serving

Calories	166.0
Protein	27.5 g
Carbohydrates	2.6 g
Fat – Total	2.6 g
Cholesterol	68.4 mg
Dietary Fiber	0.1 g
Sodium	78.8 mg

Percent of Calories

68%	Protein
6%	Carbohydrate
14%	Fat
12%	Alcohol

Fat Breakdown

Saturated Fat	0.5 g
Monounsaturated Fat	1.2 g
Polyunsaturated Fat	0.4 g

TURKEY AND ZUCCHINI
Serves 6

1½ lb.	turkey breast, cut in bite-size pieces
12 leaves	sage (or 1 tsp. dry sage)
1 clove	garlic, peeled, left whole
2 tsp.	olive oil
1 lb.	zucchini, sliced thin
⅓ cup	black olives, sliced thick
1	lemon, sliced thin
¼ cup	dry vermouth
to taste	salt and pepper

Sauté turkey, sage and garlic in 1 teaspoon olive oil. Remove turkey from pan. Discard garlic. Add zucchini, cook over low heat in remaining 1 teaspoon of oil until tender. Return turkey mixture, add olives, lemon, vermouth, salt and pepper to taste. Cook until vermouth has partially evaporated. Serve with pasta, rice or French bread.

Cook's Note: Quick and easy. A great summer meal with fresh zucchini and fresh sage.

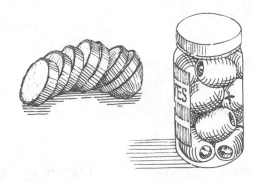

Nutrient Content Per Serving

Calories	199.0
Protein	36.4 g
Carbohydrates	4.1 g
Fat – Total	3.6 g
Cholesterol	94.1 mg
Dietary Fiber	1.3 g
Sodium	120.0 mg

Percent of Calories
74% Protein
8% Carbohydrate
17% Fat

Fat Breakdown

Saturated Fat	0.7 g
Monounsaturated Fat	2.0 g
Polyunsaturated Fat	0.6 g

GRILLED SWORDFISH STEAK SANDWICH
Serves 6

6 4-oz.	swordfish steaks
¼ cup	fish marinade *(see p. 555 or 556)*
6	rye dinner rolls
1½ cups	alfalfa sprouts
1 head	bibb lettuce
¾ cup	tomato relish *(see p. 550)*
3	black olives, sliced
2	tomatoes, sliced

Marinate swordfish in fish marinade for 5 minutes. Grill over hot coals until done. Arrange swordfish steak on rye roll. Top with tomato relish. Garnish with bibb lettuce, alfalfa sprouts, black olives and tomatoes.

Cook's Note: Grill fish 3-5 minutes per side per inch of thickness.

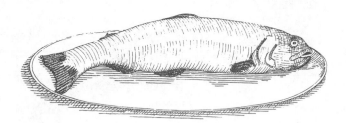

Nutrient Content Per Serving

Calories	266.0
Protein	26.4 g
Carbohydrates	19.4 g
Fat – Total	9.0 g
Cholesterol	44.2 mg
Dietary Fiber	3.3 g
Sodium	374.0 mg

Percent of Calories

40% Protein
29% Carbohydrate
31% Fat

Fat Breakdown

Saturated Fat	1.9 g
Monounsaturated Fat	4.5 g
Polyunsaturated Fat	1.6 g

JEWELS OF THE SEA WITH BUTTERY SAUCE
Serves 4

4	squid
2 oz.	mackerel, boned, skinned, cut in slices
8 oz.	white fish, boneless, cut in big pieces
3 oz.	salmon steak, cut in half
3 lbs.	lobster tail, cut in chunks

Poaching liquid:

1	lemon, sliced
1	leek, white portion only
1 branch	fresh thyme
1	bay leaf
3 branches	fresh tarragon

Sauce:

4	shallots, minced
1 tsp.	white wine vinegar
1 tsp.	dry white wine
1/2	lemon, juice of
to taste	white pepper
1 pkg	powdered butter replacement, mixed with ½ cup warm water

In a large pan that holds a steamer, combine 8 cups of water, lemon slices, leek, thyme, bay leaf and tarragon. In steamer rack, layer fish starting on the bottom with the squid, then mackerel, white fish ending with salmon on the top. Cover. Cook 25 minutes. Add lobster. Cook 5 minutes, partially covered.

Meanwhile, prepare sauce: In a small saucepan combine shallots, vinegar and white wine. Cook until most of the moisture has evaporated. Add remaining ingredients. Heat slowly.

To serve:
Remove bone from salmon and cut to yield 4 pieces.

Arrange fish on a large platter. Serve sauce separately.

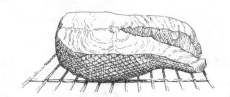

Nutrient Content Per Serving		Percent of Calories	Fat Breakdown	
Calories	276.0	46% Protein	Saturated Fat	2.0 g
Protein	31.0 g	24% Carbohydrate	Monounsaturated Fat	3.2 g
Carbohydrates	16.5 g	30% Fat	Polyunsaturated Fat	2.6 g
Fat – Total	9.1 g			
Cholesterol	127.0 mg			
Dietary Fiber	1.1 g			
Sodium	433.0 mg			

STEAMED FISH AND VEGETABLES AIOLI
Serves 6

4 sm.	potatoes, cubed
½ head	cauliflower, cut in flowerettes
½ head	broccoli, cut in flowerettes
¾ lb.	cod, in one piece
4 oz.	marlin, filet
¾ lb.	haddock filets or Sea Bass
4	carrots, cut in very thin strips
2 lbs.	mussels, in shells

Aioli:

6 cloves	garlic, minced
2 Tbl.	mayonnaise, fat-free
½	lemon, juice of
to taste	salt and pepper
dash	Tabasco™

Arrange potatoes in a steamer. Cover and steam 10 minutes. Add cauliflower, broccoli, cod and marlin. Cover and steam 5 minutes. Add haddock, carrots and mussels. Cover and steam 5 minutes or until fish is done.

To prepare sauce:
Mix the garlic with the mayonnaise in a food processor. While motor is running, add lemon juice, salt, pepper and Tabasco™ to taste. Pass sauce with fish.

Cook's Note: May want to steam fish and vegetables separately to maintain individual flavors. If you do not have a steamer, cook potatoes and remaining ingredients on a rack above a pot of boiling water.

Nutrient Content Per Serving

Calories	395.0
Protein	47.1 g
Carbohydrates	32.8 g
Fat – Total	7.9 g
Cholesterol	113.0 mg
Dietary Fiber	4.8 g
Sodium	614.0 mg

Percent of Calories

48% Protein
34% Carbohydrate
18% Fat

Fat Breakdown

Saturated Fat	1.6 g
Monounsaturated Fat	2.2 g
Polyunsaturated Fat	2.2 g

FISH ROULADES
Serves 6

6 4-oz.	white fish filets
½ lb.	marlin (or any firm fish)
2	carrots, thin, small slices
2	zucchini, sliced thin
1	leek, sliced thin
1 tsp.	olive oil
2	egg whites
1 Tbl.	skim milk
½ tsp.	nonfat dry milk powder
pinch	nutmeg
to taste	salt and pepper

Garnish:

1 bunch	parsley, chopped
1 lemon	cut in wedges

In a non-stick frying pan, sauté vegetables in olive oil for 10 minutes. Purée marlin, egg whites, milk, powdered milk and nutmeg. Add salt and pepper to taste. Mix in vegetables. Roll the filets around mixture and secure with a toothpick.

Prepare aluminum packets with cooking spray. Wrap fish rolls in aluminum foil. Close tightly. Steam 15 minutes or prepare a baking dish with non-stick spray and bake at 350° F for 15-20 minutes. To serve, open pouch and garnish with lemon and parsley.

Cook's Note: If you can't find marlin, substitute halibut.

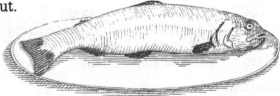

Nutrient Content Per Serving

Calories	162.0
Protein	29.0 g
Carbohydrates	5.9 g
Fat – Total	1.9 g
Cholesterol	65.1 mg
Dietary Fiber	1.4 g
Sodium	116.0 mg

Percent of Calories

74% Protein
15% Carbohydrate
11% Fat

Fat Breakdown

Saturated Fat	0.3 g
Monounsaturated Fat	0.7 g
Polyunsaturated Fat	0.5 g

SEAFOOD THERMADOR CREPES
Serves 4

12	crepes *(see p. 189)*
1 lb.	fresh white fish (cod, rockfish, butterfish, lobster, scallops etc.)

Poaching liquid:

½ cup	white wine
1 cup	water
1	lemon, sliced
1	onion, sliced
2 Tbl.	liquid margarine
3 Tbl.	flour
1¼ cup	skim milk
½ cup	nonfat dry milk
1 tsp.	powdered butter replacement
⅓ cup	white wine
¼ lb.	salad shrimp, pre-cooked
pinch	white pepper
2 Tbl.	fresh parsley, chopped
4 oz.	mozzarella, fat-free, grated very fine
1 cup	bread crumbs, fat-free

Garnish:

lemon wedges
parsley sprigs

In a skillet, poach the fish in poaching liquid. Simmer about 5 minutes or until fish is done. Remove fish, discard liquid. Cut fish into bite-size pieces.

Melt margarine in a small saucepan. Whisk in the flour and cook 1-2 minutes without browning. Add milk, powdered milk and powdered butter replacement. Whisk until thickened. Add wine, shrimp, fish, white pepper and parsley. Heat through.

Fill 12 crepes. In a shallow baking dish prepared with cooking spray, lay crepes in a single layer. Bake at 350° F for 15 minutes. Mix cheese with bread crumbs. Sprinkle on top. Bake additional 1-2 minutes until bread crumbs brown. Garnish with lemon wedges and parsley sprig.

Cook's Note: The number of crepes you end up with is dependent on how full you fill them.

Alcohol Note: The alcohol content was computed prior to cooking. Once the alcohol is heated to the boiling point, the alcohol disappears along with most of the calories from the alcohol.

Nutrient Content Per Serving (3 crepes)		**Percent of Calories**	**Fat Breakdown**	
Calories	619.0	35% Protein	Saturated Fat	2.0 g
Protein	54.1 g	43% Carbohydrate	Monounsaturated Fat	3.9 g
Carbohydrates	65.7 g	16% Fat	Polyunsaturated Fat	4.3 g
Fat – Total	11.1 g	5% Alcohol		
Cholesterol	114.0 mg			
Dietary Fiber	2.9 g			
Sodium	724.0 mg			

GRATIN OF SEAFOOD
Serves 4

2 lbs.	seafood (shrimp, crab, scallops, lobster)
1	carrot, chopped fine
1	onion, minced
2	shallots, minced
1 clove	garlic, minced
1 tsp.	olive oil
2	tomatoes, chopped, seeded
1 tsp.	tomato paste
2 Tbl.	cognac
1 Tbl.	port wine
1 cup	fish stock *(see p. 540)* or clam broth
1 tsp.	tarragon
1	bouquet garni *(see p. 15)*
2 cups	sour cream, nonfat
½ cup	skim milk
2 Tbl.	powdered butter replacement
1 Tbl.	flour
¼ cup + 2 Tbl.	egg substitute
2 Tbl.	white wine
½ lb.	mushrooms, sliced
2 Tbl.	parmesan, grated
to taste	salt and pepper

In a large non-stick frying pan sauté carrots, onions, shallots and garlic in olive oil for 3 minutes. Add tomatoes and tomato paste. Cook 3 minutes longer. Add cognac, port wine, fish stock, tarragon, and bouquet garni and simmer 20 minutes. Drain and discard the vegetables reserving liquid.

Return sauce to pan. Add sour cream and skim milk. Heat through but do not bring to a boil. Whisk in 1 tablespoon of the powdered butter replacement, flour and 1 tablespoon of water.

Meanwhile, in the top of a double boiler combine egg substitute and white wine. Whisk constantly until it thickens. Add remaining 1 tablespoon of powdered butter replacement. Transfer egg mixture to sour cream sauce. Do not cook.

Prepare a 9x13 baking dish with cooking spray. Arrange mushrooms on the bottom. Layer on the shellfish and pour sauce over top. Sprinkle top with parmesan cheese and salt and pepper to taste. Bake 20 minutes at 350° F or until hot. If top has not browned, broil a few minutes until it browns.

Cholesterol — Above the HM✓ guidelines: Occasionally a lowfat recipe is high in cholesterol. In this case the cholesterol stems from the shellfish. The level is moderately high (>150 mg per serving) but may fit into your weekly average of 150 mg per day.

Cook's Note: May use any combination of crayfish, lobster, shrimp and scallops.

Alcohol Note: The alcohol content was computed prior to cooking. Once the alcohol is heated to the boiling point, the alcohol disappears along with most of the calories from the alcohol.

Nutrient Content Per Serving		Percent of Calories	Fat Breakdown	
Calories	436.0	53% Protein	Saturated Fat	1.5 g
Protein	58.5 g	28% Carbohydrate	Monounsaturated Fat	2.1 g
Carbohydrates	31.4 g	12% Fat	Polyunsaturated Fat	1.3 g
Fat – Total	5.9 g	7% Alcohol		
Cholesterol	220.0 mg			
Dietary Fiber	2.8 g			
Sodium	924.0 mg			

SEAFOOD PASTA
Serves 6

1 lb.	pasta (rigatoni)
½ lb.	calamari (squid), sliced in rounds
½ lb.	scallops
¼ lb.	small shrimp, peeled and deveined
¼ lb.	small clams, without shells
¼ lb.	mussels, without shells
1 leaf	sage (½ tsp. dry sage)
3 cloves	garlic, minced
1	onion, diced fine
1 tsp.	olive oil
¼ cup	white wine
3	tomatoes, peeled, seeded, chopped
1 Tbl.	red pepper flakes
to taste	salt and pepper
½ lb.	mushrooms, sliced
1 cup	marsala wine
to taste	fresh basil, chopped

Cook pasta al dente.

In a non-stick frying pan, brown sage, 2 cloves of garlic and onion in olive oil. Add squid, scallops and white wine. Cook off wine.

Add tomatoes, 1 cup water, red pepper flakes and salt and pepper to taste. Cook 10 minutes.

Meanwhile, in another non-stick frying pan prepared with cooking spray, sauté mushrooms and remaining clove of garlic. Remove mushrooms to a platter. To pan add shrimp, mussels and clams. Cook until done. Add marsala, calamari mixture and mushrooms. Heat through.

Serve over pasta. Garnish with fresh basil.

Cook's Note: A wonderful assortment of seafood.

Cholesterol — Above the HM✓ guidelines: Occasionally a lowfat recipe is high in cholesterol. In this case the cholesterol stems from the shellfish. The level is moderately high (>150 mg per serving) but may fit into your weekly average of 150 mg per day.

Alcohol Note: The alcohol content was computed prior to cooking. Once the alcohol is heated to the boiling point, the alcohol disappears along with most of the calories from the alcohol.

Nutrient Content Per Serving		Percent of Calories	Fat Breakdown	
Calories	367.0	32% Protein	Saturated Fat	1.0 g
Protein	29.6 g	40% Carbohydrate	Monounsaturated Fat	1.8 g
Carbohydrates	37.0 g	14% Fat	Polyunsaturated Fat	1.7 g
Fat – Total	5.6 g	14% Alcohol		
Cholesterol	173.0 mg			
Dietary Fiber	2.9 g			
Sodium	340.0 mg			

PEACHES AND COD
Serves 4

4 4-oz.	cod steaks
4	fresh peaches, sliced
1 tsp.	olive oil
1 tsp.	powdered butter replacement
½	lemon, juice of
1 tsp.	fennel seed, ground
1 branch	fresh thyme
to taste	salt and pepper
4	tomatoes, cut in wedges

Wash cod and pat dry. Combine olive oil, powdered butter replacement, lemon juice and spices. Marinate cod for 10 minutes (5 minutes each side). Grill cod over hot coals for 10-12 minutes or until done.

Meanwhile, in a non-stick pan prepared with cooking spray, cook tomatoes slowly. In another non-stick pan coated with butter-flavored cooking spray, slowly heat peaches until warmed through (can also be done in the microwave). Keep peaches and tomatoes warm while cod cooks.

Arrange cod on a plate surrounded by tomatoes and peaches. Pour marinade over top.

Nutrient Content Per Serving

Calories	169.0
Protein	21.9 g
Carbohydrates	16.1 g
Fat – Total	2.5 g
Cholesterol	48.8 mg
Dietary Fiber	3.1 g
Sodium	77.9 mg

Percent of Calories

50% Protein
37% Carbohydrate
13% Fat

Fat Breakdown

Saturated Fat	0.4 g
Monounsaturated Fat	1.1 g
Polyunsaturated Fat	0.6 g

FISH A L'ORANGE
Serves 6

1½ lbs.   fish fillets, (orange roughy, halibut, sole, cod)

Sauce:
¼ cup   nonfat dry milk powder
⅔ cup   fresh orange juice
1 Tbl.   liquid margarine
1½ Tbl.   unbleached flour
2 tsp.   orange zest
1 tsp.   tarragon

Place fish in a baking dish coated with cooking spray. Bake at 400° F for 8-10 minutes per inch of thickness or until fish flakes easily with a fork.

To prepare sauce:
Stir nonfat dry milk powder into orange juice. Set aside. Heat margarine in a small sauce pan. Stir in flour and cook 1-2 minutes or until bubbly. Remove from heat and add orange juice mixture, whisking constantly until smooth. Return to low heat; cook and stir until thickened, 3-4 minutes. Add orange zest and tarragon. Serve over fish.

Nutrient Content Per Serving

Calories	166.0
Protein	24.4 g
Carbohydrates	5.2 g
Fat – Total	4.6 g
Cholesterol	36.5 mg
Dietary Fiber	0.2 g
Sodium	85.2 mg

Percent of Calories

61% Protein
13% Carbohydrate
26% Fat

Fat Breakdown

Saturated Fat	0.7 g
Monounsaturated Fat	1.5 g
Polyunsaturated Fat	1.8 g

CREAMY DIJON HALIBUT
Serves 4

2 lb.   halibut steak

Sauce:
½ cup   sour cream, nonfat
¼ cup   mayonnaise, nonfat
2 Tbl.   lemon juice, fresh
1 tsp.   dry mustard
1 Tbl.   flour
½ tsp.   garlic, minced
1 Tbl.   dijon mustard
½ tsp.   onion powder

Combine all sauce ingredients. Arrange halibut in a baking dish coated with non-stick cooking spray. Cover with sauce. Bake at 425° F for 20 minutes or until fish is cooked.

Cook's Note: Quick and easy and oh so creamy!

Nutrient Content Per Serving

Calories	339.0
Protein	52.6 g
Carbohydrates	8.4 g
Fat – Total	6.9 g
Cholesterol	93.0 mg
Dietary Fiber	0.2 g
Sodium	395.0 mg

Percent of Calories

69% Protein
11% Carbohydrate
20% Fat

Fat Breakdown

Saturated Fat	1.0 g
Monounsaturated Fat	2.4 g
Polyunsaturated Fat	2.1 g

HERBED SALMON STEAKS
Serves 6

6 4-oz.	salmon steaks
4 med.	shrimp
to taste	salt and pepper
2 Tbl.	flour
1 clove	garlic
2	shallots
¼ tsp.	powdered butter replacement
2 Tbl.	dry white wine
2 Tbl.	parsley, basil, chervil, chives and tarragon

Peel, devein and butterfly shrimp. Lightly salt and pepper salmon. Coat with flour. Set aside.

Crush garlic and shallots together. Combine powdered butter replacement and wine. Add to garlic and shallots. Use as baste for salmon and shrimp. Cook fish over hot coals 5-7 minutes per side. Sprinkle with herbs.

Cook's Note: Serve with green vegetables like snow peas. The herb mixture is your choice. Use any combination. You should have 2 tablespoons total.

Although the % of calories from fat is above 30, fat from the salmon (a good fat source) accounts for 9.74 grams.

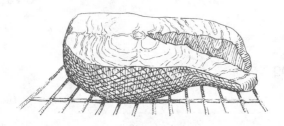

Nutrient Content Per Serving

Calories	212.0
Protein	25.9 g
Carbohydrates	2.3 g
Fat – Total	9.9 g
Cholesterol	81.1 mg
Dietary Fiber	0.1 g
Sodium	64.8 mg

Percent of Calories

51% Protein
5% Carbohydrate
43% Fat

Fat Breakdown

Saturated Fat	1.7 g
Monounsaturated Fat	4.7 g
Polyunsaturated Fat	2.2 g

SALMON WITH HERB SAUCE
Serves 4

4 4-oz.   salmon filets

Herb sauce:
1 Tbl.   shallots, chopped fine
1 clove garlic, minced
2 Tbl.   fresh parsley, chopped
¼ tsp.   salt
¼ tsp.   freshly ground pepper
1 Tbl.   powdered butter replacement
¼ cup   white wine

Garnish:
2   lemons, quartered

Blend all sauce ingredients, except the powdered butter replacement and wine in a food processor. Transfer to a pan and add the remaining sauce ingredients. Heat to dissolve the powdered butter replacement.

Wash the salmon and pat dry. Brush both sides of fish with sauce. Grill over hot coals or under broiler for 5 minutes per side. Baste when turned. Pass the sauce on the side. Serve garnished with the lemon wedges.

Cook's Note: This is great accompanied by crusty bread. All the fat in this recipe is from the salmon.

Alcohol Note: The alcohol content was computed prior to cooking. Once the alcohol is heated to the boiling point, the alcohol disappears along with most of the calories from the alcohol.

Although the % of calories from fat is above 30, fat from the salmon (a good fat source) accounts for 9.74 grams.

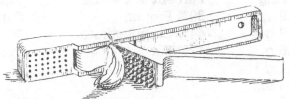

Nutrient Content Per Serving
Calories	209.0
Protein	24.3 g
Carbohydrates	2.0 g
Fat – Total	9.8 g
Cholesterol	70.5 mg
Dietary Fiber	.1 g
Sodium	203.0 mg

Percent of Calories
48% Protein
4% Carbohydrate
43% Fat
5% Alcohol

Fat Breakdown
Saturated Fat	1.7 g
Monounsaturated Fat	4.7 g
Polyunsaturated Fat	2.1 g

SALMON AND LEEK QUICHE
Serves 6

½ lb.	salmon, smoked and sliced
4	leeks

Batter:

¾ cup	egg substitute
2 cups	skim milk
¼ cup	sour cream, nonfat
⅛ tsp.	nutmeg
to taste	salt and pepper
1 Tbl.	powdered butter replacement

Slice leeks in 1-inch slices. In non-stick pan prepared with cooking spray, sauté leeks over low heat until cooked and somewhat dry.

In a bowl, combine batter ingredients and mix well. Prepare a decorative baking dish with cooking spray. Arrange three-quarters of the salmon and the leeks on the bottom. Add batter. Cook 25 minutes at 400° F. Decorate top with salmon. Serve directly from baking dish.

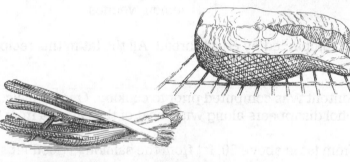

Nutrient Content Per Serving		**Percent of Calories**	**Fat Breakdown**	
Calories	158.9	39% Protein	Saturated Fat	0.7 g
Protein	15.3 g	44% Carbohydrate	Monounsaturated Fat	1.1 g
Carbohydrates	17.6 g	17% Fat	Polyunsaturated Fat	1.0 g
Fat – Total	3.1 g			
Cholesterol	10.5 mg			
Dietary Fiber	2.0 g			
Sodium	427.0 mg			

SEARED SALMON SUPREME
Serves 2

8 oz.	salmon fillet
1 Tbl.	soy sauce, light
3 Tbl.	lemon juice
1½ cups	frozen spinach, thawed
1½ Tbl.	ricotta cheese, nonfat

Garnish:

1 Tbl.	salmon caviar (optional)

Spray salmon with olive oil flavored cooking spray and quickly sear on grill or under broiler until lightly browned. In a frying pan, mix the light soy sauce and lemon juice. Add salmon and sear until lightly caramelized, then remove from the pan.

In the same pan, sauté the spinach quickly and arrange with the salmon on a serving plate. Top each serving with a dollop of nonfat ricotta cheese. Garnish with salmon caviar. (optional)

Cook's Note: All the fat comes from the salmon. This is "good fat": omega-3 fatty acids. See the nutrition discussion for more information *(see p. 3)*. You may use 1 pound of fresh spinach in place of the frozen spinach. Steam the spinach before using.

Although the % of calories from fat is above 30, fat from the salmon (a good fat source) accounts for 7.22 grams and 1.43 grams are from the optional caviar.

Nutrient Content Per Serving

Calories	215.0
Protein	27.3 g
Carbohydrates	4.8 g
Fat – Total	9.7 g
Cholesterol	113.0 mg
Dietary Fiber	1.2 g
Sodium	526.0 mg

Percent of Calories

51% Protein
9% Carbohydrate
41% Fat

Fat Breakdown

Saturated Fat	2.0 g
Monounsaturated Fat	3.0 g
Polyunsaturated Fat	3.6 g

SAUTÉED SCALLOPS
Serves 4

2 lbs.	sea scallops
1	leek, white only, chopped
1	shallot, chopped
1 tsp.	garlic, minced
1	carrot, grated
1 tsp.	olive oil
2 Tbl.	white wine
1 Tbl.	white wine vinegar
1 tsp.	powdered butter replacement
2 tsp.	sun-dried tomatoes, soaked in water, chopped
to taste	salt and pepper

In a large non-stick frying pan, sauté leeks, shallots, garlic and carrot in olive oil until tender. Add wine, vinegar, powdered butter replacement, sundried tomatoes, salt and pepper to taste. Heat through. Add scallops, simmer 5 minutes or until opaque. Serve immediately over rice or pasta.

Cook's Note: Purchase sundried tomatoes as "dried in package," not packed in oil.

Alcohol Note: The alcohol content was computed prior to cooking. Once the alcohol is heated to the boiling point, the alcohol disappears along with most of the calories from the alcohol.

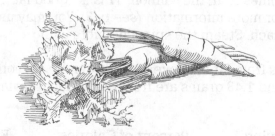

Nutrient Content Per Serving

Calories	289.0					
Protein	37.5 g					
Carbohydrates	12.7 g					
Fat – Total	8.4 g					
Cholesterol	72.2 mg					
Dietary Fiber	1.5 g					
Sodium	449.0 mg					

Percent of Calories

53% Protein
18% Carbohydrate
27% Fat
 2% Alcohol

Fat Breakdown

Saturated Fat	1.4 g
Monounsaturated Fat	3.4 g
Polyunsaturated Fat	2.5 g

Shrimp Provencal
Serves 4

1 lb.	large shrimp, peeled, deveined
1 med.	onion, chopped
1 tsp.	olive oil
2 cloves	garlic, minced
2 lg.	tomatoes, peeled, chopped
pinch	hot pepper flakes
¼ cup	cognac
½ cup	dry white wine
1 tsp.	thyme
to taste	salt and pepper
1 tsp.	powdered butter replacement

Sauté onion in olive oil. Add garlic, cook 1 minute. Add remaining ingredients except shrimp. Simmer 20 minutes, or until sauce thickens. Add shrimp, cook 2-5 minutes until pink. Serve immediately.

Cook's Note: Serve with rice or garlic bread

Cholesterol — Above the HM✔ guidelines: Occasionally a lowfat recipe is high in cholesterol. In this case the cholesterol stems from the shellfish. The level is moderately high (>150 mg per serving) but may fit into your weekly average of 150 mg per day.

Alcohol Note: The alcohol content was computed prior to cooking. Once the alcohol is heated to the boiling point, the alcohol disappears along with most of the calories from the alcohol..

Nutrient Content Per Serving		**Percent of Calories**	**Fat Breakdown**	
Calories	217.0	45% Protein	Saturated Fat	0.6 g
Protein	24.3 g	17% Carbohydrate	Monounsaturated Fat	1.2 g
Carbohydrates	9.0 g	14% Fat	Polyunsaturated Fat	1.0 g
Fat – Total	3.5 g	24% Alcohol		
Cholesterol	173.0 mg			
Dietary Fiber	1.9 g			
Sodium	184.0 mg			

SOLE AND SPINACH ROLLS
Serves 4

4 4-oz.	sole, filets
½ lb.	fresh spinach
⅓ cup	sour cream, nonfat
1 Tbl.	skim milk
1	carrot, peeled, long curls or shreds
to taste	salt and pepper
¼ tsp.	powdered butter replacement
1 sprig	fresh basil
2	tomatoes, cubed

Wash fish and pat dry. De-stem spinach and cut in strips. Using a whisk thin sour cream with a small amount of skim milk. Lay fish flat on cutting board (inside should be up). Layer spinach, carrot peels, salt and pepper on fish. Sprinkle with powdered butter replacement. Roll filets and tie with string or secure with small toothpicks. Place in aluminum foil, prepared with cooking spray. Arrange tomatoes around filets. Drizzle sour cream over top. Add basil before closing foil around fish. Cook at 400° F for 8-15 minutes or until fish is done.

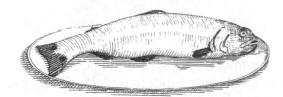

Nutrient Content Per Serving

Calories	148.0
Protein	24.9 g
Carbohydrates	8.7 g
Fat – Total	1.8 g
Cholesterol	54.4 mg
Dietary Fiber	2.9 g
Sodium	163.0 mg

Percent of Calories

66% Protein
23% Carbohydrate
11% Fat

Fat Breakdown

Saturated Fat	0.4 g
Monounsaturated Fat	0.3 g
Polyunsaturated Fat	0.6 g

TUNA CATALANA
Serves 4

4 8-oz.	Ahi tuna steaks
1 tsp.	olive oil
½ lb.	pearl onions
1 Tbl.	garlic, minced
½ lb.	sweet red peppers, cut in small cubes
1 Tbl.	tomato paste
15 oz.	tomatoes, canned, peeled
few drops	Tabasco™
to taste	salt

Garnish:

2 Tbl.	fresh parsley (1 Tbl. dried parsley)
1 Tbl.	tart pickles, diced fine

Peel onions and leave whole. Heat the olive oil in a non-stick skillet, add onions, garlic and peppers. Sauté for 5 minutes. In a separate bowl, combine tomato paste, tomato, Tabasco™ and salt to taste. Add sautéd vegetables to tomato mixture.

Arrange tuna steaks in a non-stick pan coated with cooking spray. Cover fish with tomato mixture. Cover pan and cook over low heat for 20 minutes until done. Arrange fish on a heated platter and spoon sauce around it. Combine parsley and pickles, and use to garnish fish.

Cook's Note: Serve over pasta or rice. An easy, elegant company dish.

Nutrient Content Per Serving

Calories	316.0
Protein	41.9 g
Carbohydrates	13.8 g
Fat – Total	9.9 g
Cholesterol	64.6 mg
Dietary Fiber	3.3 g
Sodium	272.0 mg

Percent of Calories

54% Protein
18% Carbohydrate
29% Fat

Fat Breakdown

Saturated Fat	2.4 g
Monounsaturated Fat	3.6 g
Polyunsaturated Fat	3.1 g

BEEF BOURGUIGNON
Serves 6

1½ lbs.	beef top round, lean
2 Tbl.	flour
to taste	salt and pepper
1 tsp.	olive oil
1 clove	garlic, minced
2 cups	bourguignon (dry red wine)
1	bouquet garni *(see p. 15)*
1 cup	pickled pearl onions
2 cups	button mushrooms
1 tsp.	sugar
1 Tbl.	powdered butter replacement
1 Tbl.	tomato paste

Trim meat of all visible fat, and cut into large cubes. Dredge in flour seasoned with salt and pepper to taste. In a non-stick pan brown meat in olive oil. Add garlic for final minute of browning. Add 1 cup of the wine and bouquet garni. Cover and simmer 2 hours. Add water if necessary to prevent sticking.

After 2 hours, add onions, remaining mushrooms, remaining cup of wine, sugar, powdered butter replacement and tomato paste. Continue to simmer until meat is tender (approximately 30 minutes). Remove bouquet garni before serving.

Cook's Note: Serve with potatoes or over noodles and with a green salad.

Alcohol Note: The alcohol content was computed prior to cooking. Once the alcohol is heated to the boiling point, the alcohol disappears along with most of the calories from the alcohol.

Nutrient Content Per Serving

Calories	297.0
Protein	37.1 g
Carbohydrates	7.8 g
Fat – Total	6.5 g
Cholesterol	95.2 mg
Dietary Fiber	0.9 g
Sodium	158.0 mg

Percent of Calories

51% Protein
11% Carbohydrate
20% Fat
11% Alcohol

Fat Breakdown

Saturated Fat	2.0 g
Monounsaturated Fat	2.7 g
Polyunsaturated Fat	0.4 g

Sautéed Elk Medallions
Serves 8

8 3-oz.	elk loin medallions (may also use venison)
to taste	salt and pepper
2 Tbl.	flour

Sauce:

3 Tbl.	shallots, chopped
1 cup	carrots, diced
1 tsp.	coriander seed, crushed
1 tsp.	olive oil
4 cups	beef stock *(see p. 536)*
1 Tbl.	tomato paste
¼ cup	plum sauce
½ cup	apple juice
½ cup	red wine
¼ tsp.	thyme, dry
dash	red pepper flakes

Garnish: (optional)
carrot curls
black sesame seeds

In a large roasting pan, over medium heat, sauté the shallots, carrots and coriander seed in the olive oil. Add the remaining sauce ingredients. Cover and simmer for 3-4 hours. Periodically remove any built up foam. Strain through a sieve and chill quickly in an ice bath.

Season the elk medallion with salt and pepper if desired. Dust lightly in flour and sauté to the desired temperature. Pat dry with a paper towel and place on dinner plate. Ladle the sauce on top. Garnish with carrot curls. Sprinkle a little bit of black sesame on top.

Cook's Note: Serve with potatoes and seasonal vegetables. Plum sauce is found in the oriental section of the grocery store. Game meat is extremely low in fat. An excellent choice.

Alcohol Note: The alcohol content was computed prior to cooking. Once the alcohol is heated to the boiling point, the alcohol disappears along with most of the calories from the alcohol.

Nutrient Content Per Serving		**Percent of Calories**	**Fat Breakdown**	
Calories	222.0	48% Protein	Saturated Fat	0.9 g
Protein	26.4 g	25% Carbohydrate	Monounsaturated Fat	1.1 g
Carbohydrates	13.8 g	15% Fat	Polyunsaturated Fat	1.4 g
Fat – Total	3.7 g	12% Alcohol		
Cholesterol	62.1 mg			
Dietary Fiber	1.1 g			
Sodium	75.8 mg			

Pork a l'Orange
Serves 4

1 lb.	pork tenderloin
4 Tbl.	flour
½ lg.	onion, chopped fine
½ cup	beef stock *(see p. 536)*, (may substitute chicken stock *(see p. 538)* if desired)
1 cup	orange juice
to taste	salt and pepper
dash	Tabasco™
1 tsp.	powdered butter replacement
2 tsp.	orange zest
1 tsp.	apricot marmalade
1	apple, unpeeled, sliced in rounds
1	orange, peeled, sliced in rounds

Trim pork of all visible fat. Cut into 2-ounce medallions. Pound each one thin and sprinkle with flour.

In non-stick frying pan coated with cooking spray, brown pork over medium-low heat. Remove from pan. Add onions and sauté until translucent. Add stock, 2 tablespoons of the flour and stir 1 minute to cook flour. Add orange juice and bring to a boil until thickened. Reduce heat, add salt and pepper to taste, Tabasco™, powdered butter replacement, orange zest and apricot marmalade.

In a baking dish, arrange pork and pour sauce over top. Cover and cook 20 minutes at 300° F. Remove cover and arrange apples and oranges on top of pork. Cook another 10 minutes. Serve with rice.

Cook's Note: Purchase pork tenderloin already trimmed. It is shaped in a long tube and is in a clear bag. May substitute chicken stock (the kind in a jar) for veal stock. Reconstitute according to directions on the jar.

Nutrient Content Per Serving

Calories	298.0
Protein	33.7 g
Carbohydrates	25.0 g
Fat – Total	6.1 g
Cholesterol	89.6 mg
Dietary Fiber	2.2 g
Sodium	70.2 mg

Percent of Calories

46% Protein
34% Carbohydrate
19% Fat

Fat Breakdown

Saturated Fat	2.0 g
Monounsaturated Fat	2.3 g
Polyunsaturated Fat	0.8 g

GRILLED VEAL SCALLOPS
Serves 4

12 oz.	veal scallops, trimmed of all visible fat

Marinade:

2 tsp.	shallots
2 tsp.	garlic
2 tsp.	fresh rosemary, chopped
1 Tbl.	sundried tomatoes, re-hydrated
1	lemon, juice of
to taste	salt and pepper

Season the veal scallops with salt and pepper to taste. Combine the remaining ingredients in a blender and purée until smooth. Spread the paste on the veal scallops and let marinate for 15 minutes. Grill over hot coals until heated through.

Cook's Note: Goes well with Risi Bisi Rice *(see p. 198)*.

The % of calories as fat is above 30, but this is still considered a lowfat meal with only 7.9 grams of fat per serving.

Nutrient Content Per Serving

Calories	201.0
Protein	28.8 g
Carbohydrates	2.2 g
Fat – Total	7.9 g
Cholesterol	106.0 mg
Dietary Fiber	0.5 g
Sodium	90.0 mg

Percent of Calories

59% Protein	
5% Carbohydrate	
36% Fat	

Fat Breakdown

Saturated Fat	2.2 g
Monounsaturated Fat	2.8 g
Polyunsaturated Fat	0.7 g

CANDIED ACORN SQUASH

Serves 4

1 med.	acorn squash
¼ cup	candied ginger
to taste	salt and pepper
1 tsp.	olive oil
¼ cup	parsley
1 Tbl.	lemon juice
½ cup	water

Preheat the oven to 350° F.

Pierce acorn squash with a cake tester. Punch holes through to the middle. (This will allow air to escape and prevent squash from exploding.) Microwave whole squash for 10 minutes or until the meat is tender. Cut open and remove seeds. Remove skin and cut pulp into bite-sized chunks.

Combine all other ingredients. Mix in squash. Bake at 350° F covered for 30 minutes or until heated through.

Nutrient Content Per Serving		**Percent of Calories**	**Fat Breakdown**	
Calories	110.0	6% Protein	Saturated Fat	0.2 g
Protein	2.0 g	83% Carbohydrate	Monounsaturated Fat	0.9 g
Carbohydrates	26.0 g	10% Fat	Polyunsaturated Fat	0.2 g
Fat – Total	1.4 g			
Cholesterol	0.0 mg			
Dietary Fiber	7.0 g			
Sodium	9.1 mg			

ASPARAGUS WITH SHALLOTS AND TARRAGON
Serves 4

1 lb.	asparagus
3 Tbl.	shallots, chopped
1 Tbl.	fresh tarragon, chopped
1 tsp.	olive oil
¼ cup	white wine
2 tsp.	powdered butter replacement

Steam or microwave asparagus until just tender. Arrange on a serving platter. In a non-stick frying pan, sauté shallots and tarragon in olive oil. Add the wine and powdered butter replacement. Bring to a boil. Pour over asparagus.

Alcohol Note: The alcohol content was computed prior to cooking. Once the alcohol is heated to the boiling point, the alcohol disappears along with most of the calories from the alcohol.

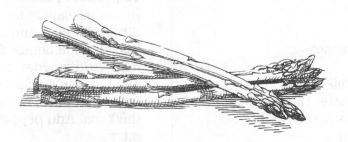

Nutrient Content Per Serving

Calories	57.9
Protein	3.1 g
Carbohydrates	7.9 g
Fat – Total	1.5 g
Cholesterol	0.0 mg
Dietary Fiber	2.2 g
Sodium	14.5 mg

Percent of Calories

19%	Protein
47%	Carbohydrate
20%	Fat
14%	Alcohol

Fat Breakdown

Saturated Fat	0.2 g
Monounsaturated Fat	0.8 g
Polyunsaturated Fat	0.2 g

BROCCOLI AU GRATIN CREPES
Serves 16

1 recipe   all-purpose crepes *(see p. 189)*

Filling:
4 cups	broccoli, chopped (fresh or frozen)
1 med.	onion, chopped fine
½ tsp.	garlic, minced
1 tsp.	olive oil
½ cup	water

Sauce:
2 Tbl.	flour
1½ Tbl.	liquid margarine
¾ cup	skim milk
⅓ cup	nonfat dry milk
1 tsp.	powdered butter replacement
½ cup	chicken stock *(see p. 538)*
¼ tsp.	white pepper

Prepare crepes according to recipe.

To prepare filling:
Heat oil in a non-stick skillet, sauté onion and garlic until soft. Add water and broccoli, cover and cook until water evaporates. Cook 1-2 minutes until broccoli is tender.

To prepare sauce:
In a small saucepan, heat the margarine. Stir in the flour and cook for 2 minutes. Dissolve the nonfat dry milk in the skim milk. Add powdered butter replacement and chicken stock. Whisk milk mixture into roux. Cook, stirring constantly, until it thickens. Add pepper and broccoli mixture.

Fill crepes and arrange in a 9x13 pan prepared with cooking spray. Add 1/8-inch water, stock or white wine. Cover and bake at 350° F for 10-15 minutes or until warm.

Cook's Note: This recipe makes 16 crepes. They can be served immediately or prepared ahead of time and warmed when ready to serve.

Nutrient Content Per Serving		**Percent of Calories**	**Fat Breakdown**	
Calories	116.0	19% Protein	Saturated Fat	0.4 g
Protein	5.5 g	59% Carbohydrate	Monounsaturated Fat	1.2 g
Carbohydrates	17.3 g	22% Fat	Polyunsaturated Fat	1.0 g
Fat – Total	2.8 g			
Cholesterol	1.1 mg			
Dietary Fiber	1.2 g			
Sodium	61.1 mg			

RED CABBAGE AND APPLES
Serves 4

½ head	red cabbage, shredded, coarse
2	apples, peeled, chopped
1 lg.	onion, chopped
½ cup	raisins
1 Tbl.	honey
to taste	salt and pepper
¼ cup	red wine vinegar

Combine all ingredients in a 4-quart sauce pan or ovenproof casserole. Bring to a boil. Lower heat and simmer covered for 1 hour. Serve hot.

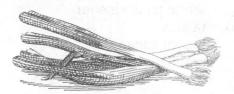

Nutrient Content Per Serving

Calories	148.0
Protein	2.0 g
Carbohydrates	38.1 g
Fat – Total	0.5 g
Cholesterol	0.0 mg
Dietary Fiber	4.5 g
Sodium	26.1 mg

Percent of Calories

5% Protein
92% Carbohydrate
3% Fat

Fat Breakdown

Saturated Fat	0.1 g
Monounsaturated Fat	0.0 g
Polyunsaturated Fat	0.2 g

SWEET AND SOUR CARROTS
Serves 6

4	carrots, sliced in ¼-inch rounds
¼ cup	onion, minced
½ tsp.	nutmeg
1 tsp.	oil
2 Tbl.	white wine vinegar
¼ cup	raisins
1 Tbl.	brown sugar
1 tsp.	powdered butter replacement

In a non-stick pan, sauté carrots, onions and nutmeg in oil until onions begin to brown. Add vinegar. Cover and cook until carrots are tender.

Soak raisins in ½ cup warm water until plump. Drain and add to cooked carrots. Add brown sugar and powdered butter replacement. Heat through. Serve hot.

Nutrient Content Per Serving

Calories	58.0
Protein	0.8 g
Carbohydrates	12.8 g
Fat – Total	0.9 g
Cholesterol	0.0 mg
Dietary Fiber	2.0 g
Sodium	21.7 mg

Percent of Calories

5% Protein
82% Carbohydrate
13% Fat

Fat Breakdown

Saturated Fat	0.1 g
Monounsaturated Fat	0.2 g
Polyunsaturated Fat	0.5 g

Glazed Carrots
Serves 6

12	carrots, peeled, cut in 2-inch pieces
1½ cups	chicken stock *(see p. 538)*
2 Tbl.	powdered butter replacement
3 Tbl.	brown sugar
¼ tsp.	salt
to taste	black pepper
1	onion, sliced thin

Garnish:

3 Tbl.	fresh parsley, chopped

In a saucepan, combine all ingredients except parsley. Bring to a boil. Cover and simmer 20-30 minutes until carrots are tender. Stir occasionally. Serve garnished with fresh parsley.

Nutrient Content Per Serving

Calories	100.0
Protein	2.9 g
Carbohydrates	21.8 g
Fat – Total	0.7 g
Cholesterol	0.0 mg
Dietary Fiber	4.8 g
Sodium	355.0 mg

Percent of Calories

11% Protein
83% Carbohydrate
 6% Fat

Fat Breakdown

Saturated Fat	0.2 g
Monounsaturated Fat	0.2 g
Polyunsaturated Fat	0.2 g

GINGERED CARROTS AND APPLES
Serves 4

2 cups	carrots, sliced thin on an angle
⅓ cup	orange juice
⅓ cup	lemon juice
2 tsp.	fresh ginger root, slivered
2 med.	apples, peeled, sliced ¼-inch thick
1 Tbl.	scallions, diced

Combine all ingredients in a medium frying pan. Simmer, covered until carrots are just tender. Add water if necessary to keep from burning. Serve vegetables with their juice.

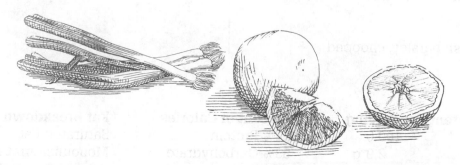

Nutrient Content Per Serving

Calories	75.6
Protein	0.9 g
Carbohydrates	19.1 g
Fat – Total	0.4 g
Cholesterol	0.0 mg
Dietary Fiber	3.1 g
Sodium	20.1 mg

Percent of Calories

4%	Protein
91%	Carbohydrate
4%	Fat

Fat Breakdown

Saturated Fat	0.1 g
Monounsaturated Fat	0.0 g
Polyunsaturated Fat	0.1 g

CARROTS WITH "CREAM"

Serves 4

1 lb.	baby carrots, peeled
1 cup	chicken stock *(see p. 538)*
1 tsp.	sugar
to taste	salt and pepper
½ cup	sour cream, nonfat

Garnish:

1 Tbl.	fresh parsley, chopped

In a saucepan, combine carrots, chicken stock, sugar, salt and pepper to taste. Cook uncovered 15 minutes or until tender and liquid evaporated. Add sour cream and heat through. Garnish with parsley.

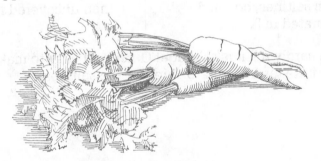

Nutrient Content Per Serving

Calories	80.6
Protein	4.4 g
Carbohydrates	15.7 g
Fat – Total	0.6 g
Cholesterol	0.0 mg
Dietary Fiber	3.6 g
Sodium	254.0 mg

Percent of Calories

21% Protein
74% Carbohydrate
6% Fat

Fat Breakdown

Saturated Fat	0.1 g
Monounsaturated Fat	0.2 g
Polyunsaturated Fat	0.2 g

CRAB AND CABBAGE CASSEROLE
Serves 6

4 cups	green cabbage, shredded
1 cup	fresh crab meat, cut in small cubes or shredded
¼ cup	parmesan cheese, grated
1½ tsp.	paprika
1 tsp.	celery seed
to taste	salt
¼ tsp.	pepper
2 cups	low-sodium saltines, crushed
3½ cups	skim evaporated milk

Combine all ingredients except saltines and evaporated milk. Alternate mixture with crushed crackers in casserole dish prepared with cooking spray.

Heat skim evaporated milk in saucepan over low heat and pour over casserole. Bake covered for 30 minutes at 350° F, then uncovered for 10 minutes.

Cook's Note: You can hardly tell it is cabbage! Quick and easy to make. Serve with grilled fish or chicken. May substitute fat-free potato chips for the saltines.

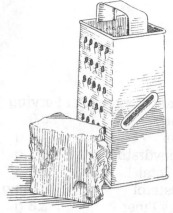

Nutrient Content Per Serving

Calories	264.0
Protein	15.1 g
Carbohydrates	36.4 g
Fat – Total	6.4 g
Cholesterol	33.3 mg
Dietary Fiber	2.1 g
Sodium	477.0 mg

Percent of Calories
23% Protein
55% Carbohydrate
22% Fat

Fat Breakdown

Saturated Fat	2.9 g
Monounsaturated Fat	1.9 g
Polyunsaturated Fat	1.1 g

STUFFED EGGPLANT WITH TWO SAUCES
Serves 6

3	eggplants (use the long and thin variety)
2 cloves	garlic, minced
2	onions, diced
1 Tbl.	olive oil
1 tsp.	thyme
to taste	salt and pepper
1 bunch	fresh basil, chopped
1	lemon

Sauce:

3	sweet red peppers, roasted (*see p. 13*)
3	yellow peppers, roasted (*see p. 13*)
⅓ cup	sour cream, nonfat
3 Tbl.	skim milk

Put yellow peppers in blender. Add ⅓ cup sour cream and enough skim milk to make it thin. Add salt and pepper to taste. Refrigerate. Repeat for red sauce using red peppers.

To prepare eggplant, slice off end (do not peel). Cut in half lengthwise. Scoop out seeds to make 6 small boats and save pulp. In a food processor mash eggplant pulp with garlic and onions. In a non-stick frying pan, sauté the pulp in olive oil for 10 minutes. Add thyme, salt and pepper to taste. Remove from heat, add basil and lemon juice. Stuff eggplant and arrange in ovenproof pan prepared with cooking spray. Bake 45 minutes at 400° F. Chill. Serve accompanied by the yellow pepper sauce and the red pepper sauce.

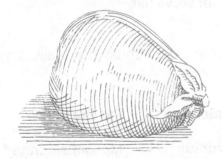

Cook's Note: Makes a beautiful accompaniment to any chicken or fish meal.

Nutrient Content Per Serving		Percent of Calories		Fat Breakdown	
Calories	103.0	12% Protein		Saturated Fat	0.4 g
Protein	3.4 g	66% Carbohydrate		Monounsaturated Fat	1.7 g
Carbohydrates	18.9 g	22% Fat		Polyunsaturated Fat	0.4 g
Fat – Total	2.8 g				
Cholesterol	0.1 mg				
Dietary Fiber	6.2 g				
Sodium	19.4 mg				

ONION OMELETTE
Serves 4

2 med.	onions, sliced thin
1 oz.	turkey, sliced thin
few leaves	fresh mint, chopped
1½ tsp.	olive oil
2	tomatoes, chopped
8	egg whites
1 tsp.	canola oil
pinch	turmeric
2 oz.	swiss cheese, lowfat, grated
1 tsp.	fresh basil, chopped
to taste	salt and pepper

In a medium non-stick frying pan over medium heat, sauté onions, turkey and mint in olive oil until onions are translucent. Add tomatoes and cook down. Set aside on a plate.

In a bowl, beat together egg whites and oil. Sprinkle in turmeric a little at a time, beating well after each addition.

Coat a non-stick frying pan with cooking spray. Heat pan over medium heat. Pour in egg white mixture. Cover and cook over low heat until about half set. Add onion mixture, cheese and basil. Cover and continue cooking until eggs are set and filling is warm. May fold omelette in half or serve flat.

Cook's Note: May serve as the main dish (for two people) for Sunday breakfast. May use egg substitute in place of egg whites, canola oil and turmeric.

Nutrient Content Per Serving

Calories	130.0
Protein	14.4 g
Carbohydrates	9.2 g
Fat – Total	3.9 g
Cholesterol	11.0 mg
Dietary Fiber	1.8 g
Sodium	158.0 mg

Percent of Calories

44% Protein
28% Carbohydrate
27% Fat

Fat Breakdown

Saturated Fat	0.8 g
Monounsaturated Fat	2.2 g
Polyunsaturated Fat	0.6 g

ROASTED ONIONS
Serves 6

4 lg.	yellow onions, sliced thick
1 Tbl.	garlic, minced
1 Tbl.	olive oil
1 tsp.	sugar
1 sprig	thyme (½ tsp. dry)
to taste	salt and pepper

Mix together garlic, olive oil, sugar, thyme and salt and pepper to taste.

Arrange onions on a large non-stick baking sheet. Brush with oil mixture. Bake at 400° F for 10-15 minutes or until onions are tender.

Cook's Note: The onions are sweet and mild, you'll be surprised!

% Calories as Fat — Above the HM✔ guidelines: Although this recipe has a high percentage of calories as fat (>30%), the total fat is less than 5 grams per serving. This will easily fit within your allotment of 45 grams per day. This happens most often in low-calorie recipes.

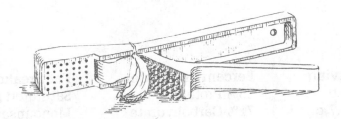

Nutrient Content Per Serving

Calories	63.3
Protein	1.8 g
Carbohydrates	9.9 g
Fat – Total	2.4 g
Cholesterol	0.0 mg
Dietary Fiber	1.8 g
Sodium	3.3 mg

Percent of Calories

8% Protein
60% Carbohydrate
33% Fat

Fat Breakdown

Saturated Fat	0.3 g
Monounsaturated Fat	1.7 g
Polyunsaturated Fat	0.3 g

PEAS AND ONIONS
Serves 6

6 cups	green peas, fresh or frozen
⅓ lb.	pearl onions, canned
1	heart of lettuce, quartered
1 Tbl.	powdered butter replacement
to taste	salt and pepper

Drain onions. Place peas and onions in a microwave dish. Cover with a small amount of water. Cook on high for 5 minutes or until almost cooked. Add lettuce heart, powdered butter replacement and salt and pepper to taste. Heat 1 minute.

Cook's Note: Heart of lettuce is the center part, without the core. Has a subtle flavor.

Nutrient Content Per Serving

Calories	121.0
Protein	7.7 g
Carbohydrates	22.0 g
Fat – Total	0.6 g
Cholesterol	0.0 mg
Dietary Fiber	7.6 g
Sodium	231.0 mg

Percent of Calories

25% Protein
71% Carbohydrate
 4% Fat

Fat Breakdown

Saturated Fat	0.1 g
Monounsaturated Fat	0.1 g
Polyunsaturated Fat	0.3 g

CHÂTEAU POTATOES
Serves 6

6	potatoes
½ Tbl.	olive oil
to taste	garlic powder
to taste	salt and freshly ground pepper
½ tsp.	sweet paprika
½ cup	chicken stock *(see p. 538)*

Garnish:

parsley flakes

Slice potatoes ¼-inch thick. Add remaining ingredients and mix well. Bake, covered, at 350° F for 60 minutes or until tender. Garnish with parsley flakes.

Cook's Note: Serve with poultry, beef or seafood.

Nutrient Content Per Serving

Calories	143.0
Protein	2.8 g
Carbohydrates	30.8 g
Fat – Total	1.3 g
Cholesterol	0.0 mg
Dietary Fiber	2.6 g
Sodium	9.8 mg

Percent of Calories

8%	Protein
85%	Carbohydrate
8%	Fat

Fat Breakdown

Saturated Fat	0.8 g
Monounsaturated Fat	0.1 g
Polyunsaturated Fat	0.0 g

POTATOES AU GRATIN

Serves 6

2 lbs.	white potatoes, sliced in thin rounds
4 oz.	regular swiss cheese, grated fine
4 oz.	fat-free swiss cheese, grated fine
½ cup	sour cream, nonfat
1 cup	skim milk
1 lg.	onion, diced fine
1 Tbl.	powdered butter replacement
to taste	salt and pepper

Parboil potatoes in microwave until just tender. Prepare a casserole dish with cooking spray. Combine the cheeses and reserve 1 ounce regular swiss. Combine sour cream and skim milk. Prepare casserole in the following layers: potato, onion, mixed cheese, salt and pepper to taste, powdered butter replacement. Repeat 4 times. Pour milk mixture over potatoes. Top with reserved cheese. Bake at 375° F covered with aluminum foil for 30 minutes. Remove aluminum foil and brown under broiler for 5 minutes.

Nutrient Content Per Serving

Calories	295.0
Protein	15.9 g
Carbohydrates	47.7 g
Fat – Total	5.0 g
Cholesterol	20.2 mg
Dietary Fiber	3.5 g
Sodium	599.0 mg

Percent of Calories

21% Protein
64% Carbohydrate
15% Fat

Fat Breakdown

Saturated Fat	3.1 g
Monounsaturated Fat	1.4 g
Polyunsaturated Fat	0.2 g

GRATIN OF POTATOES, ONIONS AND TOMATOES
Serves 4

1 lb.	new potatoes, sliced in ¼-inch rounds
1 med.	onion, sliced thin
6 sprigs	fresh thyme, chopped
to taste	salt and pepper
2 lg.	tomatoes, chopped
½ cup	white wine
½ cup	gruyere cheese, grated

Parboil the potatoes.

Prepare a 10-inch gratin dish with olive oil flavored cooking spray. Arrange ½ of the potatoes on the bottom of the dish. Cover with half of the onions, thyme, salt and pepper to taste and tomatoes. Repeat for a second layer.

Add wine and cheese. Bake at 400° F for 40-50 minutes or until vegetables are tender.

Alcohol Note: The alcohol content was computed prior to cooking. Once the alcohol is heated to the boiling point, the alcohol disappears along with most of the calories from the alcohol.

Nutrient Content Per Serving

Calories	191.0
Protein	7.4 g
Carbohydrates	26.5 g
Fat – Total	4.8 g
Cholesterol	14.9 mg
Dietary Fiber	3.5 g
Sodium	60.4 mg

Percent of Calories

15% Protein
54% Carbohydrate
22% Fat
 9% Alcohol

Fat Breakdown

Saturated Fat	2.6 g
Monounsaturated Fat	1.4 g
Polyunsaturated Fat	0.4 g

RATATOUILLE

Serves 6

2 sm.	zucchini, cut in chunks
2 sm.	eggplant, cut in chunks
2 tsp.	olive oil
1	sweet red pepper, sliced in strips
1	yellow pepper, sliced in strips
1	green pepper, sliced in strips
4 cloves	garlic, sliced thin
2	white onions, sliced thick
4	tomatoes, peeled and seeded, cut in chunks
pinch	sugar
to taste	salt and pepper

In a large pot, heat oil. Sauté zucchini and eggplant. Remove from pan and set aside. Drain liquid from pan. Heat peppers, garlic and onion for 5 minutes. Add tomatoes and stir. Return zucchini and eggplant. Add sugar, salt and pepper to taste. Cook very slowly, uncovered, for 1 hour. May serve hot or cold.

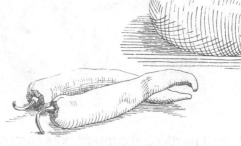

Cook's Note: May add basil, oregano or mint if desired.

Nutrient Content Per Serving

Calories	105.0
Protein	3.1 g
Carbohydrates	21.3 g
Fat – Total	2.3 g
Cholesterol	0.0 mg
Dietary Fiber	8.0 g
Sodium	14.8 mg

Percent of Calories

10% Protein
72% Carbohydrate
18% Fat

Fat Breakdown

Saturated Fat	0.4 g
Monounsaturated Fat	1.2 g
Polyunsaturated Fat	0.5 g

SNOW PEAS AND SHALLOTS
Serves 8

2 lb.	snow peas
1 tsp.	olive oil
4	shallots, chopped fine
¼ cup	skim milk
1 tsp.	nonfat dry milk
1 tsp.	powdered butter replacement
½ cup	chicken stock *(see p. 538)*
2	tomatoes, diced
2 Tbl.	fresh basil chopped
to taste	salt and pepper

Wash snow peas and remove strings and ends. Heat oil in non-stick frying pan. Sauté shallots until translucent. Add snow peas and sauté for 2 minutes. Mix milk, nonfat dry milk and powdered butter replacement. Add milk mixture and stock. Cook 15 minutes covered. Add tomatoes, basil, salt and pepper to taste.

Cook's Note: Make this when fresh snow peas are available. The frozen ones are too mushy.

Nutrient Content Per Serving

Calories	67.3
Protein	4.2 g
Carbohydrates	11.1 g
Fat – Total	1.0 g
Cholesterol	0.2 mg
Dietary Fiber	3.4 g
Sodium	64.1 mg

Percent of Calories

24% Protein
63% Carbohydrate
13% Fat

Fat Breakdown

Saturated Fat	0.2 g
Monounsaturated Fat	0.5 g
Polyunsaturated Fat	0.2 g

RUSTIC VEGETABLES
Serves 6

1	eggplant, peeled, cubed
2	zucchini, sliced in rounds
3	tomatoes, sliced in rounds
1	sweet red pepper, sliced in strips
1	yellow pepper, sliced in strips
2	onions, cut in rings
1 clove	garlic, minced
1½ oz.	gouda, grated
12 branches	parsley
12 branches	basil
to taste	salt and pepper

Arrange vegetables in a decorative manner on a baking dish sprayed with cooking spray. Mix garlic, gouda, parsley, basil, salt and pepper. Sprinkle on top of vegetables. Cover with foil. Cook 30 minutes at 350° F. Broil until brown. Serve hot.

Cook's Note: May roast the peppers if desired.

Nutrient Content Per Serving

Calories	83.0
Protein	3.8 g
Carbohydrates	13.4 g
Fat – Total	2.5 g
Cholesterol	8.1 mg
Dietary Fiber	4.7 g
Sodium	68.8 mg

Percent of Calories

17% Protein
59% Carbohydrate
25% Fat

Fat Breakdown

Saturated Fat	1.3 g
Monounsaturated Fat	0.6 g
Polyunsaturated Fat	0.3 g

Spring Vegetables
Serves 4

1 tsp.	olive oil
2	onions, peeled, cut in large pieces
2	turnips, peeled, cut in large pieces
2 cups	carrots, peeled, cut in 1-inch pieces
2 med.	white potatoes, peeled, cut in small chunks
1½ cups	peas, frozen or fresh
1½ cups	fresh green beans
2 Tbl.	powdered butter replacement, mixed with ¼ cup hot water

Heat oil in a non-stick pan. Sauté onions for 1 minute. Add turnips and carrots, cook 3 minutes. Add potatoes, 1½ cups water, salt and pepper to taste and cook on medium low for 8 minutes covered. Add peas and green beans and cook 5 minutes. Heat powdered butter replacement and pour over vegetables. Garnish with chervil.

Garnish:

6 branches	fresh chervil

Cook's Note: May use either fresh or frozen peas and green beans. If using fresh, increase the cooking time by 10 minutes. Serve vegetables with fish or meat.

Nutrient Content Per Serving

Calories	230.0
Protein	7.6 g
Carbohydrates	51.1 g
Fat – Total	0.6 g
Cholesterol	0.1 mg
Dietary Fiber	9.7 g
Sodium	165.0 mg

Percent of Calories

13% Protein
85% Carbohydrate
 2% Fat

Fat Breakdown

Saturated Fat	0.1 g
Monounsaturated Fat	0.0 g
Polyunsaturated Fat	0.3 g

STEAMED VEGETABLES WITH A LIGHT SAUCE
Serves 4

4 sm.	white potatoes, peeled	
4	scallions	
2½ cups	cauliflower, flowers	
2	fennel bulbs, quartered	
4	tomatoes	
4½ cups	fresh spinach leaves, deveined	

Cut all vegetables into bite-size pieces. Steam potatoes and scallions for 15 minutes. Add cauliflower and fennel to steam pot, cook for 5 minutes. Add tomatoes and spinach, cook for 5 minutes. May be served hot or room temperature.

Sauce:

½ bunch	watercress, de-stemmed
1 sprig	parsley, de-stemmed
1 sprig	chervil
6 oz.	nonfat yogurt, plain, drained
6 oz.	sour cream, nonfat
½	lemon, juice of
2 tsp.	olive oil
to taste	salt and pepper

Sauce:
Combine watercress and parsley, wrap in aluminum foil. Add to steamer for 3 minutes. Remove. Purée with chervil. Whisk herbs into yogurt and sour cream. Add lemon juice, olive oil, salt and pepper to taste. Pass the sauce on the side.

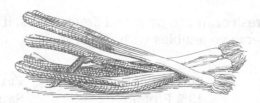

Nutrient Content Per Serving

Calories	280.0
Protein	13.9 g
Carbohydrates	54.8 g
Fat – Total	3.5 g
Cholesterol	0.8 mg
Dietary Fiber	12.3 g
Sodium	219.0 mg

Percent of Calories

18% Protein
72% Carbohydrate
10% Fat

Fat Breakdown

Saturated Fat	0.5 g
Monounsaturated Fat	1.8 g
Polyunsaturated Fat	0.6 g

ZUCCHINI AU GRATIN
Serves 4

4 cups	zucchini or summer squash, sliced thin
1 tsp.	olive oil
1	onion, sliced thin
2 Tbl.	water
to taste	white pepper

Garnish:

1 Tbl.	parmesan cheese, grated
pinch	paprika

Cook's Note: Quick and easy.

In a non-stick pan, heat oil over medium heat. Sauté onion until translucent. Add remaining ingredients and cook until zucchini is barely tender (about 10 minutes.) Turn occasionally with a spatula to cook evenly. Garnish with cheese and paprika. Serve at once.

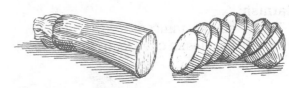

Nutrient Content Per Serving

Calories	53.5
Protein	2.5 g
Carbohydrates	8.1 g
Fat – Total	1.9 g
Cholesterol	1.2 mg
Dietary Fiber	2.0 g
Sodium	32.5 mg

Percent of Calories

17% Protein
54% Carbohydrate
29% Fat

Fat Breakdown

Saturated Fat	0.5 g
Monounsaturated Fat	1.0 g
Polyunsaturated Fat	0.2 g

ZUCCHINI AND POTATO GRATIN
Serves 6

1 lb.	zucchini, sliced thin
1 lb.	potatoes, peeled, sliced thin
1 tsp.	olive oil
1 clove	garlic, minced
¼ cup	chicken stock *(see p. 538)*
1 tsp.	thyme
1 tsp.	powdered butter replacement
to taste	salt and pepper

Garnish:

1 Tbl.	chives, minced
2 oz.	parmesan cheese, grated

Prepare a casserole dish with cooking spray. Alternate slices of potato and zucchini in casserole.

To prepare sauce:
Combine oil, garlic, stock, thyme, powdered butter replacement and salt and pepper to taste. Pour over vegetables. Bake, uncovered, at 350° F for 40 minutes. When stock evaporates, add chives and garnish with parmesan. Cook 2 minutes.

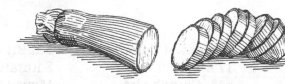

Nutrient Content Per Serving

Calories	146.0
Protein	6.8 g
Carbohydrates	22.0 g
Fat – Total	3.8 g
Cholesterol	7.4 mg
Dietary Fiber	2.5 g
Sodium	220.0 mg

Percent of Calories

18% Protein
59% Carbohydrate
23% Fat

Fat Breakdown

Saturated Fat	2.0 g
Monounsaturated Fat	1.4 g
Polyunsaturated Fat	0.2 g

DIJON VINAIGRETTE
Yields ½ cup

1 Tbl.	dijon-style mustard
2 Tbl.	red wine vinegar
1 Tbl.	olive oil
¼ cup	water
to taste	salt and pepper
to taste	fresh ground black pepper

Combine all ingredients until smooth.

% Calories as Fat — Above the HM✓ guidelines: Although this recipe has a high percentage of calories as fat (>30%), the total fat is less than 5 grams per serving. This will easily fit within your allotment of 45 grams per day. This happens most often in low-calorie recipes.

Nutrient Content
Per 2 Tablespoons

Calories	33.8
Protein	0.2 g
Carbohydrates	0.7 g
Fat – Total	3.6 g
Cholesterol	0.0 mg
Dietary Fiber	0.1 g
Sodium	49.0 mg

Percent of Calories

2% Protein
8% Carbohydrate
90% Fat

Fat Breakdown

Saturated Fat	0.5 g
Monounsaturated Fat	2.6 g
Polyunsaturated Fat	0.3 g

BLACK FOREST CREPES
Serves 8

1 recipe	dessert crepe batter *(see p. 190)*	Prepare crepes according to recipe.

Filling:

30 oz.	sweet dark cherries, pitted, drained (save juice)
¼ cup	powdered sugar
2 Tbl.	cornstarch
¾ cup	cherry juice
½ cup	amaretto
1 cup	fat-free sour cream
1 oz.	semi-sweet chocolate, grated

In a small saucepan, combine powdered sugar and cornstarch. Add cherry juice, amaretto and cherries. Cook until thickened. Fill crepes. Top with dollop of sour cream and grated chocolate.

Cook's Note: May use fresh or frozen cherries. Avoid the canned variety because they are packed in syrup and add unnecessary calories. Use the juice from thawing the cherries, instead.

Alcohol Note: The alcohol content was computed prior to cooking. Once the alcohol is heated to the boiling point, the alcohol disappears along with most of the calories from the alcohol.

Nutrient Content Per Crepe		Percent of Calories	Fat Breakdown	
Calories	253.0	11% Protein	Saturated Fat	1.0 g
Protein	7.4 g	70% Carbohydrate	Monounsaturated Fat	0.8 g
Carbohydrates	46.4 g	9% Fat	Polyunsaturated Fat	0.6 g
Fat – Total	2.8 g	10% Alcohol		
Cholesterol	0.8 mg			
Dietary Fiber	1.8 g			
Sodium	70.4 mg			

CREPES GRAND MARNIER
Serves 8

1 recipe   dessert crepes *(see p. 190)*
(see p. 190)
           (substitute Grand Marnier for
           vanilla and use orange zest)

Filling:

1 cup	skim milk
¼ cup	egg substitute
1 Tbl.	sugar
1 Tbl.	flour
4 Tbl.	Grand Marnier
4	egg whites
1 Tbl.	powdered sugar
1	orange, zest of

Prepare crepes according to recipe.

Heat milk in the top of a double boiler. In a bowl combine egg substitute, sugar and flour. Add to milk. Heat, whisking constantly until mixture thickens (about 20 minutes). Add Grand Marnier. Let cool. Preheat oven to 450° F.

Beat egg whites until stiff. Fold into egg mixture. Fill crepes (just fold in half). Place crepes in a baking dish prepared with cooking spray. Bake 4-5 minutes. Sprinkle with powdered sugar and orange zest.

Cook's Note: May substitute orange juice for Grand Marnier.

Alcohol Note: The alcohol content was computed prior to cooking. Once the alcohol is heated to the boiling point, the alcohol disappears along with most of the calories from the alcohol.

Nutrient Content Per Serving

Calories	147.0
Protein	9.0 g
Carbohydrates	21.1 g
Fat – Total	1.7 g
Cholesterol	28.0 mg
Dietary Fiber	0.5 g
Sodium	142.0 mg

Percent of Calories

25%	Protein
59%	Carbohydrate
11%	Fat
5%	Alcohol

Fat Breakdown

Saturated Fat	0.4 g
Monounsaturated Fat	0.5 g
Polyunsaturated Fat	0.5 g

FRENCH CREAM CREPES WITH RASPBERRY SAUCE
Serves 6
Yield: 2 cups filling
Makes 12 crepes

1 recipe	dessert crepe batter *(see p. 190)*

Filling:

2 cups	skim milk
2 sticks	cinnamon
1	vanilla bean
½ cup	egg substitute
1 tsp.	powdered butter replacement
½ cup	sugar
½ cup	flour

Raspberry sauce:

2 10-oz. pkgs.	frozen raspberries, thawed
2 Tbl.	cornstarch
1 Tbl.	sugar

Prepare crepes according to recipe.

Add vanilla bean and cinnamon sticks to milk. Scald milk by heating over low heat for 15 minutes. Let cool. In a bowl, beat egg substitute. Add powdered butter replacement, sugar and flour while beating. Add cooled milk. Transfer to the top of a double boiler. Cook until thickened, stirring constantly. Cool. Fill crepes. Chill until ready to serve.

Thaw raspberries. In a pan, combine cornstarch and sugar. Add raspberries including juice. Heat until thick. Cool. Spoon over crepes just prior to serving.

Nutrient Content Per 2 Crepes		Percent of Calories	Fat Breakdown	
Calories	472.0	14% Protein	Saturated Fat	0.6 g
Protein	17.0 g	81% Carbohydrate	Monounsaturated Fat	0.5 g
Carbohydrates	95.6 g	5% Fat	Polyunsaturated Fat	1.0 g
Fat – Total	2.4 g			
Cholesterol	3.6 mg			
Dietary Fiber	5.6 g			
Sodium	169.0 mg			

PEACH CREPES
Serves 8

1 recipe	dessert crepe batter *(see p. 190)*

Filling:

½ cup	mandarin oranges, save juice for syrup
¾ cup	skimmed evaporated canned milk
⅛ cup	nonfat dry milk
1 lb.	peaches, sliced thin or 1 16-oz. bag frozen, sliced peaches
1 Tbl.	powdered butter replacement
2 tsp.	vanilla

Prepare crepes according to recipe.

Purée mandarin oranges until smooth. In a saucepan, heat all filling ingredients including reserved orange syrup. Fill crepes, garnish and serve.

Cook's Note: Serve with low-calorie syrup or sprinkled with powdered sugar. May also be served with a dollop of fat-free sour cream. Garnish with peach slices, if desired.

Nutrient Content Per Serving		**Percent of Calories**	**Fat Breakdown**	
Calories	227.0	21% Protein	Saturated Fat	0.3 g
Protein	11.6 g	75% Carbohydrate	Monounsaturated Fat	0.2 g
Carbohydrates	42.6 g	4% Fat	Polyunsaturated Fat	0.4 g
Fat – Total	1.1 g			
Cholesterol	3.3 mg			
Dietary Fiber	1.9 g			
Sodium	127.0 mg			

FRUIT PACKAGES
Serves 6

1	cantaloupe
1½ cups	raspberries
1 cup	currants
1 cup	strawberries

Sauce:

½ cup	strawberries
2 Tbl.	cream cheese, fat-free
¼ cup	sugar
⅛ tsp.	almond extract

Using a melon baller scoop out melon. Wash and slice strawberries.

To prepare sauce:
Combine ½ cup of strawberries with cream cheese, sugar and almond extract in food processor. Process until smooth.

Make 6 aluminum foil pouches. Arrange cut fruit in pouches. Drizzle sauce over fruit and close pouches. Place packets in steamer. Cover and steam for 5 minutes. Serve hot in individual pouches.

Cook's Note: May use any fruit you choose.

Nutrient Content Per Serving		**Percent of Calories**	**Fat Breakdown**	
Calories	109.0	10% Protein	Saturated Fat	0.1 g
Protein	2.9 g	85% Carbohydrate	Monounsaturated Fat	0.1 g
Carbohydrates	25.0 g	5% Fat	Polyunsaturated Fat	0.3 g
Fat – Total	0.6 g			
Cholesterol	1.7 mg			
Dietary Fiber	4.4 g			
Sodium	65.5 mg			

Melon Baskets
Serves 4

2 lg.	cantaloupes
6	peaches
1 oz.	sweet white wine
1	lemon, juice of
2 Tbl.	peach liquor
1 cup	strawberries, leave whole
4 tsp.	almonds, sliced and toasted
	mint leaves

Cut melons in half and scoop out using melon baller. Cut outside edges in zig-zags. Reserve ⅓ of melon balls and freeze remaining melon balls for 1 hour. In a separate bowl, slice peaches and freeze 1 hour.

To make cantaloupe ice:
Put frozen cantaloupe in food processor. Add wine and purée.

To make peach ice:
Put frozen peaches in food processor. Add lemon juice, peach liquor and purée.

Transfer 1 scoop of each ice into melon bowl. Top with remaining melon balls, strawberries, almonds and mint. Serve immediately or may chill in freezer for 10-15 minutes.

Cook's Note: May use frozen peaches or nectarines when fresh peaches are out of season.

Alcohol Note: The alcohol content was computed prior to cooking. Once the alcohol is heated to the boiling point, the alcohol disappears along with most of the calories from the alcohol.

Nutrient Content Per Serving		**Percent of Calories**	**Fat Breakdown**	
Calories	257.0	7% Protein	Saturated Fat	0.3 g
Protein	5.2 g	77% Carbohydrate	Monounsaturated Fat	1.2 g
Carbohydrates	55.4 g	9% Fat	Polyunsaturated Fat	0.8 g
Fat – Total	2.9 g	7% Alcohol		
Cholesterol	0.0 mg			
Dietary Fiber	6.2 g			
Sodium	59.7 mg			

NECTARINES WITH RED WINE SAUCE

Serves 4

6	nectarines
2½ cups	red wine
⅓ cup	sugar
2 Tbl.	cognac
1	vanilla bean, cut in 2 pieces
4	black peppercorns
1 stick	cinnamon
2	cloves
4	cardamon seeds

Garnish:

2 Tbl.	currants (optional)
1 branch	rosemary
1 branch	mint leaves

Blanch fresh nectarines 1 minute. Remove skin. Quarter and remove pits. In a saucepan, combine wine, sugar, cognac, vanilla bean, peppercorns, cinnamon, cloves and cardamon. Bring to a boil, then reduce to low heat. Add nectarines, cook 5 minutes. Drain and reserve juice. Discard spices from juice and chill in a serving dish. Arrange fruits in juice. Serve chilled. May garnish with currants, rosemary and mint.

Cook's Note: May use frozen peaches or nectarines if desired.

Alcohol Note: The alcohol content was computed prior to cooking. Once the alcohol is heated to the boiling point, the alcohol disappears along with most of the calories from the alcohol.

Nutrient Content Per Serving

Calories	286.0
Protein	2.2 g
Carbohydrates	42.9 g
Fat – Total	0.9 g
Cholesterol	0.0 mg
Dietary Fiber	3.9 g
Sodium	7.6 mg

Percent of Calories

3% Protein
57% Carbohydrate
3% Fat
37% Alcohol

Fat Breakdown

Saturated Fat	0.2 g
Monounsaturated Fat	0.3 g
Polyunsaturated Fat	0.5 g

WINE POACHED PEARS
Serves 6

6	bartlett pears, whole
2 cups	red wine
2 Tbl.	lemon juice
½ cup	sugar
3 Tbl.	Grand Marnier
½ tsp.	vanilla extract
2	cloves, whole
½ tsp.	cinnamon

Garnish:

fresh mint leaves

Using a metal potato peeler, remove core starting from the bottom of pear, but leave stems attached. Place pears in a saucepan, in a single layer. Add remaining ingredients. Slowly bring to a boil. Reduce heat, cover and simmer 20 minutes.

Arrange pears in a serving dish. Pour cooking liquid over the top. Let cool. Place in refrigerator to chill. Baste from time to time while chilling. Serve chilled. Garnish with fresh mint leaves, if desired.

Alcohol Note: The alcohol content was computed prior to cooking. Once the alcohol is heated to the boiling point, the alcohol disappears along with most of the calories from the alcohol.

Nutrient Content Per Serving

Calories	234.0
Protein	0.8 g
Carbohydrates	45.2 g
Fat – Total	0.7 g
Cholesterol	0.0 mg
Dietary Fiber	5.1 g
Sodium	4.4 mg

Percent of Calories

1% Protein
73% Carbohydrate
2% Fat
23% Alcohol

Fat Breakdown

Saturated Fat	0.0 g
Monounsaturated Fat	0.1 g
Polyunsaturated Fat	0.2 g

APPLE MOUSSE
Serves 8

2 Tbl.	slivered almonds
8 med.	sweet apples, peeled and chopped
2 Tbl.	apricot preserves
3 Tbl.	rum
4	egg whites
pinch	salt
1 tsp.	sugar

Sauce:

2 Tbl.	sugar
2	tart apples, sliced

Toast the almonds in a toaster oven or on a dry non-stick frying pan.

In a non-stick frying pan, cook the chopped apples and apricot preserves until soft. Remove from heat. Purée in a food processor until smooth. Let cool. Stir in rum.

Beat egg whites until foamy. Add salt and sugar and continue beating until stiff. Fold egg whites into puréed apples. Pour into serving dishes and chill.

To prepare the sauce:
In a medium frying pan, heat the sugar until it melts. Add apple slices and toasted almonds. Stir until coated. Top chilled mousse with hot caramelized apples. Serve at once.

Alcohol Note: The alcohol content was computed prior to cooking. Once the alcohol is heated to the boiling point, the alcohol disappears along with most of the calories from the alcohol.

Nutrient Content Per Serving

Calories	153.0
Protein	2.5 g
Carbohydrates	31.6 g
Fat – Total	1.6 g
Cholesterol	0.0 mg
Dietary Fiber	3.4 g
Sodium	163.0 mg

Percent of Calories

6% Protein
77% Carbohydrate
9% Fat
8% Alcohol

Fat Breakdown

Saturated Fat	0.2 g
Monounsaturated Fat	0.7 g
Polyunsaturated Fat	0.4 g

CARAMEL BANANA PARFAIT
Serves 4

Sauce:

¾ cup	skim milk
1 Tbl.	powdered butter replacement
½ cup	brown sugar
½ tsp.	salt
¼ cup	nonfat dry milk
½ cup	egg substitute
1 tsp.	vanilla

Filling:

4	bananas, ripe

Caramel sauce:

Dissolve powdered milk in skim milk. Put all sauce ingredients in top of double boiler. Cook, whisking constantly until it thickens. Slice bananas lengthwise and cut in 1-inch pieces. Add bananas to sauce. Cook until heated through.

Layer in parfait glasses starting with nonfat vanilla frozen yogurt or nonfat vanilla ice cream and alternating with bananas. Serve immediately.

Cook's Note: Cut bananas when ready to add to sauce. They brown easily. Can be covered with orange juice or lemon juice to keep them from browning but the juice will change the flavor.

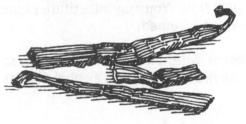

Nutrient Content Per Serving

Calories	246.0
Protein	9.2 g
Carbohydrates	51.8 g
Fat – Total	1.7 g
Cholesterol	2.6 mg
Dietary Fiber	2.2 g
Sodium	409.0 mg

Percent of Calories

14% Protein
80% Carbohydrate
 6% Fat

Fat Breakdown

Saturated Fat	0.5 g
Monounsaturated Fat	0.4 g
Polyunsaturated Fat	0.6 g

CHERRY FLAN
Serves 6

1 lb.	black cherries, pitted (may use fresh, canned or frozen)
¾ cup	all-purpose flour
½ cup	sugar
pinch	salt
¾ cup	egg substitute
¼ cup	cognac
1 tsp.	vanilla
2 cups	skim milk
2 Tbl.	powdered sugar

In a mixing bowl, blend together flour, sugar and salt. Add egg substitute. Add cognac, vanilla and milk and beat until smooth.

Prepare a deep 9-inch pie pan with butter-flavor cooking spray. Spread cherries on the bottom. Pour batter over cherries. Bake at 375° F for 60 minutes or until flan is browned, but still soft. Cool. Sprinkle top with powdered sugar.

Cook's Note: You may substitute plums, prunes, apricots or grapes for the cherries. Drain the cherries if canned.

Alcohol Note: The alcohol content was computed prior to cooking. Once the alcohol is heated to the boiling point, the alcohol disappears along with most of the calories from the alcohol.

Nutrient Content Per Serving

Calories	286.0
Protein	8.7 g
Carbohydrates	51.3 g
Fat – Total	4.4 g
Cholesterol	2.1 mg
Dietary Fiber	1.3 g
Sodium	280.0 mg

Percent of Calories

12% Protein
70% Carbohydrate
14% Fat
 4% Alcohol

Fat Breakdown

Saturated Fat	0.9 g
Monounsaturated Fat	1.0 g
Polyunsaturated Fat	2.2 g

CHERRY SOUFFLE
Serves 4

½ lb.	cherries, ripe, pitted
1 Tbl.	Kirsch
¼ cup	nonfat dry milk
1 cup	skim milk
½ cup	sugar
1 Tbl.	powdered butter replacement
½ cup	egg substitute
4	egg whites, room temperature
¼ tsp.	cream of tartar

Soak cherries in Kirsch. Prepare souffle pan with cooking spray. Sprinkle 1 tablespoon of sugar in souffle dish and shake it around. Preheat oven to 400° F.

Dissolve powdered milk in skim milk and heat. When milk is warm, add sugar and powdered butter replacement. Let cool. Add cherries and Kirsch. Whisk in egg substitute.

In a clean bowl, beat egg whites until stiff. Add cream of tartar. Fold cherry mixture into egg whites. Transfer to souffle pan and bake 30 minutes.

Cook's Note: Souffle falls quickly. Be ready to present the entire dish to the table. May also prepare individual souffle dishes. May use frozen cherries, packed without sugar. Thaw and drain before using. Kirsch is a cherry-flavored liqueur. May substitute orange-flavored liqueurs such as Grand Marnier or Triple Sec, if desired.

Alcohol Note: The alcohol content was computed prior to cooking. Once the alcohol is heated to the boiling point, the alcohol disappears along with most of the calories from the alcohol.

Nutrient Content Per Serving

Calories	332.0
Protein	20.9 g
Carbohydrates	57.6 g
Fat – Total	1.9 g
Cholesterol	7.3 mg
Dietary Fiber	0.7 g
Sodium	318.0 mg

Percent of Calories

- 25% Protein
- 69% Carbohydrate
- 5% Fat
- 1% Alcohol

Fat Breakdown

Saturated Fat	0.6 g
Monounsaturated Fat	0.5 g
Polyunsaturated Fat	0.7 g

PEACH GRATIN PARFAIT
Serves 8

Filling:

1 lb.   peaches, sliced

Sauce:

½ lb.   cream cheese, nonfat
2 Tbl.   brown sugar
½ tsp.   cinnamon

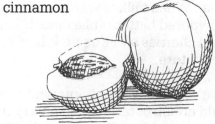

Combine cream cheese, cinnamon and brown sugar in food processor. Process until smooth. Chill.

Heat peaches in microwave. Layer peaches and sauce alternately in parfait glasses. Top with sauce.

To serve as crepes:
Layer peaches on crepe. Top with cream cheese mixture. Fold in packets. Arrange in a baking dish prepared with cooking spray. Bake 20 minutes at 300° F.

Cook's Note: May substitute mangos, nectarines, bananas or apricots. Liqueur flavors may be used in place of cinnamon.

Nutrient Content Per Serving		**Percent of Calories**	**Fat Breakdown**	
Calories	168.0	24% Protein	Saturated Fat	0.4 g
Protein	10.0 g	68% Carbohydrate	Monounsaturated Fat	0.4 g
Carbohydrates	27.9 g	8% Fat	Polyunsaturated Fat	0.4 g
Fat – Total	1.4 g			
Cholesterol	32.4 mg			
Dietary Fiber	1.3 g			
Sodium	264.0 mg			

RASPBERRY MERINGUE
Serves 4

1 lb.	raspberries
3 lg	graham crackers
2 Tbl.	currant jelly
3	egg whites
½ cup	sugar
¼ tsp.	cream of tartar
1 tsp.	vanilla
1 Tbl.	powdered sugar

Prepare a round 9-inch baking dish with butter-flavor cooking spray. Crush graham crackers and cover bottom of baking dish. Mix raspberries with the currant jelly. Arrange raspberries over the crumbs.

To prepare meringue:
Beat egg whites until they form stiff peaks. While beating, add sugar, cream of tartar and vanilla. Spoon meringue over raspberries and sprinkle powdered sugar on top. Bake at 300° F for 20 minutes or until meringue begins to brown. Garnish with a mint sprig.

Cook's Note: A nice dessert after a fish dinner.

Nutrient Content Per Serving

Calories	218.0
Protein	4.1 g
Carbohydrates	50.1 g
Fat – Total	1.2 g
Cholesterol	0.0 mg
Dietary Fiber	5.5 g
Sodium	76.4 mg

Percent of Calories
7% Protein
88% Carbohydrate
5% Fat

Fat Breakdown

Saturated Fat	0.2 g
Monounsaturated Fat	0.3 g
Polyunsaturated Fat	0.4 g

FRENCH CREAM MERINGUE TARTS
Serves 12

1 recipe   French Cream *(see p. 266)*

9   egg whites, room temperature
¾ tsp.   cream of tartar
1⅛ cups   sugar

½ recipe   Raspberry Sauce *(see p. 266)*

Preheat oven to 200° F. Line baking sheets with parchment paper. Secure paper.

In a clean glass mixing bowl, beat egg whites until foamy. Gradually add cream of tartar and sugar. Beat until stiff peaks form.

Spread mixture into 24 circles (like pancakes) on the parchment paper. Bake for 3 hours. Turn oven off and let meringue shells sit in the oven for 12 hours. Remove from paper.

Prepare french cream. Chill.

To assemble: Place a meringue on a serving dish. Cover with a thick layer of french cream. Cover with another meringue. Top with raspberry topping.

Cook's Note: A beautiful, colorful presentation. May use any fruit sauce you desire.

Nutrient Content Per Serving

Calories	189.0
Protein	6.0 g
Carbohydrates	40.8 g
Fat – Total	0.5 g
Cholesterol	0.8 mg
Dietary Fiber	1.2 g
Sodium	83.0 mg

Percent of Calories

12%	Protein
85%	Carbohydrate
2%	Fat

Fat Breakdown

Saturated Fat	0.1 g
Monounsaturated Fat	0.1 g
Polyunsaturated Fat	0.2 g

CHERRY CUSTARD CAKE
Serves 8

2 cups	sour cherries, pitted, frozen, or canned
1 cup	egg substitute
1½ cups	skim milk
½ cup	flour, sifted
¼ cup	sugar
1 Tbl.	vanilla extract
1 tsp.	brandy
	powdered sugar

Thaw cherries. Drain and reserve juice.

To prepare batter:
Combine egg substitute, milk, flour, sugar, vanilla and brandy. Blend with mixer at high speed for 1 minute. Scrape sides of bowl and continue to blend for another minute. Thoroughly coat an 8x8-inch baking dish with cooking spray. Pat the cherries dry and spread them evenly in the bottom of the baking pan. Slowly pour batter over cherries. Bake in a preheated 350° F oven for about 1½ hours. The cake is done when the batter has set to a custard-like consistency.

Let the cake cool in its pan until lukewarm. Run the flat edge of a knife around the sides of the pan to free the cake. Invert a large serving platter over the pan and grasping the pan and plate together turn them over. Lift off the pan. Dust the top of the cake with the powdered sugar and serve immediately.

Cook's Note: May make cherry juice to drink using the reserved juice. Sweeten the reserved cherry juice with corn syrup to desired taste. Chill, and serve as a beverage.

Nutrient Content Per Serving		**Percent of Calories**	**Fat Breakdown**	
Calories	117.0	22% Protein	Saturated Fat	0.3 g
Protein	6.4 g	66% Carbohydrate	Monounsaturated Fat	0.4 g
Carbohydrates	18.9 g	11% Fat	Polyunsaturated Fat	0.6 g
Fat – Total	1.4 g			
Cholesterol	1.1 mg			
Dietary Fiber	0.9 g			
Sodium	79.7 mg			

Red Aspic
Serves 6

2 cups	wine, blush
½ lb.	cherries, pitted
½ cup	currants
½ lb.	raspberries
½ lb.	strawberries
½ cup	sugar
1 pkg.	gelatin, plain, unflavored
1 sprig	fresh mint

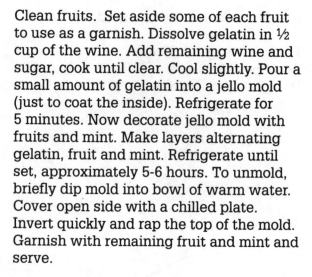

Clean fruits. Set aside some of each fruit to use as a garnish. Dissolve gelatin in ½ cup of the wine. Add remaining wine and sugar, cook until clear. Cool slightly. Pour a small amount of gelatin into a jello mold (just to coat the inside). Refrigerate for 5 minutes. Now decorate jello mold with fruits and mint. Make layers alternating gelatin, fruit and mint. Refrigerate until set, approximately 5-6 hours. To unmold, briefly dip mold into bowl of warm water. Cover open side with a chilled plate. Invert quickly and rap the top of the mold. Garnish with remaining fruit and mint and serve.

Cook's Note: May want to chill 5 minutes between layers.

Alcohol Note: The alcohol content was computed prior to cooking. Once the alcohol is heated to the boiling point, the alcohol disappears along with most of the calories from the alcohol.

Nutrient Content Per Serving		Percent of Calories	Fat Breakdown	
Calories	187.0	5% Protein	Saturated Fat	0.1 g
Protein	2.3 g	66% Carbohydrate	Monounsaturated Fat	0.1 g
Carbohydrates	32.4 g	3% Fat	Polyunsaturated Fat	0.3 g
Fat – Total	0.8 g	26% Alcohol		
Cholesterol	0.0 mg			
Dietary Fiber	3.9 g			
Sodium	7.0 mg			

ITALY

To see Italy is good, but to eat it and drink it is better.

Eat it in a crust of home-baked bread baptized with olive oil, in soft melon sweet and warmed by the sun, in the lake-laughing freshness of little poached scampi and in cheeses firm, soft, fresh, aged.

Drink it in its wines, in guileless white wines that dance across your palate and in brash, boasting reds with fetching bouquets.

At the Italian market, carts, stalls and shops brim over with breads, toys, leather goods, curios and fabrics all arranged in the confused way of gifts under a Christmas tree. A fruit vendor piles his pyramids of blood oranges. He halves the top ones to show their garnet flesh.

The cuisine of the Italian peninsula — its western side the longest Mediterranean coastline of any country — is the conjunction of the fruit of its plains, hills and seacoast.

The staples are rice, wheat and corn. The flavors come from a myriad of fishes and cheeses, vegetables of every stripe, wines (no other country in the world produces more), mushrooms, herbs and fruits.

This predominance has a long history.

The Roman historian Juvenal said that the Romans were enamored of two things: "their bread and their circuses." Indeed, the conquest of other nations — especially in North Africa — traces the Romans' near lust for wheat and the necessity of procuring additional lands on which to grow it. What is today Tunisia was ancient Carthage and was called, after its conquest by Rome, "the bread-basket of the Empire."

The Roman development of wheat flour, as distinct from the use of barley flour, and the making of that flour into bread, is a Roman legacy felt today.

▼ THE ITALIAN TABLE

You will find the most elaborate and the most simple preparations side by side on most restaurant menus. Native home cookery is plain, pleasant and delicious. All revolves around the kitchen and its soups, vegetables and pasta.

Oh, the pasta. It is possible to eat five different sorts of pasta, prepared five different ways, in and for one meal: steaming bowls of pasta e fagioli; thick-ribboned linguine with a sauce enriched with calamari; spirals of fusilli with asparagus spears and broccoli florets; and ribbed penne with basil and sage. An Italian meal most often ends in cheese and fruit, not much else. At the end of the meal, too, come the bottles of vin santo, some biscotti and much conversation. Always conversation.

One evening at dinner, a friend left the table to step outside for a moment. One at a time, the waiters would come out the door to see if he was all right. No Italian would consider separating himself from the table at the end of a meal.

Bill St. John
Food and Wine Editor
Rocky Mountain News

TABLE OF CONTENTS

TABLE OF CONTENTS

— MOST COMMONLY USED ITEMS FOR ITALIAN RECIPES —

▼ **FRESH SUPPLIES**
anchovy paste
basil
garlic
lemons
parmesan cheese
parsley
scallions
shallots
thyme
tomatoes

▼ **PANTRY SUPPLIES**
artichokes
beans, white

bread crumbs
powdered butter replacement
Marsala wine
olive oil
olives, black
oregano
pasta
pepper, fresh ground black
semolina flour
tomato paste
tomatoes, canned
tomatoes, sun-dried
vinegar, balsamic
vinegar, red wine
wine, dry white

— MENU SUGGESTIONS —

▼ **CASUAL DINING**
Minestrone
Lemon Chicken Scallopini
Risotto
Cherry Ice

▼ **FORMAL**
Reception
Marinated Mushrooms
Tomato Canapes
Baked Oysters
Grilled Vegetable Salad
Baby Clam Soup served with Pesto Bread
Seared Veal Chop with Rosemary Garlic
Fancy Polenta
Marinated Carrots
Sicilian Cassata with Semi-Sweet Chocolate
    Frosting

▼ **SUMMER DINING**
Artichoke Alioli with Steamed Artichoke
    Leaves
Creamy Pepper Soup
Rainbow Trout with Mushrooms
Spinach Gnocchi
Sauteed Zucchini
Strawberries with Red Wine

▼ **WINTER DINING**
Baked Oysters
Lentil Soup
Warm Foccacia
Beef Slices in Wine
Chocolate Amaretto Budino

▼ **QUICK BUT AUTHENTIC**
Zuppa Pizzialo
Grilled Swordfish Salad
Peach Ice

Vegetable Antipasto Platter
Serves 4

8	scallions
16	radishes
8	pimento-stuffed olives
8	pickled peppers
8	carrot sticks
8	celery sticks
8	cauliflower flowerettes
8	button mushrooms
8	thin slices part-skim mozzarella (4 oz. total)

Cut all items decoratively and arrange on a serving platter. Serve with fresh Italian bread.

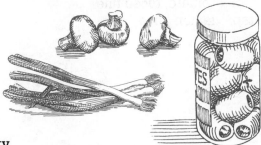

Cook's Note: May add a lowfat potted cheese for variety.

% Calories as Fat — This recipe is above the HealthMark recommendation of 30% calories as fat. The majority of the fat is from the mozzarella.

Nutrient Content Per Serving

Calories	140.0
Protein	9.7 g
Carbohydrate	14.1 g
Fat – Total	6.0 g
Cholesterol	16.4 mg
Dietary Fiber	4.0 g
Sodium	398.0 mg

Percent of Calories

26% Protein
38% Carbohydrate
36% Fat

Fat Breakdown

Saturated Fat	3.1 g
Monounsaturated Fat	1.9 g
Polyunsaturated Fat	0.5 g

ARTICHOKE AGLIO
Serves 4

4	fresh artichokes
6 Tbl.	fat-free mayonnaise
1 tsp.	olive oil
4 Tbl.	tomato, diced fine
2 tsp.	lemon juice

Neatly trim spikes from artichoke leaves. Cut off stem so artichoke will sit flat. Steam artichokes until tender, approximately 15 minutes.

Whip together mayonnaise, olive oil and lemon juice.

To serve:
Remove the artichoke leaves and fan to the outside of the plate making a flower. Scoop out the choke from the middle of the artichoke. Place a dollop of the mayonnaise mixture on the artichoke bottom. Garnish with diced tomato.

Cook's Note: May substitute white wine for the olive oil if you choose. May use as a vegetable accompaniment to a meal. This is a nice twist to plain high-fat drawn butter with a fresh artichoke. May increase the alioli and use large artichokes to serve as a vegetable dish. When arranged on a pretty plate, this is a beautiful sight.

Nutrient Content Per Serving

Calories	89.0
Protein	4.3 g
Carbohydrates	18.1 g
Fat – Total	1.4 g
Cholesterol	0.0 mg
Dietary Fiber	6.4 g
Sodium	369.0 mg

Percent of Calories

17% Protein
71% Carbohydrate
12% Fat

Fat Breakdown

Saturated Fat	0.2 g
Monounsaturated Fat	0.8 g
Polyunsaturated Fat	0.2 g

ARTICHOKE DIP
Serves 8

2 cups	1% fat cottage cheese
⅓ cup	nonfat plain yogurt, drained
1½ tsp.	fresh lemon juice
2 Tbl.	fresh parsley, chopped
2 cloves	garlic, minced
2 tsp.	onion powder
1 14-oz. can	artichoke hearts
1 10-oz. can	water chestnuts, drained
¼ cup	parmesan cheese, grated
to taste	salt

Squeeze all liquid from artichokes. Combine all ingredients in a food processor. Process until smooth. Serve with raw vegetables for dippers.

Cook's Note: It looks very nice served in a purple cabbage bowl. This has a milk flavor. You may substitute fat-free sour cream for the yogurt but the calories will increase. You may also change the flavor by including some nonfat cream cheese, or substitute the nonfat cream cheese for part of the cottage cheese.

To drain yogurt: Place a cheese cloth or coffee filter in a sieve or colander. Set colander over a bowl. Pour yogurt into the cheesecloth. Cover with plastic wrap. Place in the refrigerator. Let drain at least 4 hours (overnight is better).

Nutrient Content Per Serving		Percent of Calories	Fat Breakdown	
Calories	113.0	38% Protein	Saturated Fat	1.0 g
Protein	11.1 g	49% Carbohydrate	Monounsaturated Fat	0.5 g
Carbohydrates	14.4 g	13% Fat	Polyunsaturated Fat	0.1 g
Fat – Total	1.7 g			
Cholesterol	5.3 mg			
Dietary Fiber	4.0 g			
Sodium	340.0 mg			

ARTICHOKE SPREAD
Serves 12

2 cans	artichoke hearts, rinsed and drained
¾ cup	parmesan cheese, grated
1 cup	fat-free mayonnaise
1 clove	garlic, minced
¼ tsp.	garlic powder
¼ tsp.	paprika

Squeeze all liquid from artichokes. Place all ingredients except paprika in a food processor. Process until smooth. Transfer to a shallow baking dish. Sprinkle top with paprika. Bake at 350° F for 20 minutes. Serve hot with lowfat crackers, melba rounds or bread rounds.

Nutrient Content Per Serving

Calories	68.4
Protein	3.9 g
Carbohydrates	9.8 g
Fat – Total	2.0 g
Cholesterol	4.9 mg
Dietary Fiber	3.4 g
Sodium	379.0 mg

Percent of Calories

22% Protein
54% Carbohydrate
25% Fat

Fat Breakdown

Saturated Fat	1.2 g
Monounsaturated Fat	0.6 g
Polyunsaturated Fat	0.1 g

CHEESY ARTICHOKES
Makes 6 appetizers

12-16   baby fresh artichokes
        (2 inches diameter)
4 oz.   cream cheese, nonfat
¼ cup   fresh chives, chopped
2 Tbl.   powdered butter replacement
⅓ cup   parmesan cheese, grated

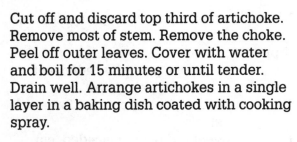

Cut off and discard top third of artichoke. Remove most of stem. Remove the choke. Peel off outer leaves. Cover with water and boil for 15 minutes or until tender. Drain well. Arrange artichokes in a single layer in a baking dish coated with cooking spray.

In a food processor, blend cream cheese, chives and powdered butter replacement. Fill artichokes with this mixture. Sprinkle evenly with parmesan cheese. Bake in the serving dish at 375° F for 20-25 minutes or until topping is golden.

Cook's Note: This makes a beautiful presentation. May also be used as the vegetable dish if served with a grilled fish or chicken entrée.

Nutrient Content Per Serving

Calories	67.9
Protein	6.0 g
Carbohydrates	7.0 g
Fat – Total	1.8 g
Cholesterol	7.7 mg
Dietary Fiber	2.6 g
Sodium	264.0 mg

Percent of Calories

35% Protein
41% Carbohydrate
23% Fat

Fat Breakdown

Saturated Fat	1.1 g
Monounsaturated Fat	0.5 g
Polyunsaturated Fat	0.1 g

HOT VEGETABLES WITH ANCHOVY-GARLIC DIP
Serves 8

1 head   romaine lettuce, separate leaves

Dippers:
1   cucumber, peeled, seeded, cut
              into 2x½-inch strips
2   carrots, peeled, cut into 2x½-inch
              strips
1   sweet red pepper, seeded, cut
              into 2x½-inch strips
1   green bell pepper, seeded, cut
              into 2x½-inch strips
4 stalks celery, cut into 2x½-inch strips
1 bunch scallions, leave whole
12   cherry tomatoes
¼ lb.   fresh mushrooms, cut into bite-
              size pieces
1 pkg.   plain Italian bread sticks

Dip:
2 cups   skim evaporated milk
½ cup   nonfat dry milk
1 tsp.   olive oil
8   flat anchovies, rinsed, finely
              chopped
2 tsp.   cornstarch
1 tsp.   garlic, minced
1 tsp.   red pepper flakes

Line a serving dish with lettuce leaves.
Arrange dippers on top. Serve bread sticks
on a separate plate or basket.

To prepare dip:
Heat olive oil in a non-stick pan over
medium-low heat. Gently sauté garlic and
anchovies. Blend in cornstarch. Dissolve
nonfat dry milk in skim milk. Add milk
mixture and stir until thickened. Serve
warm (preferably in a warming dish) with
cold vegetables.

Cook's Note: Other vegetables that may be used include fennel, broccoli, cauliflower or
radishes.

Nutrient Content Per Serving		Percent of Calories	Fat Breakdown	
Calories	176.0	25% Protein	Saturated Fat	0.4 g
Protein	11.2 g	65% Carbohydrate	Monounsaturated Fat	0.8 g
Carbohydrates	29.4 g	10% Fat	Polyunsaturated Fat	0.5 g
Fat – Total	1.9 g			
Cholesterol	6.9 mg			
Dietary Fiber	2.8 g			
Sodium	380.0 mg			

CAPONATA
Serves 8

2	whole eggplants, peeled, cubed in ½-inch cubes
3 cups	Italian plum tomatoes, chopped
1 lg.	onion, chopped
1 cup	mushrooms, chopped
1 sm.	zucchini, cubed, not peeled
2 Tbl.	capers, rinsed and drained
¼ cup	black olives, sliced thin
3 cloves	garlic, minced
½ tsp.	olive oil
1 Tbl.	anchovy paste
¼ cup	red wine vinegar
1½ tsp.	sugar
½ tsp.	thyme
4 Tbl.	fresh basil, chopped
2 Tbl.	fresh parsley, chopped
2 Tbl.	pine nuts
to taste	salt

Heat tomatoes in a non-stick pan. Mash as they cook.

Meanwhile, coat a large baking dish with non-stick cooking spray. Put eggplant in baking dish. Add onion, mushrooms, zucchini, capers and olives.

Sauté garlic in olive oil. Add anchovy paste, vinegar and sugar. Toss with the vegetables. Cover baking dish. Bake at 350° F for 1½ hours, stirring every 30 minutes. It is finished when vegetables are tender and fragrant. Allow to cool. Add thyme, basil, parsley and pine nuts. Place in a serving dish. Cover and refrigerate. Serve with lowfat crackers, melba toast or bread rounds.

Cook's Note: This is a very traditional Italian appetizer. It makes a great accompaniment to most Italian entrées. For a different twist you may add one small can of water-packed tuna.

Nutrient Content Per Serving

Calories	66.5
Protein	2.5 g
Carbohydrates	11.2 g
Fat – Total	2.3 g
Cholesterol	1.3 mg
Dietary Fiber	2.9 g
Sodium	149.0 mg

Percent of Calories

- 13% Protein
- 59% Cargohydrate
- 28% Fat

Fat Breakdown

Saturated Fat	0.4 g
Monounsaturated Fat	1.2 g
Polyunsaturated Fat	0.6 g

TOMATO BRUSCHETTA
Serves 8

1 loaf   Italian bread
2 lg.   cloves garlic, minced
2 tsp.   olive oil
2   tomatoes
2 Tbl.   fresh basil

Slice bread in 1-inch thick slices. Place bread slices on a baking sheet. Combine the garlic and olive oil. Using a pastry brush, spread the olive oil over the bread slices. Grill under the broiler until the bread begins to brown around the edges. Purée the tomatoes and basil. Spread on bread. Broil 1 minute until warmed. Serve immediately.

Variations: (To use in place of tomatoes or in addition)
- Canned tomatoes, drained
- Chopped olives
- Roasted peppers
- Chopped artichokes
- May substitute shallots for garlic
- Add oregano
- Top with ½ oz. lowfat mozzarella cheese

Cook's Note: May add pesto, but that will increase the fat content.

Nutrient Content Per Serving		**Percent of Calories**	**Fat Breakdown**	
Calories	180.0	13% Protein	Saturated Fat	0.7 g
Protein	5.6 g	71% Carbohydrate	Monounsaturated Fat	1.3 g
Carbohydrates	31.7 g	17% Fat	Polyunsaturated Fat	1.0 g
Fat – Total	3.3 g			
Cholesterol	0.0 mg			
Dietary Fiber	2.0 g			
Sodium	353.0 mg			

TOMATO AND ROASTED PEPPER CROSTINI
Serves 4

1 loaf	Italian bread
1 tsp.	olive oil
2 cloves	garlic
2 lg.	yellow peppers, roasted, sliced julienne
¼ cup	black olives, sliced
4	plum tomatoes, sliced lengthwise, very thin
1 Tbl.	capers, chopped
1 Tbl.	fresh basil, chopped

Slice bread in 1-inch slices. Combine olive oil, garlic, basil and capers. Lightly brush oil mixture onto the bread. It will seem like it is barely enough. Broil bread until it starts to brown (about 1-2 minutes). Arrange peppers, tomatoes and olives on top. Broil 3-5 minutes. Serve hot.

Variations:
- Sun-dried tomatoes and bell peppers
- Tomato relish *(see p. 550)*

Cook's Note: These long slices can be difficult to handle, so you may want to slice into rounds. This is a fun dish for a party.

Nutrient Content Per Serving

Calories	368.0
Protein	11.6 g
Carbohydrates	66.6 g
Fat – Total	6.4 g
Cholesterol	0.0 mg
Dietary Fiber	4.3 g
Sodium	755.0 mg

Percent of Calories

13% Protein	
72% Carbohydrate	
16% Fat	

Fat Breakdown

Saturated Fat	1.3 g
Monounsaturated Fat	2.5 g
Polyunsaturated Fat	1.8 g

Marinated Mushrooms
Serves 4

1 lb.	button mushrooms

Marinade:

1 tsp.	olive oil
⅔ cup	water
2	lemons, juice of
1	bay leaf
2 cloves	garlic, crushed, not minced
2	scallions, cut in 2-inch lengths
6	peppercorns
to taste	salt

In a small saucepan, combine all marinade ingredients. Bring to a boil, cover and simmer 15 minutes. Strain marinade through a sieve, reserving liquid. Return strained liquid to saucepan. Drop in mushrooms, stir occasionally until marinade cools. When cooled to room temperature, refrigerate. Remove mushrooms from marinade. Serve chilled, with toothpicks.

Cook's Note: You may want to use this as a separate appetizer or as part of an antipasto platter. You may also choose to increase the amount of marinade and add other vegetables such as cauliflower, peppers, eggplant or zucchini.

Nutrient Content Per Serving

Calories	49.2
Protein	2.6 g
Carbohydrates	8.6 g
Fat – Total	1.7 g
Cholesterol	0.0 mg
Dietary Fiber	1.7 g
Sodium	5.6 mg

Percent of Calories

18% Protein
58% Carbohydrate
25% Fat

Fat Breakdown

Saturated Fat	0.2 g
Monounsaturated Fat	0.8 g
Polyunsaturated Fat	0.3 g

BAKED MUSHROOM CAPS
Serves 4

16 lg.	mushrooms
½ tsp.	olive oil
1 clove	garlic, minced
2 Tbl.	fresh parsley, chopped
¼ tsp.	salt
1 Tbl.	fresh thyme, chopped (¼ tsp. dried)
1 Tbl.	fresh oregano, chopped (¼ tsp. dried)
pinch	fresh ground black pepper
⅛ tsp.	nutmeg
⅓ cup	bread crumbs, unseasoned
2 Tbl.	parmesan cheese, grated
2 Tbl.	white wine

Wash mushrooms. Remove stems and chop them. Sauté chopped mushroom stems in olive oil until most of the moisture is gone and the mushrooms begin to brown. Add garlic, parsley, salt, thyme, oregano, pepper, nutmeg and bread crumbs. Stuff mushroom caps. Sprinkle with parmesan. Add wine to baking pan to keep mushrooms from drying out. Bake at 400° F for 20 minutes. Serve hot.

Variations:
- Chopped mushroom stems
- Cream cheese, nonfat
- Chopped olives
- Diced tomatoes
- Chopped artichoke hearts

Cook's Note: This is a traditional mushroom cap recipe. Use your imagination to obtain variety. Be creative!

Nutrient Content Per Serving		Percent of Calories	Fat Breakdown	
Calories	75.4	20% Protein	Saturated Fat	0.9 g
Protein	4.1 g	53% Carbohydrate	Monounsaturated Fat	0.9 g
Carbohydrates	10.6 g	27% Fat	Polyunsaturated Fat	0.4 g
Fat – Total	2.4 g			
Cholesterol	2.5 mg			
Dietary Fiber	1.8 g			
Sodium	267.0 mg			

BAKED OYSTERS
Serves 4

2 dozen	oysters, shucked and cleaned
1 cup	bread crumbs, unseasoned
2 tsp.	olive oil
1 tsp.	garlic, minced
2 Tbl.	fresh parsley, chopped
2 Tbl.	parmesan cheese, grated
2 tsp.	lemon zest
to taste	salt and pepper

Toast bread crumbs in a dry non-stick frying pan. Remove to a dish and let cool. In the non-stick pan, heat the olive oil. Sauté garlic. Combine garlic, bread crumbs, parsley, parmesan, lemon zest and salt and pepper to taste.

Rinse oysters and pat dry. Coat with bread crumb mixture. Bake on a non-stick cookie sheet at 450° F for 10-12 minutes. Serve with a spicy cocktail sauce.

Cook's Note: Oysters come in two sizes. Atlantic oysters are small while Pacific oysters are large. We used Pacific oysters in this recipe. If you can only obtain small oysters, use twice as many.

Nutrient Content Per Serving

Calories	220.0
Protein	17.8 g
Carbohydrates	21.5 g
Fat – Total	6.5 g
Cholesterol	76.9 mg
Dietary Fiber	0.9 g
Sodium	379.0 mg

Percent of Calories

33% Protein
40% Carbohydrate
27% Fat

Fat Breakdown

Saturated Fat	1.7 g
Monounsaturated Fat	2.0 g
Polyunsaturated Fat	1.4 g

SALMON SPREAD
Serves 12

1 15-oz. can	red salmon or smoked salmon
8 oz.	cream cheese, nonfat
1 Tbl.	lemon juice
1 tsp.	onion powder
2 tsp.	prepared horseradish
¼ tsp.	liquid smoke

Garnish:

3 Tbl.	fresh parsley, chopped

Remove skin and bones from salmon. Combine all ingredients until smooth. Chill several hours. Shape like a fish or make into a ball and roll in parsley. Serve with fresh bread, plain crackers or raw vegetables.

Cook's Note: This appetizer goes well with an antipasto platter.

% Calories as Fat — Above the HM✔ guidelines: Although this recipe has a high percentage of calories as fat (>30%), the total fat is less than 5 grams per serving. This will easily fit within your allotment of 45 grams per day. This happens most often in low-calorie recipes.

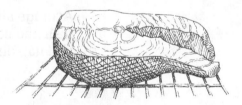

Nutrient Content Per Serving

Calories	72.5
Protein	10.0 g
Carbohydrates	1.1 g
Fat – Total	2.6 g
Cholesterol	18.9 mg
Dietary Fiber	0.1 g
Sodium	305.0 mg

Percent of Calories

59% Protein	
6% Carbohydrate	
35% Fat	

Fat Breakdown

Saturated Fat	0.6 g
Monounsaturated Fat	1.1 g
Polyunsaturated Fat	0.8 g

TOMATO CANAPÉS
Serves 6

6	ripe tomatoes, sliced thick
6 lg.	shrimp, peeled and deveined
6 slices	mozzarella (3 oz. total)
6	black olives, sliced thin
1	hot pepper
4 sm.	white onions, mashed
6 leaves	fresh basil
6 leaves	fresh sage
to taste	salt and pepper
6 lg.	mushrooms, sliced thin
1 clove	garlic, minced
1 Tbl.	fresh Italian parsley
3	scallions, chopped

Slice tomatoes into 24 slices. Separate into groups of 6.

Group 1: Grill shrimp. Put on a toothpick with a leaf of sage. Set each shrimp on a tomato slice.

Group 2: On 6 other tomato slices, arrange a thin slice of mozzarella cheese. Garnish with a slice of hot pepper and a basil leaf.

Group 3: Combine onion and olives. Arrange on another 6 tomato slices.

Group 4: Sauté mushrooms with scallions, garlic and parsley. Arrange on another 6 tomato slices.

Arrange all tomato slices on a flat glass dish and serve immediately. Provide forks and napkins for this dish.

Cook's Note: This sounds complicated, but is very impressive. Plan to make some of the toppings ahead. You may want to serve this with a loaf of hot Italian bread *(see p. 322).*

Nutrient Content Per Serving		Percent of Calories	Fat Breakdown	
Calories	96.9	27% Protein	Saturated Fat	1.6 g
Protein	7.0 g	44% Carbohydrate	Monounsaturated Fat	1.1 g
Carbohydrates	11.4 g	30% Fat	Polyunsaturated Fat	0.4 g
Fat – Total	3.4 g			
Cholesterol	18.8 mg			
Dietary Fiber	2.6 g			
Sodium	119.0 mg			

AUTUMN SOUP
Serves 6

1 lb.	extra-lean ground beef
1 cup	onions, chopped
4 cups	beef stock *(see p. 536)*
1 cup	carrots, sliced
1 cup	celery, sliced
1 cup	potatoes, cubed
½ tsp.	pepper
1	bay leaf
pinch	dry basil
1 16-oz. can	tomatoes
to taste	salt

Brown meat in a non-stick skillet. Add onions, cook 5 minutes. Transfer to a large soup pot, add beef stock, carrots, celery, potatoes and seasonings. Mix thoroughly then bring to a boil. Cover and simmer for 20 minutes. Add tomatoes, simmer 10 minutes or until vegetables are tender.

Cook's Note: May substitute ground buffalo or ground turkey breast. This is a wonderful cool-weather meal that displays the colors of autumn.

Nutrient Content Per Serving		**Percent of Calories**	**Fat Breakdown**	
Calories	191.0	53% Protein	Saturated Fat	0.3 g
Protein	25.5 g	42% Carbohydrate	Monounsaturated Fat	0.2 g
Carbohydrates	20.0 g	5% Fat	Polyunsaturated Fat	0.3 g
Fat – Total	1.1 g			
Cholesterol	64.8 mg			
Dietary Fiber	3.6 g			
Sodium	726.0 mg			

CREAMY BROCCOLI-LEEK SOUP
Serves 6

1½ lbs.	broccoli, chopped
4 cups	chicken stock *(see p. 538)*
3 lg.	leeks, chopped
6 lg.	mushrooms, chopped
¼ lb.	lowfat swiss cheese, grated
2 Tbl.	liquid margarine
¼ cup	flour
1 Tbl.	skim milk
1 tsp.	nonfat dry milk
to taste	salt and freshly ground pepper

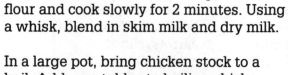

In a small saucepan, melt margarine. Add flour and cook slowly for 2 minutes. Using a whisk, blend in skim milk and dry milk.

In a large pot, bring chicken stock to a boil. Add vegetables to boiling chicken stock. Cook until vegetables are soft and easily fall apart.

Using a whisk, add flour mixture to soup and stir until completely dissolved. Transfer soup to a blender, bit by bit. Purée until smooth. Return to pan and simmer. Add cheese. Cook until cheese melts. Add salt and pepper to taste.

Cook's Note: This can be made ahead or served as a leftover. Simply reheat on the stove top. Using a microwave to reheat may cause curdling.

Nutrient Content Per Serving

Calories	168.0
Protein	11.1 g
Carbohydrates	21.5 g
Fat – Total	5.5 g
Cholesterol	6.8 mg
Dietary Fiber	5.2 g
Sodium	135.0 mg

Percent of Calories

25% Protein
48% Carbohydrate
28% Fat

Fat Breakdown

Saturated Fat	1.4 g
Monounsaturated Fat	1.6 g
Polyunsaturated Fat	2.1 g

BABY CLAM SOUP
Serves 8

5 lbs.	clams in shells, scrubbed
1 Tbl.	olive oil
¼ lb.	carrots, cut julienne
¼ lb.	celery, sliced
1	onion, cut julienne
¼	fennel, diced (knob only)
¼	leek, cut julienne
1 clove	garlic, roasted *(see p. 13)*
¼ Tbl.	fresh thyme
1 Tbl.	fresh oregano, chopped
¼ Tbl.	fresh marjoram, chopped
2	lemons, juice of
to taste	freshly ground black pepper
1 cup	pernod (optional)
2 cups	white wine
4 cups	clam juice
2	peppers, roasted, chopped *(see p. 13)*
1 14-oz. can	plum tomatoes, low-sodium, chopped
1 qt.	fish stock *(see p. 540)*
1½ Tbl.	butter
2 Tbl.	flour
2 cups	skim evaporated milk
½ cup	nonfat dry milk (dissolved in the milk)
1 Tbl.	powdered butter replacement
to taste	salt
4	lemons, use the zest of and chop fine

In a large pot, heat the olive oil over medium heat. Add carrots, celery, onion, fennel, leeks, garlic, thyme, oregano, marjoram and lemon juice. Sauté until vegetables begin to soften but do not brown. Add ground black pepper and clams, mix well. Add pernod (if using), white wine and clam juice. Cover and cook until clams fully open. Do not overcook. Remove clams from pan. Remove the clams from their shells. Keep them moist in a little clam juice in a separate bowl. Discard any unopened clams. Add the roasted peppers, tomatoes and fish stock. Reduce liquid until it becomes thick like a soup.

Make a roux with the 1½ Tbl. of butter and 2 tablespoons of flour. Cook 2 minutes. Add milk, powdered milk and powdered butter replacement. Cook until it begins to thicken. This will make a light white sauce. Stir white sauce into the soup. Return clams to soup. Heat through.

Season with salt, pepper and a little lemon juice.

Garnish:
1 slice crusty french bread with a mix of parsley, lemon zest and parmesan.

Cook's Note: Pernod is a French fennel liqueur (may substitute Annisette).

Nutrient Content Per Serving		**Percent of Calories**	**Fat Breakdown**	
Calories	514.0	36% Protein	Saturated Fat	2.1 g
Protein	46.3 g	34% Carbohydrate	Monounsaturated Fat	2.3 g
Carbohydrates	44.2 g	16% Fat	Polyunsaturated Fat	1.6 g
Fat – Total	7.9 g			
Cholesterol	106.0 mg			
Dietary Fiber	3.5 g			
Sodium	345.0 mg			

ESCAROLE AND BEANS
Serves 8

2 lbs.	escarole/curly endive, chopped rough
½ lb.	turkey Italian sausage
½ lb.	extra-lean ground beef
1 sm.	onion, chopped fine
1 tsp.	garlic, minced
15 oz.	navy beans, canned
15 oz.	tomato sauce

Brown ground beef and sausage. Drain. Add onion and garlic, and cook until onion browns. Add tomato sauce. In a separate pan, parboil escarole for 10 minutes. Combine escarole with other ingredients. Drain beans and add to pan. Cook until escarole is tender, about 30 minutes.

Cook's Note: Purchase fresh Italian turkey sausage or chicken sausage from your meat market, the flavor will be considerably better. Purchase vegetarian canned beans. Rinse and drain before using. You may also use dry beans and cook them first. Serve with a salad and Italian bread for a complete meal.

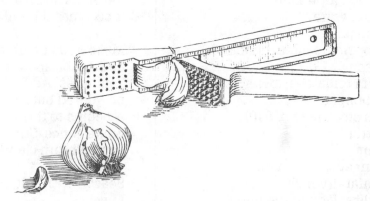

Nutrient Content Per Serving

Calories	239.0
Protein	21.1 g
Carbohydrates	22.5 g
Fat – Total	7.9 g
Cholesterol	45.4 mg
Dietary Fiber	7.3 g
Sodium	386.0 mg

Percent of Calories

34% Protein
37% Carbohydrate
29% Fat

Fat Breakdown

Saturated Fat	2.7 g
Monounsaturated Fat	2.8 g
Polyunsaturated Fat	1.4 g

GOOGOOTS
(Italian Stew)
Serves 8

1 lb.	turkey Italian sausage, cut in 1-inch pieces
1 med.	onion, chopped
1 clove	garlic, minced
2 med.	zucchini, cubed
3	carrots, cut in chunks
1 cup	celery, cubed
3 med.	potatoes, cut in cubes
1 15-oz. can	tomato sauce
3 cups	chicken stock *(see p. 538)*
1 15-oz. can	crushed tomatoes
2 Tbl.	dried parsley
2 tsp.	dried oregano
1 Tbl.	dried basil
to taste	salt and pepper

In a large soup pot, sauté sausage over medium heat, until done. Add onions and garlic and continue to sauté until onions are limp. Add remaining ingredients. Liquid should cover the vegetables. May need to add water. Partially cover pot and simmer 40-50 minutes or until vegetables are tender.

Serve with hot Italian bread *(see p. 322).*

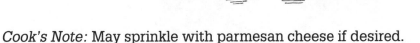

Cook's Note: May sprinkle with parmesan cheese if desired.

Nutrient Content Per Serving

Calories	261.0
Protein	19.1 g
Carbohydrates	29.9 g
Fat – Total	7.7 g
Cholesterol	47.6 mg
Dietary Fiber	4.6 g
Sodium	396.0 mg

Percent of Calories

29% Protein
45% Carbohydrate
26% Fat

Fat Breakdown

Saturated Fat	2.3 g
Monounsaturated Fat	2.4 g
Polyunsaturated Fat	2.1 g

LENTIL SOUP
Serves 8

1 lb. (2 cups)	brown lentils, uncooked
1 med.	onion, chopped fine
1 med.	carrot, chopped coarse
1 clove	garlic, minced
1 cup	celery, chopped coarse
1 Tbl.	olive oil
½ cup	tomatoes, peeled, seeded and chopped
1 tsp.	fresh parsley, chopped
to taste	salt and pepper

Simmer lentils uncovered in 2 quarts of water for 1 hour. In a non-stick frying pan sauté onion, carrot, garlic and celery in the olive oil. Add tomatoes and parsley. Cook 10 minutes. Add vegetables to the lentils and salt to taste. Cover and simmer 15-20 minutes or until lentils are tender.

Cook's Note: This soup also works well with split peas. You may purée all or half of the soup for a smooth and creamy texture.

Nutrient Content Per Serving

Calories	91.8
Protein	5.7 g
Carbohydrates	16.3 g
Fat – Total	2.1 g
Cholesterol	0.0 mg
Dietary Fiber	3.4 g
Sodium	24.9 mg

Percent of Calories

21% Protein
61% Carbohydrate
18% Fat

Fat Breakdown

Saturated Fat	0.3 g
Monounsaturated Fat	1.3 g
Polyunsaturated Fat	0.3 g

MINESTRONE
Serves 8

2 cups	dried white beans or canned beans, drained, rinsed
1 Tbl.	olive oil
2 cloves	garlic, minced
1 lg.	onion, sliced thin
2 stalks	celery, diced
1	carrot, diced
2 sprigs	fresh rosemary, chopped fine
1 med.	tomato, chopped coarse
½ head	savoy cabbage, shredded
3	leeks, chopped fine
3 sm.	zucchini, diced
2 Tbl.	fresh basil, chopped
3 sprigs	parsley, chopped fine
1	clove
to taste	salt and pepper
1 cup	V-8 juice, low-sodium
¾ cup	noodles, any small variety

Soak dry beans overnight. Discard water and rinse beans. Boil until tender (approximately 1 hour). In a non-stick frying pan, sauté garlic and onions in oil. Remove one-half of the beans and purée. Drain boiling water from remaining beans. Combine all ingredients except noodles in large soup pan. Add enough fresh water to cover vegetables. Simmer 30 minutes or until vegetables are tender. Add noodles and cook until just tender.

Cook's Note: What could be more Italian? You may change the heartiness of the soup by varying the amounts of vegetables and beans. Add some warm Italian bread *(see p. 322)* for a complete meal.

Nutrient Content Per Serving		**Percent of Calories**	**Fat Breakdown**	
Calories	323.0	20% Protein	Saturated Fat	0.3 g
Protein	16.3 g	75% Carbohydrate	Monounsaturated Fat	0.5 g
Carbohydrates	62.5 g	5% Fat	Polyunsaturated Fat	0.6 g
Fat – Total	1.9 g			
Cholesterol	0.0 mg			
Dietary Fiber	14.6 g			
Sodium	55.8 mg			

Pasta Fajioli Soup
Serves 6

1 cup	white beans, uncooked
2½ qts.	water
½ lb.	turkey ham, low-sodium, cut in ¼-inch cubes
½ cup	onions, chopped
½ cup	celery, chopped
1 tsp.	garlic, minced
1 tsp.	olive oil
½ cup	small pasta (elbows or rotini), uncooked
a few	grindings fresh black pepper
1 tsp.	oregano, dry
3 tsp.	parmesan cheese, grated
2 cups	tomatoes, chopped, peeled and seeded

Clean and sort beans. Discard any stones and shriveled beans.

In a 4-quart soup pot, boil beans in water for 2 minutes. Remove from heat, soak 1½ hours. Drain beans and discard water.

Add 2 quarts fresh water to beans. Heat oil in a non-stick pan. Add turkey ham, onions, celery and garlic. Sauté until onion begins to brown. Add this to beans. Add pepper and oregano. Bring beans to a boil. Simmer for 1½ hours or until beans are tender.

Using a slotted spoon, remove one-half of the beans, purée them and return to the pot. Add pasta and tomatoes. Simmer until pasta is tender (5-10 minutes). Serve hot, sprinkled with a little parmesan.

Cook's Note: If you discard the soaking water, you will reduce the gassiness of the beans. If you use canned beans, drain and rinse well before starting. This may be used as a main dish if served with Italian bread *(see p. 322)*, pesto bread *(see p. 323)* or bread sticks.

Nutrient Content Per Serving		**Percent of Calories**	**Fat Breakdown**	
Calories	217.0	30% Protein	Saturated Fat	1.1 g
Protein	16.5 g	55% Carbohydrate	Monounsaturated Fat	1.2 g
Carbohydrates	30.3 g	15% Fat	Polyunsaturated Fat	1.0 g
Fat – Total	3.8 g			
Cholesterol	22.0 mg			
Dietary Fiber	8.2 g			
Sodium	414.0 mg			

CREAMY PEPPER SOUP
Serves 4

1 lg.	sweet yellow pepper
1 lg.	sweet red pepper
3 cups	chicken stock *(see p. 538)*
1 lg.	green pepper, chopped
1 med.	onion, chopped fine
1 sm.	potato, peeled, chopped fine
¼ cup	fat-free tofu
2 Tbl.	skim milk
to taste	salt and pepper

In a food processor, purée yellow pepper. Set aside. Similarly purée red pepper and set aside. Heat chicken stock. Add green pepper, onion and potato. Cover and simmer until tender (approximately 20 minutes).

In the food processor purée tofu with milk until creamy. Stir into the soup and heat through.

Spoon soup into serving bowls. Garnish each bowl with a spoonful of yellow and red peppers.

Cook's Note: Don't worry, you'll never notice the tofu. It just acts as a creamy base.

Nutrient Content Per Serving		**Percent of Calories**	**Fat Breakdown**	
Calories	70.4	12% Protein	Saturated Fat	0.1 g
Protein	2.3 g	83% Carbohydrate	Monounsaturated Fat	0.1 g
Carbohydrates	15.7 g	5% Fat	Polyunsaturated Fat	0.1 g
Fat – Total	0.4 g			
Cholesterol	0.1 mg			
Dietary Fiber	2.0 g			
Sodium	8.9 mg			

TOMATO SOUP
Serves 8

1 med.	onion, chopped fine
1 tsp.	olive oil
1 clove	garlic, minced
4 lbs.	plum tomatoes, peeled, seeded and chopped
⅛ tsp.	salt
1	bay leaf
½ tsp.	thyme
1 Tbl.	fresh mint leaves, chopped
1 Tbl.	fresh basil, chopped
2	whole cloves
4	black peppercorns
¼ cup	fresh parsley, chopped coarse
1½ cups	chicken stock *(see p. 538)*

In a small non-stick frying pan, sauté onion in olive oil until soft. Add garlic. Transfer to a soup pot and add remaining ingredients. Cook until vegetables are tender. Remove cloves, peppercorns and bay leaf. Purée two-thirds of the soup. Return puréed portion to pan. Serve hot with warmed crusty bread.

Cook's Note: May substitute canned tomatoes for fresh tomatoes, but then omit the salt. This is not the tomato soup you find at the store. Expect a tomato base, not a cream base. You will be impressed by the fresh taste of tomato.

Nutrient Content Per Serving		Percent of Calories	Fat Breakdown	
Calories	61.4	13% Protein	Saturated Fat	0.2 g
Protein	2.3 g	68% Carbohydrate	Monounsaturated Fat	0.6 g
Carbohydrates	12.1 g	19% Fat	Polyunsaturated Fat	0.4 g
Fat – Total	1.5 g			
Cholesterol	0.2 mg			
Dietary Fiber	3.2 g			
Sodium	263.0 mg			

ZUPPA PIZZIALO
Serves 8

1½ cups	onion, chopped fine
6 cloves	garlic, minced
1 tsp.	olive oil
2 15-oz. cans	condensed tomato soup, low-sodium
2 15-oz. cans	diced tomatoes
1 15-oz. can	kidney beans, low-sodium, rinsed and drained
1 15-oz. can	garbanzo beans, rinsed and drained
1½ cup	croutons, non-fat or homemade *(see p. 534)*
2 Tbl.	Italian seasoning
½ tsp.	cayenne pepper
to taste	salt and pepper
3 cups	chicken stock *(see p. 538)*
1½ cups	fat-free mozzarella cheese, shredded

In a small non-stick frying pan, sauté onion and garlic in oil. In a large soup pot, combine all ingredients except croutons and cheese. Simmer 20 minutes. Ladle soup into individual ovenproof bowls and top with croutons and cheese. Bake at 450° F for 10 minutes or until cheese begins to bubble.

Cook's Note: This is a great potluck item.

Non-fat croutons can be found in the "diet" section of the grocery store. Or you may broil some bread cubes of your own, see croutons *(see p. 534)*. Serve with Italian bread *(see p. 322)* or add pasta to the soup and use as a meatless main dish. You may add more vegetables such as green pepper, zucchini or green beans.

Nutrient Content Per Serving

Calories	292.0
Protein	15.5 g
Carbohydrates	50.7 g
Fat – Total	4.3 g
Cholesterol	2.5 mg
Dietary Fiber	11.7 g
Sodium	328.0 mg

Percent of Calories

20% Protein
67% Carbohydrate
13% Fat

Fat Breakdown

Saturated Fat	0.6 g
Monounsaturated Fat	1.3 g
Polyunsaturated Fat	1.6 g

CAESAR SALAD

Serves 4

1 head	romaine lettuce
	Paprika Seasoned Croutons
	(see p. 534)
8 Tbl.	Caesar Dressing *(see p. 410)*
2 tsp.	parmesan cheese, grated

Clean and dry romaine. Cut into 1½-inch-long chunks. Place in a large bowl. Prepare croutons using paprika seasoning mix. Add 1 serving of croutons per salad and caesar dressing. Toss and serve.

Cook's Note: May add other salad items as you wish: artichoke hearts, radishes, olives, cucumbers, etc. Serve it the traditional way. Bring a large over-sized salad bowl to the table. Pour on the dressing and toss. Scoop out individual servings and top with freshly ground black pepper.

% Calories as Fat — Above the HM✓ guidelines: Although this recipe has a high percentage of calories as fat (>30%), the total fat is less than 5 grams per serving. This will easily fit within your allotment of 45 grams per day. This happens most often in low-calorie recipes.

Nutrient Content Per Serving

Calories	150.0
Protein	5.4 g
Carbohydrates	21.0 g
Fat – Total	5.7 g
Cholesterol	2.4 mg
Dietary Fiber	2.6 g
Sodium	230.0 mg

Percent of Calories

14% Protein
54% Carbohydrate
33% Fat

Fat Breakdown

Saturated Fat	1.0 g
Monounsaturated Fat	3.4 g
Polyunsaturated Fat	0.9 g

MOZZARELLA WITH TOMATO AND BASIL

Serves 4

12 oz.	mozzarella, fat-free, sliced thin
4 leaves	radicchio
4 leaves	bibb lettuce
2	tomatoes, sliced in rounds
1 med.	onion, sliced in rounds
4 tsp.	olive oil
to taste	freshly ground pepper
4 sprigs	basil

On a large dinner plate, arrange radicchio and bibb lettuce leaves decoratively. Neatly layer mozzarella, tomato and onion over lettuce. Top with oil and freshly ground pepper. Garnish with basil.

Cook's Note: If you prefer part-skim mozzarella the fat content will increase by 3.4 grams per serving.

Nutrient Content Per Serving

Calories	186.0
Protein	28.1 g
Carbohydrates	8.8 g
Fat – Total	4.8 g
Cholesterol	15.0 mg
Dietary Fiber	1.3 g
Sodium	609.0 mg

Percent of Calories

59% Protein
18% Carbohydrate
23% Fat

Fat Breakdown

Saturated Fat	0.7 g
Monounsaturated Fat	3.4 g
Polyunsaturated Fat	0.5 g

MUSHROOM SALAD

Serves 4

½ lb. (2½ cups)	fresh mushrooms, sliced thin
2 Tbl.	fresh parsley, chopped
2 Tbl.	fresh basil, chopped
¼ cup	scallions, sliced thin

Marinade:

3 tsp.	olive oil
2 tsp.	fresh lemon juice
2 Tbl.	cold water
1 Tbl.	balsamic vinegar
¼ tsp.	salt

Combine all marinade ingredients. Combine vegetables and herbs. Mix the two together. Allow mushrooms to marinate for 1-2 hours. Serve chilled.

Cook's Note: Although the percent of calories as fat is high, the total grams of fat are low. The whole salad is really the mushrooms. Do not expect a salad dressing. The mushrooms will absorb the marinade, and that will provide moisture and flavor.

% Calories as Fat — Above the HM✔ guidelines: Although this recipe has a high percentage of calories as fat (>30%), the total fat is less than 5 grams per serving. This will easily fit within your allotment of 45 grams per day. This happens most often in low-calorie recipes.

Nutrient Content Per Serving		**Percent of Calories**	**Fat Breakdown**	
Calories	47.5	10% Protein	Saturated Fat	0.5 g
Protein	1.3 g	27% Carbohydrate	Monounsaturated Fat	2.5 g
Carbohydrates	3.6 g	62% Fat	Polyunsaturated Fat	0.4 g
Fat – Total	3.6 g			
Cholesterol	0.0 mg			
Dietary Fiber	0.9 g			
Sodium	137.0 mg			

TUNA-BEAN SALAD
Serves 6

3 cups	white beans, (Great Northern) canned, rinsed and drained
½ med.	red onion, sliced thin
3 Tbl.	red wine vinegar
6 leaves	romaine lettuce
1	tomato, cut in wedges
1	lemon, juice of
dash	fresh ground black pepper
6½ oz.	solid white tuna, water-pack, drained
1 clove	garlic, minced
2 Tbl.	fresh parsley, chopped
2 Tbl.	fresh basil, chopped
2	plum tomatoes, chopped
1 tsp.	fresh sage, chopped
1 Tbl.	capers, rinsed and drained

Marinate onion in vinegar for 30 minutes. Mix remaining ingredients. Chill at least 2 hours to blend flavors. Line plates with romaine lettuce and tomato wedges. Spoon salad onto lettuce-lined plates. Top with onion slices.

Cook's Note: Can be served as a main dish salad, especially for summertime. Can be prepared a day ahead. Goes well with lamb or chicken. Salad is even better the second day.

Nutrient Content Per Serving

Calories	204.0
Protein	17.5 g
Carbohydrates	32.5 g
Fat – Total	1.2 g
Cholesterol	9.2 mg
Dietary Fiber	8.7 g
Sodium	225.0 mg

Percent of Calories

33% Protein
62% Carbohydrate
5% Fat

Fat Breakdown

Saturated Fat	0.3 g
Monounsaturated Fat	0.1 g
Polyunsaturated Fat	0.5 g

BASIL PASTA SALAD
Serves 10

1 lb.	shell macaroni, uncooked
3	scallions
4	plum tomatoes
2 lg.	carrots
¼ cup	fresh basil, chopped

Dressing:

2	plum tomatoes
1 lg. clove	garlic, minced
¼ cup	balsamic vinegar
1½ tsp.	olive oil
1½ tsp.	pesto sauce
¼ cup	fresh basil
¼ tsp.	black pepper, crushed

Cook shell macaroni al dente. Cool. Dice scallions, plum tomatoes and carrots, add to pasta. Toss well and refrigerate until ready to serve.

Combine all dressing ingredients in food processor or blender. Process until smooth. Pour over pasta. Serve cold.

Cook's Note: This makes a pretty summer potluck item. It has a refreshing flavor.

Nutrient Content Per Serving

Calories	87.5
Protein	2.8 g
Carbohydrates	16.2 g
Fat – Total	1.5 g
Cholesterol	0.2 mg
Dietary Fiber	1.6 g
Sodium	13.5 mg

Percent of Calories

12% Protein
73% Carbohydrate
15% Fat

Fat Breakdown

Saturated Fat	0.2 g
Monounsaturated Fat	0.8 g
Polyunsaturated Fat	0.3 g

Pasta Salad
Serves 12

1 lb.	rotini noodles
1 tsp.	olive oil
1 28-oz. can	tomatoes, peeled, seeded and chopped
3 lg.	carrots, peeled, chopped coarse
1 bunch	scallions, sliced fine
½ cup	fresh parsley, chopped fine
1½ cups	purple cabbage, chopped medium
2 lg. cloves	garlic, minced
2 Tbl.	balsamic vinegar
8 oz.	fat-free mozzarella, cubed small
⅓ cup	fresh basil, chopped fine

Boil noodles, rinse in cold water. Toss with olive oil. Combine all ingredients in a large bowl. Chill. Serve cold.

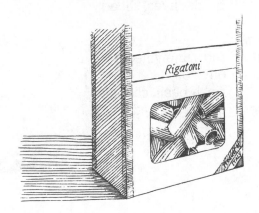

Cook's Note: This makes a great potluck item. It is very colorful.

Nutrient Content Per Serving

Calories	135.0
Protein	8.1 g
Carbohydrates	17.2 g
Fat – Total	4.1 g
Cholesterol	10.2 mg
Dietary Fiber	2.4 g
Sodium	216.0 mg

Percent of Calories

23% Protein
50% Carbohydrate
27% Fat

Fat Breakdown

Saturated Fat	2.2 g
Monounsaturated Fat	1.3 g
Polyunsaturated Fat	0.3 g

ITALIAN-STYLE POTATO SALAD
Serves 6

3 med.	potatoes, peeled, cubed
3 med.	tomatoes, cubed
1	sweet yellow pepper, cubed
5 lg.	black olives, sliced

Dressing:

¼ cup	red wine vinegar
1 Tbl.	olive oil
2 tsp.	fresh basil, chopped
1 clove	garlic, minced

Parboil the potatoes until tender. Rinse and cool, combine cooled potatoes with tomatoes, peppers and olives.

To prepare dressing:
Combine all dressing ingredients.

Pour dressing over potatoes. Mix carefully so as not to break the potatoes. Chill at least 1 hour. Serve cold.

Nutrient Content Per Serving

Calories	101.0
Protein	1.9 g
Carbohydrates	18.4 g
Fat – Total	2.9 g
Cholesterol	0.0 mg
Dietary Fiber	1.7 g
Sodium	32.2 mg

Percent of Calories
7% Protein
68% Carbohydrate
25% Fat

Fat Breakdown

Saturated Fat	0.4 g
Monounsaturated Fat	2.0 g
Polyunsaturated Fat	0.3 g

RED, WHITE AND GREEN SALAD
Serves 4

8	plum tomatoes, peeled
2 oz.	lowfat mozzarella cheese, sliced
8	basil leaves
4 tsp.	Italian Salad dressing *(choose from p. 408, p. 409 or p. 412)*

Slice tomatoes thin. Arrange on individual salad plates. Slice mozzarella into triangles. Layer cheese on top of tomatoes. Top with basil. Drizzle salad dressing on top.

Cook's Note: Quick and easy. It makes a beautiful presentation.

% Calories as Fat — Above the HM✓ guidelines: Although this recipe has a high percentage of calories as fat (>30%), the total fat is less than 5 grams per serving. This will easily fit within your allotment of 45 grams per day. This happens most often in low-calorie recipes.

Nutrient Content Per Serving (includes salad dressing)

Calories	68.9
Protein	5.1 g
Carbohydrates	6.6 g
Fat – Total	3.1 g
Cholesterol	7.8 mg
Dietary Fiber	1.7 g
Sodium	85.6 mg

Percent of Calories

27% Protein
35% Carbohydrate
37% Fat

Fat Breakdown

Saturated Fat	1.6 g
Monounsaturated Fat	0.9 g
Polyunsaturated Fat	0.3 g

Spinach Fajioli

Serves 4

1 cup	white beans, cooked
1 bunch	fresh spinach leaves, deveined
4	plum tomatoes, sliced
¾ cup	mushrooms, sliced
¼ med.	red onion, sliced thin
½ cup	Basil Vinaigrette *(see p. 408)*

Marinade:

⅓ cup	white wine vinegar
¼ med.	white onion, sliced thick
¼ tsp.	onion powder
¼ tsp.	garlic powder
¼ tsp.	fresh ground black pepper

Garnish:
fresh parsley sprigs

Combine marinade ingredients. Add cooked beans. Cover and refrigerate at least 4 hours.

Toss together spinach, tomatoes, mushrooms and red onion. Add Basil Vinaigrette and toss gently. Garnish with parsley sprigs.

Cook's Note: May substitute canned navy beans. Purchase vegetarian-style beans and rinse before using. To serve as a complete meal, add water-packed tuna or any grilled fish from this book.

Nutrient Content Per Serving

Calories	129.0
Protein	8.4 g
Carbohydrates	23.1 g
Fat – Total	2.0 g
Cholesterol	0.6 mg
Dietary Fiber	4.9 g
Sodium	75.9 mg

Percent of Calories

23%	Protein
64%	Carbohydrate
13%	Fat

Fat Breakdown

Saturated Fat	0.3 g
Monounsaturated Fat	0.9 g
Polyunsaturated Fat	0.5 g

FRESH GRILLED SWORDFISH SALAD
Serves 6

6 4-oz.	swordfish steaks
½ cup	fish marinade *(see p. 555)*
1 head	radicchio leaves, torn
1 head	bibb lettuce leaves, torn
2 heads	belgian endive, torn
1	sweet pepper, julienne
2	carrots, julienne
1	leek, julienne
3 stalks	celery, chopped

Garnish:

4	orange segments
4	tomatoes, julienne
¼ bunch	chives, chopped
¾ cup	Basil Vinaigrette *(see p. 408)*

Marinate the swordfish steak in the fish marinade for 5 minutes. Quickly grill the swordfish over hot coals until the center becomes opaque (approximately 7 minutes per side).

Arrange the lettuce and vegetables nicely on individual plates. Lay the swordfish on top. Garnish with the orange segments, tomato julienne and chives. Top each with 2 tablespoons of Basil Vinaigrette.

Cook's Note: This can be a complete dinner if served with Italian bread *(see p. 322)* or Pesto bread *(see p. 323)*. It is a wonderful meal to serve on a summer evening out on the patio.

Nutrient Content Per Serving

Calories	224.0
Protein	24.9 g
Carbohydrates	15.5 g
Fat – Total	7.4 g
Cholesterol	45.0 mg
Dietary Fiber	3.4 g
Sodium	144.0 mg

Percent of Calories

44% Protein
27% Carbohydrate
29% Fat

Fat Breakdown

Saturated Fat	1.6 g
Monounsaturated Fat	3.5 g
Polyunsaturated Fat	1.5 g

GRILLED VEGETABLE SALAD

Serves 6

1	fennel, cut on bias
1	yellow squash, sliced lengthwise
2	plum tomatoes, peeled, sliced
12	baby zucchini, cut in half lengthwise
1 lb.	fresh spinach, chopped in large chunks
¾ cup	Old Fashioned Balsamic Dressing *(see p. 409)*
to taste	salt and pepper

Garnish:

grenadine onions *(see p. 533)*
button marigolds

Season the yellow squash, zucchini and fennel with a little salt, pepper and a dash of balsamic vinegar. Grill vegetables over hot coals on both sides until soft, then chill.

Arrange the grilled vegetables on a dinner plate with sliced tomatoes around the outside. Arrange spinach in the center and garnish the top with sprinkles of grenadine onions *(see p. 533)* and a few button marigolds.

Serve with 2 tablespoons of salad dressing for each plate.

Cook's Note: Fennel is a seasonal item. It is usually in the stores during the spring. However, specialty stores will often carry it year-round.

% Calories as Fat — Above the HM✔ guidelines: Although this recipe has a high percentage of calories as fat (>30%), the total fat is less than 5 grams per serving. This will easily fit within your allotment of 45 grams per day. This happens most often in low-calorie recipes.

Nutrient Content Per Serving

Calories	71.4
Protein	4.0 g
Carbohydrates	10.0 g
Fat – Total	3.0 g
Cholesterol	0.0 mg
Dietary Fiber	4.7 g
Sodium	83.8 mg

Percent of Calories

19% Protein
48% Carbohydrate
33% Fat

Fat Breakdown

Saturated Fat	0.4 g
Monounsaturated Fat	1.8 g
Polyunsaturated Fat	0.4 g

FOCACCIA

Serves 8

3 cups	all-purpose flour
1 pkg.	dry active yeast
1½ tsp.	salt
2 Tbl.	olive oil
1 cup	lukewarm water

Dissolve yeast in ½ cup of the warm water. Let rest 5 minutes.

Place 1½ cups of the flour in a large bowl. Make a well in the center and add the yeast mixture. Incorporate the flour, working it into a ball. Knead on a floured surface for 10 minutes. Dust the bowl with flour and place the ball of dough in the bowl to rise. Cover with a damp cloth and allow to rise in a warm draft-free place until it has doubled in bulk (approximately 2 hours).

Punch down and incorporate the remaining 1½ cups of flour, remaining water, olive oil and salt. Knead for 8 minutes. Let rise again until doubled in bulk.

Punch down and turn dough onto a floured surface. Roll into a 12-inch-diameter circle. It should be at least ½-inch thick. Season the top with any herbs or seasonings you like. Bake on a tile at 400° F for 20-25 minutes or until it turns golden brown.

Serve with a meal or as a snack.

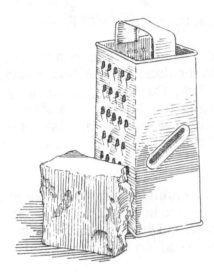

Variations:
- Top with a dusting of parmesan.
- Top with herbs such as parsley, oregano, basil, rosemary or thyme.
- Grated onions or a mist of olive oil or olives is a nice twist.
- Use your imagination.

Nutrient Content Per Serving		Percent of Calories	Fat Breakdown	
Calories	203.0	10% Protein	Saturated Fat	0.5 g
Protein	5.2 g	72% Carbohydrate	Monounsaturated Fat	2.6 g
Carbohydrates	36.1 g	17% Fat	Polyunsaturated Fat	0.5 g
Fat – Total	3.9 g			
Cholesterol	0.0 mg			
Dietary Fiber	1.5 g			
Sodium	401.0 mg			

ITALIAN BREAD

Serves 8

1 pkg.	active dry yeast
1 cup	lukewarm water
1½ tsp.	salt
1 Tbl.	olive oil
3 cups	bread flour

In a small bowl, dissolve the yeast in ½ cup of the warm water. Allow to rest for 5 minutes.

Place 1½ cups of the flour in a large bowl. Make a well in the center and add the yeast mixture. Incorporate into the flour making a ball. Knead on a floured surface for 10 minutes. Dust the bowl with flour and place kneaded dough in bowl. Cover with a damp cloth and allow to rise in a draft-free place until double in bulk (approximately 2 hours). The dough will look sponge-like and full of air bubbles.

Punch down and add remaining ingredients. Knead another 10 minutes. Shape dough into a ball and return it to the bowl. Cover with a damp cloth and allow to rise again until double in bulk (approximately 2 hours).

Preheat the oven to 450° F.

Knead the dough again for a minute. Divide the dough in half. Shape each half into a long, thin loaf (approximately 8 inches long). Let shaped loaf rest 5 minutes. Make a lengthwise slit in the top of the loaf. Brush tops of loaves with water.

Bake in a preheated oven for 12 minutes. Then reduce heat to 375° F and bake for an additional 45 minutes. Allow bread to cool on a cooling rack.

Variations:
  ▪ Use 1 cup whole wheat flour and 2 cups of bread flour.

Cook's Note: This bread cooks best when placed on a baking stone or tiles in a completely preheated oven.

Nutrient Content Per Serving		**Percent of Calories**	**Fat Breakdown**	
Calories	188.0	11% Protein	Saturated Fat	0.3 g
Protein	5.2 g	78% Carbohydrate	Monounsaturated Fat	1.3 g
Carbohydrates	36.1 g	11% Fat	Polyunsaturated Fat	0.3 g
Fat – Total	2.2 g			
Cholesterol	0.0 mg			
Dietary Fiber	1.5 g			
Sodium	401.0 mg			

PESTO BREAD
Serves 8

2 Tbl.	yeast
3 cups	flour
2 Tbl.	gluten
½ tsp.	salt
2 Tbl.	sugar
2 Tbl.	nonfat dry milk
1 Tbl.	olive oil
3 Tbl.	pesto
1 cup	lukewarm water

Dissolve pesto in olive oil. Dissolve yeast in ¼ cup of lukewarm water. Let stand 5 minutes. Combine dry ingredients in a bowl. Make a well in the center. Add wet ingredients. Mix well. Shape into a ball. Turn onto a floured surface and knead for 10 minutes. Cover with a damp cloth and let rise until doubled. Punch down and knead for 10 minutes. Shape and let rise 1 hour. Bake at 350° F for 30-40 minutes.

Cook's Note: This will work well in a bread maker. You must first combine the pesto and olive oil in a small bowl. Then add ingredients to the bread machine in the order listed. May use bread flour in place of flour and gluten.

Nutrient Content Per Serving

Calories	247.0
Protein	8.1 g
Carbohydrates	42.0 g
Fat – Total	5.0 g
Cholesterol	2.0 mg
Dietary Fiber	2.0 g
Sodium	185.0 mg

Percent of Calories

13% Protein
68% Carbohydrate
18% Fat

Fat Breakdown

Saturated Fat	1.0 g
Monounsaturated Fat	3.0 g
Polyunsaturated Fat	0.5 g

BASIC PIZZA DOUGH
Makes 4 12-inch crusts
Serves 12

2 Tbl.	dry yeast
2 cups	lukewarm water
1 Tbl.	salt
4½ cups	bread flour
1 Tbl.	olive oil

Dissolve yeast in warm water. Let stand 5 minutes. Combine with remaining ingredients. Form a ball. Knead until elastic. Cover with a moist towel and let rest in a warm spot for 30 minutes.

Roll and shape into 4 individual 10-inch crusts. Sprinkle cornmeal on baking sheet. Arrange crusts on top. Top with your favorite lowfat pizza toppings. Bake at 400° F for 20 minutes.

Suggested HealthMark Pizza Toppings:
- Tomatoes and basil
- Garlic, tomatoes and olive oil
- Sun-dried tomatoes, scallions and olives
- Roasted peppers, artichokes and tomatoes
- Mushrooms, olives and green peppers
- Spinach, tomatoes and olives
- Tomatoes, basil and mushrooms

Cook's Note: Use your imagination for toppings. Have fun! May freeze extra crusts after rolling and shaping. To use, simply thaw, add toppings and bake.

▼ This recipe is used for the following items:
Artichoke Pizza (see p. 325)
Tomato and Mushroom Pizza (see p. 326)

Nutrient Content Per Serving

Calories	184.0				
Protein	5.3 g				
Carbohydrates	36.3 g				
Fat – Total	1.6 g				
Cholesterol	0.0 mg				
Dietary Fiber	1.7 g				
Sodium	534.0 mg				

Percent of Calories
12% Protein
80% Carbohydrate
8% Fat

Fat Breakdown

Saturated Fat	0.2 g
Monounsaturated Fat	0.9 g
Polyunsaturated Fat	0.3 g

ARTICHOKE PIZZA
Serves 4

1	pizza crust *(see p. 324)*
1 Tbl.	olive oil
1 lb.	ripe tomatoes, peeled, seeded, mashed or puréed
½ cup	artichoke hearts, drained, quartered
1½ cups	button mushrooms, washed, left whole
1 Tbl.	capers
few sprigs	basil
to taste	oregano

Preheat oven at 400° F. Prepare pizza crust. Spread on pizza pan. Brush olive oil on dough. Arrange remaining ingredients on crust. Bake 20 minutes.

Nutrient Content Per Serving

Calories	216.0
Protein	6.3 g
Carbohydrates	37.8 g
Fat – Total	5.2 g
Cholesterol	0.0 mg
Dietary Fiber	4.5 g
Sodium	454.0 mg

Percent of Calories

11% Protein
68% Carbohydrate
21% Fat

Fat Breakdown

Saturated Fat	0.7 g
Monounsaturated Fat	3.2 g
Polyunsaturated Fat	0.8 g

TOMATO AND MUSHROOM PIZZA
Serves 4

1   pizza crust *(see p. 324)*
½ lb.   mushrooms, sliced thin
1 lb.   tomatoes, sliced thin
3 oz.   lowfat mozzarella cheese, grated
2 Tbl.   oregano
1 Tbl.   thyme
1 tsp.   olive oil

Preheat oven at 400° F. Prepare pizza crust. Spread on pizza pan. Sauté mushrooms in olive oil for 10 minutes. Arrange ingredients in order: tomatoes, mozzarella and mushrooms. Sprinkle with oregano, thyme. Bake 20 minutes or until crust is golden brown.

Cook's Note: Fat-free mozzarella makes the pizza too rubbery. Use your imagination for lowfat cheese mixtures.

Nutrient Content Per Serving

Calories	253.0
Protein	12.3 g
Carbohydrates	37.3 g
Fat – Total	6.8 g
Cholesterol	11.5 mg
Dietary Fiber	4.1 g
Sodium	525.0 mg

Percent of Calories

19% Protein
57% Carbohydrate
24% Fat

Fat Breakdown

Saturated Fat	2.8 g
Monounsaturated Fat	2.6 g
Polyunsaturated Fat	0.8 g

ZUCCHINI BREAD
Serves 12
Makes 1 loaf

¼ cup	canola oil
½ cup	brown sugar
½ cup	non-fat dry milk
4	egg whites, slightly beaten
2½ cups	zucchini, grated, patted dry
2 cups	all-purpose flour
2 tsp.	baking soda
¼ tsp.	baking powder
1 Tbl.	cinnamon
2 tsp.	nutmeg
¼ tsp.	cloves
⅛ tsp.	ginger powder
½ cup	lowfat buttermilk
2 tsp.	vanilla

To make in a bread machine:
Follow directions for your machine and add ingredients according to the following groups.

Group 1: canola oil, sugar and dry milk.
Group 2: egg whites
Group 3: zucchini
Group 4: remaining ingredients

Conventional method:
Combine all dry ingredients. Combine all wet ingredients, except zucchini. Mix the dry and wet ingredients together. Add the zucchini. Preheat oven to 350° F. Bake in a loaf pan prepared with cooking spray, for 1 hour. Bake for 20-30 minutes if using muffin tins.

Variations:
- Add ½ cup raisins or dates to increase sweetness.
- May use any variety of flours: oat bran, whole-wheat.
- May add wheat germ.
- May add lemon peel for more tart, less sweet taste.

Cook's Note: Serve for breakfast or as a snack for guests with coffee or tea.

Nutrient Content Per Serving

Calories	174.0			
Protein	5.7 g			
Carbohydrates	26.4 g			
Fat – Total	4.9 g			
Cholesterol	1.2 mg			
Dietary Fiber	1.1 g			

Sodium
191.0   mg

Percent of Calories
13% Protein
61% Carbohydrate
26% Fat

Fat Breakdown

Saturated Fat	0.5 g
Monounsaturated Fat	2.7 g
Polyunsaturated Fat	1.5 g

BASIC RISOTTO
Serves 6

Basic ingredients:

2 cups	rice, short grain
2 tsp.	olive oil
6 cups	hot stock *(see variations on following pages)*

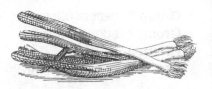

In a large non-stick frying pan, heat oil over medium heat. Add rice and cook, stirring constantly until rice becomes opaque (a few minutes). While stirring the rice, add the stock. Bring to a boil, cover and simmer until rice is tender and most of the liquid has been absorbed. Meanwhile, prepare flavor variation of your choice. Stir into the rice. Serve hot.

Cook's Note: A good risotto should be a little runny. The type of rice used to make a true risotto is a short-grain starchy rice. It cooks up like a pasta.

Nutrient Content Per Serving		Percent of Calories	Fat Breakdown	
Calories	244.0	8% Protein	Saturated Fat	0.3 g
Protein	4.6 g	85% Carbohydrate	Monounsaturated Fat	1.2 g
Carbohydrates	50.3 g	7% Fat	Polyunsaturated Fat	0.3 g
Fat – Total	1.9 g			
Cholesterol	0.0 mg			
Dietary Fiber	0.9 g			
Sodium	3.1 mg			

MUSHROOM RISOTTO
Serves 6

1 recipe   basic risotto *(see p. 328)*

Hot stock:

½ tsp.	olive oil
½ cup	onion, diced fine
1 cup	white wine
3 cups	chicken stock *(see p. 538)*

Mushroom mixture:

½ tsp.	olive oil
½ cup	onion, diced fine
1 clove	garlic, minced
½ lb.	mushrooms, sliced thin
½ cup	dry white wine
to taste	salt and pepper

Finish:

½ cup	parmesan cheese, grated

Hot stock:
Prepare rice according to risotto directions.

Sauté onion in oil until soft. Add wine and reduce to ½ cup. Add chicken stock and heat.

Mushroom mixture:
Sauté onion in oil until soft. Add garlic and mushrooms. Cook until most of the moisture has disappeared. Add wine and salt and pepper to taste. Combine with rice. Blend in parmesan on top.

Alcohol Note: The alcohol content was computed prior to cooking. Once the alcohol is heated to the boiling point, the alcohol disappears along with most of the calories from the alcohol.

Nutrient Content Per Serving		Percent of Calories	Fat Breakdown	
Calories	345.0	11% Protein	Saturated Fat	2.0 g
Protein	9.1 g	64% Carbohydrate	Monounsaturated Fat	2.5 g
Carbohydrates	54.4 g	14% Fat	Polyunsaturated Fat	0.4 g
Fat – Total	5.4 g	11% Alcohol		
Cholesterol	6.6 mg			
Dietary Fiber	1.7 g			
Sodium	163.0 mg			

SPINACH-HERB RISOTTO
Serves 6

1 recipe   basic risotto *(see p. 328)*

Hot stock:
6 cups   chicken stock *(see p. 538)*

Herb mixture:
1 tsp.   olive oil
¾ cup   scallions, chopped fine
½ cup   parsley, chopped
1½ cups   fresh spinach, chopped

Finish:
¼ cup   basil, chopped fine
¼ cup   parmesan cheese, grated

Prepare rice according to risotto directions.

Herb mixture:
Sauté scallions in olive oil until soft. Add parsley and spinach. Cook until greens are wilted. Add to rice. Blend in basil and parmesan.

Nutrient Content Per Serving

Calories	279.0
Protein	7.1 g
Carbohydrates	52.3 g
Fat – Total	4.0 g
Cholesterol	3.3 mg
Dietary Fiber	1.9 g
Sodium	96.5 mg

Percent of Calories

10% Protein
76% Carbohydrate
13% Fat

Fat Breakdown

Saturated Fat	1.2 g
Monounsaturated Fat	2.2 g
Polyunsaturated Fat	0.4 g

VEGETABLE RISOTTO
Serves 6

1 recipe   basic risotto *(see p. 328)*

Hot liquid:
6 cups   vegetable stock *(see p. 542)*

Vegetable mixture:
1 tsp.	olive oil
¼ cup	onion, chopped
¼ cup	carrots, chopped
¼ cup	celery, chopped
½ cup	frozen peas, thawed
1 med.	zucchini, chopped fine
2 lg.	tomatoes, diced

Finish:
¼ cup	parmesan cheese, grated
2 Tbl.	parsley, chopped

Prepare rice according to risotto directions.

Vegetable mixture:
Sauté onions in oil until soft. Add remaining vegetables and cook until barely tender. Combine with rice. Blend in parsley and parmesan cheese.

Nutrient Content Per Serving
Calories	356.0
Protein	7.9 g
Carbohydrates	57.0 g
Fat – Total	7.0 g
Cholesterol	3.3 mg
Dietary Fiber	2.9 g
Sodium	105.0 mg

Percent of Calories
9% Protein
65% Carbohydrate
18% Fat

Fat Breakdown
Saturated Fat	1.6 g
Monounsaturated Fat	0.5 g
Polyunsaturated Fat	2.5 g

CACCIATORE RISOTTO
Serves 6

1 recipe   basic risotto *(see p. 328)*

Hot liquid:
6 cups   chicken stock *(see p. 538)*

Chicken mixture:
3   chicken breasts, boneless,
           skinless, diced
½ tsp.   olive oil
2 cloves   garlic, minced
1 cup   tomato sauce *(see p. 552 or*
           p. 417)

Finish:
¼ cup   parmesan cheese, grated
2 Tbl.   parsley, chopped

Prepare rice according to risotto directions.

Chicken mixture:
Sauté chicken in oil until thoroughly cooked. Add garlic, tomato sauce and parsley. Heat through. Add to rice. Blend in parmesan cheese and parsley.

Nutrient Content Per Serving
Calories	354.0
Protein	20.6 g
Carbohydrates	54.5 g
Fat – Total	5.2 g
Cholesterol	37.5 mg
Dietary Fiber	1.7 g
Sodium	153.0 mg

Percent of Calories
24% Protein
63% Carbohydrate
13% Fat

Fat Breakdown
Saturated Fat	1.5 g
Monounsaturated Fat	2.6 g
Polyunsaturated Fat	0.6 g

FENNEL RISOTTO
Serves 6

1 recipe   basic risotto *(see p. 328)*

Hot liquid:
6 cups   vegetable stock *(see p. 542)* or
           chicken stock *(see p. 538)*

Fennel mixture:
4 sm.   fennel bulbs
½ tsp.   olive oil
½ cup   onion, chopped
½ cup   white wine
¼ cup   parmesan, grated

Garnish:
¼ cup   parsley, chopped

Prepare rice according to risotto directions.

Fennel mixture:
To prepare fennel, remove stalks and outer layers of bulb. Cut bulb in half and remove the core. Slice lengthwise into slivers. Blanch in boiling water for 4 minutes. Drain water. Sauté the onion in olive oil. Add wine and bring to a boil. Add fennel. Add to rice. Blend in parmesan cheese. Garnish with fresh parsley.

Alcohol Note: The alcohol content was computed prior to cooking. Once the alcohol is heated to the boiling point, the alcohol disappears along with most of the calories from the alcohol.

Nutrient Content Per Serving

Calories	402.0
Protein	8.8 g
Carbohydrates	64.8 g
Fat – Total	7.5 g
Cholesterol	3.3 mg
Dietary Fiber	8.2 g
Sodium	165.0 mg

Percent of Calories

- 9% Protein
- 64% Carbohydrate
- 17% Fat
- 11% Alcohol

Fat Breakdown

Saturated Fat	1.6 g
Monounsaturated Fat	2.8 g
Polyunsaturated Fat	2.4 g

PEPPERED CORN RISOTTO
Serves 6

2 cups   rice, short-grain

Hot stock:
6 cups   chicken stock *(see p. 538)*

Corn and pepper mixture:
1 10-oz.   pkg. frozen corn
½ tsp.   olive oil
½ cup   onions, minced
1 clove   garlic, minced
1 med.   sweet red pepper, diced

Finish:
¼ cup   parmesan cheese, grated
2 Tbl.   basil, chopped

Corn and peppers:
In a medium non-stick frying pan, heat olive oil. Sauté onions and garlic until soft. Add raw rice, 2 cups of stock, red pepper and corn. Cook until rice is creamy. Add remaining stock. Cook until all liquid is absorbed. Blend in parmesan cheese. Garnish with fresh basil.

Nutrient Content Per Serving

Calories	301.0
Protein	8.1 g
Carbohydrates	62.3 g
Fat – Total	2.1 g
Cholesterol	3.3 mg
Dietary Fiber	2.8 g
Sodium	83.8 mg

Percent of Calories

11% Protein
83% Carbohydrate
6% Fat

Fat Breakdown

Saturated Fat	1.0 g
Monounsaturated Fat	0.8 g
Polyunsaturated Fat	0.2 g

SHRIMP RISOTTO
Serves 6

Fish stock:

4 cups	fish stock *(see p. 540)*
½ cup	dry white wine
2 sm.	onions, sliced thick
1	carrot, sliced thick
2 sprigs	parsley
1	bay leaf

Shrimp mixture:

1 lb.	medium shrimp, peeled, deveined
2 cups	rice, short grain
1 Tbl.	powdered butter replacement
1 Tbl.	olive oil
½ tsp.	garlic, minced
½ cup	fresh parmesan cheese, grated

Combine all fish stock ingredients. Bring to a boil and simmer covered 30 minutes. Pass through a strainer, reserving liquid.

In a large non-stick frying pan, heat 2 teaspoons of olive oil. Add rice and cook, stirring constantly until rice turns opaque. Add fish stock and powdered butter replacement. Bring to a boil, then simmer uncovered until all liquid is absorbed and rice is tender.

Meanwhile, in a smaller non-stick frying pan, heat remaining 1 teaspoon of olive oil. Sauté the shrimp and garlic until the shrimp are pink. Cover and set aside.

Stir the shrimp and all its juices into the rice mixture. Sprinkle with parmesan. Serve at once.

Alcohol Note: The alcohol content was computed prior to cooking. Once the alcohol is heated to the boiling point, the alcohol disappears along with most of the calories from the alcohol.

Nutrient Content Per Serving

Calories	417.0
Protein	23.8 g
Carbohydrates	55.3 g
Fat – Total	7.5 g
Cholesterol	122.0 mg
Dietary Fiber	1.6 g
Sodium	286.0 mg

Percent of Calories

23% Protein
54% Carbohydrate
17% Fat
 6% Alcohol

Fat Breakdown

Saturated Fat	2.4 g
Monounsaturated Fat	2.9 g
Polyunsaturated Fat	1.5 g

PEASANT POLENTA
Serves 4

5 cups cold water or vegetable stock
1 cup   yellow cornmeal (or polenta)
1 tsp.   salt

Bring half of the water to a boil. Mix the other half of water with the polenta. Stir until smooth. Pour polenta into the boiling water. Add salt. Bring to a boil, stirring constantly. Simmer 1 hour. It is done when it is very thick and starts to pull away from the sides of the pan. Pour it onto a platter and let cool. Slice to serve.

Variations:
- Add ½ cup grated parmesan cheese when cooking.
- Add 1 teaspoon fresh rosemary and 1 teaspoon fresh sage before cooking.

Cook's Note: This is a simple dish. It is similar to a cornmeal mush and goes well with stews and spicy dishes. It is excellent with sauce from Orange Roughy *(see p. 380)* and a good accompaniment to Pepperonata *(see p. 397).*

▼ This recipe is used for the following item:
Polenta Pie (see p. 338)

Nutrient Content Per Serving		Percent of Calories	Fat Breakdown	
Calories	126.0	9% Protein	Saturated Fat	0.1 g
Protein	2.9 g	86% Carbohydrate	Monounsaturated Fat	0.1 g
Carbohydrates	26.8 g	4% Fat	Polyunsaturated Fat	0.2 g
Fat – Total	0.6 g			
Cholesterol	0.0 mg			
Dietary Fiber	1.8 g			
Sodium	534.0 mg			

FANCY POLENTA
Serves 8

5 cups	skim milk
1½ cups	semolina flour
1 Tbl.	olive oil
1	egg yolk, well-beaten
¼ cup	parmesan cheese, grated
2 Tbl.	parmesan cheese, grated
8 cups	mushroom ragout *(see p. 552)*

In a large sauce pan, scald the milk. Slowly incorporate the semolina with a whisk to prevent lumps from forming. Cook until thick (about 20 minutes). Pour into a bowl, add the egg yolk, olive oil and ¼ cup parmesan cheese. Mix well. Pour batter into a 9x13 baking dish prepared with cooking spray. Smooth out batter and sprinkle top with 2 tablespoons of parmesan cheese. Bake at 375° F for 20-30 minutes or until set. Cut into squares and serve with mushroom ragout.

Cook's Note: It is a great accompaniment to spicy meals.

Nutrient Content Per Serving

Calories	203.0
Protein	10.8 g
Carbohydrates	30.3 g
Fat – Total	3.9 g
Cholesterol	31.7 mg
Dietary Fiber	0.8 g
Sodium	138.0 mg

Percent of Calories

22% Protein
61% Carbohydrate
17% Fat

Fat Breakdown

Saturated Fat	1.3 g
Monounsaturated Fat	1.9 g
Polyunsaturated Fat	0.4 g

POLENTA PIE
Serves 8

1 recipe	Peasant Polenta *(see p. 336)*
2	shallots, chopped fine
2 cloves	garlic, minced
1 Tbl.	olive oil
½ cup	sun-dried tomatoes, chopped
3	tomatoes, chopped
¼ tsp.	fresh thyme
¼ tsp.	fresh rosemary
¼ tsp.	fresh sage
1½ lbs.	mushrooms, sliced
to taste	salt and pepper
¼ cup	white wine
½ cup	skim milk
¼ bunch	chives

In a medium non-stick frying pan, sauté the shallots and garlic in the olive oil. Add the sun-dried tomatoes, fresh tomatoes and the fresh herbs. Heat until sun-dried tomatoes are plump. Add mushrooms and season with salt and pepper to taste. Add the white wine and skim milk. Reduce until it starts getting thick. Sprinkle chives on top. Pour onto a platter and top with the polenta.

Cook's Note: Use porcini mushrooms for a more authentic version. Use only 4 ounces dried weight. Serve over pasta, rice or chicken in place of polenta.

Nutrient Content Per Serving

Calories	248.0
Protein	12.3 g
Carbohydrates	35.5 g
Fat – Total	5.8 g
Cholesterol	32.0 mg
Dietary Fiber	2.0 g
Sodium	221.0 mg

Percent of Calories

20% Protein	
57% Carbohydrate	
21% Fat	

Fat Breakdown

Saturated Fat	1.5 g
Monounsaturated Fat	3.2 g
Polyunsaturated Fat	0.6 g

SEMOLINA GNOCCHI
Serves 8

4 cups	skim milk
1 cups	semolina flour
¾ cup	parmesan cheese, grated
½ tsp.	salt
½ cup	egg substitute
1 tsp.	olive oil

In a large saucepan, scald milk. While stirring, pour in the semolina. Whisk until all milk is absorbed and mixture becomes thick (10-12 seconds). Remove from heat and stir in the ½ cup of parmesan cheese, salt and egg substitute.

Prepare a 11x17 baking sheet with cooking spray. Spread batter evenly. Cover and refrigerate 2 hours. Cut into 1-inch diameter circles. Arrange in a prepared 9x13 baking dish. Slightly overlap the circles. Spray with olive oil. Sprinkle remaining parmesan cheese on top. Bake at 450° F for 15-20 minutes or until the gnocchi begin to turn golden brown.

Cook's Note: This has the consistency of twice-baked potatoes. It is very tasty.

Nutrient Content Per Serving

Calories	190.0	**Percent of Calories**		**Fat Breakdown**	
Protein	12.4 g	27% Protein		Saturated Fat	2.3 g
Carbohydrates	21.9 g	47% Carbohydrate		Monounsaturated Fat	1.7 g
Fat – Total	5.5 g	26% Fat		Polyunsaturated Fat	1.1 g
Cholesterol	9.9 mg				
Dietary Fiber	0.5 g				
Sodium	401.0 mg				

POTATO GNOCCHI
Serves 8

4 lbs.	potatoes
½ cup	egg substitute
½ tsp.	salt
2 cups	all-purpose flour

Peel and cube potatoes. Boil until tender. Mash until very smooth. Allow moisture to evaporate. (They need to be dry.)

Mix together mashed potatoes, egg substitute, salt and 1½ cups of the flour. Mix well. Turn onto a floured board. Knead, incorporating the remaining ½ cup of flour. (Dough should be soft.)

Divide dough into 4 sections. Roll each into a long rope approximately ¾ inch in diameter. Cut into 1-inch pieces. To make the traditional shape, press and roll each square over the tines of a fork. The square should curl around your finger like a shell macaroni. May also roll them around your finger pressing on the counter.

Boil in a large pot until the gnocchi rise to the surface (approximately 30-45 minutes). They will be heavy.

Variations:
- Serve with olive oil and parmesan cheese, a bechamel sauce, an alfredo sauce or a marinara sauce.
- Makes a fine main course or a side dish.

Cook's Note: These freeze very well. Freeze before boiling. To use, toss frozen gnocchi into boiling water.

Nutrient Content Per Serving		Percent of Calories	Fat Breakdown	
Calories	333.0	11% Protein	Saturated Fat	0.4 g
Protein	8.8 g	84% Carbohydrate	Monounsaturated Fat	0.4 g
Carbohydrates	69.7 g	6% Fat	Polyunsaturated Fat	1.2 g
Fat – Total	2.2 g			
Cholesterol	0.3 mg			
Dietary Fiber	4.3 g			
Sodium	175.0 mg			

SPINACH GNOCCHI
Serves 4

¾ lb.   spinach, chopped
4 cups   flour
2 tsp.   olive oil
¼ cup   egg substitute
¼ cup   parmesan, grated

Thaw spinach and squeeze out all moisture. Mix together flour, oil, egg substitute and spinach, parmesan and some water if needed. Make a soft dough. Let rest for 30 minutes.

Form into little balls, like dumplings. Boil a large pot of water. Drop dumplings into the water. Cook approximately 20 minutes. Remove with a slotted spoon. Serve plain, with parmesan cheese or a marinara sauce.

Cook's Note: Excellent, yet simple to make.

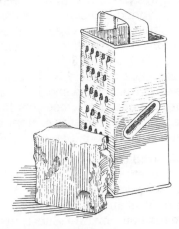

Nutrient Content Per Serving

Calories	551.0
Protein	19.9 g
Carbohydrates	101.0 g
Fat – Total	7.2 g
Cholesterol	5.2 mg
Dietary Fiber	5.6 g
Sodium	222.0 mg

Percent of Calories

15% Protein
74% Carbohydrate
12% Fat

Fat Breakdown

Saturated Fat	2.0 g
Monounsaturated Fat	2.7 g
Polyunsaturated Fat	1.8 g

PASTA DOUGH
Serves 6

1½ cups   semolina flour
1½ cups   all-purpose flour
½ tsp.   salt
4   egg whites or ½ cup egg
              substitute
1 tsp.   olive oil
½ cup   warm water

If making without a pasta machine: Mix
ingredients together until the consistency is
like cornmeal. Roll out dough to ⅛-inch thick
and cut into noodles.

If using a pasta machine: Combine the flour
and flavoring in machine and mix for 4 minutes.
Add three-quarters of egg whites, salt and oil.
Mix for 4 minutes. Add remaining egg whites,
salt and oil. Mix for 3 minutes and check
consistency. It should be the consistency of
coarse cornmeal and should stick together
when squeezed between your fingers. You may
need to adjust moisture content by adding more
water or more flour. Begin extruding process.

BEET (red color)
2 sm. beets
Boil unpeeled beets until tender. Reserve beet
water. Peel and purée. Incorporate beet purée
into the flour mixture. Substitute beet cooking
water for plain water.

HERB PASTA (speckled green)
6 Tbl. fresh chopped herbs
Choose from: parsley, sorrel, thyme, sage,
basil, marjoram or fennel. Incorporate herbs
into the flour.

RED PEPPER Linguini (orange)
7-oz. jar roasted red peppers
Drain and purée red peppers. Incorporate as
you combine the wet and dry ingredients.

SAFFRON PASTA (yellow)
Pinch of saffron and pinch of turmeric
Incorporate spices into the dry flour.

SPINACH (green)
5-oz. pkg. frozen spinach, chopped.
Thaw and purée spinach. Squeeze out all
moisture. Reserve spinach water. Work
spinach into flour before adding egg whites.
Substitute spinach water for plain water.

TOMATO PASTA (orange)
2-oz. can tomato paste
Incorporate tomato paste as you combine the
wet and dry ingredients.

WHOLE WHEAT (brown)
Substitute 1½ cups whole wheat pastry flour
for the all-purpose flour.

ZUCCHINI PASTA (speckled green)
1 med. zucchini
Grate unpeeled zucchini. Blanch or microwave.
Drain and squeeze dry, reserving liquid.
Incorporate zucchini into flour. Substitute
zucchini cooking water for plain water.

▼ This recipe is used for the following
items:
Pasta with Tomatoes (see p. 345)
Chicken Tortellini (see p. 349)
Turkey, Gorgonzola Ravioli with Red
*   Pepper Sauce (see p. 351)*
Chicken Florentine Style (see p. 364)

Nutrient Content Per Serving

Calories	282.0
Protein	10.9 g
Carbohydrates	54.3 g
Fat – Total	1.5 g
Cholesterol	0.0 mg
Dietary Fiber	1.9 g
Sodium	215.0 mg

Percent of Calories
16% Protein
79% Carbohydrate
 5% Fat

Fat Breakdown

Saturated Fat	0.2 g
Monounsaturated Fat	0.6 g
Polyunsaturated Fat	0.4 g

GRILLED VEGETARIAN SANDWICH

Serves 6

6	poppy-seed rolls
6 slices	eggplant, sliced thin
12 slices	zucchini
3	tomatoes, sliced
2 Tbl.	fat-free mayonnaise
1 bag	alfalfa sprouts
to taste	salt and pepper

Vegetable Relish:

¼ cup	broccoli, chopped
¼ cup	carrots, chopped
¼ cup	cauliflower, chopped
¼ cup	tomato, diced
¼ cup	Balsamic Ginger Vinaigrette *(see p. 559)*

Marinade:

1 tsp.	olive oil
pinch	salt
few grindings	pepper

Combine all the Vegetable Relish ingredients and let stand for about 30 minutes before using.

Preheat the grill. Marinate the eggplant, zucchini and tomatoes slices for 10 minutes. Grill quickly over hot coals. Remove and set aside. Cut the poppy-seed rolls in half. Spread mayonnaise on the rolls and layer the vegetables on it. Garnish with alfalfa sprouts and Vegetable Relish.

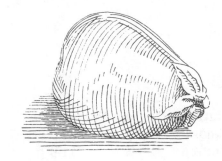

Cook's Note: This recipe is very light and refreshing.

Nutrient Content Per Serving		Percent of Calories	Fat Breakdown	
Calories	184.0	12% Protein	Saturated Fat	0.7 g
Protein	5.7 g	69% Carbohydrate	Monounsaturated Fat	2.0 g
Carbohydrates	32.6 g	19% Fat	Polyunsaturated Fat	0.7 g
Fat – Total	3.9 g			
Cholesterol	0.3 mg			
Dietary Fiber	4.1 g			
Sodium	349.0 mg			

ANGEL-HAIR PASTA WITH FRESH BASIL TOMATO SAUCE

Serves 4

¾ lb. angel-hair pasta, uncooked
2 cups tomato ragout *(see p. 552)*
2 tsp. olive oil

Garnish:
8 Tbl. tomato, chopped
2 Tbl. chives, chopped

Cook's Note: Quick and easy. A basic Italian pasta dish.

Cook angel-hair pasta in water, al dente. Drain. Add ragout. Garnish each serving with 2 tablespoons of chopped tomatoes and a dash of chives.

Nutrient Content Per Serving

Calories	385.0
Protein	11.9 g
Carbohydrates	71.5 g
Fat – Total	6.3 g
Cholesterol	0.0 mg
Dietary Fiber	5.7 g
Sodium	4.1 mg

Percent of Calories

12% Protein	
73% Carbohydrate	
14% Fat	

Fat Breakdown

Saturated Fat	0.9 g
Monounsaturated Fat	3.5 g
Polyunsaturated Fat	1.2 g

PASTA WITH TOMATOES
Serves 4

1 lb.	tomato pasta *(see p. 342)*

Sauce:

1 clove	garlic, minced
½ tsp.	olive oil
1 lb.	plum tomatoes, peeled, seeded and chopped
to taste	salt and pepper
1 Tbl.	fresh basil, chopped
3 oz.	pecorino cheese, grated

Sauce:
In a non-stick pan, sauté garlic in olive oil until cooked but not browned. Add tomatoes, salt and pepper. Cook over low heat for 10 minutes.

Cook pasta al dente. Drain. Add sauce. Sprinkle with basil and pecorino cheese.

Cook's Note: May substitute romano cheese for pecorino cheese.

Nutrient Content Per Serving

Calories	446.0
Protein	19.5 g
Carbohydrates	69.8 g
Fat – Total	9.7 g
Cholesterol	22.1 mg
Dietary Fiber	4.5 g
Sodium	456.0 mg

Percent of Calories

18% Protein
63% Carbohydrate
20% Fat

Fat Breakdown

Saturated Fat	4.2 g
Monounsaturated Fat	3.8 g
Polyunsaturated Fat	0.9 g

WHOLE-WHEAT PASTA WITH VEGETABLES

Serves 4

1 lb.	whole-wheat pasta, uncooked
¾ cup	vegetable stock *(see p. 542)*
	(or chicken stock, *see p. 538*)
1 Tbl.	shallots, minced
3 cloves	garlic, minced
2 cups	mushrooms, sliced thick
½	lemon, juice of
½ tsp.	red pepper flakes
24 spears	asparagus, cut in large pieces
3½ cups	broccoli, cut in large pieces
3 cups	plum tomatoes (or 28-oz. can of
	pear tomatoes with their juice)

Garnish:

8	black olives, chopped
1 Tbl.	lite soy sauce

Cook pasta al dente. Heat stock and add shallots, garlic, mushrooms, lemon juice and red pepper flakes. Reduce stock by half. Steam or microwave asparagus and broccoli until barely tender. Ten minutes before serving add vegetables, pasta and tomatoes to stock. Serve garnished with chopped olives and soy sauce.

Cook's Note: Quick and easy. The spiciness can be varied by the amount of red pepper flakes used.

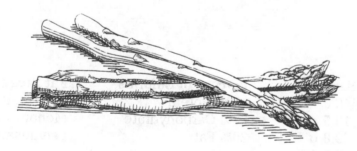

Nutrient Content Per Serving

Calories	451.0
Protein	21.4 g
Carbohydrates	91.6 g
Fat – Total	4.1 g
Cholesterol	0.0 mg
Dietary Fiber	15.5 g
Sodium	228.0 mg

Percent of Calories

17% Protein
74% Carbohydrate
 7% Fat

Fat Breakdown

Saturated Fat	0.6 g
Monounsaturated Fat	1.2 g
Polyunsaturated Fat	1.5 g

PASTA E FAJIOLI
Serves 6

1 lb.	elbow macaroni
1 clove	garlic, minced
½ cup	onion, chopped
1 tsp.	olive oil
2 cups	all-purpose red sauce *(see p. 416 or p. 417)*
1 14-oz. can	vegetarian navy beans
1 cup	parmesan, grated (optional)

In a non-stick pan, sauté garlic and onion in olive oil. Add marinara sauce and beans. Simmer for 30 minutes.

In a separate pot, cook the pasta al dente (about 10 minutes). Combine sauce, beans and pasta. Sprinkle with grated cheese if desired.

Cook's Note: This is an excellent vegetarian meal. High in fiber too! The analysis does not include the optional parmesan cheese. Addition of 1 cup of grated parmesan will add 5 grams of fat per serving.

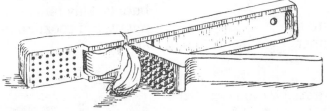

Nutrient Content Per Serving

Calories	440.0
Protein	20.3 g
Carbohydrates	78.1 g
Fat – Total	5.5 g
Cholesterol	15.3 mg
Dietary Fiber	10.4 g
Sodium	412.0 mg

Percent of Calories

18% Protein
71% Carbohydrate
11% Fat

Fat Breakdown

Saturated Fat	1.4 g
Monounsaturated Fat	2.0 g
Polyunsaturated Fat	1.6 g

MANICOTTI OR STUFFED SHELLS

Serves 8

1 12-oz. pkg.	manicotti shells or jumbo shell macaroni

Filling:

½ med.	onion, chopped
2 cloves	garlic, minced
1 tsp.	olive oil
1 lb.	nonfat ricotta cheese
1 lb.	lowfat cottage cheese
½ lb.	fat-free mozzarella, grated
4	egg whites
2 Tbl.	parsley, dry
1 Tbl.	oregano, dry
⅓ cup	parmesan, grated
to taste	salt and pepper

Topping:

2 Tbl.	parmesan, grated for top
4 cups	tomato ragout *(see p. 552)*

Cook shells al dente. Add cold water to pan. Let cool until you are able to hold them.

Meanwhile, sauté garlic and onion in olive oil. Mix together all filling ingredients. Cover bottom of a 9x12-inch pan with sauce. Stuff shells with filling. Arrange in pan. Dot some sauce over top of shells. Sprinkle with 2 tablespoons of the parmesan cheese. Bake covered at 350° F for 30 minutes or until cheese is hot and bubbly. May remove cover for final 5 minutes of cooking. Pass remaining sauce at table.

Cook's Note: In order to maintain flavor and sacrifice fat calories, it is important to use both nonfat and lowfat cheeses.

Nutrient Content Per Serving

Calories	319.0
Protein	35.9 g
Carbohydrates	29.3 g
Fat – Total	7.3 g
Cholesterol	36.7 mg
Dietary Fiber	3.1 g
Sodium	833.0 mg

Percent of Calories

44% Protein
36% Carbohydrate
20% Fat

Fat Breakdown

Saturated Fat	2.7 g
Monounsaturated Fat	2.8 g
Polyunsaturated Fat	1.6 g

CHICKEN TORTELLINI
Serves 9

Filling:

2¼ cups	chicken, chopped fine (3 chicken breasts, boneless, skinless, and poached in stock for 15 minutes)
½ cup	parmesan cheese, grated
¼ cup	egg substitute
⅛ tsp.	lemon peel, grated
⅛ tsp.	ground nutmeg
to taste	salt
to taste	freshly ground black pepper
1 double recipe	of pasta dough *(see p. 342)*
1 recipe	all-purpose sauce *(see p. 416)*

Filling:

Thoroughly combine the chicken, cheese, egg substitute, lemon peel and nutmeg. Season with salt and pepper to taste. Roll out one-quarter of the dough on a floured board until it is ¹⁄₁₆-inch thick. Cut into 2-inch rounds with a biscuit cutter. Place ¼ teaspoon of the chicken mixture in the center of each round. Moisten the edges of each round. Fold the circles in half and press the edges firmly together. Shape into rings by stretching the tips of each half circle and wrapping around your index finger. Gently press the tips together. The tortellini are best if they are cooked at once, but they may be covered and refrigerated for a day.

To cook:

Bring water to a boil in a large pot. Add a drop or two of olive oil. Drop in the tortellini and stir gently with a wooden spoon for a moment to make sure they do not stick to one another. Boil, gently stirring occasionally, for about 8 minutes or until tender. Drain them into a colander. Serve with sauce of your choice. Anything from tomato base to a bechamel sauce is tasty.

Nutrient Content Per Serving
(Calculations done with ½ cup All-Purpose Sauce per serving)

Calories	204.0
Protein	14.5 g
Carbohydrates	28.9 g
Fat – Total	2.9 g
Cholesterol	20.9 mg
Dietary Fiber	1.6 g
Sodium	135.0 mg

Percent of Calories

29% Protein
58% Carbohydrate
13% Fat

Fat Breakdown

Saturated Fat	1.3 g
Monounsaturated Fat	0.7 g
Polyunsaturated Fat	0.5 g

RICOTTA CHEESE TORTELLINI WITH SUN-DRIED TOMATO SAUCE

Serves 6

2 lbs.	lowfat ricotta cheese tortellini
1 cup	sun-dried tomatoes
4	shallots, chopped
6 cloves	garlic, minced
1 Tbl.	olive oil
¼ cup	sweet white wine
¼ cup	chicken stock *(see p. 538)*
½ cup	skim milk
2 Tbl.	nonfat dry milk
¼ bunch	fresh basil, chopped

In a non-stick frying pan, sauté shallots and garlic with olive oil. Add sun-dried tomatoes, white wine, chicken stock, skim milk and dry milk. Reduce sauce to half. Add the fresh basil and simmer for 10 minutes. Transfer sauce to a blender and purée until smooth. Return sauce to the skillet and add the pre-cooked tortellini. Toss quickly and serve immediately with your choice of parmesan or Italian bread.

Cook's Note: Another quick and easy recipe!

Alcohol Note: The alcohol content was computed prior to cooking. Once the alcohol is heated to the boiling point, the alcohol disappears along with most of the calories from the alcohol.

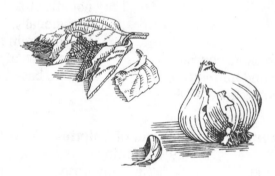

Nutrient Content Per Serving

Calories	272.0
Protein	12.6 g
Carbohydrates	43.8 g
Fat – Total	4.7 g
Cholesterol	0.9 mg
Dietary Fiber	3.5 g
Sodium	389.0 mg

Percent of Calories

18% Protein
64% Carbohydrate
15% Fat
 2% Alcohol

Fat Breakdown

Saturated Fat	0.5 g
Monounsaturated Fat	1.8 g
Polyunsaturated Fat	0.6 g

TURKEY, GORGONZOLA RAVIOLI WITH RED PEPPER SAUCE
Serves 6

Filling:

1 lb.	turkey breast, ground fine
2 oz.	gorgonzola cheese, grated
½	onion, chopped fine
2	egg whites
¼ cup	white wine
dash	nutmeg
to taste	salt and pepper
1 recipe	pasta dough *(see p. 342)*
1	egg white, whipped

Sauce:

1 tsp.	garlic, minced
¼ med.	onion, diced
2	sweet red peppers, diced
¼ cup	white wine
2 cups	chicken stock *(see p. 538)*
¼ tsp.	cumin
3 Tbl.	fennel bulb, diced fine
to taste	salt and pepper
1 Tbl.	powdered butter replacement

To prepare filling:
Combine all ingredients in a food processor. Blend until smooth.

To prepare ravioli:
Roll out pasta dough into two thin sheets (¹⁄₁₆-inch thick), on a flour-dusted table. Arrange spoonfuls of filling on one sheet of dough. Brush dough between filling with egg white. Cover with the remaining sheet of dough. Using a ravioli cutter, roll and cut into squares. You will have little pillow-shaped ravioli. If using a pasta machine, make lasagna noodles and proceed as above.

In a large pot, boil the ravioli quickly until done.

To prepare the sauce:
In a non-stick frying pan, sauté the onion, garlic, peppers and fennel. Add the wine and chicken stock. Reduce. Season with cumin, salt and pepper to taste. Add the powdered butter replacement. In a blender or food processor, blend or purée until smooth.

To serve:
Return the ravioli to a skillet, add the sauce and bring to a boil. Cook slowly for 10 minutes. Serve immediately with freshly grated parmesan.

Nutrient Content Per Serving	
Calories	382.0
Protein	35.9 g
Carbohydrates	42.0 g
Fat – Total	5.3 g
Cholesterol	73.3 mg
Dietary Fiber	2.3 g
Sodium	296.0 mg

Percent of Calories
39% Protein
45% Carbohydrate
13% Fat

Fat Breakdown	
Saturated Fat	2.3 g
Monounsaturated Fat	1.6 g
Polyunsaturated Fat	0.7 g

VEGETARIAN LASAGNA
Serves 6

1 14-oz. can	tomatoes, low-sodium, undrained
1 12-oz. can	tomato sauce, low-sodium
1 tsp.	dried oregano
1 tsp.	dried basil leaves
dash	black pepper
1 lg.	onion, chopped
1½ tsp.	garlic, minced
2 sm.	zucchini, chopped
8 oz.	mushrooms, sliced
1 lg.	carrot, chopped
1	green pepper, chopped
1 cup	nonfat mozzarella cheese, shredded
2 cups	nonfat cottage cheese
¼ cup	1% milk
1 cup	parmesan cheese, grated
8 oz.	lasagna noodles, uncooked

Garnish:

Parsley sprigs (optional)

In a medium saucepan over low heat, simmer tomatoes with juice, tomato sauce, oregano, basil and black pepper for 5 minutes. In microwave, cook onion, garlic, zucchini, mushrooms, carrot and green pepper until just tender. Stir vegetables into tomato mixture. Simmer 15 minutes. Combine mozzarella, milk, cottage cheese and parmesan cheese in large bowl. Blend well.

Spoon about 1 cup sauce into the bottom of a 9x12 baking pan. Place a layer of noodles over sauce, then one-half of the cheese mixture and one-half of the remaining sauce. Repeat layers of noodles, cheese mixture and sauce. Bake in preheated 350° F oven 30-45 minutes or until bubbly. Let stand 10 minutes. Garnish with parsley.

Cook's Note: May substitute or add other vegetables for those above. Serving sizes are large. The sodium is a bit high due to the cheese and tomatoes. If you must restrict sodium, skip this recipe *(see HealthMark Dietary Goals p. 3)* for more information).

Nutrient Content Per Serving		**Percent of Calories**	**Fat Breakdown**	
Calories	371.0	31% Protein	Saturated Fat	5.4 g
Protein	29.4 g	47% Carbohydrate	Monounsaturated Fat	2.5 g
Carbohydrates	44.2 g	22% Fat	Polyunsaturated Fat	0.7 g
Fat – Total	9.3 g			
Cholesterol	26.4 mg			
Dietary Fiber	6.0 g			
Sodium	714.0 mg			

BROCCOLI-SPINACH LASAGNA
Serves 8

1 lb.	spinach lasagna noodles

Filling:

1 oz.	dried porcini mushrooms
2 cups	boiling water
1 lb.	broccoli flowerettes, chopped
1 tsp.	olive oil
2 med.	shallots, chopped
5 cloves	garlic, minced
1½ lb.	fresh mushrooms, sliced
¼ cup	dry white wine
½ tsp.	thyme
½ tsp.	rosemary
½ cup	parsley, chopped
few grindings	black pepper
3½ cups	fresh spinach, chopped
1½ cups	parmesan cheese, grated
3 cups	bechamel sauce *(see p. 554)*

Filling:

Soak dried porcini mushrooms in boiling water while preparing remainder of filling. Parboil broccoli and spinach. Set aside. In a non-stick frying pan, sauté shallots in olive oil. When they are translucent, add garlic. Sauté until garlic begins to brown. Add fresh mushrooms. Sauté until limp. Drain dried mushrooms reserving soaking liquid. Chop dried mushrooms if needed. Add to pan with fresh mushrooms. Add ½ cup soaking liquid to pan.

In a separate saucepan, reduce remaining soaking liquid to ½ cup. Add to mushrooms with the wine, thyme, rosemary, parsley and pepper. Continue to sauté until all liquid has disappeared.

Prepare Bechamel Sauce. Mix ½ cup of sauce into mushrooms and ½ cup into broccoli.

To prepare the lasagna:

Spray a non-stick 9x13 pan with cooking spray. Have water boiling for lasagna noodles. Add a few lasagna noodles at a time. Layer noodles, cover with some bechamel, then mushrooms and chopped broccoli. Sprinkle with some parmesan. Continue layering, making 4-6 layers. Top off with sauce covered with some parmesan. Bake at 400° F for 25 minutes. Let stand 10 minutes before serving.

Nutrient Content Per Serving

Calories	302.0
Protein	19.9 g
Carbohydrates	32.9 g
Fat – Total	10.7 g
Cholesterol	37.6 mg
Dietary Fiber	5.1 g
Sodium	520.0 mg

Percent of Calories

25% Protein
42% Carbohydrate
31% Fat

Fat Breakdown

Saturated	4.9 g
Monounsaturated Fat	3.3 g
Polyunsaturated Fat	1.6 g

LINGUINI WITH CALAMARI

Serves 6

2 lbs.	linguini, uncooked
1 lb.	calamari, cut in rounds
to taste	Tabasco™
4 lg. cloves	garlic, minced
½ tsp.	olive oil
1 Tbl.	lemon juice
½ cup	chicken stock *(see p. 538)*
½ cup	white wine
to taste	salt and pepper

Garnish:

2	tomatoes, peeled, seeded, chopped
	chives chopped

Cook the linguini al dente according to package directions, omitting added salt and fat.

In a non-stick pan, quickly sauté calamari with olive oil. Add salt and pepper to taste, garlic, Tabasco™ and lemon juice. Combine the linguini and calamari mixture and mix well. Garnish with tomatoes and chives.

Cholesterol — Above the HM⁄ guidelines: Occasionally a lowfat recipe is high in cholesterol. In this case the cholesterol stems from the shellfish. The level is moderately high (>150 mg per serving) but may fit into your weekly average of 150 mg per day.

Alcohol Note: The alcohol content was computed prior to cooking. Once the alcohol is heated to the boiling point, the alcohol disappears along with most of the calories from the alcohol.

Nutrient Content Per Serving

Calories	696.0
Protein	34.8 g
Carbohydrates	119.0 g
Fat – Total	6.5 g
Cholesterol	212.0 mg
Dietary Fiber	11.0 g
Sodium	339.0 mg

Percent of Calories

20%	Protein
69%	Carbohydrate
8%	Fat
3%	Alcohol

Fat Breakdown

Saturated Fat	1.2 g
Monounsaturated Fat	1.7 g
Polyunsaturated Fat	2.3 g

SPAGHETTI CON COZZE

Serves 4

2 lbs.	mussels in their shells
14 oz.	spaghetti, uncooked
3 lg. cloves	garlic, minced
½ tsp.	olive oil
8 oz.	tomatoes, peeled and chopped
to taste	salt and pepper
1 tsp.	sugar (optional)
small bunch	parsley, chopped fine
2 Tbl.	sun-dried tomatoes, chopped
1 tsp.	basil, dry
1 tsp.	oregano, dry

Begin water for spaghetti.

Scrub mussels and remove beards. Steam mussels in 2 cups of water until they open. Discard any unopened ones. Remove cooked mussels from their shells and set aside. Reserve the cooking liquid.

Begin to cook the spaghetti.

To prepare the sauce:
Strain and boil the cooking liquor (the liquid the mussels were cooked in) until it is reduced to 1 cup. In a non-stick frying pan, sauté garlic in the oil for 2 minutes. Add tomatoes, salt and pepper to taste, sugar, the reduced cooking liquor, parsley, sun-dried tomatoes, basil and oregano. Cook until the tomatoes soften. Add the mussels and immediately remove sauce from heat, so as not to cook the mussels any further.

As soon as the spaghetti is cooked al dente, drain and add to the sauce. Stir briefly over high heat and serve immediately.

Cook's Note: The sodium is coming from the mussels themselves.

Nutrient Content Per Serving		Percent of Calories	Fat Breakdown	
Calories	588.0	28% Protein	Saturated Fat	1.3 g
Protein	40.9 g	60% Carbohydrate	Monounsaturated Fat	1.8 g
Carbohydrates	87.0 g	12% Fat	Polyunsaturated Fat	2.1 g
Fat – Total	7.4 g			
Cholesterol	63.5 mg			
Dietary Fiber	7.6 g			
Sodium	690.0 mg			

Fresh Garden Pasta Primavera with Shrimp

Serves 4

1 lb.	spaghetti, uncooked
2 cloves	garlic, minced
1 tsp.	olive oil
1 cup	cauliflower or broccoflower flowers
½ cup	carrots, peeled, chopped in chunks
1 cup	fresh snow peas
1 cup	zucchini, cut in rounds then quartered
4	plum tomatoes, cut in chunks
½ lb.	baby shrimp, frozen or precooked
2 Tbl.	fresh basil, chopped
¼ cup	fresh chives, chopped

Sauce:

⅓ cup	powdered milk
1¼ cups	skim milk
2 Tbl.	liquid margarine
2 Tbl.	flour
1 Tbl.	powdered butter replacement
¼ tsp.	white pepper
½ cup	parmesan cheese, grated fine

Garnish:

fresh parsley

In a non-stick pan, sauté garlic in oil until it starts to brown. Add cauliflower and carrots. Cook 5 minutes. Add snow peas and zucchini. Cook 3 minutes. Add tomato, shrimp, basil and chives. Cook until vegetables are just tender, but still crisp.

Meanwhile, cook pasta al dente.

To prepare sauce:
Dissolve powdered milk in skim milk. Heat margarine, whisk in flour. Cook 2 minutes stirring constantly. Gradually whisk in milk until incorporated without lumps. Add powdered butter replacement and pepper. Whisk over medium heat until it begins to thicken. Add parmesan cheese and cook until cheese is melted and sauce is smooth.

To serve:
Drain pasta. Add three-quarters of vegetables and most of the sauce. Toss. Top with remaining vegetables and remaining sauce. Garnish with fresh parsley. Serve with Italian bread and green salad.

Nutrient Content Per Serving		**Percent of Calories**	**Fat Breakdown**	
Calories	396.0	27% Protein	Saturated Fat	1.6 g
Protein	26.6 g	53% Carbohydrate	Monounsaturated Fat	3.1 g
Carbohydrates	52.9 g	20% Fat	Polyunsaturated Fat	3.4 g
Fat – Total	8.7 g			
Cholesterol	114.0 mg			
Dietary Fiber	6.2 g			
Sodium	328.0 mg			

ANGEL-HAIR PASTA
WITH SEARED SCALLOPS AND PRAWNS
Serves 4

1 lb.	angel-hair pasta, uncooked
12	sea scallops
12	jumbo prawns, peeled, deveined
1	shallot, diced fine
1 clove	garlic, minced
2 tsp.	olive oil
½ cup	white wine
dash	samba olé (hot pepper sauce)
1 cup	tomato ragout *(see p. 552)*
pinch	fresh cilantro, chopped
to taste	salt and pepper

Garnish:

cilantro sprigs
salmon rose *(see p. 14)*

In a non-stick frying pan, sauté scallops, shrimp, shallots and garlic, in olive oil. Meanwhile, cook the pasta al dente. Remove the seafood and set aside. Add the white wine and samba olé. Reduce a little and add tomato ragout. Cook for 5-10 minutes and season with cilantro, salt and pepper to taste. Return seafood to pan. Heat through.

To serve:
Cover the bottoms of individual serving plates with a swirl of sauce and swish the pasta in the center of the plate. Arrange the seafood nicely around pasta. Garnish with cilantro sprigs and place a salmon rose on top of the pasta for color and taste.

Nutrient Content Per Serving

Calories	560.0
Protein	26.7 g
Carbohydrates	91.9 g
Fat – Total	6.8 g
Cholesterol	48.6 mg
Dietary Fiber	8.8 g
Sodium	161.0 mg

Percent of Calories

19% Protein
66% Carbohydrate
11% Fat

Fat Breakdown

Saturated Fat	1.0 g
Monounsaturated Fat	3.2 g
Polyunsaturated Fat	1.6 g

CHICKEN ARTICHOKE CASSEROLE

Serves 4

4	chicken breasts, skinless, boneless
1 cup	artichoke hearts (may use canned)
⅓ cup	flour
2½ cups	low-sodium chicken broth, defatted
1 oz.	cheddar cheese, sharp, grated
¼ cup	dry wine or vermouth
½ cup	mozzarella cheese, lowfat, grated
¼ cup	romano cheese, grated
2 Tbl.	scallions, diced
1 tsp.	paprika
1 tsp.	thyme, dry
1 tsp.	parsley, dry
1 Tbl.	romano or parmesan cheese, grated

Arrange chicken in a baking dish prepared with cooking spray. Dot with artichokes.

In a saucepan, blend flour and chicken broth. Heat until thick, whisking constantly. Remove from heat, add cheddar cheese, wine, mozzarella, ¼ cup romano cheese and scallions. Pour sauce over chicken. Top with spices and remaining grated cheese. Bake uncovered at 350° F for 35 minutes or until bubbly.

Nutrient Content Per Serving

Calories	304.0
Protein	38.0 g
Carbohydrates	15.2 g
Fat – Total	8.9 g
Cholesterol	91.6 mg
Dietary Fiber	3.2 g
Sodium	321.0 mg

Percent of Calories

50% Protein
20% Carbohydrate
27% Fat

Fat Breakdown

Saturated Fat	4.8 g
Monounsaturated Fat	2.3 g
Polyunsaturated Fat	0.6 g

SEARED CHICKEN BREAST
Serves 6

6	chicken breasts, boneless, skinless
½ cup	artichoke hearts, diced

Gremoulata:

¼ cup	bread crumbs
1 Tbl.	fresh rosemary, chopped
2 Tbl.	fresh parsley, chopped
½ Tbl.	roasted garlic
1 Tbl.	parmesan cheese, freshly grated
1	lemon, zest of, chopped
½ Tbl.	olive oil

Sauce:

½ tsp.	olive oil
1 tsp.	shallots, minced
2 Tbl.	carrots, diced
¼ tsp.	herbs (your choice)
1 tsp.	tomato paste
2 oz.	Marsala wine
2 cups	veal stock *(see p. 536)*
to taste	salt and pepper

In a non-stick pan, sauté artichoke hearts in olive oil. Set aside for garnish.

Gremoulata:
Combine all ingredients. Mix well. Keep refrigerated.

Season the chicken breast with salt and pepper to taste. Dust with flour and cook in a non-stick frying pan over medium heat until done. Remove from pan, top with a thin layer of gremoulata. Brown under broiler until golden.

To prepare sauce:
Sauté shallots and carrots in olive oil until tender. Add herbs and tomato paste. Allow to brown slightly. Add Marsala and veal stock. Reduce to 1½ cups. Strain. Add salt and pepper to taste.

To assemble, place the sauce on the plate. Add an artichoke on top of sauce. Arrange the chicken breast on top of the artichoke. Serve with turnip, potato purée and seasonal vegetables. Garnish with rosemary sprigs and curled red beets.

Cook's Note: May purchase demi-glace in the specialty section of most supermarkets. Use in place of veal stock. The gremoulata may also be used for a variety of meats and seafood.

Alcohol Note: The alcohol content was computed prior to cooking. Once the alcohol is heated to the boiling point, the alcohol disappears along with most of the calories from the alcohol.

Nutrient Content Per Serving		Percent of Calories	Fat Breakdown	
Calories	205.0	54% Protein	Saturated Fat	0.9 g
Protein	27.8 g	15% Carbohydrate	Monounsaturated Fat	1.8 g
Carbohydrates	6.6 g	20% Fat	Polyunsaturated Fat	1.2 g
Fat – Total	4.4 g	11% Alcohol		
Cholesterol	66.6 mg			
Dietary Fiber	1.0 g			
Sodium	136.0 mg			

CHICKEN CACCIAMANI
Serves 4

4	chicken breasts, boneless, skinless
4	egg whites
¼ cup	bread crumbs
1 lb.	fresh mushrooms, sliced
2 cups	chicken stock *(see p. 538)*
4 oz.	lowfat mozzarella cheese, grated fine

Cut chicken into strips. Drop into a bowl of egg whites. Soak chicken in the refrigerator for 2 hours or overnight.

Dip chicken in bread crumbs. Broil or cook in a non-stick skillet prepared with cooking spray, for 5 minutes each side or until bread crumbs brown. Place in a non-stick baking dish. Cover with sliced mushrooms. Pour chicken stock over top. Top with mozzarella cheese. Cover and bake 30 minutes at 350° F. Uncover and bake an additional 10 minutes allowing the cheese to brown nicely.

Cook's Note: Quick and easy! May be prepared ahead and baked at the last minute for company.

Nutrient Content Per Serving

Calories	389.0
Protein	48.6 g
Carbohydrates	26.8 g
Fat – Total	9.3 g
Cholesterol	83.7 mg
Dietary Fiber	2.5 g
Sodium	593.0 mg

Percent of Calories

50% Protein
28% Carbohydrate
22% Fat

Fat Breakdown

Saturated Fat	4.2 g
Monounsaturated Fat	2.8 g
Polyunsaturated Fat	1.3 g

CHICKEN CACCIATORE
Serves 8

8	chicken breasts, boneless and skinless
1 Tbl.	olive oil
1 med.	onion, chopped
2 cloves	garlic, minced
3 leaves	sage
1 8-oz. can	tomato paste
1 cup	water
2 cups	tomatoes, chopped
1 cup	mushrooms, sliced thick
½ cup	red wine

In a large non-stick frying pan, gently sauté chicken breasts in 2 teaspoons of the olive oil. Remove chicken to a baking dish prepared with cooking spray. Using the same pan, sauté onions in the remaining olive oil until translucent. Add to baking dish. Add remaining ingredients to the baking dish. Cover dish and bake at 325° F for 30-45 minutes, or until done.

Cook's Note: This may be prepared in a crock pot after chicken and onions have been sautéed. It makes a nice accompaniment to polenta.

Alcohol Note: The alcohol content was computed prior to cooking. Once the alcohol is heated to the boiling point, the alcohol disappears along with most of the calories from the alcohol.

Nutrient Content Per Serving

Calories	193.0
Protein	29.1 g
Carbohydrates	8.6 g
Fat – Total	3.6 g
Cholesterol	68.4 mg
Dietary Fiber	2.0 g
Sodium	251.0 mg

Percent of Calories

60% Protein
18% Carbohydrate
17% Fat
 5% Alcohol

Fat Breakdown

Saturated Fat	0.7 g
Monounsaturated Fat	1.7 g
Polyunsaturated Fat	0.7 g

CHICKEN CALABRESE
Serves 4

4	chicken breasts, skinless

Marinade:
1 Tbl.	olive oil
½ cup	black olives, sliced in half
1 cup	marsala or sherry
1 Tbl.	garlic, minced
1	shallot, minced
1 Tbl.	oregano, dried
1 Tbl.	rosemary, dried

Garnish:
1 Tbl.	parsley, dry
1 tsp.	paprika

Combine marinade ingredients. Place chicken in marinade for at least 1 hour. Bake chicken in the marinade for 1 hour at 350° F. Turn pieces or baste every 20 minutes. Discard entire marinade. Serve only the chicken. Sprinkle with parsley and paprika before serving.

Cook's Note: You may wish to pound the chicken breasts before marinating for a more tender result.

Alcohol Note: The alcohol content was computed prior to cooking. Once the alcohol is heated to the boiling point, the alcohol disappears along with most of the calories from the alcohol.

Nutrient Content Per Serving		**Percent of Calories**	**Fat Breakdown**	
Calories	224.0	50% Protein	Saturated Fat	1.1 g
Protein	27.7 g	5% Carbohydrate	Monounsaturated Fat	4.2 g
Carbohydrates	2.7 g	27% Fat	Polyunsaturated Fat	0.8 g
Fat – Total	6.7 g	17% Alcohol		
Cholesterol	68.4 mg			
Dietary Fiber	0.7 g			
Sodium	191.0 mg			

CHICKEN CREOLE
Serves 8

8	chicken breasts, skinless
1 pkg.	onion-mushroom soup mix
2¼ cups	boiling water
1 16-oz. can	whole tomatoes, peeled, seeded, drained, chopped
1 cup	white rice, uncooked
1 cup	green pepper, chopped

Prepare a baking dish with cooking spray. Arrange chicken in a single layer. Preheat oven to 350° F.

Meanwhile, in a bowl, combine soup mix, water, tomatoes, rice and green pepper. Pour around chicken. Bake covered at 350° F for 30-40 minutes or until chicken and rice are tender.

Cook's Note: A simple one-pot dish for a winter day.

Nutrient Content Per Serving

Calories	232.0
Protein	29.7 g
Carbohydrates	22.4 g
Fat – Total	1.8 g
Cholesterol	68.4 mg
Dietary Fiber	1.3 g
Sodium	250.0 mg

Percent of Calories

53% Protein
40% Carbohydrate
7% Fat

Fat Breakdown

Saturated Fat	0.5 g
Monounsaturated Fat	0.5 g
Polyunsaturated Fat	0.5 g

CHICKEN FLORENTINE STYLE
Serves 4

4 lg.	chicken breasts, skinless and boneless
1 oz.	dried mushrooms
1 Tbl.	olive oil
2 cloves	garlic, left whole
1 sm.	onion, chopped fine
½ cup	Marsala wine
¾ lb.	tomatoes, peeled, seeded and chopped
2 sprigs	parsley
to taste	salt and pepper

Soak mushrooms in warm water for 30 minutes. Squeeze dry and cut into thin strips.

In a large non-stick frying pan, heat oil and gently sauté the chicken. Add garlic and onion. Discard garlic as it begins to brown. Continue cooking until onion is limp. Add remaining ingredients. Season with salt and pepper if desired. Simmer 30 minutes, or until chicken is tender. Sauce should be fairly thick. Add water to thin if necessary.

Cook's Note: Serve with fresh pasta *(see p. 342).* For a more colorful presentation, try spinach pasta, tomato pasta or red pepper linguini.

Alcohol Note: The alcohol content was computed prior to cooking. Once the alcohol is heated to the boiling point, the alcohol disappears along with most of the calories from the alcohol.

Nutrient Content Per Serving		**Percent of Calories**	**Fat Breakdown**	
Calories	228.0	51% Protein	Saturated Fat	0.9 g
Protein	29.1 g	21% Carbohydrate	Monounsaturated Fat	2.9 g
Carbohydrates	11.8 g	20% Fat	Polyunsaturated Fat	0.8 g
Fat – Total	5.2 g	8% Alcohol		
Cholesterol	68.4 mg			
Dietary Fiber	2.3 g			
Sodium	87.5 mg			

Red, White and Green Salad *(page 317)*
Orange Roughy with a Fennel-Tomato Sauce *(page 380)*
Grilled Vegetable Salad *(page 320)*

Vegetable Antipasto Platter *(page 285)*
Lemon Chicken Flambé *(page 370)*

Chicken Italiano *(page 369)*
Italian-Style Potato Salad *(page 316)*

Chicken Cacciatore *(page 361)*
Tuna-Bean Salad *(page 313)*
Sautéed Zucchini *(page 406)*

CHICKEN ITALIANO
Serves 4

4   chicken breasts, skinless, boneless
¼ cup   parmesan or romano cheese, grated
¼ cup   cornmeal
2 Tbl.   parsley, dry
2 tsp.   oregano, dry
1 clove garlic, minced
½ tsp.   pepper
2   egg whites, beaten

In a flat bowl, combine grated cheese, cornmeal, parsley, oregano, garlic and pepper. Dip chicken in egg whites, then in cornmeal mixture. Place in an 8x8 baking dish prepared with cooking spray. Bake at 375° F for 30-40 minutes or until chicken is done.

Cook's Note: Quick and easy. Serve with Zuppa Pizzialo *(see p. 309)* or Broccoli al Vino *(see p. 389).*

Nutrient Content Per Serving

Calories	177.0
Protein	33.3 g
Carbohydrates	1.4 g
Fat – Total	3.4 g
Cholesterol	73.3 mg
Dietary Fiber	0.4 g
Sodium	244.0 mg

Percent of Calories

78% Protein	
3% Carbohydrate	
18% Fat	

Fat Breakdown

Saturated Fat	1.6 g
Monounsaturated Fat	0.9 g
Polyunsaturated Fat	0.4 g

LEMON CHICKEN FLAMBÉ
Serves 6

6	chicken breasts, boneless, skinless
6 Tbl.	flour
	onion powder
	oregano, dry
	basil, dry
	black pepper
⅓ cup	dry white wine
4 Tbl.	fresh lemon juice
2 tsp.	lemon zest
2 cloves	garlic, minced
1½ cups	mushrooms, sliced
12	artichoke hearts, canned or frozen
1 Tbl.	fresh parsley, chopped
¼ cup	brandy

Pound chicken breasts until flat. Dredge chicken in flour. Shake off excess flour. Sprinkle chicken with onion powder, oregano, basil and pepper to taste. Bake on a rack for 30 minutes at 375° F.

In a medium frying pan, combine wine, lemon juice and garlic. Simmer 4-5 minutes. Add mushrooms, artichoke hearts and parsley. Cook 3 minutes.

To Serve:
Place chicken breasts in sauce. Add zest. Heat brandy and ignite it with a match. While flaming, pour brandy into sauce. Allow flames to die down, then ladle sauce over chicken. Serve over fresh fettucine or rice.

Cook's Note: For a dramatic effect flame the brandy at the table. Very impressive!

Alcohol Note: The alcohol content was computed prior to cooking. Once the alcohol is heated to the boiling point, the alcohol disappears along with most of the calories from the alcohol.

Nutrient Content Per Serving

Calories	228.0
Protein	30.8 g
Carbohydrates	14.7 g
Fat – Total	2.0 g
Cholesterol	68.4 mg
Dietary Fiber	4.3 g
Sodium	116.0 mg

Percent of Calories

54%	Protein
26%	Carbohydrate
8%	Fat
13%	Alcohol

Fat Breakdown

Saturated Fat	0.5 g
Monounsaturated Fat	0.4 g
Polyunsaturated Fat	0.6 g

CHICKEN MARSALA
Serves 6

6 5-oz.	chicken breasts, boneless, skinless
¼ cup	flour
1 tsp.	olive oil
1 Tbl.	shallots, chopped
1 tsp.	garlic, chopped
1 cup	mushrooms, sliced
¼ cup	Marsala wine
1 cup	chicken stock *(see p. 538)*
1 Tbl.	Italian parsley, chopped

Dust the chicken breasts with flour. In a non-stick frying pan, sauté chicken in the olive oil until golden brown on both sides. Remove and set aside. Add shallots, garlic and mushrooms and sauté until limp. Quickly add marsala and reduce a little. Add chicken stock, parsley and return chicken to the pan. Cover and simmer for 5-10 minutes. Serve immediately.

Alcohol Note: The alcohol content was computed prior to cooking. Once the alcohol is heated to the boiling point, the alcohol disappears along with most of the calories from the alcohol.

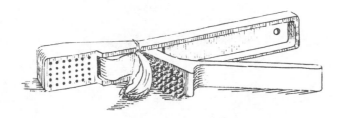

Nutrient Content Per Serving

Calories	200.0
Protein	34.3 g
Carbohydrates	6.6 g
Fat – Total	2.73 g
Cholesterol	82.2 mg
Dietary Fiber	0.8 g
Sodium	94.9 mg

Percent of Calories

70% Protein
14% Carbohydrate
13% Fat
 3% Alcohol

Fat Breakdown

Saturated Fat	0.6 g
Monounsaturated Fat	1.0 g
Polyunsaturated Fat	0.6 g

CHICKEN MODENA STYLE
Serves 4

4 4-oz.	chicken breasts, boneless, skinless
3	egg whites, lightly beaten
1 cup	bread crumbs
¼ cup	Marsala wine
1 Tbl.	tomato paste
1 cup	chicken stock *(see p. 538)*
to taste	salt and pepper

Using a meat pounder, flatten chicken breasts. Nick edges of the chicken to prevent curling. Dip chicken in egg whites, then in bread crumbs. In a non-stick pan coated with cooking spray, gently brown chicken. Add Marsala, cook 1 minute. Add remaining ingredients. Season with salt and pepper. Simmer 5-10 minutes.

Cook's Note: Quick, easy and so delicious.

Alcohol Note: The alcohol content was computed prior to cooking. Once the alcohol is heated to the boiling point, the alcohol disappears along with most of the calories from the alcohol.

Nutrient Content Per Serving

Calories	250.0
Protein	32.0 g
Carbohydrates	19.7 g
Fat – Total	2.8 g
Cholesterol	65.7 mg
Dietary Fiber	1.3 g
Sodium	360.0 mg

Percent of Calories

53% Protein
33% Carbohydrate
10% Fat
 4% Alcohol

Fat Breakdown

Saturated Fat	0.8 g
Monounsaturated Fat	0.9 g
Polyunsaturated Fat	0.7 g

CHICKEN PARMIGIANA
Serves 4

4 lg.	chicken breasts, boneless, skinless
½ cup	flour
to taste	salt and pepper
½ cup	parmesan cheese, grated
½ cup	bread crumbs
¼ tsp.	nutmeg, ground
4	egg whites, lightly beaten

Garnish:

lemon wedges

Combine flour, bread crumbs, nutmeg, salt and pepper to taste. Dip chicken in egg whites, then in bread-crumb mixture. Place chicken breasts on wax paper. Refrigerate for 2 hours to allow coating to solidify.

Arrange on broiler pan that has been prepared with cooking spray. Broil 6 inches away from heat for 10 minutes on each side. Serve with lemon wedges.

Cook's Note: A delicious lowfat version of Parmigiana. May also be served with All-Purpose Sauce *(see p. 416).*

Nutrient Content Per Serving		**Percent of Calories**	**Fat Breakdown**	
Calories	308.0	52% Protein	Saturated Fat	3.0 g
Protein	38.9 g	29% Carbohydrate	Monounsaturated Fat	1.7 g
Carbohydrates	21.8 g	18% Fat	Polyunsaturated Fat	0.7 g
Fat – Total	6.1 g			
Cholesterol	78.2 mg			
Dietary Fiber	1.0 g			
Sodium	467.0 mg			

ROSEMARY CHICKEN
Serves 4

1 tsp.	olive oil
2 cloves	garlic, cut in half
2 sprigs	rosemary, whole
4	chicken breasts, boneless, skinless
to taste	salt and pepper
6 oz.	dry white wine

In a non-stick pan, sauté the garlic and rosemary in 1 teaspoon olive oil for 30 seconds. Set aside rosemary and garlic. Add chicken and sauté until browned. Return rosemary and garlic to the pan. Add wine, salt and pepper to taste. Simmer uncovered for 30 minutes. Serve with Italian bread.

Cook's Note: Grow a pot of rosemary on your patio. You'll enjoy the convenience of always having fresh rosemary on hand.

Alcohol Note: The alcohol content was computed prior to cooking. Once the alcohol is heated to the boiling point, the alcohol disappears along with most of the calories from the alcohol.

Nutrient Content Per Serving

Calories	171.0
Protein	27.4 g
Carbohydrates	0.8 g
Fat – Total	2.6 g
Cholesterol	68.4 mg
Dietary Fiber	0.1 g
Sodium	78.8 mg

Percent of Calories

67%	Protein
2%	Carbohydrate
14%	Fat
17%	Alcohol

Fat Breakdown

Saturated Fat	0.5 g
Monounsaturated Fat	1.2 g
Polyunsaturated Fat	0.4 g

Lemon Chicken Scallopini
Serves 6

1½ lbs.	chicken breasts, skinless, boneless
⅓ cup	flour
to taste	white pepper
to taste	salt
1½ cups	chicken stock *(see p. 538)*
½ cup	sherry
3 Tbl.	lemon juice
1 Tbl.	lemon zest
1 tsp.	powdered butter replacement
2 tsp.	cornstarch

Garnish:

1	lemon, sliced thin
few sprigs	fresh parsley

Pound chicken breasts flat. Dredge scallops in flour. Season with white pepper and salt to taste.

In a non-stick pan prepared with cooking spray, gently brown the chicken. Transfer to a large frying pan when browned. Add chicken stock, sherry, lemon juice, lemon zest and powdered butter replacement. Simmer 10-15 minutes.

Immediately before serving add 2 teaspoons of cornstarch to thicken. Serve garnished with lemon slices and parsley.

Cook's Note: A nice alternative to veal scallopini.

Alcohol Note: The alcohol content was computed prior to cooking. Once the alcohol is heated to the boiling point, the alcohol disappears along with most of the calories from the alcohol.

Nutrient Content Per Serving		**Percent of Calories**	**Fat Breakdown**	
Calories	171.0	65% Protein	Saturated Fat	0.4 g
Protein	27.1 g	19% Carbohydrate	Monounsaturated Fat	0.4 g
Carbohydrates	7.7 g	8% Fat	Polyunsaturated Fat	0.4 g
Fat – Total	1.5 g	8% Alcohol		
Cholesterol	65.7 mg			
Dietary Fiber	0.3 g			
Sodium	79.0 mg			

GRILLED TURKEY BREAST WITH HERBS
Serves 4

4 4-oz.	turkey breast cutlets
½ tsp.	olive oil
4	lemon wedges

Herb Sauce:

2 Tbl.	capers, drained
2 Tbl.	pickled onions, chopped
¾ cup	parsley, chopped
¼ cup	basil, chopped
¼ cup	balsamic vinegar
1 Tbl.	olive oil
to taste	salt and pepper

Brush turkey cutlets with olive oil. Grill over hot coals 5 minutes per side.

To prepare sauce:
Blend all ingredients. Pass in a gravy boat.

To serve:
Arrange turkey on a platter. Squeeze some lemon over the top. Pass the sauce on the side.

Cook's Note: Quick and easy. The sauce also tastes great on grilled chicken or fish. A great meal for a hot summer evening.

Nutrient Content Per Serving		Percent of Calories	Fat Breakdown	
Calories	216.0	66% Protein	Saturated Fat	1.0 g
Protein	34.8 g	11% Carbohydrate	Monounsaturated Fat	3.2 g
Carbohydrates	5.6 g	23% Fat	Polyunsaturated Fat	0.7 g
Fat – Total	5.5 g			
Cholesterol	97.2 mg			
Dietary Fiber	0.9 g			
Sodium	138.0 mg			

GRILLED ITALIAN FISH SANDWICH
Serves 6

6 2-oz.	tuna steaks
6 2-oz.	swordfish steaks
to taste	salt and pepper
3 Tbl.	fish marinade *(see p. 556)*
6 med.	sourdough rolls

Anchovy mayonnaise:

4 Tbl.	fat-free mayonnaise
6	anchovy filets, drained
2 Tbl.	fresh lemon juice
1 head	bibb lettuce
2 med.	tomatoes, sliced thin
1 med.	Italian pickled pepper
6 ½-oz. slices	fontina cheese

Season the tuna and swordfish steaks with salt and pepper to taste. Place in the fish marinade for about 2-5 minutes. Grill quickly over hot coals. Set aside.

To prepare anchovy mayonnaise:
Combine all ingredients in a blender and purée until smooth.

Cut each roll into three equal slices and toast on the grill until light brown. Spread the anchovy mayonnaise on each piece. Arrange fish on the bottom layer. Cover with the middle section of the roll. Place a piece of lettuce, tomato and pickled pepper on the middle section and cover with the top of the roll. Secure sandwich with toothpicks and serve.

Cook's Note: You may substitute 1 clove of garlic or 2 shallots for anchovies if you prefer.

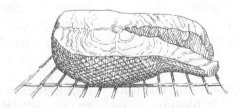

Nutrient Content Per Serving

Calories	375.0
Protein	34.1 g
Carbohydrates	30.6 g
Fat – Total	12.2 g
Cholesterol	63.4 mg
Dietary Fiber	2.4 g
Sodium	765.0 mg

Percent of Calories

37% Protein
33% Carbohydrate
30% Fat

Fat Breakdown

Saturated Fat	4.6 g
Monounsaturated Fat	4.2 g
Polyunsaturated Fat	2.4 g

CIOPPINO
Serves 6

1 tsp.	olive oil
1 lg.	onion, chopped
2 cloves	garlic, minced
1 lg.	bell pepper, chopped
2 ribs	celery, chopped
½ cup	parsley, chopped
½ cup	dried mushrooms
2 med.	carrots, sliced
1 cup	dry red wine
1 28-oz. can	tomatoes, crushed
1 28-oz. can	tomato purée
1½ cups	chicken stock *(see p. 538)* or fish stock *(see p. 540)*
1 tsp.	oregano, dried
¼ tsp.	rosemary, dried
1	bay leaf
1 tsp.	basil, dry
1 tsp.	thyme, dry
pinch	cayenne pepper
12	crab claws, in shells
1 lb.	shrimp, shelled and deveined
½ lb.	scallops
12	clams, cleaned, in shells
1 lb.	mussels, cleaned, in shells
1½ lbs.	fish (halibut, snapper, bass or any firm fish)

Garnish:
fresh parsley
basil
fresh ground black pepper

Soak dried mushrooms in water. Drain and chop. In a large soup pot, sauté onions in the olive oil. Add garlic, bell pepper, celery, parsley, mushrooms and carrots. Sauté 5 minutes. Add wine, tomatoes, tomato purée, stock, oregano, rosemary, bay leaf, basil and thyme. Simmer, uncovered until vegetables are tender (approximately 30 minutes).

Add cayenne pepper and crab, cook 3 minutes. Add shrimp, scallops, mussels and clams. Cook until clams open and crab claws are red. Discard any clams or mussels that do not open. Add remaining fish. Cook 5 minutes longer.

Serve in a deep bowl accompanied by crusty bread. Garnish with fresh parsley, basil and fresh ground black pepper.

Cook's Note: This has many ingredients, but it is a simple dish to prepare. You'll want to wear a bib to eat this dish. The sodium is high because king crab is high in sodium. Other types of crab contain half the sodium of king crab. Cholesterol is high due to the shellfish.

Nutrient Content Per Serving		Percent of Calories	Fat Breakdown	
Calories	717.0	64% Protein	Saturated Fat	1.5 g
Protein	113.0 g	18% Carbohydrate	Monounsaturated Fat	2.6 g
Carbohydrates	31.2 g	14% Fat	Polyunsaturated Fat	3.7 g
Fat – Total	11.2 g	4% Alcohol		
Cholesterol	365.0 mg			
Dietary Fiber	7.0 g			
Sodium	2159.0 mg			

POACHED LOBSTER OVER RED LINGUINI
Serves 4

4 med.	lobster tails
½ lb.	red pepper linguini, uncooked

Aromatic Fennel Reduction:

1 bulb	fennel, cleaned, chopped
2 cloves	garlic, minced
1 Tbl.	vanilla-bean oil *(see p. 563)*
2 Tbl.	pernod (anise flavored liqueur)
1 bunch	basil, chopped
1 cup	chicken stock *(see p. 538)*
½ cup	sweet port wine
1 cup	Gewurztraminer (or any sweet white wine)
2	lemons, juice of
to taste	salt and pepper

Garnish:

carrot curls
marigolds, sliced

Aromatic Fennel Reduction:
In a non-stick frying pan, over medium heat, sauté the fennel and garlic in vanilla-bean oil for 5 minutes. Add the remaining ingredients. Let it simmer 20 minutes or until the aroma is well formed. Strain, reserving the liquid, and season with salt and pepper to taste.

Skewer the lobster tail with a bamboo stick (so it doesn't curl). Steam for 5-10 minutes. Don't overcook. Cool, to touch, remove lobster from shell.

Cook pasta al dente. Ladle half of the fennel reduction onto individual dinner plates. Arrange a swirl of pasta on top. Place the lobster tail on top of pasta. Ladle remaining fennel reduction over top. Garnish with curled carrots and sliced marigolds.

Cook's Note: May increase spice by garnishing with red pepper flakes.

Alcohol Note: The alcohol content was computed prior to cooking. Once the alcohol is heated to the boiling point, the alcohol disappears along with most of the calories from the alcohol.

Nutrient Content Per Serving		**Percent of Calories**	**Fat Breakdown**	
Calories	482.0	31% Protein	Saturated Fat	0.9 g
Protein	36.8 g	44% Carbohydrate	Monounsaturated Fat	3.0 g
Carbohydrates	53.1 g	11% Fat	Polyunsaturated Fat	0.9 g
Fat – Total	5.8 g	14% Alcohol		
Cholesterol	143.0 mg			
Dietary Fiber	6.5 g			
Sodium	505.0 mg			

ORANGE ROUGHY WITH A FENNEL-TOMATO SAUCE
Serves 4

4 6-oz.	orange roughy fillets
½ tsp.	olive oil

Sauce:

¼ med.	onion
2 lg.	fennel bulbs
1 clove	garlic
3 lg.	tomatoes
1 tsp.	lemon juice
to taste	salt and pepper

To prepare the sauce:
Place all sauce ingredients in a food processor. Pulse to chop until it becomes the consistency of a salsa. Transfer sauce to a saucepan. Bring to a boil, then simmer uncovered 10 minutes.

Brush fillets with olive oil. Grill over hot coals or broil the orange roughy approximately 5 minutes per side.

To serve:
Arrange fish on a platter. Pour sauce over top.

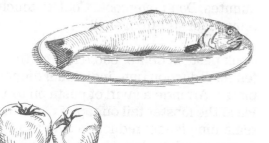

Cook's Note: Serve with Peasant Polenta *(see p. 336)* and Pepperonata *(see p. 397)* for a colorful presentation.

Nutrient Content Per Serving		**Percent of Calories**	**Fat Breakdown**	
Calories	217.0	63% Protein	Saturated Fat	0.2 g
Protein	34.5 g	26% Carbohydrate	Monounsaturated Fat	1.5 g
Carbohydrates	14.1 g	11% Fat	Polyunsaturated Fat	0.2 g
Fat – Total	2.7 g			
Cholesterol	44.2 mg			
Dietary Fiber	6.3 g			
Sodium	208.0 mg			

SHERRIED SCALLOPS
Serves 4

1⅓ lbs.	sea scallops
4 cloves	garlic, minced
4	scallions, diced fine
1 tsp.	olive oil
2 Tbl.	lemon juice
½ cup	sherry
½ cup	fish stock *(see p. 540)*

In a non-stick frying pan, sauté garlic and scallions in oil. Add scallops and cook until almost done. Add lemon juice, sherry and fish stock. Simmer 2-3 minutes. Serve immediately.

Cook's Note: This goes well with risotto or over pasta.

Alcohol Note: The alcohol content was computed prior to cooking. Once the alcohol is heated to the boiling point, the alcohol disappears along with most of the calories from the alcohol.

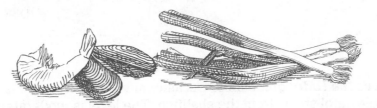

Nutrient Content Per Serving		Percent of Calories	Fat Breakdown	
Calories	173.0	60% Protein	Saturated Fat	0.3 g
Protein	25.1 g	15% Carbohydrate	Monounsaturated Fat	0.9 g
Carbohydrates	6.2 g	13% Fat	Polyunsaturated Fat	0.6 g
Fat – Total	2.5 g	12% Alcohol		
Cholesterol	48.6 mg			
Dietary Fiber	0.4 g			
Sodium	241.0 mg			

SHRIMP SCAMPI
Serves 4

1 lb.	shrimp, peeled, deveined
1 tsp.	olive oil
¼ cup	scallions, minced
5 cloves	garlic, minced
1	lemon, juice of
1¼ cups	white wine
2 Tbl.	fresh parsley, chopped
1	lemon, zest of
¼ tsp.	red pepper flakes

Garnish:

    lemon wedges

In a non-stick frying pan, heat oil and sauté scallions and garlic. Add shrimp, lemon juice and wine. Cook until shrimp turns pink. Add parsley, lemon zest and red pepper flakes. Stir. Serve over rice or pasta. Garnish with lemon wedges.

Cholesterol — Above the HM✓ guidelines: Occasionally a lowfat recipe is high in cholesterol. In this case the cholesterol stems from the shellfish. The level is moderately high (>150 mg per serving) but may fit into your weekly average of 150 mg per day.

Nutrient Content Per Serving

Calories	151.0
Protein	23.5 g
Carbohydrates	3.9 g
Fat – Total	3.2 g
Cholesterol	173.0 mg
Dietary Fiber	0.6 g
Sodium	171.0 mg

Percent of Calories

64% Protein
11% Carbohydrate
19% Fat

Fat Breakdown

Saturated Fat	0.5 g
Monounsaturated Fat	1.1 g
Polyunsaturated Fat	0.9 g

SEAFOOD BAKE
Serves 4

2 lbs.	halibut steak
½ lb.	medium shrimp, shelled and deveined
12 small	hard-shell clams in shells, well-scrubbed
2 Tbl.	powdered butter replacement
2 cloves	garlic, minced
2 Tbl.	fresh lemon juice
1 tsp.	lemon zest

Sauce:

2 Tbl.	liquid margarine
1 clove	garlic, squeezed
2 Tbl.	flour
½ cup	skim milk
¼ cup	nonfat dry milk
2 Tbl.	parmesan cheese, grated
2 Tbl.	dry white wine
⅓ cup	fish juices

Garnish:

fresh parsley (optional)

Combine powdered butter replacement, garlic, lemon juice and lemon zest. Prepare a foil pouch or baking bag with cooking spray. Place halibut steaks on foil. Spread lemon mixture over steaks. Arrange shrimp on top of halibut. Top with clams. Fold over foil or seal pouch. Pierce pouch to allow steam to escape. Bake at 350° F for 40 minutes. Remove juices for sauce.

Dissolve nonfat dry milk in skim milk and set aside. In a small sauce pan, melt margarine. Add garlic and sauté 1 minute. Whisk in flour and cook 2 minutes. Slowly whisk in milk. After sauce thickens, add wine stirring constantly so as not to curdle. Add parmesan until melted. Add fish juices as you please to attain the desired thickness of the sauce.

Serve fish in individual dishes covered with ⅓ cup sauce. Garnish with fresh parsley.

Cholesterol — Above the HM✔ guidelines: Occasionally a lowfat recipe is high in cholesterol. In this case the cholesterol stems from the shellfish. The level is moderately high (>150 mg per serving) but may fit into your weekly average of 150 mg per day.

Nutrient Content Per Serving

Calories	466.0
Protein	67.9 g
Carbohydrates	13.4 g
Fat – Total	13.3 g
Cholesterol	172.0 mg
Dietary Fiber	0.3 g
Sodium	421.0 mg

Percent of Calories

60% Protein
12% Carbohydrate
27% Fat

Fat Breakdown

Saturated Fat	2.6 g
Monounsaturated Fat	5.0 g
Polyunsaturated Fat	5.0 g

TROUT WITH MUSHROOMS

Serves 4

4 8-oz.	trout, boneless
	flour
1 tsp.	olive oil
¾ cup	scallions, sliced thin
½ lb.	mushrooms, sliced thin
1 Tbl.	lemon juice
¼ cup	bread crumbs
1 Tbl.	powdered butter replacement

Wash trout and pat dry. Dredge in flour. In a non-stick frying pan, sauté trout in 1 teaspoon olive oil for 10 minutes (5 minutes per side) or until golden brown. Remove trout to a baking dish that will hold trout in a single layer.

In the same non-stick skillet, sauté scallions until they soften (may need to add some cooking spray). Add mushrooms and lemon juice. When all vegetables are soft, arrange on top of trout.

Wipe skillet clean with a paper towel. Brown bread crumbs over low heat. Mix in powdered butter replacement. Cover vegetables with bread crumbs. Bake at 425° F for 10 minutes or until heated through.

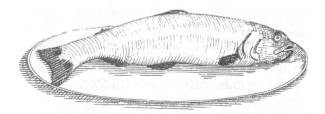

Cook's Note: Serve with mushroom rissoto *(see p. 329).*

The % calories as fat are slightly high. The portion size is large (8 ounces of trout per serving). Of the total 9.9 grams of fat, 8 grams are from the trout, which is considered a good fat.

Nutrient Content Per Serving		**Percent of Calories**	**Fat Breakdown**	
Calories	297.0	55% Protein	Saturated Fat	2.6 g
Protein	40.2 g	14% Carbohydrate	Monounsaturated Fat	3.0 g
Carbohydrates	10.0 g	31% Fat	Polyunsaturated Fat	2.0 g
Fat – Total	9.9 g			
Cholesterol	189.0 mg			
Dietary Fiber	1.5 g			
Sodium	206.0 mg			

SAUSAGE AND PEPPER SANDWICH
Serves 4

1 lb.	loose turkey Italian sausage
3 cups	green peppers, sliced
3 med.	onions, sliced thin
1 tsp.	oregano, dry
1 cup	tomato ragout *(see p. 552)* or all-purpose sauce *(see p. 416)*
8 slices	Italian bread, ½-inch-thick slices

In a non-stick pan, brown sausage. Drain any grease and pat with paper towels. Add green peppers and onions. Sauté until soft. Add oregano and tomato sauce. Simmer about 10 minutes with cover on until done. If it becomes dry, add water in small amounts. Make a sandwich on Italian bread.

Cook's Note: Purchase fresh, not frozen, turkey sausage from your butcher. Make sure the sausage was made without added fat. I've used hot turkey sausage, sweet turkey sausage and even a chicken and basil sausage for this recipe. Search until you find a turkey sausage you really like!

Nutrient Content Per Serving

Calories	466.0
Protein	40.4 g
Carbohydrates	49.3 g
Fat – Total	11.9 g
Cholesterol	96.4 mg
Dietary Fiber	5.7 g
Sodium	493.0 mg

Percent of Calories

35% Protein
42% Carbohydrate
23% Fat

Fat Breakdown

Saturated Fat	3.5 g
Monounsaturated Fat	3.2 g
Polyunsaturated Fat	3.7 g

BEEF SLICES IN WINE

Serves 6

1 lb.	flank steak, cut into ¼-inch slices, cross-grain
2 cloves	garlic, minced
¼ cup	fresh parsley, chopped
¼ tsp.	salt
¼ tsp.	rosemary, dry
¼ tsp.	basil, dry
¼ tsp.	oregano, dry
1 cup	tomato sauce
1 cup	dry red wine
½ lb.	mushrooms, sliced

In a large non-stick frying pan, sauté steak slices. Add all ingredients except mushrooms and simmer 1 hour. Add mushrooms 5 minutes before serving.

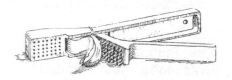

Cook's Note: Serve over pasta, rice or with Italian bread. The aroma in your home will be exquisite!

Although this recipe has 34% calories as fat, it is lowfat for a beef dish.

Alcohol Note: The alcohol content was computed prior to cooking. Once the alcohol is heated to the boiling point, the alcohol disappears along with most of the calories from the alcohol.

Nutrient Content Per Serving

Calories	208.0
Protein	22.1 g
Carbohydrates	5.9 g
Fat – Total	7.9 g
Cholesterol	50.9 mg
Dietary Fiber	1.4 g
Sodium	404.0 mg

Percent of Calories

42% Protein
17% Carbohydrate
34% Fat
 7% Alcohol

Fat Breakdown

Saturated Fat	3.3 g
Monounsaturated Fat	3.1 g
Polyunsaturated Fat	0.4 g

PASTA WITH BEEF AND CAPERS
Serves 4

1 lb.	spaghetti, uncooked
8 oz.	lean top round
4 lg.	tomatoes, peeled, seeded, mash pulp
2 cloves	garlic, minced
2 Tbl.	capers
2 Tbl.	fresh oregano, chopped
½ cup	parmesan cheese, grated
1 sprig	Italian parsley, chopped
to taste	pepper
pinch	cayenne pepper

Cut meat in very thin slices, then cut into cubes. Prepare a non-stick pan with cooking spray and cook meat for 3-5 minutes, or until it turns pink. Add tomatoes, garlic, capers, oregano, one-half of the parsley, salt and pepper to taste, and cayenne pepper. Simmer 10 minutes.

Meanwhile, boil spaghetti al dente. Drain.

To serve:
Place spaghetti in a warm bowl. Add beef and caper sauce, sprinkle with parsley and parmesan cheese.

Cook's Note: Meat is easier to slice thin if it has been partially frozen.

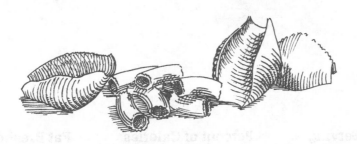

Nutrient Content Per Serving

Calories	620.0
Protein	37.6 g
Carbohydrates	101.0 g
Fat – Total	7.3 g
Cholesterol	52.5 mg
Dietary Fiber	11.0 g
Sodium	373.0 mg

Percent of Calories

24% Protein
65% Carbohydrate
11% Fat

Fat Breakdown

Saturated Fat	2.6 g
Monounsaturated Fat	1.9 g
Polyunsaturated Fat	1.3 g

VEAL MEDALLIONS
WITH PORT WINE SAUCE AND ARTICHOKES
Serves 6

6 4-oz.   veal medallions

Sauce:
1 tsp.   shallots, chopped
1 tsp.   garlic, chopped
1-3   artichoke bottoms, ⅓ cup
            canned or fresh, diced fine
½ tsp.   olive oil
¾ cup   port wine
1 cup   beef stock *(see p. 536)*
to taste   salt and pepper
            flour
½ tsp.   olive oil

To prepare the sauce:
In a non-stick pan, sauté the shallots, garlic and artichoke bottoms in ½ teaspoon olive oil until lightly brown. Add port wine. Reduce to one-half of the amount. Add the beef stock. Reduce to one-half the amount. Season with salt and pepper to taste. Purée sauce in a blender until smooth.

Dust veal scallops lightly with flour. Sauté the veal in a non-stick pan with another ½ teaspoon olive oil until done. Serve immediately with sauce.

Nutrient Content Per Serving
Calories	257.0
Protein	32.3 g
Carbohydrates	8.2 g
Fat – Total	8.0 g
Cholesterol	118.0 mg
Dietary Fiber	3.3 g
Sodium	155.0 mg

Percent of Calories
50% Protein
13% Carbohydrate
28% Fat

Fat Breakdown
Saturated Fat	2.9 g
Monounsaturated Fat	3.0 g
Polyunsaturated Fat	0.9 g

BROCCOLI AL VINO
Serves 4

6 cups	broccoli flowerettes
1 tsp.	garlic, minced
1 Tbl.	olive oil
1½ cups	dry white wine
¼ tsp.	salt
to taste	pepper

In a non-stick pan, sauté garlic in olive oil for 1 minute. Add broccoli and toss until it glistens. Add remaining ingredients. Simmer, covered until broccoli is tender and liquid is reduced to ½ cup.

Alcohol Note: The alcohol content was computed prior to cooking. Once the alcohol is heated to the boiling point, the alcohol disappears along with most of the calories from the alcohol.

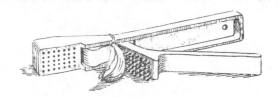

Nutrient Content Per Serving

Calories	127.0
Protein	4.0 g
Carbohydrates	7.7 g
Fat – Total	3.8 g
Cholesterol	0.0 mg
Dietary Fiber	3.7 g
Sodium	173.0 mg

Percent of Calories

12%	Protein
22%	Carbohydrate
25%	Fat
41%	Alcohol

Fat Breakdown

Saturated Fat	0.5 g
Monounsaturated Fat	2.5 g
Polyunsaturated Fat	0.5 g

BROCCOLI MEDLEY
Serves 4

3 cups	broccoli flowerettes
1 clove	garlic, minced
¼ med.	red onion, sliced thin
1 tsp.	olive oil
3	plum tomatoes, cubed 1-inch size
¼ lb.	mushrooms, sliced thick
1 tsp.	dried oregano
2 Tbl.	dry white wine

In a non-stick pan, sauté garlic and onion in olive oil over low heat until garlic is browned. Add broccoli, sauté 2 minutes. Add remaining ingredients and cover. Steam in juices of the mushrooms, tomatoes and white wine until broccoli is just tender.

Alcohol Note: The alcohol content was computed prior to cooking. Once the alcohol is heated to the boiling point, the alcohol disappears along with most of the calories from the alcohol.

Nutrient Content Per Serving

Calories	55.8
Protein	3.2 g
Carbohydrates	8.2 g
Fat – Total	1.7 g
Cholesterol	0.0 mg
Dietary Fiber	3.1 g
Sodium	23.9 mg

Percent of Calories

19% Protein
50% Carbohydrate
23% Fat
 8% Alcohol

Fat Breakdown

Saturated Fat	0.2 g
Monounsaturated Fat	0.9 g
Polyunsaturated Fat	0.3 g

MARINATED CARROTS
Serves 4

3 cups	carrots, sliced in rounds
1 cup	water
1 cup	dry white wine
½ cup	white wine vinegar
2 sprigs	parsley
2 sprigs	thyme
1 branch	sage
1	bay leaf
4 sprigs	mint
2 cloves	garlic, left whole and bruised
2 Tbl.	sugar
to taste	salt and pepper

Combine all ingredients in a saucepan. Cover and simmer until carrots are tender-crunchy. Remove carrots from pan. Reduce sauce to a syrupy consistency. Let cool. Pour sauce over carrots and let marinate overnight. Remove chunks of garlic before serving.

Alcohol Note: The alcohol content was computed prior to cooking. Once the alcohol is heated to the boiling point, the alcohol disappears along with most of the calories from the alcohol.

Nutrient Content Per Serving		**Percent of Calories**	**Fat Breakdown**	
Calories	123.0	4% Protein	Saturated Fat	0.0 g
Protein	1.5 g	65% Carbohydrate	Monounsaturated Fat	0.0 g
Carbohydrates	21.2 g	2% Fat	Polyunsaturated Fat	0.1 g
Fat – Total	0.2 g	29% Alcohol		
Cholesterol	0.0 mg			
Dietary Fiber	3.9 g			
Sodium	80.6 mg			

SWEET AND SOUR CABBAGE
Serves 8

1 tsp.	olive oil
½ cup	onions, sliced thin
1 head	green cabbage, sliced thin
3 lg.	tomatoes, peeled, seeded, chopped coarse
½ cup	water
4 Tbl.	white wine vinegar
few grindings	fresh ground black pepper
1 tsp.	celery seed (optional)
1 Tbl.	honey

Heat oil in a large non-stick pan. Gently sauté onions until soft. Add cabbage, tomatoes, vinegar and water. Simmer until cabbage is tender, approximately 15 minutes. Drizzle honey over mixture. Cook 1 minute.

Nutrient Content Per Serving

Calories	45.3
Protein	1.5 g
Carbohydrates	9.5 g
Fat – Total	0.9 g
Cholesterol	0.0 mg
Dietary Fiber	1.9 g
Sodium	16.1 mg

Percent of Calories

11% Protein	
73% Carbohydrate	
16% Fat	

Fat Breakdown

Saturated Fat	0.1 g
Monounsaturated Fat	0.5 g
Polyunsaturated Fat	0.2 g

BAKED FENNEL
Serves 6

6 med.   fennel bulbs
1 cup   chicken stock *(see p. 538)*
1 Tbl.   powdered butter replacement
3 Tbl.   parsley, chopped

Remove core and stems from fennel. Cut into quarters. Place fennel in a baking dish. Add remaining ingredients. Bake at 400° F for 15 minutes or until fennel is tender.

Cook's Note: When fennel is cooked, its flavor mellows.

Nutrient Content Per Serving

Calories	77.2
Protein	3.0 g
Carbohydrates	18.2 g
Fat – Total	0.5 g
Cholesterol	0.0 mg
Dietary Fiber	9.8 g
Sodium	133.0 mg

Percent of Calories

14% Protein
81% Carbohydrate
 5% Fat

Fat Breakdown

Saturated Fat	0.0 g
Monounsaturated Fat	0.0 g
Polyunsaturated Fat	0.0 g

GREEN BEANS AND ANISE SEEDS
Serves 6

2 lbs.	fresh green beans or wax beans
1 tsp.	olive oil
1 med.	onion, chopped fine
1 tsp.	anise seeds, crushed
to taste	salt and pepper
1 Tbl.	tomato paste
2 Tbl.	water

Cut beans into 1-inch pieces. Steam or microwave beans until tender. Heat oil in a large non-stick frying pan. Sauté onions until soft. Add beans, anise seed and salt and pepper to taste. Cook, stirring constantly, for 5 minutes. Mix tomato paste with water. Stir into beans. Cover and heat 3-5 minutes.

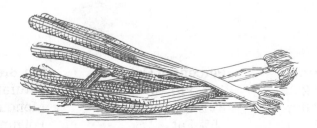

Nutrient Content Per Serving

Calories	62.1
Protein	3.0 g
Carbohydrates	12.6 g
Fat – Total	1.0 g
Cholesterol	0.0 mg
Dietary Fiber	5.1 g
Sodium	31.1 mg

Percent of Calories

17% Protein
70% Carbohydrate
13% Fat

Fat Breakdown

Saturated Fat	0.1 g
Monounsaturated Fat	0.6 g
Polyunsaturated Fat	0.2 g

GARLIC THYME GREEN BEANS
Serves 4

3 cups	green beans, frozen or blanched
1 tsp.	olive oil
2 cloves	garlic, minced
1	shallot, minced
3 sprigs	fresh thyme
1 Tbl.	white wine
to taste	salt and pepper

In a medium non-stick frying pan, heat oil. Sauté garlic, shallots and thyme until soft. Add green beans, sauté 3-5 minutes until tender. Add wine for moisture. Remove from heat and serve immediately.

Nutrient Content Per Serving

Calories	39.7
Protein	1.6 g
Carbohydrates	6.3 g
Fat – Total	1.2 g
Cholesterol	0.0 mg
Dietary Fiber	2.6 g
Sodium	5.3 mg

Percent of Calories

14% Protein
56% Carbohydrate
25% Fat

Fat Breakdown

Saturated Fat	0.2 g
Monounsaturated Fat	0.8 g
Polyunsaturated Fat	0.1 g

LIMA BEAN BAKE
Serves 4

1 10-oz. pkg.	frozen lima beans
1 16-oz. can	tomatoes, chopped
2 Tbl.	basil, chopped
1 tsp.	marjoram, dry
½ cup	parmesan cheese, grated
to taste	salt
a few grindings	black pepper

Microwave lima beans for 10 minutes on high setting. Mix with remaining ingredients. Place in a casserole dish prepared with cooking spray. Bake at 350° F for 30 minutes.

Nutrient Content Per Serving

Calories	146.0
Protein	10.6 g
Carbohydrates	17.4 g
Fat – Total	4.2 g
Cholesterol	9.8 mg
Dietary Fiber	5.8 g
Sodium	369.0 mg

Percent of Calories

28% Protein
47% Carbohydrate
25% Fat

Fat Breakdown

Saturated Fat	2.5 g
Monounsaturated Fat	1.1 g
Polyunsaturated Fat	0.3 g

PEPPERONATA
Serves 6

10	bell peppers, red and green, cut in strips
3 lg.	onions, sliced thin
2 cloves	garlic, sliced
2 med.	tomatoes, chopped
1 tsp.	marjoram, dried
to taste	salt
to taste	white pepper
1 tsp.	olive oil

In a large non-stick frying pan heat olive oil. Sauté peppers, onions and garlic over low heat. Cover and cook for 20 minutes. Add remaining ingredients. Cover and cook 15 minutes.

Cook's Note: This is a good side dish especially with a bland fish or meat dish. It can be cooked ahead easily.

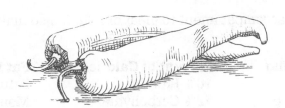

Nutrient Content Per Serving

Calories	80.7				
Protein	2.5 g				
Carbohydrates	17.1 g				
Fat – Total	1.3 g				
Cholesterol	0.0 mg				
Dietary Fiber	3.9 g				
Sodium	8.8 mg				

Percent of Calories
- 11% Protein
- 76% Carbohydrate
- 13% Fat

Fat Breakdown

Saturated Fat	0.2 g
Monounsaturated Fat	0.6 g
Polyunsaturated Fat	0.3 g

PEPPERS AND TOMATOES
Serves 6

1 lb.	bell peppers, chopped coarse
1 lb.	tomatoes, chopped fine
1 med.	onion, chopped
1 clove	garlic, minced
1 tsp.	olive oil
1 tsp.	sugar
1 Tbl.	fresh basil, chopped
to taste	black pepper

In a non-stick pan, brown onion and garlic in oil. Add remaining ingredients. Cover and simmer 30 minutes. Serve hot or cold.

Cook's Note: This is a nice accompaniment to meat or fish. It also makes a great sandwich.

Nutrient Content Per Serving

Calories	53.4
Protein	1.6 g
Carbohydrates	10.8 g
Fat – Total	1.2 g
Cholesterol	0.0 mg
Dietary Fiber	2.5 g
Sodium	9.0 mg

Percent of Calories

10% Protein
72% Carbohydrate
18% Fat

Fat Breakdown

Saturated Fat	0.2 g
Monounsaturated Fat	0.6 g
Polyunsaturated Fat	0.3 g

ITALIAN POTATO SALAD
Serves 6

3 lg.	Idaho potatoes, peeled, sliced
2 med.	tomatoes, sliced
1	yellow pepper, roasted, sliced in strips *(see p. 13)*
¼ cup	balsamic vinegar
1 Tbl.	olive oil
2 tsp.	fresh basil, chopped
to taste	salt and pepper
1 clove	garlic, minced
¼ cup	black olives, sliced

Boil potatoes until tender. Combine remaining ingredients and chill. Add hot potatoes. Mix and serve immediately.

Nutrient Content Per Serving

Calories	101.0
Protein	1.9 g
Carbohydrates	18.1 g
Fat – Total	2.9 g
Cholesterol	0.0 mg
Dietary Fiber	1.7 g
Sodium	32.2 mg

Percent of Calories

7% Protein
68% Carbohydrate
25% Fat

Fat Breakdown

Saturated Fat	0.4 g
Monounsaturated Fat	2.0 g
Polyunsaturated Fat	0.3 g

SAUTÉED SPINACH AND TOMATOES
Serves 4

8 cups	fresh spinach, washed, stems removed
4 cloves	garlic, minced
4	scallions, diced
1 tsp.	olive oil
2	tomatoes, chopped coarse
to taste	salt and pepper

In a large non-stick frying pan, sauté scallions in olive oil until tender. Add garlic, sauté 30 seconds. Add spinach and tomato. Cook until spinach wilts and tomato softens.

Cook's Note: I recommend adding this to rice or pasta. It makes a nice topping. It also goes well with fish or poultry.

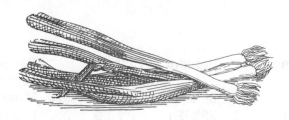

Nutrient Content Per Serving

Calories	53.9
Protein	4.0 g
Carbohydrates	8.2 g
Fat – Total	1.8 g
Cholesterol	0.0 mg
Dietary Fiber	4.0 g
Sodium	95.5 mg

Percent of Calories

25% Protein
51% Carbohydrate
24% Fat

Fat Breakdown

Saturated Fat	0.2 g
Monounsaturated Fat	0.9 g
Polyunsaturated Fat	0.4 g

Spinach Formato
Serves 4

1 10-oz. pkg.	frozen spinach, thawed, chopped, squeezed dry
2 Tbl.	bread crumbs
½ tsp.	olive oil
¼ cup	onions, chopped fine
1 clove	garlic, minced

Sauce:

1 Tbl.	margarine, liquid
1½ Tbl.	flour
¾ cup	skim milk
¼ cup	nonfat dry milk powder, dissolved in skim milk
¼ cup + 2 Tbl.	egg substitute
¼ cup	parmesan cheese, freshly grated
few grindings	black pepper
3	egg whites

Preheat oven to 325° F. Prepare a metal mold with cooking spray. Dust with bread crumbs. In a non-stick pan, heat oil and gently sauté onions and garlic until transparent. Add spinach and cook 3 minutes. Remove pan from heat.

Meanwhile, prepare sauce. In a non-stick pan, melt margarine. Stir in flour. Heat 2 minutes. Add skim milk, stirring with a whisk until sauce begins to thicken. Remove from heat and stir in egg substitute, parmesan cheese and spinach mixture. Season with pepper to taste. Cool slightly.

In a clean bowl, beat the egg whites until stiff. Fold in egg whites. Pour mixture into prepared baking mold. Place mold in a pan with simmering water. The water should come three-fourths of the way up the side of the mold. Cover spinach and bake in middle of oven for 1 hour. Spinach should be firm to the touch when done.

To serve:
Unmold by running a knife around the side of mold. Turn onto serving dish. Serve in wedges.

Nutrient Content Per Serving

Calories	179.0
Protein	15.2 g
Carbohydrates	15.7 g
Fat – Total	6.5 g
Cholesterol	7.4 mg
Dietary Fiber	2.2 g
Sodium	377.0 mg

Percent of Calories

33% Protein
34% Carbohydrate
32% Fat

Fat Breakdown

Saturated Fat	2.1 g
Monounsaturated Fat	2.3 g
Polyunsaturated Fat	1.9 g

CREPES FLORENTINE
Serves 16

1 recipe	all-purpose crepes *(see p. 191)*
12 cups	fresh spinach or 20 oz. frozen spinach
to taste	salt and pepper
1 cup	lowfat ricotta cheese
⅓ cup	nonfat sour cream
¼ cup + 2 Tbl.	egg substitute
⅛ tsp.	nutmeg
2 Tbl.	fresh parmesan cheese, grated

Steam spinach. Squeeze dry. Add salt and pepper to taste. Mix in ricotta, sour cream, egg substitute and nutmeg. Fill 16 crepes. Roll up.

Prepare baking dish with cooking spray. Arrange crepes in the baking dish. Sprinkle top of crepes with parmesan cheese. Bake at 350° F for 15-20 minutes (until crepes are heated through).

Cook's Note: Prepared crepes can be found in the supermarket at times. They seem to be a seasonal item found in the summer.

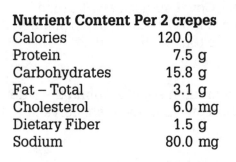

Nutrient Content Per 2 crepes

Calories	120.0
Protein	7.5 g
Carbohydrates	15.8 g
Fat – Total	3.1 g
Cholesterol	6.0 mg
Dietary Fiber	1.5 g
Sodium	80.0 mg

Percent of Calories

25% Protein
52% Carbohydrate
23% Fat

Fat Breakdown

Saturated Fat	1.1 g
Monounsaturated Fat	1.1 g
Polyunsaturated Fat	0.6 g

SPAGHETTI SQUASH
Serves 6

1   spaghetti squash
6 cups   marinara sauce *(see p. 417)*

Pierce spaghetti squash with a fork. Bake at 350° F for 1½ hours. Cut open and run a fork through the pulp to form spaghetti-like strands. Serve with marinara sauce.

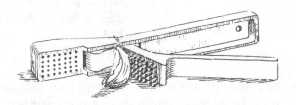

Nutrient Content Per Serving

Calories	176.0
Protein	4.4 g
Carbohydrates	31.6 g
Fat – Total	5.5 g
Cholesterol	0.0 mg
Dietary Fiber	8.5 g
Sodium	224.0 mg

Percent of Calories

9% Protein
65% Carbohydrate
25% Fat

Fat Breakdown

Saturated Fat	0.8 g
Monounsaturated Fat	3.3 g
Polyunsaturated Fat	0.9 g

STUFFED TOMATOES
Serves 4

4 lg.	ripe tomatoes
2 Tbl.	parsley, chopped
2 cloves	garlic, minced
1 Tbl.	capers, rinsed
½	dry hot chili pepper, minced
¼ cup	bread crumbs
½ tsp.	oregano
to taste	salt and pepper
2 tsp.	olive oil

Cut each tomato in half. Remove seeds. Combine remaining ingredients. Stuff the tomatoes.

Prepare a baking dish with cooking spray. Arrange tomatoes in baking dish. Bakes at 350° F for 30 minutes. Serve warm, not hot.

% Calories as Fat — Above the HM✔ guidelines: Although this recipe has a high percentage of calories as fat (>30%), the total fat is less than 5 grams per serving. This will easily fit within your allotment of 45 grams per day. This happens most often in low-calorie recipes.

Nutrient Content Per Serving

Calories	85.0
Protein	2.3 g
Carbohydrates	13.6 g
Fat – Total	3.1 g
Cholesterol	0.0 mg
Dietary Fiber	2.5 g
Sodium	96.3 mg

Percent of Calories

10% Protein
59% Carbohydrate
31% Fat

Fat Breakdown

Saturated Fat	0.5 g
Monounsaturated Fat	1.9 g
Polyunsaturated Fat	0.5 g

Zucchini Boats
Serves 8

1 med.	zucchini, scoop out insides
1 sm.	zucchini, cubed
1	onion, diced fine
1 tsp.	olive oil
1 cup	fresh mushrooms, sliced
4	plum tomatoes, cubed
2 cloves	garlic, minced
1 Tbl.	fresh basil, chopped
½ tsp.	dry oregano
to taste	salt and pepper

Place zucchini boats in a microwave-safe baking dish filled with ½ inch of water. Blanch in microwave for 5 minutes. In a non-stick frying pan, sauté onion in oil until transparent. Add garlic, cook 1 minute. Add chopped zucchini and cook until zucchini starts to soften. Add mushrooms, tomato, garlic, basil, oregano, salt and pepper to taste. Cook until most of the moisture has evaporated. Spoon mixture into zucchini boats. Can be served immediately or may bake at 350° F for 10-15 minutes.

Variation:
- You may wish to stuff baby zucchini boats with a mixture of bread crumbs, minced garlic, fresh mint and parsley for a nice variety.

Cook's Note: This goes nicely with rice. It makes a great potluck item. May sprinkle grated parmesan or romano cheese on top if desired.

Nutrient Content Per Serving		**Percent of Calories**	**Fat Breakdown**	
Calories	21.9	14% Protein	Saturated Fat	0.1 g
Protein	0.8 g	58% Carbohydrate	Monounsaturated Fat	0.4 g
Carbohydrates	3.6 g	28% Fat	Polyunsaturated Fat	0.1 g
Fat – Total	0.8 g			
Cholesterol	0.0 mg			
Dietary Fiber	0.9 g			
Sodium	3.9 mg			

Sautéed Zucchini
Serves 6

3 sm.	zucchini, sliced in ¼-inch rounds
1 tsp.	olive oil
2 cloves	garlic, minced
1 tsp.	fresh rosemary, chopped
to taste	salt and pepper

In a large non-stick frying pan heat olive oil. Sauté garlic and rosemary. Add zucchini and sauté for 5 minutes. Add salt and pepper to taste.

% Calories as Fat — Above the HM✔ guidelines: Although this recipe has a high percentage of calories as fat (>30%), the total fat is less than 5 grams per serving. This will easily fit within your allotment of 45 grams per day. This happens most often in low-calorie recipes.

Nutrient Content Per Serving

Calories	11.5
Protein	0.5 g
Carbohydrates	0.8 g
Fat – Total	0.9 g
Cholesterol	0.0 mg
Dietary Fiber	0.2 g
Sodium	0.7 mg

Percent of Calories

16% Protein
26% Carbohydrate
58% Fat

Fat Breakdown

Saturated Fat	0.1 g
Monounsaturated Fat	0.6 g
Polyunsaturated Fat	0.1 g

ZUCCHINI CREOLE
Serves 6

6 cups	zucchini, cubed
1 Tbl.	olive oil
1 clove	garlic, chopped
1 cup	tomatoes, cubed
½ cup	celery, sliced
⅛ tsp.	pepper
¼ tsp.	basil
¼ tsp.	thyme
¼ tsp.	marjoram
¼ tsp.	sugar

In a large non-stick frying pan, heat oil over medium heat. Add garlic and zucchini. Cook 5 minutes. Add remaining ingredients. Cook until vegetables are tender, approximately 5 minutes. Do not overcook.

% Calories as Fat — Above the HM✓ guidelines: Although this recipe has a high percentage of calories as fat (>30%), the total fat is less than 5 grams per serving. This will easily fit within your allotment of 45 grams per day. This happens most often in low-calorie recipes.

Nutrient Content Per Serving

Calories	47.4
Protein	1.9 g
Carbohydrates	5.9 g
Fat – Total	2.6 g
Cholesterol	0.0 mg
Dietary Fiber	2.1 g
Sodium	15.4 mg

Percent of Calories

14% Protein
44% Carbohydrate
43% Fat

Fat Breakdown

Saturated Fat	0.4 g
Monounsaturated Fat	1.7 g
Polyunsaturated Fat	0.3 g

Basil Vinaigrette
Serves 4
Yield: ⅔ cup

⅓ cup   balsamic vinegar
2 cloves garlic, minced
½ tsp.   anchovy paste
⅓ cup   fresh basil, chopped
1 tsp.   olive oil

Combine all ingredients in blender. Chill. Serve over salad.

Cook's Note: Don't be afraid of the anchovy paste — you may find that you like it. This may be stored 3-5 days in the refrigerator.

% Calories as Fat — Above the HM✔ guidelines: Although this recipe has a high percentage of calories as fat (>30%), the total fat is less than 5 grams per serving. This will easily fit within your allotment of 45 grams per day. This happens most often in low-calorie recipes.

▼ This recipe is used for the following items:
Red, White and Green Salad (see p. 317)
Spinach Fajioli (see p. 318)
Fresh Grilled Swordfish Salad (see p. 319)
Cucumber-Tomato Salad (see p. 459)

Nutrient Content Per 1½ Tablespoons		Percent of Calories	Fat Breakdown	
Calories	18.0	9% Protein	Saturated Fat	0.2 g
Protein	0.5 g	36% Carbohydrate	Monounsaturated Fat	0.9 g
Carbohydrates	1.8 g	55% Fat	Polyunsaturated Fat	0.1 g
Fat – Total	1.3 g			
Cholesterol	0.9 mg			
Dietary Fiber	0.2 g			
Sodium	37.2 mg			

OLD-FASHIONED BALSAMIC DRESSING
Serves 22
Yield: 1¼ cups

1 cup	balsamic vinegar
1 Tbl.	shallots, chopped
dash	pepper
1 bunch	fresh basil, chopped
1 tsp.	fresh thyme, chopped
2 Tbl.	gingerroot, peeled, grated
1 tsp.	light brown sugar
¼ cup	olive oil

Combine all ingredients, except the oil, in a blender. Purée well. While the motor is running, add the oil slowly. Keep refrigerated and sprinkle on top of salad immediately before serving.

Cook's Note: Purchase fresh gingerroot and store it in the freezer. It is easier to grate when frozen.

% Calories as Fat — Above the HM✔ guidelines: Although this recipe has a high percentage of calories as fat (>30%), the total fat is less than 5 grams per serving. This will easily fit within your allotment of 45 grams per day. This happens most often in low-calorie recipes.

▼ This recipe is used for the following items:
Red, White and Green Salad (see p. 317)
Grilled Vegetable Salad (see p. 320)

Nutrient Content Per Tablespoon		**Percent of Calories**	**Fat Breakdown**	
Calories	24.1	1% Protein	Saturated Fat	0.3 g
Protein	0.0 g	13% Carbohydrate	Monounsaturated Fat	1.8 g
Carbohydrates	0.9 g	86% Fat	Polyunsaturated Fat	0.2 g
Fat – Total	2.5 g			
Cholesterol	0.0 mg			
Dietary Fiber	0.0 g			
Sodium	0.2 mg			

CAESAR DRESSING
(From Paul's Place Restaurant in Denver, Colorado)
Serves 8
Yield: 1 cup

½ cup	lemon juice
⅓ cup	water
1 Tbl.	olive oil
1½ tsp.	anchovy paste (to taste)
½ tsp.	black pepper
¾ tsp.	garlic, minced
¾ tsp.	dijon mustard
¾ tsp.	Worcestershire sauce™
1 Tbl.	red wine vinegar

Combine all ingredients. Whisk or shake together and serve. Keep unused dressing in the refrigerator.

Cook's Note: It will only keep 3-5 days, after which the dressing becomes bitter.

% Calories as Fat — Above the HM✔ guidelines: Although this recipe has a high percentage of calories as fat (>30%), the total fat is less than 5 grams per serving. This will easily fit within your allotment of 45 grams per day. This happens most often in low-calorie recipes.

▼ This recipe is used for the following item:
Caesar Salad (see p. 310)

Nutrient Content Per 2 Tablespoons		Percent of Calories	Fat Breakdown	
Calories	22.5	5% Protein	Saturated Fat	0.3 g
Protein	0.3 g	30% Carbohydrate	Monounsaturated Fat	1.3 g
Carbohydrates	1.9 g	65% Fat	Polyunsaturated Fat	0.2 g
Fat – Total	1.8 g			
Cholesterol	0.5 mg			
Dietary Fiber	0.1 g			
Sodium	44.9 mg			

GARLIC DRESSING
Serves 10
Yield: 1¼ cups

¼ cup	olive oil
½ cup	wine vinegar
1½ tsp.	salt
6 cloves	garlic, halved
1 tsp.	dry mustard
½ cup	water
2 tsp.	creole mustard

Combine all ingredients in a tightly covered glass container. Store in refrigerator. Let stand for several days. To serve, shake well.

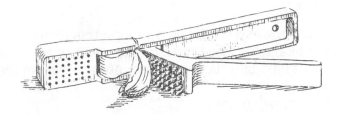

% Calories as Fat — Above the HM✔ guidelines: Although this recipe has a high percentage of calories as fat (>30%), the total fat is less than 5 grams per serving. This will easily fit within your allotment of 45 grams per day. This happens most often in low-calorie recipes.

Nutrient Content Per 2 Tablespoons		Percent of Calories		Fat Breakdown	
Calories	52.5	1%	Protein	Saturated Fat	0.7 g
Protein	0.1 g	10%	Carbohydrate	Monounsaturated Fat	4.0 g
Carbohydrates	1.3 g	89%	Fat	Polyunsaturated Fat	0.5 g
Fat – Total	5.4 g				
Cholesterol	0.0 mg				
Dietary Fiber	0.1 g				
Sodium	327.0 mg				

ITALIAN SALAD DRESSING
Serves 8
Yield: 1 cup

2 Tbl.	olive oil
¼ cup	red wine vinegar
3 Tbl.	lemon juice
1 Tbl.	cooking wine
½ tsp.	Worcestershire sauce™
2 tsp.	dijon mustard
1 tsp.	anchovy paste
2 Tbl.	fresh basil, chopped

Combine all ingredients. Shake well and serve.

% Calories as Fat — Above the HM✔ guidelines: Although this recipe has a high percentage of calories as fat (>30%), the total fat is less than 5 grams per serving. This will easily fit within your allotment of 45 grams per day. This happens most often in low-calorie recipes.

▼ This recipe is used for the following item:
Red, White and Green Salad (see p. 317)

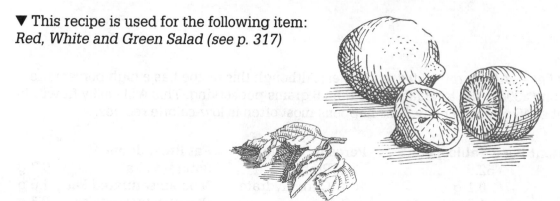

Nutrient Content Per Serving

Calories	39.4
Protein	0.4 g
Carbohydrates	1.4 g
Fat – Total	3.7 g
Cholesterol	0.4 mg
Dietary Fiber	0.2 g
Sodium	22.1 mg

Percent of Calories

4%	Protein
13%	Carbohydrate
80%	Fat

Fat Breakdown

Saturated Fat	0.5 g
Monounsaturated Fat	2.7 g
Polyunsaturated Fat	0.4 g

TOMATO-BASIL SALAD DRESSING
Serves 4
Yield: 1 cup

¼ cup   fresh basil, chopped
3   scallions, chopped
1   tomato, seeded, chopped
1 tsp.   garlic, minced
¼ cup   fresh parsley, chopped
1 Tbl.   olive oil
2 Tbl.   balsamic vinegar
4 Tbl.   water

Combine all ingredients in a small blender jar or food processor. Purée until smooth.

Serve over greens or raw vegetable salads.

% Calories as Fat — Above the HM guidelines: Although this recipe has a high percentage of calories as fat (>30%), the total fat is less than 5 grams per serving. This will easily fit within your allotment of 45 grams per day. This happens most often in low-calorie recipes.

Nutrient Content Per Serving

Calories	42.5
Protein	0.6 g
Carbohydrates	2.9 g
Fat – Total	3.5 g
Cholesterol	0.0 mg
Dietary Fiber	0.8 g
Sodium	6.2 mg

Percent of Calories

5% Protein
25% Carbohydrate
69% Fat

Fat Breakdown

Saturated Fat	0.5 g
Monounsaturated Fat	2.5 g
Polyunsaturated Fat	0.4 g

ALFREDO-TYPE SAUCE

Serves 6

Yield: 2 cups

1 cup	skim milk
¼ cup	nonfat dry milk
1 tsp.	chicken base, fat-free
2 Tbl.	flour
1½ Tbl.	liquid margarine
¼ cup	fresh romano cheese, grated
¼ cup	fat-free Italian topping
¼ cup	nonfat cream cheese
1 clove	garlic, minced
dash	white pepper
to taste	salt

Dissolve nonfat dry milk in skim milk. Set aside.

Melt margarine in a small saucepan. Sauté garlic for 1 minute. Whisk in flour to make a paste. Cook, stirring constantly for 1 minute. Carefully whisk in milk mixture and chicken base. Cook until it begins to thicken. Add romano, Italian topping, cream cheese and white pepper. Cook until cheese has melted and sauce is creamy.

Cook's Note: Thin with milk to desired consistency. Fat-free grated Italian topping is found in your supermarket next to the dry parmesan cheese in a can.

% Calories as Fat — Above the HM✔ guidelines: Although this recipe has a high percentage of calories as fat (>30%), the total fat is less than 5 grams per serving. This will easily fit within your allotment of 45 grams per day. This happens most often in low-calorie recipes.

Nutrient Content Per Serving

Calories	121.0
Protein	9.5 g
Carbohydrates	10.5 g
Fat – Total	4.2 g
Cholesterol	10.4 mg
Dietary Fiber	0.1 g
Sodium	266.0 mg

Percent of Calories

32% Protein
36% Carbohydrate
32% Fat

Fat Breakdown

Saturated Fat	1.3 g
Monounsaturated Fat	1.4 g
Polyunsaturated Fat	1.3 g

SWEET AND SOUR HERB SAUCE
Serves 6
Yield: 1 cup

3 Tbl.	mixed fresh herbs, such as basil, mint and parsley, chopped
1 slice	white bread, crusts removed
3 Tbl.	balsamic vinegar
1 Tbl.	sugar
½ tsp.	anchovy paste
2 tsp.	olive oil
to taste	salt and pepper

Blend all the ingredients together.

Cook's Note: Vary the quantities of the ingredients of this sauce according to your liking. It works great brushed on toasted bread to make a strong flavored bruschetta. It may also be served with cold meat, fish or boiled vegetables. Use it as a marinade and basting sauce for white fish.

% Calories as Fat — Above the HM✔ guidelines: Although this recipe has a high percentage of calories as fat (>30%), the total fat is less than 5 grams per serving. This will easily fit within your allotment of 45 grams per day. This happens most often in low-calorie recipes.

Nutrient Content Per Serving		Percent of Calories	Fat Breakdown	
Calories	35.8	6% Protein	Saturated Fat	0.2 g
Protein	0.5 g	53% Carbohydrate	Monounsaturated Fat	1.1 g
Carbohydrates	4.9 g	41% Fat	Polyunsaturated Fat	0.2 g
Fat – Total	1.7 g			
Cholesterol	0.4 mg			
Dietary Fiber	0.1 g			
Sodium	36.1 mg			

ALL-PURPOSE RED SAUCE
Serves 8

1 lb.	hot turkey Italian sausage
1 lg.	onion, diced
4-6 cloves	garlic, minced
1 18-oz. can	low-sodium tomatoes, peeled, seeded
1 15-oz. can	tomato sauce or purée
1 12-oz. can	tomato paste
4 cups	water
1 Tbl.	dried parsley
2 tsp.	dried basil
1 tsp.	dried oregano
1 tsp.	black pepper

Cut sausage into 1-inch lengths. Cook over low heat to brown. In a food processor, process garlic and onion. Add to sausage and brown. Process tomatoes in food processor. Add to sausage. Add remaining ingredients to pan. Simmer, partially covered for 1½-2 hours. To thicken, remove cover. Stir occasionally to prevent sticking.

Cook's Note: Use this sauce for any recipe that calls for a tomato sauce. It is superb over plain pasta served either with or without the sausage. You can make a big pot and freeze it for later use.

▼ This recipe is used for the following items:
Pasta e Fajioli (see p. 347)
Chicken Tortellini (see p. 349)
Chicken Parmigiana (see p. 373)
Sausage and Pepper Sandwich (see p. 385)

Nutrient Content Per Serving

Calories	195.0
Protein	20.0 g
Carbohydrates	20.8 g
Fat – Total	4.7 g
Cholesterol	48.2 mg
Dietary Fiber	4.9 g
Sodium	716.0 mg

Percent of Calories

39% Protein
40% Carbohydrate
21% Fat

Fat Breakdown

Saturated Fat	1.5 g
Monounsaturated Fat	1.0 g
Polyunsaturated Fat	1.5 g

MARINARA SAUCE FOR FISH
Serves 4
Yield: 2 cups

1 15-oz. can	tomatoes
1 med.	onion, sliced
1 clove	garlic, minced
½ Tbl.	olive oil
1 can	anchovy fillets, rinsed and drained, cut into small pieces
to taste	salt and pepper
½ tsp.	oregano
½ tsp.	sugar

In a non-stick pan, sauté onion and garlic in oil about 5 minutes. Add tomatoes. Simmer gently for 1 hour. Add anchovies, salt and pepper to taste. Cook 10 minutes. Stir in oregano. Simmer over low heat until ready to serve over spaghetti or fish dish.

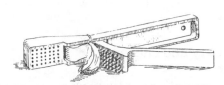

% Calories as Fat — Above the HM✔ guidelines: Although this recipe has a high percentage of calories as fat (>30%), the total fat is less than 5 grams per serving. This will easily fit within your allotment of 45 grams per day. This happens most often in low-calorie recipes.

▼ This recipe is used for the following items:
Cacciatore Risotto (see p. 332)
Pasta e Fajioli (see p. 347)
Spaghetti Squash (see p. 403)

Nutrient Content Per Serving		**Percent of Calories**	**Fat Breakdown**	
Calories	67.1	21% Protein	Saturated Fat	0.5 g
Protein	3.7 g	44% Carbohydrate	Monounsaturated Fat	1.6 g
Carbohydrates	7.8 g	35% Fat	Polyunsaturated Fat	0.5 g
Fat – Total	2.8 g			
Cholesterol	6.8 mg			
Dietary Fiber	1.9 g			
Sodium	467.0 mg			

FIREY OLIVE OIL RELISH
Serves 8
Yield: 1 cup

1 med.	onion, chopped fine
½	hot red pepper, diced
⅓ cup	parsley, chopped fine
3 cloves	garlic, minced
¾ oz.	capers, drained
¼ cup + 2 Tbl.	red wine vinegar
1½ tsp.	red pepper flakes
2 tsp.	oregano, fresh, chopped
1	bay leaf
3 tsp.	dry mustard
½ tsp.	fresh lemon juice
to taste	salt
2 Tbl.	olive oil

Combine all ingredients except oil. Mix well, then add oil.

Cook's Note: Serve with seafood, poultry and cheeses.

% Calories as Fat — Above the HM✔ guidelines: Although this recipe has a high percentage of calories as fat (>30%), the total fat is less than 5 grams per serving. This will easily fit within your allotment of 45 grams per day. This happens most often in low-calorie recipes.

Nutrient Content Per 2 Tablespoons

Calories	46.2
Protein	0.5 g
Carbohydrates	4.0 g
Fat – Total	3.5 g
Cholesterol	0.0 mg
Dietary Fiber	0.7 g
Sodium	35.6 mg

Percent of Calories

4%	Protein
32%	Carbohydrate
64%	Fat

Fat Breakdown

Saturated Fat	0.5 g
Monounsaturated Fat	2.5 g
Polyunsaturated Fat	0.3 g

SICILIAN CASSATA
WITH SEMISWEET CHOCOLATE FROSTING
Serves 10

Cake:

1 lb.	fat-free pound cake

Filling:

¾ lb.	lowfat ricotta cheese
¼ cup	sugar
1 tsp.	orange extract
1 Tbl.	orange-flavored liqueur (Strega, Triple Sec, Grand Marnier)
2 Tbl.	candied citron, lemon or orange peel, chopped peel
2 Tbl.	semisweet chocolate chips

Frosting:

¼ cup	cocoa powder
¼ cup	brown sugar
1½ tsp.	honey
⅓ cup	skimmed evaporated milk
2 Tbl.	semisweet chocolate chips
¼ cup + 2 Tbl.	very strong black coffee (espresso is best)
1 tsp.	vanilla
2 Tbl.	orange liqueur
1 Tbl.	cornstarch

Slice cake in thirds lengthwise (to make a 3-layer cake). Combine ricotta cheese, sugar and flavors with a fork until smooth. Stir in lemon peel and chocolate chips. Spread one-half on bottom layer of cake, cover with middle cake layer. Spread remaining one-half next, then cover with top layer of cake. Chill.

Frosting:
In a small saucepan, combine all frosting ingredients, except cornstarch. Heat, stirring constantly until smooth. Carefully add 1 tablespoon cornstarch and continue heating until it thickens. Allow to cool to room temperature before frosting cake.

Frost top of cake, letting some drip down sides.

Cook's Note: Candied citron, candied lemon peel and candied orange peel are seasonal. They are only available during the winter holiday season.

Nutrient Content Per Serving		Percent of Calories	Fat Breakdown	
Calories	260.0	11% Protein	Saturated Fat	2.7 g
Protein	7.5 g	71% Carbohydrate	Monounsaturated Fat	1.4 g
Carbohydrates	48.0 g	16% Fat	Polyunsaturated Fat	0.3 g
Fat – Total	4.7 g			
Cholesterol	10.6 mg			
Dietary Fiber	1.2 g			
Sodium	397.0 mg			

CHOCOLATE AMARETTO BUDINO
Serves 8

Cake:

2 cups	flour
1 Tbl.	baking powder
1 cup	sugar
¼ cup	cocoa powder
1¾ cups	skim milk
1 Tbl.	Amaretto
1 tsp.	vanilla
1 tsp.	almond extract
2 Tbl.	canola oil
½ cup	fat-free sour cream
2 Tbl.	powdered butter replacement

Topping:

¾ cup	sugar
1¼ cups	cocoa powder
2 Tbl.	Amaretto
1 cup	brown sugar
⅓ cup	brewed espresso

Garnish:

2 cups	nonfat vanilla frozen yogurt

To prepare cake:

In a large bowl, sift together flour, baking powder, 1 cup sugar and ¼ cup cocoa powder.

In a separate bowl, beat together milk, 1 Tbl. Amaretto, vanilla, almond extract, canola oil, sour cream and powdered butter replacement. Mix dry and wet ingredients together with a fork. Pour batter into an 8x8 baking dish that has been prepared with butter-flavor cooking spray. Smooth out the top and set aside.

To prepare topping:

In a saucepan, combine remaining ¾ cup sugar, 1¼ cups cocoa powder, 2 Tbl. Amaretto, brown sugar and espresso. Heat, stirring constantly until sugar and cocoa powder are dissolved. Pour over the batter.

Bake at 350° F for 30 minutes. Serve hot or warm with a scoop of nonfat frozen vanilla yogurt.

Cook's Note: For low altitude, add 1 tsp. baking powder + ¼ cup sugar and decrease milk by ¼ cup in the cake batter.

Nutrient Content Per Serving		Percent of Calories	Fat Breakdown	
Calories	498.0	9% Protein	Saturated Fat	2.0 g
Protein	12.3 g	79% Carbohydrate	Monounsaturated Fat	3.0 g
Carbohydrates	106.0 g	11% Fat	Polyunsaturated Fat	1.2 g
Fat – Total	6.5 g			
Cholesterol	2.1 mg			
Dietary Fiber	6.5 g			
Sodium	261.0 mg			

Orange Glazed Cake
Serves 8

6	oranges
8 slices	angel food cake

Syrup:

2 cups	water
½ cup	sugar
1½ cups	orange juice
1½ tsp.	vanilla

Peel oranges. Separate into segments and cut into bite-sized pieces. Reserve peel of 3 oranges and grate.

In a saucepan, combine syrup ingredients. Add the peel. Simmer 5 minutes. Pass sauce through a strainer to remove peel. Return sauce to the pan. Add orange segments. Simmer until tender.

Cook's Note: This may also be served over nonfat frozen yogurt.

Nutrient Content Per Serving

Calories	255.0
Protein	4.4 g
Carbohydrates	59.8 g
Fat – Total	0.6 g
Cholesterol	0.0 mg
Dietary Fiber	2.7 g
Sodium	398.0 mg

Percent of Calories

7%	Protein
91%	Carbohydrate
2%	Fat

Fat Breakdown

Saturated Fat	0.1 g
Monounsaturated Fat	0.1 g
Polyunsaturated Fat	0.2 g

ALMOND BISCOTTI
Makes 42 cookies

¾ cup	almonds, sliced
½ cup	almond paste
6	egg whites or ¾ cup egg substitute
¾ cup	brown sugar
2 tsp.	lemon zest
1 tsp.	almond extract
1⅔ cups	flour
⅓ cup	cornstarch
½ tsp.	baking powder
¼ tsp.	salt

Toast almonds on a baking sheet at 350° F until golden brown. Let cool.

In a large mixing bowl, stir almond paste with a fork until smooth. Beat in egg whites until completely incorporated. Using an electric mixer, gradually beat in sugar until fluffy. Add lemon zest and almond extract.

In a separate bowl, combine flour, cornstarch, baking powder and salt. Add this to the first bowl and blend well. Fold in nuts. Dough should be gooey and hard to mix, but not stiff and dry.

Prepare a cookie sheet with cooking spray. Spread the dough in long strips 14 inches long by 2½ inches wide. Allow 2 inches between strips of dough. Bake at 350° F for 20 minutes or until golden brown. Turn oven heat down to 325° F and bake another 5 minutes. Allow baking sheet to cool on racks for 5 minutes.

Transfer cookie strips to a cutting board. Using a serrated knife slice at a 45° angle into ½-inch thick cookies. Lay cookies cut-side down on the cookie sheet and place in 325° F oven for 10 minutes to dry out. Turn cookies over after 5 minutes. Cool and store in a tin. Keeps well.

Cook's Note: Since these are so low in fat, they are very crisp. Serve them with an ice or flavored coffee. If they get too hard, transfer to an air-tight container and add a few drops of water. If your batter of almond paste and egg whites is too lumpy, simply place in a blender to smooth it out.

Nutrient Content Per Cookie

Calories	55.3
Protein	1.7 g
Carbohydrates	8.7 g
Fat – Total	1.7 g
Cholesterol	0.0 mg
Dietary Fiber	0.7 g
Sodium	27.2 mg

Percent of Calories

12% Protein
62% Carbohydrate
27% Fat

Fat Breakdown

Saturated Fat	0.2 g
Monounsaturated Fat	1.1 g
Polyunsaturated Fat	0.4 g

CHOCOLATE AMARETTO BISCOTTI
Serves 42

¾ cup	almonds, sliced
½ cup	almond paste
½ cup	egg substitute (or 4 egg whites)
¾ cup	brown sugar
2 tsp.	lemon zest
1 tsp.	almond extract
2 Tbl.	Amaretto
4 oz.	bittersweet chocolate, melted
2 cups	flour
⅓ cup	cornstarch
1½ tsp.	baking powder
¼ tsp.	salt

Toast almonds on a baking sheet at 350° F until golden brown. Let cool.

In a large mixing bowl, stir almond paste with a fork until smooth. Beat in egg whites until completely incorporated. Using an electric mixer, gradually beat in sugar until fluffy. Add melted chocolate (slightly cooled), lemon zest, almond extract and Amaretto.

In a separate bowl, combine flour, cornstarch, baking powder and salt. Add this to the first bowl and blend well. Fold in nuts. Dough should be gooey and hard to mix, but not stiff and dry.

Prepare a cookie sheet with cooking spray. Spread the dough in long strips 14 inches long by 2½ inches wide. Allow 2 inches between strips of dough. Bake at 350° F for 20 minutes or until golden brown. Turn oven heat down to 325° F and bake another 5 minutes. Allow baking sheet to cool on racks for 5 minutes.

Transfer cookie strips to a cutting board. Using a serrated knife slice at a 45° angle into ½-inch-thick cookies. Lay cookies cut-side down on the cookie sheet and place in 325° F oven for 10 minutes to dry out. Turn cookies over after 5 minutes. Cool and store in a tin. Keeps well.

Cook's Note: Since these are so low in fat, they are very crisp. Serve with an ice or a flavored coffee. If they get too hard, transfer to an air-tight container and add a few drops of water. If your batter of almond paste and egg whites is too lumpy, simply place in a blender to smooth it out.

Variations: You may substitute pine nuts for almonds.

Alcohol Note: The alcohol content was computed prior to cooking. Once the alcohol is heated to the boiling point, the alcohol disappears along with most of the calories from the alcohol.

Nutrient Content Per Cookie

Calories	74.0
Protein	1.8 g
Carbohydrates	11.1 g
Fat – Total	2.8 g
Cholesterol	0.0 mg
Dietary Fiber	0.8 g
Sodium	34.8 mg

Percent of Calories

9% Protein	
57% Carbohydrate	
32% Fat	
2% Alcohol	

Fat Breakdown

Saturated Fat	0.8 g
Monounsaturated Fat	1.5 g
Polyunsaturated Fat	0.4 g

AMARETTI (ALMOND MACAROONS)
Makes 30

1½ cups	blanched almonds
1½ cups	sugar
¼ tsp.	salt
1 tsp.	almond extract
3	egg whites
½ cup	flour

Process almonds in food processor until ground coarse. Combine all ingredients. Batter should be stiff enough not to flow. If too soft, add more flour. With lightly floured hands, shape into 1-inch balls. Arrange on a non-stick cookie sheet 2-3 inches apart. Bake at 350° F for 18-20 minutes.

Cook's Note: Serve with zabaglione *(see p. 435).* You may wish to spray your cookie sheet before baking. It makes it easier to remove the cookies.

% Calories as Fat — Above the HM✔ guidelines: Although this recipe has a high percentage of calories as fat (>30%), the total fat is less than 5 grams per serving. This will easily fit within your allotment of 45 grams per day. This happens most often in low-calorie recipes.

Nutrient Content Per Cookie

Calories	92.3
Protein	2.3 g
Carbohydrates	13.0 g
Fat – Total	3.8 g
Cholesterol	0.0 mg
Dietary Fiber	0.7 g
Sodium	28.6 mg

Percent of Calories

10% Protein
54% Carbohydrate
36% Fat

Fat Breakdown

Saturated Fat	0.4 g
Monounsaturated Fat	2.5 g
Polyunsaturated Fat	0.8 g

ANISE COOKIES
Makes 60

¾ cup	canola oil
8	egg whites
1 tsp.	vanilla
1 oz.	Anisette
4 cups	all-purpose flour
1½ cups	sugar
4 tsp.	baking powder
1 tsp.	baking soda
1 tsp.	anise seed, ground to a powder

In a large bowl, combine oil, egg whites, vanilla and Anisette. In a separate bowl, combine remaining ingredients. Mix together well. Using a tablespoon, drop batter onto a non-stick cookie sheet. Bake at 350° F for 15-20 minutes.

Variations:
- May substitute Amaretto + 1 tsp. almond flavor in place of Anisette and anise seed.
- May add 1 Tbl. orange rind or 1 Tbl. lemon peel for yet another flavor.

Cook's Note: If you are using an electric mixer, you may want to use dough hooks. It gets pretty thick.

% Calories as Fat — Above the HM✔ guidelines: Although this recipe has a high percentage of calories as fat (>30%), the total fat is less than 5 grams per serving. This will easily fit within your allotment of 45 grams per day. This happens most often in low-calorie recipes.

Nutrient Content Per Cookie		Percent of Calories	Fat Breakdown	
Calories	77.7	6% Protein	Saturated Fat	0.2 g
Protein	1.3 g	54% Carbohydrate	Monounsaturated Fat	1.6 g
Carbohydrates	11.6 g	39% Fat	Polyunsaturated Fat	0.8 g
Fat – Total	2.8 g			
Cholesterol	0.0 mg			
Dietary Fiber	0.2 g			
Sodium	49.5 mg			

PITZELLAS
Makes 48

3 cups   egg substitute
2 cups   sugar
½ cup   liquid margarine
4 tsp.   anise seed, ground
2 tsp.   anise flavor
2 Tbl.   baking powder
3 cups   flour
1 Tbl.   orange zest

Pour egg substitute into a mixing bowl. Beat while adding sugar and liquid margarine. Allow sugar to dissolve. Add remaining ingredients.

Heat pitzella iron. Spray with cooking spray. Use 1 heaping tablespoon per pitzella. Squeeze iron tight and cook until slightly browned. Cool flat on a rack.

Variations:
- Substitute almond extract for anise seed and anise flavor.

Nutrient Content Per Pitzella
Calories	91.7
Protein	2.8 g
Carbohydrates	14.6 g
Fat – Total	2.5 g
Cholesterol	0.2 mg
Dietary Fiber	0.3 g
Sodium	99.4 mg

Percent of Calories
12% Protein
63% Carbohydrate
25% Fat

Fat Breakdown
Saturated Fat	0.4 g
Monounsaturated Fat	0.8 g
Polyunsaturated Fat	1.1 g

PEARS WITH RICOTTA CHEESE TOPPING
Serves 4

4	ripe pears
1	lemon
2 qts.	cold water

Topping:

8 oz.	nonfat ricotta cheese
2 Tbl.	skim milk
1 Tbl.	powdered sugar

Garnish:

2 Tbl.	toasted almonds
1 tsp.	lemon zest

To prepare topping:
Whisk together ricotta cheese, skim milk and powdered sugar until smooth. Store in refrigerator until ready to serve.

To prepare pears:
Slice lemon in half. Add lemon and its juice to the water. Peel and remove core from pears. Cut in half. Drop pears into the lemon water and let soak for 2 hours in the refrigerator.

To serve:
Place 2 pear halves on a serving dish. Top with a dollop of cheese mixture. Garnish with toasted almonds and lemon zest.

Nutrient Content Per Serving

Calories	202.0
Protein	8.1 g
Carbohydrates	33.6 g
Fat – Total	5.4 g
Cholesterol	0.1 mg
Dietary Fiber	6.0 g
Sodium	264.0 mg

Percent of Calories

15% Protein
62% Carbohydrate
23% Fat

Fat Breakdown

Saturated Fat	0.3 g
Monounsaturated Fat	1.9 g
Polyunsaturated Fat	0.7 g

STRAWBERRIES AND WINE
Serves 4

4 cups	strawberries, sliced
1 tsp.	sugar
1 cup	red wine

Sprinkle sugar over berries. Add wine. Chill.

Serve in individual dishes.

Cook's Note: May substitute raspberries for strawberries.

Alcohol Note: The alcohol content was computed prior to cooking. Once the alcohol is heated to the boiling point, the alcohol disappears along with most of the calories from the alcohol.

Nutrient Content Per Serving		**Percent of Calories**	**Fat Breakdown**	
Calories	89.7	4% Protein	Saturated Fat	0.0 g
Protein	1.0 g	51% Carbohydrate	Monounsaturated Fat	0.1 g
Carbohydrates	12.2 g	5% Fat	Polyunsaturated Fat	0.3 g
Fat – Total	0.5 g	40% Alcohol		
Cholesterol	0.0 mg			
Dietary Fiber	3.7 g			
Sodium	4.4 mg			

CHERRY ICE
Serves 4

4 cups	sour cherries
1 cup	sugar
1 Tbl.	lemon juice, fresh
2 Tbl.	brandy (optional)

Purée cherries in food processor. To eliminate skins, push through a food mill. Heat cherry pulp with sugar, until sugar dissolves. Cook 2 minutes longer. Freeze in ice cube trays.

When ready to serve, unmold cubes into a food processor. Add lemon juice and brandy. Process until smooth. Serve immediately in decorative dessert cups. Garnish with a cherry or mint sprig.

Cook's Note: May use frozen cherries. This has a refreshing, tart flavor. It is great after a "rich" meal. If you use sweet cherries decrease the sugar to ⅓ cup or eliminate it completely.

Nutrient Content Per Serving

Calories	282.0
Protein	1.4 g
Carbohydrates	67.2 g
Fat – Total	0.7 g
Cholesterol	0.0 mg
Dietary Fiber	3.0 g
Sodium	2.2 mg

Percent of Calories

2%	Protein
90%	Carbohydrate
2%	Fat
6%	Alcohol

Fat Breakdown

Saturated Fat	0.2 g
Monounsaturated Fat	0.2 g
Polyunsaturated Fat	0.2 g

PEACH ICE
Serves 6

1 lb. bag	peach slices, frozen
¼ cup	peach schnapps
1 tsp.	vanilla
¼ cup	honey
1 Tbl.	lime juice
	water as needed

Place all ingredients in blender or food processor. Add water as needed and process to a thick consistency. Garnish with mint leaves and/or fresh slices of peach.

Garnish:

mint leaves
fresh peach slices

Cook's Note: May substitute nectarines for peaches.

Alcohol Note: The alcohol content was computed prior to cooking. Once the alcohol is heated to the boiling point, the alcohol disappears along with most of the calories from the alcohol.

Nutrient Content Per Serving

Calories	109.0
Protein	0.5 g
Carbohydrates	23.1 g
Fat – Total	0.1 g
Cholesterol	0.0 mg
Dietary Fiber	1.1 g
Sodium	5.2 mg

Percent of Calories

2%	Protein
81%	Carbohydrate
1%	Fat
16%	Alcohol

Fat Breakdown

Saturated Fat	0.0 g
Monounsaturated Fat	0.0 g
Polyunsaturated Fat	0.1 g

Marsala Custard
Serves 4

2 Tbl.	sugar
2 cups	skim milk
½ cup	marsala wine
1 cup	egg substitute
⅓ cup	sugar
1¼ tsp.	vanilla

In a small saucepan, slowly brown 2 tablespoons of sugar. Cook over medium heat until it caramelizes. Carefully pour syrup into custard cups that are prepared with cooking spray. Combine remaining ingredients. Pour into custard cups.

Place cups in a baking pan filled with hot water. Bake at 350° F for 1 hour or until knife comes out clean.

Alcohol Note: The alcohol content was computed prior to cooking. Once the alcohol is heated to the boiling point, the alcohol disappears along with most of the calories from the alcohol.

Nutrient Content Per Serving

Calories	206.0
Protein	11.4 g
Carbohydrates	29.9 g
Fat – Total	2.2 g
Cholesterol	2.8 mg
Dietary Fiber	0.0 g
Sodium	171.0 mg

Percent of Calories

22% Protein
59% Carbohydrate
10% Fat
 9% Alcohol

Fat Breakdown

Saturated Fat	0.5 g
Monounsaturated Fat	0.6 g
Polyunsaturated Fat	1.0 g

RICOTTA ESPRESSO MOUSSE
Serves 4

15 oz.	lowfat ricotta cheese
½ cup	powdered sugar
¼ cup	espresso, brewed
2 Tbl.	Sambuca (or Anisette)

Garnish:

4 tsp.	pistachios, chopped

Place all ingredients except pistachios in a food processor. Blend until smooth. Spoon into decorative dessert glasses. Chill 2 hours. Garnish with pistachios.

Variations:
- May use any liqueur you prefer; Amaretto, Frangelico, etc.

Cook's Note: Expect a thin consistency. Serve with anise cookies *(see p. 425)* or biscotti *(see p. 422).*

Nutrient Content Per Serving		Percent of Calories	Fat Breakdown	
Calories	194.0	24% Protein	Saturated Fat	0.2 g
Protein	11.8 g	47% Carbohydrate	Monounsaturated Fat	0.9 g
Carbohydrates	22.9 g	24% Fat	Polyunsaturated Fat	0.2 g
Fat – Total	5.1 g			
Cholesterol	0.0 mg			
Dietary Fiber	0.3 g			
Sodium	488.0 mg			

RICOTTA PUDDING
Serves 6

3 Tbl.	cream of wheat
15 oz.	lowfat ricotta cheese
4 Tbl.	powdered sugar
6 Tbl.	egg substitute
1 Tbl.	currants (or raisins)
1 Tbl.	candied fruit
2 Tbl.	rum
1	egg white
½ cup	graham cracker crumbs

Bring 1½ cups of water to a boil. Add cream of wheat. Simmer 3 minutes. Cool. Place ricotta in a food processor. Process until smooth. Add powdered sugar and egg substitute. Process again until smooth. Stir in the currants, candied fruit, rum and cooled cream of wheat.

Beat egg white until stiff. Fold into batter. Prepare a casserole with butter-flavored cooking spray. Sprinkle bottom and sides with graham cracker crumbs. Pour batter into pan. Bake at 375° F for 1 hour.

Cook's Note: If you've ever had a fried cannoli, this tastes similar to the filling. May want to chop the currants and candied fruits to obtain smaller pieces. This will allow for more even distribution throughout the pudding. Can also be baked in individual ramekins.

Nutrient Content Per Serving

Calories	170.0
Protein	11.0 g
Carbohydrates	17.8 g
Fat – Total	4.6 g
Cholesterol	0.3 mg
Dietary Fiber	0.5 g
Sodium	440.0 mg

Percent of Calories

26% Protein
42% Carbohydrate
25% Fat

Fat Breakdown

Saturated Fat	0.4 g
Monounsaturated Fat	0.5 g
Polyunsaturated Fat	1.1 g

SEMOLINA PUDDING
Serves 6

½ cup	semolina flour
3 cups	skim milk
1	lemon, zest of, chopped
dash	salt
⅓ cup	sugar
¼ cup	egg substitute
2	egg whites

Garnish:

    fresh fruit compote or fruit sauce
        (see p. 266)

In a saucepan, combine the skim milk, lemon zest and salt. Slowly bring to a boil. Add the semolina gradually and bring back to a boil, stirring constantly for 2-3 minutes. Remove from heat and cool slightly. Add the egg substitute and one-half of the sugar.

Beat the egg whites stiff. Beat in the remaining sugar. Fold into milk mixture. Pour into serving dishes and chill for 2-3 hours.

Cook's Note: May use other flavors such as vanilla bean, hazelnut, almond, chocolate chips, raisins, or mocha in place of the lemon.

Nutrient Content Per Serving

Calories	160.0
Protein	8.3 g
Carbohydrates	28.3 g
Fat – Total	1.5 g
Cholesterol	2.4 mg
Dietary Fiber	0.4 g
Sodium	101.0 mg

Percent of Calories

21% Protein
71% Carbohydrate
 8% Fat

Fat Breakdown

Saturated Fat	0.4 g
Monounsaturated Fat	0.3 g
Polyunsaturated Fat	0.7 g

ZABAGLIONE (FROTHY EGG PUDDING)
Serves 4

1 cup	liquid egg substitute (equivalent to 4 eggs)
4 Tbl.	sugar
½ tsp.	vanilla
½ cup	dry white wine

In the top of a double boiler, combine all ingredients. Whisk until it thickens (approximately 5 minutes). Pour into stemmed glasses. Serve immediately.

Variation:
- Pour 2 tablespoons grenadine into glasses. Then add zabaglione.
- Can be prepared at the table over a denatured alcohol flame.

Cook's Note: Must use egg substitute and not egg whites for this recipe.

Alcohol Note: The alcohol content was computed prior to cooking. Once the alcohol is heated to the boiling point, the alcohol disappears along with most of the calories from the alcohol.

Nutrient Content Per Serving

Calories	120.0
Protein	7.2 g
Carbohydrates	13.2 g
Fat – Total	2.0 g
Cholesterol	0.6 mg
Dietary Fiber	0.0 g
Sodium	107.0 mg

Percent of Calories

24% Protein
45% Carbohydrate
15% Fat
16% Alcohol

Fat Breakdown

Saturated Fat	0.4 g
Monounsaturated Fat	0.5 g
Polyunsaturated Fat	1.0 g

GREECE

Greek cuisine is rather conservative when put up against the finer cookery of (its sometimes former landlords) France and Italy. All the spice-laden meat dishes, the pan-fried cheeses oozing their oils and the honey-sweet desserts that set your teeth to singing can amount to a culinary ker-plunk.

But Greek cooking, too, is Mediterranean at its best, which is to say its heartiness is healthy and wholesome. So you find vegetables everywhere, a prodigal use of herbs — and a paucity of meat. Mediterranean cooking worships the eternal trinity of wheat, olives and wine: Filo, noodles and pita breads; the ubiquitous olive oil; long, purple-black kala-matas and wines brash and bouyantly fruity.

Greeks are serious eaters. To eat in the Greek style, allow plenty of time for the meal and conversation and order lots of different appetizers and main dishes to share. Pause for a long gap of wine and more conversation, then a bevy of desserts and Greek coffee.

The Greek general and historian Xenophon (431-355 B.C.) wrote how Greek commanders had difficulty getting their soldiers to fight after lunch.

To begin a meal, there are ground yellow lentils in the manner of a Middle Eastern hummus made of chick-peas, with a liberal dose of chopped parsley. Lap it up with grilled triangles of warm pita. (Homer fed parsley to his chariot horses for added strength.)

Or enjoy a hot and gooey saganaki, the melt-down of the piquant kaseri cheese that tastes much like Italian pecorino fresco. But remember that Greek cuisine is much ado ahead of time. Serve it room temperature or warmed a bit, that's all.

Main dishes in Greece usually include vegetables, pulses, eggs and cheese: big squares of moussaka (eggplant and potatoes with ground beef) and pastitsio (macaroni and ground beef) are both liberally scented with nutmeg and cinnamon. Finding cinnamon in savory dishes isn't odd in Greece. The spice is credited with alleviating stomach disorders and reducing fevers.

Both of these classic Greek dishes are topped with a deliciously rich egg custard — the Greeks call it "bechamel," but it's nothing like the classic French preparation of the same name — that holds the whole together so that you can look down the side and see all the sedimentary layers of meat, vegetables or pasta. It's like those jars of marinated Italian artichokes, olives and giardinara.

If it's "Greek to me" you say about Mediterranean cooking, start here on the Aegean islands, perhaps the mother kitchen to the cuisine of this rich and varied sea.

Bill St. John
Food and Wine Editor
Rocky Mountain News

TABLE OF CONTENTS

TABLE OF CONTENTS

—— Most Commonly Used Items for Greek Recipes ——

▼ **FRESH SUPPLIES**

basil
eggplant
feta cheese
garlic
lemons
mint
parmesan cheese
scallions
tomatoes
vermouth, dry
wine, dry white

▼ **PANTRY SUPPLIES**

artichokes
bread crumbs
butter replacement
coriander seed
dill weed
olive oil
olives, black
olives, Greek
tomato paste
tomato sauce
tomatoes, canned
vinegar, red wine

—— Menu Suggestions ——

▼ **CASUAL**

Cucumber-Tomato Salad
Grilled Snapper with Spinach and Rice
Fruit and Yogurt

▼ **FORMAL RECEPTION**

Feta Cheese Balls
Eggplant Canapes
Stifado
Orange and Olive Salad
Bean Soup
Lobster wrapped in filo with Mixed
　　Vegetables
Baklava

▼ **SUMMER**

Mushroom Tomato Spread
Pepper Salad
Chicken with Artichokes and White Lima
　　Pilaki
Sweet Orange Compote

▼ **WINTER**

Marinated Lamb
Lentil Soup
New Year's Bread
Moussaka with Spicy Risotto
Apricopita

▼ **QUICK BUT AUTHENTIC**

Tomato Feta Salad
Baked Fish with Zucchini Casserole
Rice Pudding

ARTICHOKES AND ONIONS
Serves 4

20	baby artichokes
20	scallions, white portion only, chopped fine
1 tsp.	olive oil
3 lg.	tomatoes, peeled, chopped coarse
1 tsp.	coriander seed, ground
1	lemon, juice of
1	bouquet garni *(see p. 15)*
½ tsp.	bay leaf
½ tsp.	parsley, dry
½ tsp.	thyme, dry
3 Tbl.	white wine
to taste	salt and pepper

Cut artichokes in 2-4 pieces. Remove chokes. In a non-stick pan, sauté onions in oil for 3 minutes. Add remaining ingredients. Cover with water. Cook, covered for 20 minutes. Chill. Serve cold.

Cook's Note: May use canned, drained artichoke hearts when artichokes are out of season (not marinated artichoke hearts).

Alcohol Note: The alcohol content was computed prior to cooking. Once the alcohol is heated to the boiling point, the alcohol disappears along with most of the calories from the alcohol.

Nutrient Content Per Serving

Calories	151.0
Protein	8.2 g
Carbohydrates	29.9 g
Fat – Total	2.0 g
Cholesterol	0.0 mg
Dietary Fiber	12.4 g
Sodium	202.0 mg

Percent of Calories

19% Protein
68% Carbohydrate
10% Fat
3% Alcohol

Fat Breakdown

Saturated Fat	0.3 g
Monounsaturated Fat	1.0 g
Polyunsaturated Fat	0.4 g

BEAN DIP
Serves 8

16-oz. can white limas or butter beans
1 tsp.   olive oil
1 med.   onion, chopped fine
1 tsp.   sugar
2 tsp.   paprika
1 tsp.   dill weed

Servers and Dippers:
      red bell pepper
      baby carrots
      celery sticks
      baby corn
      zucchini sticks
      pita bread wedges

In a small non-stick frying pan, heat oil and sauté onions until soft. Remove to a large food processor bowl.

Drain and rinse lima beans. Add remaining ingredients to the food processor and process until smooth.

To prepare platter:
Cut red pepper in half and scoop out ribs and seeds. Use as a bowl to serve the dip. Arrange dippers around the bell pepper.

Nutrient Content Per Serving

Calories	68.9
Protein	3.3 g
Carbohydrates	12.5 g
Fat – Total	0.9 g
Cholesterol	0.0 mg
Dietary Fiber	4.1 g
Sodium	135.0 mg

Percent of Calories

19% Protein
70% Carbohydrate
11% Fat

Fat Breakdown

Saturated Fat	0.2 g
Monounsaturated Fat	0.5 g
Polyunsaturated Fat	0.2 g

CHEESE FILLED TRIANGLES
(TIROTRIGONA)
Serves 30
Yield: 60 triangles

1 lb.	filo dough sheets
6 oz.	feta cheese, crumbled
1 cup	1% cottage cheese, drained
6	egg whites
1 Tbl.	powdered butter replacement
1 tsp.	mint, dry
1 Tbl.	butter, melted
2 Tbl.	olive oil, in a spray bottle

In a bowl, mix together feta, cottage cheese, egg whites, powdered butter replacement and mint. Cut filo into 6 strips lengthwise approximately 2 inches wide. Keep all filo covered with wax paper and a damp cloth to keep dough from drying out. Work only with 2 strips at a time. Lay 2 strips of filo on top of each other. Spray with a mist of olive oil. Place 2 teaspoons of filling in the corner of filo strip. Fold corner over in a triangle shape. Continue folding the triangle like a flag. Repeat with remaining dough and filling.

Prepare a non-stick baking sheet with cooking spray. Lay triangles in a single layer (may take a few batches). Brush tops of triangles with melted butter. Bake at 350° F for 30 minutes or until slightly browned.

Cook's Note: Preparation time = 1 hour. Do not use egg substitute. Butter was used to enhance the flavor. You may substitute olive oil.

% Calories as Fat — Above the HM✔ guidelines: Although this recipe has a high percentage of calories as fat (>30%), the total fat is less than 5 grams per serving. This will easily fit within your allotment of 45 grams per day. This happens most often in low-calorie recipes.

Nutrient Content Per Two Triangles		**Percent of Calories**	**Fat Breakdown**	
Calories	80.9	19% Protein	Saturated Fat	1.4 g
Protein	3.5 g	45% Carbohydrate	Monounsaturated Fat	1.3 g
Carbohydrates	8.6 g	39% Fat	Polyunsaturated Fat	0.8 g
Fat – Total	3.5 g			
Cholesterol	6.4 mg			
Dietary Fiber	0.2 g			
Sodium	184.0 mg			

EGGPLANT CANAPÉS
Serves 6

1 lg.	eggplant
2 tsp.	olive oil
1 lg.	onion, chopped fine
2 sm. cloves	garlic, minced
1 lg.	sweet red pepper, chopped fine
2 Tbl.	tomato paste
¼ cup	dry sun-dried tomatoes
1 tsp.	red wine vinegar
to taste	salt and pepper
1 tsp.	olive oil

Garnish:

3 tsp.	pine nuts
	cilantro leaves

Soak sun-dried tomatoes in hot water. Chop. Slice eggplant into 18 round slices. Pat dry. Set aside.

In a medium non-stick frying pan, heat the olive oil. Sauté onion, garlic and pepper. Cook until onion is soft. Add remaining ingredients.

Place eggplant slices on a non-stick baking sheet. Lightly brush tops with olive oil. Top with tomato mixture. Cover and bake at 350° F for 40-50 minutes.

Garnish with pine nuts and cilantro leaves.

% Calories as Fat — Above the HM✔ guidelines: Although this recipe has a high percentage of calories as fat (>30%), the total fat is less than 5 grams per serving. This will easily fit within your allotment of 45 grams per day. This happens most often in low-calorie recipes.

Nutrient Content Per Serving		Percent of Calories	Fat Breakdown	
Calories	80.8	9% Protein	Saturated Fat	0.6 g
Protein	1.9 g	51% Carbohydrate	Monounsaturated Fat	2.2 g
Carbohydrates	11.4 g	41% Fat	Polyunsaturated Fat	1.0 g
Fat – Total	4.1 g			
Cholesterol	0.0 mg			
Dietary Fiber	4.2 g			
Sodium	95.6 mg			

EGGPLANT DIP
Serves 10

1 lg.	eggplant
1 clove	garlic, minced
1 med.	onion, minced
¼ cup	sesame seeds, toasted
1 Tbl.	olive oil
1 lg.	tomato, chopped
to taste	salt and pepper
½ tsp.	cumin
3 Tbl.	fresh lemon juice
dash	Tabasco™
1 Tbl.	fresh parsley, chopped

Cook's Note: This has a salsa-like texture.

Pierce eggplant. Bake at 375° F for 1 hour. Let cool. Peel and remove seeds.

Sauté garlic and onion in olive oil. Transfer all ingredients (except sesame seeds and parsley) to a blender or food processor and purée until smooth. Stir in toasted sesame seeds and parsley. Chill overnight. Serve with crackers, pita chips or pita wedges.

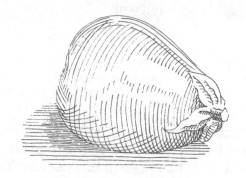

Nutrient Content Per Serving
Calories	26.4
Protein	0.7 g
Carbohydrates	5.2 g
Fat – Total	0.6 g
Cholesterol	0.0 mg
Dietary Fiber	2.1 g
Sodium	3.3 mg

Percent of Calories
10% Protein
71% Carbohydrate
19% Fat

Fat Breakdown
Saturated Fat	0.1 g
Monounsaturated Fat	0.4 g
Polyunsaturated Fat	0.1 g

FETA CHEESE BALLS
Makes 24 balls

1 cup	fat-free cream cheese
3 oz.	feta cheese, crumbled
1 clove	garlic, minced
1 tsp.	parsley, chopped
2 tsp.	mint, chopped

To Roll in:

1 Tbl.	parsley, chopped
1 Tbl.	mint, chopped

Garnish:

fresh grape leaves
yellow tomato wedges

Cook's Note: Very strong flavor!

In a mixing bowl, blend together cheeses and herbs until smooth. Chill 1 hour. Shape into 1-inch balls. Chill again for 1 hour. Mix together the parsley and mint. Roll in chopped herbs.

Garnish with fresh grape leaves and yellow tomato wedges.

Nutrient Content Per Tablespoon

Calories	26.3
Protein	3.2 g
Carbohydrates	0.9 g
Fat – Total	0.8 g
Cholesterol	6.5 mg
Dietary Fiber	0.0 g
Sodium	153.0 mg

Percent of Calories

55% Protein
15% Carbohydrate
30% Fat

Fat Breakdown

Saturated Fat	0.5 g
Monounsaturated Fat	0.2 g
Polyunsaturated Fat	0.0 g

GRAPE LEAVES STUFFED WITH RICE
Serves 36

1 jar	grape leaves
3 med.	onions, chopped fine
1 bunch	scallions, chopped fine
2 tsp.	olive oil
2 Tbl.	pine nuts
¾ cup	rice
1 Tbl.	dill, chopped
½ bunch	parsley, chopped
2 tsp.	mint, chopped
2 Tbl.	lemon juice
¾ cup	water

Cooking liquid:

½ bunch	parsley
2 Tbl.	lemon juice

Garnish:

lemon wedges

In a large non-stick frying pan, heat olive oil. Sauté onions and scallions until soft. Add pine nuts and rice. Cook 10 minutes. Add dill, parsley, mint, lemon juice and water. Cover and cook 10 minutes or until water is absorbed (rice will not be cooked).

Lay grape leaves stem side up. Place a dollop of rice mixture on leaf. Fold over 2 sides and then roll into a cylinder. In a saucepan, arrange parsley stalks on bottom. Lay leaf rolls on top of parsley. Cover with a plate to weigh them down. Add lemon juice and enough water to cover the plate. Cover and simmer 1 hour. Let rolls cool. Serve garnished with lemon wedges.

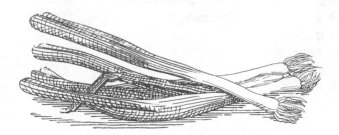

Nutrient Content Per Serving

Calories	36.2
Protein	1.2 g
Carbohydrates	6.1 g
Fat – Total	1.1 g
Cholesterol	0.0 mg
Dietary Fiber	0.3 g
Sodium	4.5 mg

Percent of Calories

12% Protein
62% Carbohydrate
26% Fat

Fat Breakdown

Saturated Fat	0.2 g
Monounsaturated Fat	0.5 g
Polyunsaturated Fat	0.3 g

MARINATED LAMB SKEWERS
Serves 4

½ lb.	boneless lamb, lean
pinch	salt
pinch	fresh ground black pepper
2 tsp.	marjoram
1 clove	garlic, minced
2 tsp.	fresh mint, chopped
1 med.	red pepper, cut in squares

Garnish:

fresh mint sprigs

Trim lamb of all visible fat. Cut meat into bite-sized cubes. Combine lamb, salt, pepper, marjoram and garlic. Coat meat thoroughly and let marinate for 2 hours.

Arrange meat and red pepper on skewers. Broil or grill using hottest setting, for 4 minutes per side. Serve at once.

Cook's Note: Small but tasty. May increase the amounts and use for an entrée. This is a dry marinade. Do not expect the lamb to soak.

% Calories as Fat — Above the HM✓ guidelines: Although this recipe has a high percentage of calories as fat (>30%), the total fat is less than 5 grams per serving. This will easily fit within your allotment of 45 grams per day. This happens most often in low-calorie recipes.

Nutrient Content Per Skewer

Calories	110.0
Protein	16.1 g
Carbohydrates	0.3 g
Fat – Total	4.4 g
Cholesterol	50.5 mg
Dietary Fiber	0.1 g
Sodium	38.8 mg

Percent of Calories

61% Protein
1% Carbohydrate
38% Fat

Fat Breakdown

Saturated Fat	1.6 g
Monounsaturated Fat	1.9 g
Polyunsaturated Fat	0.3 g

MUSHROOM TOMATO SPREAD
Serves 6

1 lb.	button mushrooms, chopped fine
4	tomatoes, peeled, seeded, chopped fine
½ tsp.	olive oil
1 sm.	onion, chopped fine
1 clove	garlic, minced
1 Tbl.	tomato paste
½ cup	white wine
4 Tbl.	fresh parsley, chopped
10 seeds	coriander, ground
to taste	salt and pepper

In a large non-stick skillet, sauté onion and garlic in oil over medium heat for 5 minutes. Add tomatoes and mushrooms, continue cooking 5 more minutes. Stir in tomato paste and wine, cook until thick (about 10-15 minutes). Add remaining ingredients, reserving half of the parsley, and cook 5 more minutes. Remove from heat and cool. Garnish with remaining parsley. Serve warm with sliced Italian bread.

Cook's Note: Grind coriander seed for a stronger flavor. Use a coffee grinder or a mortar and pestle. Can also spread this on sliced Italian bread and broil 1-2 minutes until bubbly.

Alcohol Note: The alcohol content was computed prior to cooking. Once the alcohol is heated to the boiling point, the alcohol disappears along with most of the calories from the alcohol.

Nutrient Content Per Serving

Calories	61.9
Protein	2.7 g
Carbohydrates	9.5 g
Fat – Total	1.0 g
Cholesterol	0.0 mg
Dietary Fiber	2.5 g
Sodium	34.9 mg

Percent of Calories

15% Protein
54% Carbohydrate
13% Fat
18% Alcohol

Fat Breakdown

Saturated Fat	0.1 g
Monounsaturated Fat	0.3 g
Polyunsaturated Fat	0.3 g

MARINATED VEGETABLES
Serves 8

Vegetables:

1 lb.	button mushrooms
1	zucchini, unpeeled, cut in bite-sized cubes
2 cups	cauliflower, broken into flowerettes

Stock:

3 cups	chicken stock *(see p. 538)*
½ cup	dry white wine
¼ cup	red wine vinegar
1	bay leaf
2 cloves	garlic, left whole
3	peppercorns
1 med.	onion, sliced thick
1 tsp.	olive oil

Combine all stock ingredients. Bring to a boil, reduce heat and simmer 20 minutes. Strain. Pour over vegetables and refrigerate immediately. Serve chilled with toothpicks.

Cook's Note: Use any combination of vegetables you like.

Alcohol Note: The alcohol content was computed prior to cooking. Once the alcohol is heated to the boiling point, the alcohol disappears along with most of the calories from the alcohol.

Nutrient Content Per Serving

Calories	50.6
Protein	2.4 g
Carbohydrates	6.9 g
Fat – Total	1.2 g
Cholesterol	0.3 mg
Dietary Fiber	1.7 g
Sodium	429.0 mg

Percent of Calories

17% Protein
48% Carbohydrate
19% Fat
16% Alcohol

Fat Breakdown

Saturated Fat	0.2 g
Monounsaturated Fat	0.5 g
Polyunsaturated Fat	0.3 g

BEAN SOUP
(FASOULATHA)
Serves 8

1 lb.	dry navy beans
2 qts.	water
1 cup	celery, chopped coarse
½ cup	celery leaves, chopped
2 cups	onions, chopped coarse
1 cup	carrots, chopped coarse
to taste	salt and pepper

Soak beans overnight. Discard soaking water and rinse beans well. Place all ingredients in a large soup pot. Simmer 4 hours or until beans are tender.

Cook's Note: To decrease gas produced by beans, discard the soaking water and rinse well. May substitute canned beans. Be sure to rinse and drain. Cook all ingredients except the canned beans for 35 minutes. Add beans for the last 10 minutes only, or else they will disintegrate.

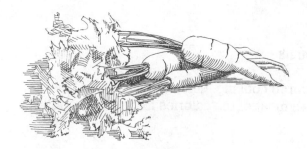

Nutrient Content Per Serving

Calories	105.0
Protein	5.7 g
Carbohydrates	20.6 g
Fat – Total	0.4 g
Cholesterol	0.0 mg
Dietary Fiber	6.4 g
Sodium	33.3 mg

Percent of Calories

21% Protein
75% Carbohydrate
4% Fat

Fat Breakdown

Saturated Fat	0.1 g
Monounsaturated Fat	0.0 g
Polyunsaturated Fat	0.2 g

CHICKEN AND LEMON SOUP
Serves 6

4 cups	chicken stock *(see p. 538)*
2 Tbl.	fresh lemon juice
½ cup	cooked, skinless, chicken breast, diced
½ cup	scallions, sliced on bias
to taste	salt and white pepper
¼ cup	feta cheese, crumbled

In a soup pot, bring chicken stock and lemon juice to a boil. Add cooked chicken and scallions. Bring to a boil again. Add salt and white pepper to taste. Remove from heat. Add feta cheese just before serving.

% Calories as Fat — Above the HM✔ guidelines: Although this recipe has a high percentage of calories as fat (>30%), the total fat is less than 5 grams per serving. This will easily fit within your allotment of 45 grams per day. This happens most often in low-calorie recipes.

Nutrient Content Per Serving

Calories	44.1
Protein	3.9 g
Carbohydrates	2.0 g
Fat – Total	2.3 g
Cholesterol	14.8 mg
Dietary Fiber	0.3 g
Sodium	121.0 mg

Percent of Calories

35%	Protein
18%	Carbohydrate
47%	Fat

Fat Breakdown

Saturated Fat	1.6 g
Monounsaturated Fat	0.5 g
Polyunsaturated Fat	0.1 g

EGG-LEMON SOUP
Serves 6

6 cups	chicken stock *(see p. 538)*
¼ cup	short-grain rice
½ cup	egg substitute
1 tsp.	olive oil
⅓ cup	lemon juice
to taste	salt and pepper

Garnish:

2 Tbl.	mint, chopped

In a large soup pot, bring chicken stock to a boil. Add rice and simmer 15 minutes. In a separate bowl, beat together egg substitute, oil, lemon juice and salt and pepper to taste. Continue beating while slowly adding 1 cup of the stock to the eggs. Once this is incorporated, remove stock from heat. Carefully whisk egg mixture into the remaining stock.

Serve garnished with mint.

Cook's Note: The result is a smooth, creamy and lemony soup. If you stir the mint around in the soup, it adds a minty flavor as well as a pretty garnish.

Nutrient Content Per Serving

Calories	44.4
Protein	2.9 g
Carbohydrates	5.1 g
Fat – Total	1.5 g
Cholesterol	0.2 mg
Dietary Fiber	0.4 g
Sodium	37.2 mg

Percent of Calories

26% Protein
45% Carbohydrate
30% Fat

Fat Breakdown

Saturated Fat	0.3 g
Monounsaturated Fat	0.8 g
Polyunsaturated Fat	0.4 g

CREAM OF SPINACH SOUP
Serves 4

1 10-oz. pkg.	frozen spinach, thawed, drained, chopped
6	scallions, minced
1 tsp.	olive oil
1 cup	chicken stock *(see p. 538)*
to taste	black pepper
1 Tbl.	fresh lemon juice
½ cup	sour cream, nonfat

Garnish:

lemon curls

In a non-stick frying pan, sauté scallions in the oil; do not brown. Add spinach, stock and pepper to taste. Bring to a boil. Reduce heat and simmer gently over low heat about 6-8 minutes. Remove from heat, add lemon juice. Remove half of the soup and purée in a blender. Return the blended soup to the pan. Whisk in sour cream. Chill. Ladle in bowls and garnish with lemon curls.

Cook's Note: You may purée entire batch for a smooth soup. It is quick and easy; a great first course.

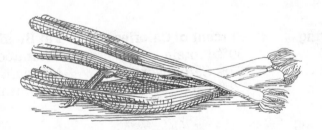

Nutrient Content Per Serving

Calories	53.6
Protein	4.6 g
Carbohydrates	7.5 g
Fat – Total	1.5 g
Cholesterol	0.2 mg
Dietary Fiber	2.0 g
Sodium	360.0 mg

Percent of Calories

30% Protein
49% Carbohydrate
22% Fat

Fat Breakdown

Saturated Fat	0.3 g
Monounsaturated Fat	0.9 g
Polyunsaturated Fat	0.2 g

Lentil Soup
(Faki)
Serves 8

2 cups	dry brown lentils
2 qts.	cold water
½ cup	carrots, diced
2 cups	onions, chopped coarse
1 cup	celery, chopped coarse
5 cloves	garlic, minced
½ tsp.	salt
few grindings	black pepper

Rinse lentils. Combine all ingredients in a large soup pot. Simmer, partially covered for 1 hour or until lentils are tender.

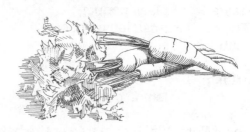

Cook's Note: Serve with French bread. It may be cooked ahead of time and makes a good leftover. May substitute chickpeas for lentils for a nice change.

Nutrient Content Per Serving

Calories	183.0
Protein	14.2 g
Carbohydrates	31.9 g
Fat – Total	0.6 g
Cholesterol	0.0 mg
Dietary Fiber	6.9 g
Sodium	6.6 mg

Percent of Calories

30% Protein
67% Carbohydrate
 3% Fat

Fat Breakdown

Saturated Fat	0.1 g
Monounsaturated Fat	0.1 g
Polyunsaturated Fat	0.3 g

OLIVE SOUP
Serves 4

4-oz. can	black olives, chopped
2 Tbl.	scallions, chopped
1 Tbl.	flour
1½ cups	chicken stock *(see p. 538)*
1	egg white, beaten
½ cup	sour cream, nonfat
½ cup	skim milk
to taste	salt and pepper

Garnish:

sour cream, nonfat
chives

In a medium saucepan prepared with cooking spray, gently sauté the scallions. Add olives and flour and cook 3 minutes. Blend. Add the stock stirring constantly over low heat until it almost reaches a boil.

Meanwhile, blend the egg white, sour cream and milk. Reduce heat. Whisk the sour cream mixture slowly and carefully into the soup being careful not to curdle. Heat to serving temperature, but do not boil. If too thick add a bit more milk. Season to taste. Ladle into bowls and garnish with fat-free sour cream and chives.

% Calories as Fat — Above the HM✔ guidelines: Although this recipe has a high percentage of calories as fat (>30%), the total fat is less than 5 grams per serving. This will easily fit within your allotment of 45 grams per day. This happens most often in low-calorie recipes.

Nutrient Content Per Serving

Calories	79.6
Protein	4.8 g
Carbohydrates	8.5 g
Fat – Total	3.4 g
Cholesterol	0.8 mg
Dietary Fiber	1.0 g
Sodium	652.0 mg

Percent of Calories

23% Protein
40% Carbohydrate
37% Fat

Fat Breakdown

Saturated Fat	0.5 g
Monounsaturated Fat	2.4 g
Polyunsaturated Fat	0.4 g

Soup of the Sea
Serves 8

1 lb.	fish (snapper, bass or halibut)
4 cups	fish stock *(see p. 540)*
½ lb.	medium shrimp, peeled, deveined
24	mussels, in shells
1 Tbl.	lemon juice, fresh
to taste	salt and pepper

Garnish:

parsley, chopped
paprika croutons (optional) *(see p. 534)*

Remove skin and bones from fish. Cut into chunks. Heat fish stock to boiling. Add fish chunks and shrimp. Simmer 5 minutes. Add cleaned mussels. Cook until they open. Discard any unopened mussels. Add lemon juice, salt and pepper to taste.

Serve in individual bowls garnished with parsley and paprika croutons.

Alcohol Note: The alcohol content was computed prior to cooking. Once the alcohol is heated to the boiling point, the alcohol disappears along with most of the calories from the alcohol.

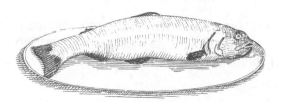

Nutrient Content Per Serving

Calories	160.0
Protein	23.5 g
Carbohydrates	3.1 g
Fat – Total	4.4 g
Cholesterol	110.0 mg
Dietary Fiber	0.2 g
Sodium	265.0 mg

Percent of Calories

61% Protein
8% Carbohydrate
26% Fat
5% Alcohol

Fat Breakdown

Saturated Fat	0.9 g
Monounsaturated Fat	1.3 g
Polyunsaturated Fat	1.5 g

BEET AND ONION SALAD

Serves 4

16 oz.	canned beets, sliced, drained
1 med.	onion, sliced in rings
1	bay leaf

Dressing:

2 cloves	garlic, minced
½ tsp.	basil, chopped
¾ cup	white wine vinegar
¼ cup	white wine
to taste	salt and pepper

To prepare dressing:
Combine all dressing ingredients.

Arrange beets and onions decoratively in a serving dish. Break bay leaf and place between some of the layers.

Pour dressing over beets. Chill.

Alcohol Note: The alcohol content was computed prior to cooking. Once the alcohol is heated to the boiling point, the alcohol disappears along with most of the calories from the alcohol.

Nutrient Content Per Serving

Calories	64.3
Protein	1.5 g
Carbohydrates	13.8 g
Fat – Total	0.2 g
Cholesterol	0.0 mg
Dietary Fiber	2.5 g
Sodium	312.0 mg

Percent of Calories

8% Protein
76% Carbohydrate
3% Fat
13% Alcohol

Fat Breakdown

Saturated Fat	0.0 g
Monounsaturated Fat	0.0 g
Polyunsaturated Fat	0.1 g

THREE-BEAN SALAD WITH FRESH TUNA STEAKS

Serves 4

1 lb.	fresh tuna steaks
1 cup	green beans
1 cup	garbanzo beans, drained, rinsed
1 cup	kidney beans, drained, rinsed
½ cup	onion, sliced
1 cup	tomato, cut in wedges
¼ cup	lemon juice
1 Tbl.	olive oil
⅔ cup	red wine vinegar
2 cloves	garlic, minced
to taste	salt and pepper

Grill tuna steaks (10 minutes per 1-inch thickness each side). Cool. Cut into cubes. Microwave green beans until just tender. Cool.

Mix all ingredients except the tuna. Season with salt and pepper to taste. Arrange beans nicely on a plate lined with lettuce or endive. Top with the cubed tuna.

Cook's Note: Serve with fresh bread for a great summer meal! Swordfish works well, too.

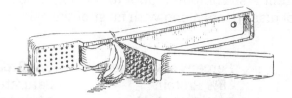

Nutrient Content Per Serving

Calories	350.0
Protein	35.0 g
Carbohydrates	30.6 g
Fat – Total	10.4 g
Cholesterol	43.1 mg
Dietary Fiber	8.0 g
Sodium	53.9 mg

Percent of Calories

39% Protein
34% Carbohydrate
26% Fat

Fat Breakdown

Saturated Fat	2.1 g
Monounsaturated Fat	4.6 g
Polyunsaturated Fat	2.9 g

Cucumber-Tomato Salad
Serves 4

1	cucumber, peeled
3 lg.	tomatoes, cubed
1 oz.	feta cheese, crumbled
3 leaves	basil, chopped
4 Tbl.	Basil Vinaigrette *(see p. 408)*

Prepare Basil Vinaigrette according to recipe.

Cut cucumbers in ¼-inch slices, then in quarters. Add remaining ingredients. Toss with Basil Vinaigrette. Serve chilled.

Cook's Note: A great summer dish!

% Calories as Fat — Above the HM✔ guidelines: Although this recipe has a high percentage of calories as fat (>30%), the total fat is less than 5 grams per serving. This will easily fit within your allotment of 45 grams per day. This happens most often in low-calorie recipes.

Nutrient Content Per Serving

Calories	66.2
Protein	2.9 g
Carbohydrates	9.6 g
Fat – Total	2.7 g
Cholesterol	6.7 mg
Dietary Fiber	2.6 g
Sodium	92.6 mg

Percent of Calories

16% Protein
52% Carbohydrate
32% Fat

Fat Breakdown

Saturated Fat	1.2 g
Monounsaturated Fat	0.8 g
Polyunsaturated Fat	0.3 g

EGGPLANT SALAD
Serves 8

2 med.	eggplants
1 lg.	tomato
1 clove	garlic, minced
1 sm.	onion, chopped fine
2 Tbl.	fresh parsley, chopped
½ tsp.	salt
¼ tsp.	black pepper
¼ cup	wine vinegar
2 Tbl.	olive oil

Pierce eggplant with a fork. Bake eggplant and tomato at 375° F for 1 hour. When cooled, peel, remove seeds and chop both the eggplant and tomato. Add remaining ingredients, mix well and chill. Serve on a bed of greens.

Cook's Note: You may serve as a dip with crackers or as an accompaniment to meat.

% Calories as Fat — Above the HM✔ guidelines: Although this recipe has a high percentage of calories as fat (>30%), the total fat is less than 5 grams per serving. This will easily fit within your allotment of 45 grams per day. This happens most often in low-calorie recipes.

Nutrient Content Per Serving

Calories	78.1
Protein	1.5 g
Carbohydrates	11.5 g
Fat – Total	3.8 g
Cholesterol	0.0 mg
Dietary Fiber	4.8 g
Sodium	140.0 mg

Percent of Calories

7% Protein
54% Carbohydrate
40% Fat

Fat Breakdown

Saturated Fat	0.3 g
Monounsaturated Fat	1.3 g
Polyunsaturated Fat	0.3 g

GREEK SALAD
(SALATA)
Serves 4

1 head	leaf lettuce
3 med.	tomatoes, chopped
1	cucumber, chopped
1 bunch	watercress, chopped
4	scallions, chopped
8	green olives, sliced
1	green bell pepper
1 oz.	feta cheese, crumbled

Dressing:

⅓ cup	fresh lemon juice
2 tsp.	olive oil
2 Tbl.	water

Garnish:

fresh ground black pepper

Combine all salad ingredients. Combine all dressing ingredients. Pour dressing over salad. Garnish with fresh ground black pepper.

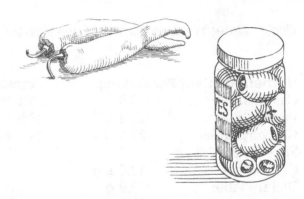

% Calories as Fat — Above the HM✓ guidelines: Although this recipe has a high percentage of calories as fat (>30%), the total fat is less than 5 grams per serving. This will easily fit within your allotment of 45 grams per day. This happens most often in low-calorie recipes.

Nutrient Content Per Serving		Percent of Calories	Fat Breakdown	
Calories	109.0	15% Protein	Saturated Fat	1.6 g
Protein	4.6 g	45% Carbohydrate	Monounsaturated Fat	2.8 g
Carbohydrates	14.0 g	40% Fat	Polyunsaturated Fat	0.7 g
Fat – Total	5.6 g			
Cholesterol	6.3 mg			
Dietary Fiber	4.1 g			
Sodium	294.0 mg			

KIDNEY BEAN SALAD
Serves 6

2 cans	kidney beans
1 7-oz. can	albacore tuna, water pack
1 med.	onion, grated
3 stalks	celery, minced
2 Tbl.	olive oil
⅔ cup	red wine vinegar

Drain and rinse beans. Drain tuna. Stir all ingredients together. Let rest at least ½ hour but overnight is better. Serve cold.

Cook's Note: You may choose to use low-sodium kidney beans.

Nutrient Content Per Serving

Calories	213.0
Protein	15.4 g
Carbohydrates	26.0 g
Fat – Total	5.7 g
Cholesterol	12.0 mg
Dietary Fiber	8.9 g
Sodium	133.0 mg

Percent of Calories

28% Protein
48% Carbohydrate
24% Fat

Fat Breakdown

Saturated Fat	0.9 g
Monounsaturated Fat	3.6 g
Polyunsaturated Fat	0.9 g

ORANGE AND OLIVE SALAD
Serves 6

1 sm.	onion, sliced in thin rings (may use grenadine onions, *see p. 533*)
4 lg.	oranges, peeled, seeded, sliced in thin rounds
½ cup	olives, sliced

Dressing:

1 Tbl.	olive oil
2 Tbl.	lemon juice
to taste	salt and pepper

Garnish:

2 Tbl.	parsley, chopped

In a small pan, simmer onion rings until tender. Discard water. (If using grenadine onions, they are ready as is.)

Dressing:
Combine all dressing ingredients. Arrange oranges, onions and olives decoratively on a plate; drizzle dressing over top. Refrigerate and marinate up to 6 hours.

Serve with its juices. Garnish with parsley.

Cook's Note: It makes an absolutely beautiful presentation with pink grenadine onions.

% Calories as Fat — Above the HM✔ guidelines: Although this recipe has a high percentage of calories as fat (>30%), the total fat is less than 5 grams per serving. This will easily fit within your allotment of 45 grams per day. This happens most often in low-calorie recipes.

Nutrient Content Per Serving		**Percent of Calories**	**Fat Breakdown**	
Calories	82.6	5% Protein	Saturated Fat	0.5 g
Protein	1.2 g	59% Carbohydrate	Monounsaturated Fat	2.6 g
Carbohydrates	13.1 g	36% Fat	Polyunsaturated Fat	0.3 g
Fat – Total	3.6 g			
Cholesterol	0.0 mg			
Dietary Fiber	2.8 g			
Sodium	74.3 mg			

PEPPER SALAD
Serves 8

1	sweet red pepper, seeded, sliced thin
1	green pepper, seeded, sliced thin
1	yellow pepper, seeded, sliced thin
¼ cup	white wine vinegar
2 med.	onions, minced fine
2 oz.	feta cheese, cut in very small cubes
1 tsp.	olive oil
1 Tbl.	fresh basil, minced
1 stalk	celery, sliced
to taste	salt and pepper

Toss peppers in vinegar and let stand for 15 minutes to tenderize. Add remaining ingredients. Serve cold.

Cook's Note: Simple, tasty and different!

% Calories as Fat — Above the HM✔ guidelines: Although this recipe has a high percentage of calories as fat (>30%), the total fat is less than 5 grams per serving. This will easily fit within your allotment of 45 grams per day. This happens most often in low-calorie recipes.

Nutrient Content Per Serving		**Percent of Calories**	**Fat Breakdown**	
Calories	44.9	14% Protein	Saturated Fat	1.2 g
Protein	1.7 g	45% Carbohydrate	Monounsaturated Fat	0.7 g
Carbohydrates	5.4 g	41% Fat	Polyunsaturated Fat	0.1 g
Fat – Total	2.2 g			
Cholesterol	6.3 mg			
Dietary Fiber	0.7 g			
Sodium	84.7 mg			

GREEK POTATO SALAD
Serves 8

2 lbs.	potatoes, peeled, cubed
1 cup	onion, chopped coarse
¾ cup	celery, chopped coarse

Dressing:

2 Tbl.	olive oil
4 Tbl.	red wine vinegar
¼ tsp.	garlic powder
2 Tbl.	fresh parsley, chopped
to taste	salt and pepper

Boil and drain potatoes. Combine with onions and celery.

Combine all dressing ingredients. Shake well. Pour over potatoes.

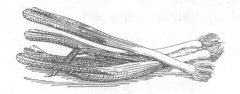

Cook's Note: This may be served hot, warm or chilled.

Nutrient Content Per Serving

Calories	138.0
Protein	2.3 g
Carbohydrates	25.4 g
Fat – Total	3.5 g
Cholesterol	0.0 mg
Dietary Fiber	2.3 g
Sodium	16.7 mg

Percent of Calories

6% Protein
71% Carbohydrate
22% Fat

Fat Breakdown

Saturated Fat	0.5 g
Monounsaturated Fat	2.5 g
Polyunsaturated Fat	0.4 g

SQUID SALAD
Serves 4

1 lb.	squid, cleaned
2 tsp.	olive oil
1 sm.	red onion, chopped
1 clove	garlic, minced
¼ cup	dry white wine
1 Tbl.	lemon juice, fresh
1 Tbl.	parsley, chopped

Garnish:

½	lemon, zest of
a few	parsley sprigs

Rinse squid and pat dry. Cut into ¼-inch-thick rings. In a medium non-stick skillet heat olive oil. Sauté onion until soft. Add squid and cook until opaque (approximately 5 minutes). Add garlic and wine. Bring to a boil, reduce heat and simmer, covered for 5-10 minutes or until squid is tender. Let dish cool.

When cool, transfer squid and onions to a serving dish. Add remaining ingredients. May chill or serve at room temperature. Garnish with lemon zest and sprigs of parsley.

Cook's Note: Purchase squid cleaned. May also use calamari steaks. Squid should be sautéed very quickly, otherwise it gets tough.

Alcohol Note: The alcohol content was computed prior to cooking. Once the alcohol is heated to the boiling point, the alcohol disappears along with most of the calories from the alcohol.

Nutrient Content Per Serving

Calories	163.0
Protein	20.8 g
Carbohydrates	7.2 g
Fat – Total	4.1 g
Cholesterol	304.0 mg
Dietary Fiber	0.6 g
Sodium	357.0 mg

Percent of Calories

52%	Protein
18%	Carbohydrate
23%	Fat
7%	Alcohol

Fat Breakdown

Saturated Fat	0.8 g
Monounsaturated Fat	1.8 g
Polyunsaturated Fat	0.9 g

SNOW PEA SALAD
Serves 4

1 lb.	fresh snow peas
1 Tbl.	olive oil
½	lemon, juice of

Garnish:

1 sm. clove	garlic, minced (optional)
2 tsp.	cilantro, chopped
2 tsp.	mint, chopped
½	lemon, zest of

Remove ends and strings from the snow peas. Heat 1 teaspoon of the oil in a large non-stick frying pan. Add snow peas and toss with the oil for 1-2 minutes. Add water to just cover the snow peas. Bring to a boil and simmer until peas are barely tender (still somewhat crisp). Drain snow peas into a colander and rinse with cold water to stop the cooking process. Place snow peas in a serving dish. Add remaining oil and lemon juice. Chill 2 hours.

To serve, garnish with chopped garlic, cilantro, mint and lemon zest.

Cook's Note: You must use fresh snow peas. The frozen type are too mushy.

% Calories as Fat — Above the HM✔ guidelines: Although this recipe has a high percentage of calories as fat (>30%), the total fat is less than 5 grams per serving. This will easily fit within your allotment of 45 grams per day. This happens most often in low-calorie recipes.

Nutrient Content Per Serving		Percent of Calories	Fat Breakdown	
Calories	80.8	16% Protein	Saturated Fat	0.5 g
Protein	3.3 g	45% Carbohydrate	Monounsaturated Fat	0.4 g
Carbohydrates	9.6 g	39% Fat	Polyunsaturated Fat	2.5 g
Fat – Total	3.6 g			
Cholesterol	0.0 mg			
Dietary Fiber	3.2 g			
Sodium	4.9 mg			

STUFFED TOMATO
Serves 4

4 lg.	tomatoes
2 med.	potatoes, peeled and cubed
4	black olives, chopped fine
1	anchovy or ½ tsp. anchovy paste
2 Tbl.	fresh parsley, chopped
2 tsp.	olive oil
3 Tbl.	white wine vinegar
¼ tsp.	salt
⅛ tsp.	black pepper
4	lettuce leaves

Wash tomatoes. Remove core. Slice off top ¼ inch. Remove seeds. Carefully cut out remaining pulp. Dice the pulp and set aside.

Boil potatoes. Cool. Combine tomato, potatoes, olives, anchovy and parsley. Whisk together oil, vinegar, salt and pepper. Add to potato mixture.

Stuff potato mixture into tomato. Garnish with a sprig of parsley, Serve chilled over a bed of lettuce leaves.

Cook's Note: A very pretty accompaniment to a summer meal.

Nutrient Content Per Serving		Percent of Calories	Fat Breakdown	
Calories	115.0	9% Protein	Saturated Fat	0.5 g
Protein	2.7 g	67% Carbohydrate	Monounsaturated Fat	2.1 g
Carbohydrates	20.7 g	24% Fat	Polyunsaturated Fat	0.5 g
Fat – Total	3.4 g			
Cholesterol	0.9 mg			
Dietary Fiber	3.0 g			
Sodium	216.0 mg			

TOMATO FETA SALAD
Serves 6

6	tomatoes, diced
3	scallions, sliced
6	calamata olives (green), remove pits, chopped
1	green bell pepper, diced
2 oz.	feta cheese, crumbled
½ cup	balsamic vinegar
2 tsp.	olive oil
2 cloves	garlic, minced
1 tsp.	black pepper
	lettuce
3	anchovies, chopped fine (optional)

Toss all ingredients together and serve with your favorite lettuce to make 6 servings.

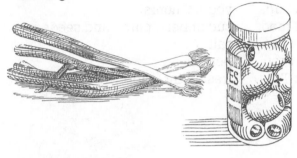

% Calories as Fat — Above the HM✔ guidelines: Although this recipe has a high percentage of calories as fat (>30%), the total fat is less than 5 grams per serving. This will easily fit within your allotment of 45 grams per day. This happens most often in low-calorie recipes.

Nutrient Content Per Serving

Calories	91.4
Protein	4.1 g
Carbohydrates	10.9 g
Fat – Total	4.6 g
Cholesterol	8.4 mg
Dietary Fiber	3.0 g
Sodium	218.0 mg

Percent of Calories

16% Protein
43% Carbohydrate
41% Fat

Fat Breakdown

Saturated Fat	1.8 g
Monounsaturated Fat	2.0 g
Polyunsaturated Fat	0.5 g

YOGURT AND CUCUMBERS
Serves 6

¼ cup	walnuts, chopped coarse
2 cloves	garlic, halved
2 tsp.	olive oil
4 cups	yogurt, nonfat
3 med.	cucumbers, pared and seeded
½ tsp.	salt
⅛ tsp.	pepper
2 Tbl.	fresh mint, chopped

Place walnuts and garlic in a food processor and process until coarsely ground. Add oil and blend until smooth. Stir in yogurt. Set aside.

Shred cucumbers. Place in colander and let stand 15 minutes, press out excess liquid. Stir cucumbers, salt and pepper into yogurt mixture. Cover and refrigerate at least 2 hours. Spoon into individual bowls. Garnish each serving with ½ tsp. chopped mint.

Nutrient Content Per Serving

Calories	157.0
Protein	11.2 g
Carbohydrates	18.0 g
Fat – Total	5.1 g
Cholesterol	2.9 mg
Dietary Fiber	1.7 g
Sodium	306.0 mg

Percent of Calories

28% Protein
44% Carbohydrate
28% Fat

Fat Breakdown

Saturated Fat	0.7 g
Monounsaturated Fat	1.9 g
Polyunsaturated Fat	2.2 g

ZUCCHINI SALAD
Serves 4

1 Tbl.	pine nuts
2 sm.	zucchini (3 cups sliced)
2 tsp.	olive oil
1 clove	garlic, minced
1 Tbl.	currants
2 tsp.	mint, chopped
1 Tbl.	lemon juice
to taste	salt and pepper
1	scallion, sliced thin (including green)

Toast pine nuts in a dry non-stick skillet. Set aside. Slice zucchini in rounds. Heat oil in a large non-stick frying pan. Sauté zucchini, garlic and currants until zucchini begins to brown. Add pine nuts, mint, lemon juice, salt and pepper to taste. Stir 1 minute. Transfer to a serving bowl. Top with scallions. Serve at room temperature or chill.

% Calories as Fat — Above the HM✔ guidelines: Although this recipe has a high percentage of calories as fat (>30%), the total fat is less than 5 grams per serving. This will easily fit within your allotment of 45 grams per day. This happens most often in low-calorie recipes.

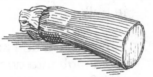 

Nutrient Content Per Serving

Calories	69.3
Protein	1.9 g
Carbohydrates	8.4 g
Fat – Total	4.6 g
Cholesterol	0.0 mg
Dietary Fiber	1.8 g
Sodium	7.1 mg

Percent of Calories

- 9% Protein
- 41% Carbohydrate
- 50% Fat

Fat Breakdown

Saturated Fat	0.7 g
Monounsaturated Fat	2.5 g
Polyunsaturated Fat	1.2 g

SWEET ANISE BREAD
Serves 16

½ cup	water
1 Tbl.	Ouzo (or Anisette)
½ tsp.	cinnamon, ground
½ tsp.	anise seed, ground
1 tsp.	orange zest
½ cup	skim milk
⅓ cup	canola oil
¾ cup	sugar
¼ tsp.	salt
1 pkg.	active dry yeast
½ cup	warm water
5¼ cups	flour
2	egg whites
2 Tbl.	water
¼ cup	slivered almonds

In a saucepan combine water, Ouzo, cinnamon, anise seed, orange zest, milk, oil, sugar and salt. Heat until sugar is dissolved. Let cool to lukewarm.

Dissolve yeast in warm water. Let rest 20 minutes.

Add yeast to the syrup. Place flour in a large bowl. Make a well in the middle and add the syrup. Incorporate into a ball. Knead the dough for 10 minutes. Prepare a bowl with cooking spray. Place ball of dough in the bowl. Cover with a damp cloth and set in a warm draft-free place to rise. Let rise 2 hours or until it has doubled in bulk.

Punch down and knead 3 minutes. Divide the dough into two parts. Roll each part into 3 ropes. Lay three ropes side by side touching each other. Repeat for other 3 ropes. Place the loaves onto a baking sheet prepared with cooking spray. Let rise 2 hours.

Brush tops of loaves with a mixture of egg white and water. Sprinkle tops with almonds. Bake at 350° F for 45 minutes.

Nutrient Content Per Serving	
Calories	252.0
Protein	5.7 g
Carbohydrates	43.2 g
Fat – Total	6.1 g
Cholesterol	0.1 mg
Dietary Fiber	1.6 g
Sodium	45.6 mg

Percent of Calories	
9% Protein	
69% Carbohydrate	
22% Fat	

Fat Breakdown	
Saturated Fat	0.5 g
Monounsaturated Fat	3.4 g
Polyunsaturated Fat	1.7 g

DILLY BREAD
Serves 8

1 pkg.	active dry yeast
1 cup	lowfat cottage cheese
2 Tbl.	sugar
2 tsp.	onion powder
2 tsp.	liquid margarine
2 Tbl.	dill weed
¾ tsp.	salt
¼ tsp.	baking soda
2	egg whites
2¼-3 cups	flour

Mix yeast with ¼ cup warm water. Set aside.

Combine all ingredients except yeast and flour in a food processor. Add flour and yeast. Knead 10 minutes. Let rise until double in size (approximately 60-90 minutes).

Punch down. Knead 5 minutes. Shape and let rise in an oiled baking bowl until doubled (45 minutes). Bake at 375° F for 30 minutes.

Cook's Note: Place a bowl of water in oven when baking bread to soften crust. Can also be made in a bread maker. Group 1: yeast. Group 2: flour. Group 3: remaining ingredients. Follow instructions in your manual.

Nutrient Content Per Serving

Calories	51.6
Protein	4.9 g
Carbohydrates	5.2 g
Fat – Total	1.3 g
Cholesterol	1.2 mg
Dietary Fiber	0.5 g
Sodium	365.0 mg

Percent of Calories

38% Protein
40% Carbohydrate
23% Fat

Fat Breakdown

Saturated Fat	0.3 g
Monounsaturated Fat	0.4 g
Polyunsaturated Fat	0.4 g

GREEK NEW YEAR'S BREAD
Makes 16 slices

8 Tbl.	sugar (divide 1 Tbl. and 7 Tbl.)
1 pkg.	active dry yeast
½ cup	skim milk
2 Tbl.	canola oil
1 Tbl.	orange zest
1 tsp.	salt
½ tsp.	ground cinnamon
¼ tsp.	ground nutmeg
4	egg whites or 1 cup egg substitute
4 cups	all-purpose flour, plus additional ¼ cup as needed

Combine ¼ cup warm water, 1 tablespoon of the sugar and yeast. Stir to dissolve yeast. Let stand until bubbly, about 5 minutes.

In a small saucepan, heat remaining sugar, milk, oil, orange zest, salt, cinnamon and nutmeg until warm. Pour into a large mixing bowl.

Set aside 2 tablespoons egg substitute (or 1 egg white). Beat remaining egg whites and yeast mixture into milk mixture.

Beat in 1½ cups flour until smooth. Stir in remaining flour to make a moderately stiff dough. Turn dough onto a lightly floured surface. Knead until smooth and satiny, approximately 8-10 minutes.

Shape dough into a ball and place in a lightly greased bowl, turning to grease all sides. Cover and let rise in warm place until doubled in bulk, about 1½ hours.

Punch dough down, cover and let rest 10 minutes. Shape dough into a ball and place on a large baking sheet prepared with cooking spray. Pat into a circle 6 inches in diameter. Brush top with water. Let stand in a warm place until almost doubled in bulk, 30 to 40 minutes.

Brush loaf with reserved beaten egg whites to make a nice golden crust.

Bake in preheated 350° F oven until golden brown, 30-35 minutes. Transfer to wire rack and cool completely.

Cook's Note: You may add raisins, nuts or candied fruit for variety.

Nutrient Content Per Slice		Percent of Calories	Fat Breakdown	
Calories	178.0	13% Protein	Saturated Fat	0.3 g
Protein	5.8 g	74% Carbohydrate	Monounsaturated Fat	1.2 g
Carbohydrates	32.4 g	13% Fat	Polyunsaturated Fat	0.9 g
Fat – Total	2.6 g			
Cholesterol	0.3 mg			
Dietary Fiber	1.1 g			
Sodium	166.0 mg			

OLIVE BREAD
Serves 12

1 tsp.	olive oil
1 med.	onion, chopped fine
1 tsp.	salt
7 cups	bread flour
1 pkg.	active dry yeast
¼ cup	warm water
1½ cups	black olives, sliced

Sauté onion in olive oil until soft. Let cool.

Mix yeast with warm water. Let stand 5 minutes. Add salt to flour. Incorporate yeast into flour, adding as much water as necessary to make a soft dough. Add onions. Knead 10 minutes. Cover with a damp cloth and let rise in a warm, draft-free place until doubled in bulk.

Punch down and add olives. Knead 5 minutes. Divide into 2 loaves. Shape into rounds. Place on a baking sheet prepared with cooking spray. Let rise 1 hour or until doubled in bulk. Mist with olive oil. Bake at 350° F for 30-40 minutes.

Nutrient Content Per Serving

Calories	293.0
Protein	8.0 g
Carbohydrates	57.7 g
Fat – Total	2.9 g
Cholesterol	0.0 mg
Dietary Fiber	2.8 g
Sodium	289.0 mg

Percent of Calories

11% Protein
80% Carbohydrate
9% Fat

Fat Breakdown

Saturated Fat	0.4 g
Monounsaturated Fat	1.7 g
Polyunsaturated Fat	0.5 g

ONION BREAD
Makes 16 slices

1 cup	skim milk
¼ cup	sugar
1 Tbl.	canola oil
1 tsp.	salt
¼ cup	dried minced onions
1 Tbl.	active dry yeast
¼ cup	warm water
3½ cups	flour
1 Tbl.	gluten flour (optional)
2	egg whites

In a small saucepan warm the milk. Add sugar, canola oil, salt and onions. Heat until sugar is dissolved. Cool.

Combine yeast with ¼ cup lukewarm water. Let stand 5 minutes. Add 1 cup of the flour to milk mixture, beat until smooth. Add egg whites to yeast mixture. Put remaining flour in a bowl. Make a well. Add all ingredients. Knead 10 minutes. Cover with a damp towel and let rise in a draft-free place until double.

Punch down. Knead 5 minutes. Shape in a ball. Let rise 45 minutes. Bake at 375° F for 40-50 minutes.

Cook's Note: If you use bread flour, eliminate the gluten flour. Can also be made in a bread maker. Group 1: yeast mixture. Group 2: flour. Group 3: remaining ingredients.

Nutrient Content Per Slice

Calories	130.0
Protein	4.2 g
Carbohydrates	25.2 g
Fat – Total	1.2 g
Cholesterol	0.3 mg
Dietary Fiber	0.9 g
Sodium	149.0 mg

Percent of Calories

13% Protein
79% Carbohydrate
8% Fat

Fat Breakdown

Saturated Fat	0.1 g
Monounsaturated Fat	0.5 g
Polyunsaturated Fat	0.4 g

PILAF
Serves 4

2 tsp.	olive oil
1 cup	rice
1 med.	onion, chopped fine
2 cups	chicken stock *(see p. 538)*
pinch	saffron (optional)
to taste	salt

In a medium non-stick saucepan (or frying pan), heat oil. Sauté rice and onions for 5 minutes. Add chicken stock, saffron and salt. Cover and simmer 20 minutes or until all water is absorbed.

▼ This recipe is used for the following items:
Artichoke Pilaf (see p. 478)
Tomato Pilaf (see p. 479)
Mussel Pilaf (see p. 480)
Chicken Pilaf (see p. 481)
Pilaf al Greco (see p. 482)

Nutrient Content Per Serving

Calories	202.0
Protein	3.7 g
Carbohydrates	39.8 g
Fat – Total	2.6 g
Cholesterol	0.0 mg
Dietary Fiber	1.1 g
Sodium	3.1 mg

Percent of Calories

8% Protein
68% Carbohydrate
21% Fat

Fat Breakdown

Saturated Fat	0.4 g
Monounsaturated Fat	1.8 g
Polyunsaturated Fat	0.3 g

ARTICHOKE PILAF
Serves 4

1 recipe	pilaf *(see p. 477)*
8	artichoke hearts, cooked
1 Tbl.	tomato paste
¼ cup	feta cheese, crumbled

Prepare pilaf with the following changes.

Add tomato paste with chicken stock. Simmer 10 minutes and add artichokes. Continue cooking remaining 10 minutes. Add feta before serving.

Nutrient Content Per Serving

Calories	267.0
Protein	7.5 g
Carbohydrates	45.5 g
Fat – Total	6.2 g
Cholesterol	13.7 mg
Dietary Fiber	3.7 g
Sodium	231.0 mg

Percent of Calories

11% Protein
68% Carbohydrate
21% Fat

Fat Breakdown

Saturated Fat	2.8 g
Monounsaturated Fat	2.5 g
Polyunsaturated Fat	0.5 g

TOMATO PILAF
Serves 4

1 recipe	pilaf *(see p. 477)*
2 cups	beef stock *(see p. 536)* instead of chicken stock
2 med.	tomatoes, chopped
to taste	fresh ground black pepper

Prepare pilaf with the following changes.

Add tomatoes 5 minutes before end of cooking time.

Alcohol Note: The alcohol content was computed prior to cooking. Once the alcohol is heated to the boiling point, the alcohol disappears along with most of the calories from the alcohol.

Nutrient Content Per Serving

Calories	252.0
Protein	4.5 g
Carbohydrates	44.9 g
Fat – Total	4.2 g
Cholesterol	0.0 mg
Dietary Fiber	2.3 g
Sodium	8.7 mg

Percent of Calories

- 7% Protein
- 72% Carbohydrate
- 15% Fat
- 6% Alcohol

Fat Breakdown

Saturated Fat	0.6 g
Monounsaturated Fat	2.1 g
Polyunsaturated Fat	1.2 g

MUSSEL PILAF
Serves 4

1 recipe	pilaf *(see p. 477)*
4 doz.	mussels, in shells
1 cup	dry white wine
½ cup	fish stock *(see p. 540)*
1 clove	garlic, minced
2 Tbl.	parsley, chopped
1 touch	lemon juice

Prepare pilaf with the following additions.

Scrub mussels and place in a large pot. Add wine, fish stock, garlic and parsley. Cover and steam the mussels for 10 minutes or until the shells open. Discard any that do not open. Remove mussels from their shells and add to finished pilaf. Let stand 10 minutes before serving.

Cook's Notes: This may be used as a complete meal. The calories are high because mussels are high in calories.

Alcohol Note: The alcohol content was computed prior to cooking. Once the alcohol is heated to the boiling point, the alcohol disappears along with most of the calories from the alcohol.

Nutrient Content Per Serving

Calories	443.0
Protein	31.0 g
Carbohydrates	49.1 g
Fat – Total	7.9 g
Cholesterol	63.5 mg
Dietary Fiber	1.2 g
Sodium	655.0 mg

Percent of Calories

29% Protein
46% Carbohydrate
16% Fat
 9% Alcohol

Fat Breakdown

Saturated Fat	1.4 g
Monounsaturated Fat	3.0 g
Polyunsaturated Fat	1.8 g

CHICKEN PILAF
Serves 4

1 recipe	pilaf *(see p. 477)*
4	chicken breasts, boneless, skinless
1 clove	garlic, minced
¼ cup	tomato paste
1 tsp.	oregano
1 tsp.	olive oil
to taste	salt and pepper

Mix together garlic, tomato paste, oregano, oil and salt and pepper to taste. Coat chicken with this mixture and bake in a prepared casserole dish.

Prepare pilaf to the point of adding the chicken stock. Add the stock and rice to the casserole. Cover and bake 30-40 minutes.

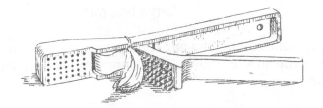

Nutrient Content Per Serving

Calories	356.0
Protein	31.7 g
Carbohydrates	43.1 g
Fat – Total	5.3 g
Cholesterol	68.4 mg
Dietary Fiber	1.8 g
Sodium	209.0 mg

Percent of Calories

36% Protein
50% Carbohydrate
14% Fat

Fat Breakdown

Saturated Fat	1.0 g
Monounsaturated Fat	3.0 g
Polyunsaturated Fat	0.8 g

PILAF AL GRECO
Serves 6

1 cup	bulgur wheat
2 tsp.	olive oil
1 med.	onion, chopped
1 med.	bell pepper, sliced in strips
1 cup	vermicelli, uncooked
3½ cups	chicken stock *(see p. 538)*
3 med.	tomatoes, peeled, cut in thin wedges
to taste	salt and pepper

Garnish:

cilantro leaves

In a large non-stick frying pan heat oil. Sauté onions and pepper until soft. Add vermicelli and stir 1 minute.

Rinse bulgur wheat and add to the pan along with chicken stock. Cover and simmer 5 minutes. Add tomatoes and continue to simmer 10 minutes or until stock is absorbed. Add salt and pepper to taste.

Serve hot, garnished with cilantro leaves.

Cook's Note: For a decorative presentation hollow out small zucchinis with an apple corer to form a tube. Firmly stuff pilaf into the zucchini tube. Bake or microwave the zucchini until tender. Slice in rounds and serve.

Nutrient Content Per Serving

Calories	175.0
Protein	5.7 g
Carbohydrates	34.8 g
Fat – Total	2.2 g
Cholesterol	0.0 mg
Dietary Fiber	5.6 g
Sodium	7.8 mg

Percent of Calories

13% Protein
76% Carbohydrate
11% Fat

Fat Breakdown

Saturated Fat	0.3 g
Monounsaturated Fat	1.2 g
Polyunsaturated Fat	0.4 g

SPICY RISOTTO WITH VEGETABLES
Serves 6

½ tsp.	olive oil
1½ cups	short-grain rice
2 cups	chicken stock *(see p. 538)*
2 tsp.	powdered butter replacement
1	bouquet garni *(see p. 15)*
to taste	salt and pepper
3 oz.	fresh Italian turkey sausage, loose
1 med.	onion, cut in rings
1 head	leaf lettuce, shredded
1 cup	peas, frozen
3	tomatoes, cut in wedges

In a non-stick frying pan, heat oil. Gently brown rice. Add hot stock, powdered butter replacement, bouquet garni and salt and pepper to taste. Cover and cook 15 minutes. (Rice may not be completely cooked.)

Transfer to a baking dish. In same frying pan, brown chopped sausage and onion. Add lettuce and peas. Cook 5 minutes.

Combine meat with rice. Arrange tomatoes on top. Bake at 350° F for 25 minutes.

Nutrient Content Per Serving

Calories	259.0
Protein	9.5 g
Carbohydrates	47.9 g
Fat – Total	3.5 g
Cholesterol	11.5 mg
Dietary Fiber	3.5 g
Sodium	137.0 mg

Percent of Calories

14% Protein
74% Carbohydrate
12% Fat

Fat Breakdown

Saturated Fat	1.0 g
Monounsaturated Fat	1.3 g
Polyunsaturated Fat	0.9 g

LAMB KEBABS
Serves 6

For lamb:
1½ lbs.   lamb

Marinade:
1 clove   garlic, minced
⅓ cup   fresh lemon juice
¼ cup   fresh oregano, chopped
to taste   pepper

Vegetables to skewer (for all variations):
cherry tomatoes
onion chunks
bell pepper, variety of colors
mushrooms
zucchini

Cut meat, fish or poultry into large cubes. Marinate at least 2 hours. Arrange vegetables with meat on skewers. Grill over hot coals 10-15 minutes or until meat is cooked.

Cook's Note: The amount of meat is small due to the high saturated fat content. Remember, the Mediterranean cuisine uses limited meat.

Nutrient Content Per Serving
Calories	284.0
Protein	34.4 g
Carbohydrates	15.7 g
Fat – Total	9.5 g
Cholesterol	101.0 mg
Dietary Fiber	3.7 g
Sodium	87.0 mg

Percent of Calories
48% Protein
22% Carbohydrate
30% Fat

Fat Breakdown
Saturated Fat	3.3 g
Monounsaturated Fat	3.9 g
Polyunsaturated Fat	0.9 g

PORK KEBABS
Serves 6

For Pork:

2 lbs.   pork roast, well trimmed

Marinade:

1   orange, juice of
1 clove   garlic, minced
1 tsp.   fresh thyme, chopped
1 tsp.   coriander seeds, ground
to taste   pepper

See directions for lamb.

Nutrient Content Per Serving

Calories	318.0
Protein	44.6 g
Carbohydrates	16.0 g
Fat – Total	7.8 g
Cholesterol	120.0 mg
Dietary Fiber	2.9 g
Sodium	94.4 mg

Percent of Calories

57% Protein
20% Carbohydrate
22% Fat

Fat Breakdown

Saturated Fat	2.6 g
Monounsaturated Fat	3.0 g
Polyunsaturated Fat	0.8 g

SWORDFISH KEBABS

Serves 6

For swordfish:

2 lbs.   swordfish

Marinade:

1   lemon, juice of
1 Tbl.   fennel, chopped (green part
            only)
1 Tbl.   chives, chopped
1 clove   garlic, minced
to taste   pepper

See directions for lamb.

Nutrient Content Per Serving

Calories	241.0
Protein	31.8 g
Carbohydrates	13.1 g
Fat – Total	6.5 g
Cholesterol	58.9 mg
Dietary Fiber	2.9 g
Sodium	146.0 mg

Percent of Calories

53% Protein
22% Carbohydrate
25% Fat

Fat Breakdown

Saturated Fat	1.7 g
Monounsaturated Fat	2.4 g
Polyunsaturated Fat	1.6 g

SHRIMP KEBABS
Serves 6

For shrimp:

2 lbs.   shrimp, peeled and deveined

Marinade:

3 Tbl.   lemon juice
1 clove   garlic, minced
1 Tbl.   fennel, chopped (green part
           only)
to taste   salt and pepper
pinch   saffron

See directions for lamb.

Cook's Note: You may add squid to the shrimp kebabs to keep the cholesterol content down. Just fold the squid to fit on the skewer.

Cholesterol — Above the HM✔ guidelines: Occasionally a lowfat recipe is high in cholesterol. In this case the cholesterol stems from the shellfish. The level is moderately high (>150 mg per serving) but may fit into your weekly average of 150 mg per day.

Nutrient Content Per Serving		Percent of Calories	Fat Breakdown	
Calories	218.0	60% Protein	Saturated Fat	0.6 g
Protein	32.6 g	27% Carbohydrate	Monounsaturated Fat	0.4 g
Carbohydrates	14.0 g	13% Fat	Polyunsaturated Fat	1.2 g
Fat – Total	3.1 g			
Cholesterol	230.0 mg			
Dietary Fiber	2.9 g			
Sodium	233.0 mg			

CHICKEN WITH ARTICHOKES
Serves 6

6 lg.	chicken breasts, boneless and skinless
1 Tbl.	olive oil

Sauce:

4	tomatoes, cut in chunks
2 cloves	garlic, minced
2 Tbl.	wine vinegar
6	artichoke hearts, canned, drained, cut in quarters
1 bunch	scallions, minced
1	lemon, juice of
⅓ cup	white wine
1 tsp.	Worcestershire sauce™
¼ tsp.	black pepper
5 drops	hot oil

Topping:

¼ cup	black olives, sliced thin
1 can	marinated artichoke hearts, drained

In a large non-stick frying pan, sauté chicken in olive oil. In a food processor combine all sauce ingredients. Prepare a baking dish with cooking spray. Arrange chicken in a single layer. Pour sauce over chicken. Sprinkle with sliced olives. Cover and bake at 325° F for 1 hour. Remove cover and bake an additional 15 minutes. Serve over rice. Garnish with marinated artichoke hearts.

Cook's Note: Most of the fat is from the marinated artichoke hearts.

Alcohol Note: The alcohol content was computed prior to cooking. Once the alcohol is heated to the boiling point, the alcohol disappears along with most of the calories from the alcohol.

Nutrient Content Per Serving		**Percent of Calories**	**Fat Breakdown**	
Calories	251.0	47% Protein	Saturated Fat	1.3 g
Protein	30.6 g	23% Carbohydrate	Monounsaturated Fat	3.1 g
Carbohydrates	15.1 g	27% Fat	Polyunsaturated Fat	2.5 g
Fat – Total	7.7 g	3% Alcohol		
Cholesterol	68.4 mg			
Dietary Fiber	6.6 g			
Sodium	361.0 mg			

BRAISED CHICKEN
Serves 4

4	chicken breasts, boneless, skinless
1 tsp.	olive oil
1 med.	onion, chopped fine
1 clove	garlic, minced
6 lg.	tomatoes, chopped
2 Tbl.	tomato paste
½ cup	dry white wine
1 tsp.	cinnamon

In a large non-stick frying pan, brown the chicken breasts in olive oil. They should not be cooked, just browned. Remove chicken to a casserole dish prepared with cooking spray. Sauté onions and garlic in the frying pan. To the onions, add tomatoes, tomato paste, wine and cinnamon. Add to the casserole. Cover and bake at 300° F for 45 minutes. Serve over pasta.

Alcohol Note: The alcohol content was computed prior to cooking. Once the alcohol is heated to the boiling point, the alcohol disappears along with most of the calories from the alcohol.

Nutrient Content Per Serving

Calories	217.0
Protein	29.6 g
Carbohydrates	13.4 g
Fat – Total	3.3 g
Cholesterol	68.4 mg
Dietary Fiber	3.5 g
Sodium	160.0 mg

Percent of Calories

54% Protein
24% Carbohydrate
14% Fat
 8% Alcohol

Fat Breakdown

Saturated Fat	0.6 g
Monounsaturated Fat	1.3 g
Polyunsaturated Fat	0.7 g

TOMATO AND FETA BAKED CHICKEN
Serves 8

8	chicken breasts, boneless and skinless
	flour
1 tsp.	olive oil
1 15-oz. can	tomatoes, peeled, seeded, chopped
2 oz.	feta, crumbled
8	Greek olives, sliced thin

Pound chicken breasts until thin. Flour chicken lightly. Sauté in a non-stick frying pan using 1 teaspoon of olive oil. Cook until browned. Transfer to a casserole dish. Arrange chicken in a single layer. Pour tomatoes over chicken. Sprinkle with feta and olives. Bake covered for 20 minutes at 350° F. Remove cover and bake an additional 10 minutes or until chicken is done.

Cook's Note: A quick and easy meal, with a very pretty presentation.

Nutrient Content Per Serving

Calories	168.0
Protein	28.9 g
Carbohydrates	2.6 g
Fat – Total	4.2 g
Cholesterol	74.7 mg
Dietary Fiber	0.7 g
Sodium	336.0 mg

Percent of Calories

71% Protein
 6% Carbohydrate
23% Fat

Fat Breakdown

Saturated Fat	1.6 g
Monounsaturated Fat	1.5 g
Polyunsaturated Fat	0.5 g

MOUSSAKA
Serves 8

1½ lbs.	ground turkey breast, skinless
2 med.	eggplants (about 1½ lbs. each), peeled and sliced ⅛-inch thick slices
1 med.	onion, peeled and finely chopped
2 tsp.	olive oil
2 med.	tomatoes, peeled, seeded and finely chopped (may use 15-oz. can, drained)
½ cup	dry white wine
¼ cup	tomato paste
2 Tbl.	fresh parsley, chopped fine
1 clove	garlic, minced
½ tsp.	dried oregano, crumbled
¼ tsp.	ground cinnamon
⅛ tsp.	ground allspice
to taste	salt and pepper
¼ cup	dry bread crumbs, unseasoned
½ cup	all-purpose flour
½ cup	parmesan cheese, grated

Yogurt Sauce:

¾ cup	egg substitute
2 Tbl.	all-purpose flour
2 cups (1 pint)	plain nonfat yogurt
½ tsp.	salt
⅛ tsp.	white pepper
⅛ tsp.	ground nutmeg

In a non-stick pan, sauté onion in 1 teaspoon of the oil over medium heat until soft. Add ground turkey. Cook until turkey is browned, stirring with a fork to keep it from clumping. Add tomatoes, wine, tomato paste, parsley, garlic, oregano, spices, salt and pepper to taste. Continue cooking, stirring frequently, until most of the liquid has evaporated. Remove from heat and stir in bread crumbs.

To prepare yogurt sauce: Pour egg substitute into a 1½-quart saucepan. Beat with a whisk while blending in flour and yogurt. Add seasonings. Cook over medium-low heat, stirring constantly, until mixture begins to thicken (do not boil), 6-8 minutes.

Dip eggplant slices in flour to coat both sides evenly. Shake off excess flour. Coat a non-stick griddle with cooking spray. Brush pan with remaining 1 teaspoon olive oil. Gently brown eggplant slices on both sides.

(continued on the next page)

MOUSSAKA
(CONTINUED)
Serves 8

To Assemble:
Arrange half of the eggplant slices in a
9x13 baking dish prepared with cooking
spray. Spread meat evenly over eggplant
and sprinkle with ¼ cup cheese. Top with
remaining eggplant. Pour Yogurt Sauce
evenly over eggplant. Top with remaining
¼ cup parmesan cheese. Bake uncovered
at 375° F for 20 minutes or until top is
golden and puffed. Remove from oven and
let stand 10 minutes. To serve, cut into
squares.

Alcohol Note: The alcohol content was computed prior to cooking. Once the alcohol is heated
to the boiling point, the alcohol disappears along with most of the calories from the alcohol.

Nutrient Content Per Serving		**Percent of Calories**	**Fat Breakdown**	
Calories	332.0	46% Protein	Saturated Fat	2.0 g
Protein	38.6 g	36% Carbohydrate	Monounsaturated Fat	1.9 g
Carbohydrates	30.0 g	15% Fat	Polyunsaturated Fat	1.0 g
Fat – Total	5.5 g	3% Alcohol		
Cholesterol	79.1 mg			
Dietary Fiber	5.8 g			
Sodium	486.0 mg			

CHICKEN WITH WALNUT SAUCE
Serves 4

4	chicken breasts, boneless, skinless

Sauce:

¼ cup	walnuts, toasted, chopped coarse
½ tsp.	walnut oil (may substitute olive oil)
½ cup	dry white wine
1 Tbl.	honey
½ tsp.	dry oregano
½ tsp.	dry mint
pinch	dill weed
pinch	cinnamon
pinch	allspice
to taste	salt and pepper

Garnish:

2 Tbl.	fresh mint, chopped

Sauce:
Combine all ingredients in a food processor and blend until smooth.

Prepare a baking dish with non-stick spray. Lay chicken breasts in a single layer. Spread chicken with walnut sauce. Cover and bake at 350° F for 30 minutes. Remove cover and bake another 10 minutes or until chicken is done.

Serve garnished with fresh mint.

Alcohol Note: The alcohol content was computed prior to cooking. Once the alcohol is heated to the boiling point, the alcohol disappears along with most of the calories from the alcohol.

Nutrient Content Per Serving		**Percent of Calories**	**Fat Breakdown**	
Calories	218.0	54% Protein	Saturated Fat	0.7 g
Protein	29.3 g	10% Carbohydrate	Monounsaturated Fat	1.5 g
Carbohydrates	5.7 g	27% Fat	Polyunsaturated Fat	3.6 g
Fat – Total	6.5 g	9% Alcohol		
Cholesterol	68.4 mg			
Dietary Fiber	0.5 g			
Sodium	78.3 mg			

BAKED FISH FILLETS
Serves 6

2 lbs.	fresh fish fillets (bass, red snapper, codfish or halibut)
½ cup	dry white wine
1 Tbl.	lemon juice, fresh
½ cup	onion, chopped
1 clove	garlic, minced
1 tsp.	olive oil
½ cup	tomato sauce
3 Tbl.	fresh parsley, chopped fine
½ tsp.	dried oregano, crumbled
2 med.	tomatoes, sliced ¼-inch thick
1	lemon, sliced thin
¼ cup	dry bread crumbs
2 Tbl.	scallions, including tops, sliced thin

Rinse fish under cold running water. Pat dry with paper towels. Coat a large baking dish with cooking spray. Add wine and fish, drizzle with lemon juice.

In a small non-stick frying pan sauté onion and garlic in oil until onion is soft. Stir in tomato sauce, 1 tablespoon of the parsley and oregano. Simmer, uncovered, 5 minutes. Spoon mixture over fish.

Arrange tomato and lemon slices over fish. Sprinkle bread crumbs, remaining parsley and scallions over tomato and lemon slices. Bake in a preheated 350° F oven for 25-30 minutes. Serve immediately.

Alcohol Note: The alcohol content was computed prior to cooking. Once the alcohol is heated to the boiling point, the alcohol disappears along with most of the calories from the alcohol.

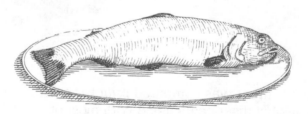

Nutrient Content Per Serving

Calories	228.0
Protein	33.0 g
Carbohydrates	9.3 g
Fat – Total	4.7 g
Cholesterol	48.4 mg
Dietary Fiber	1.7 g
Sodium	248.0 mg

Percent of Calories

59% Protein
17% Carbohydrate
19% Fat
 5% Alcohol

Fat Breakdown

Saturated Fat	0.7 g
Monounsaturated Fat	1.8 g
Polyunsaturated Fat	1.5 g

Fish And Seafood Pilaki
Serves 6

4 oz.	monkfish
3 sm.	red snapper fillets
2 med.	squid, cleaned, cut into rounds
1 dozen	mussels, in their shells
2 tsp.	olive oil
2 med.	onions, chopped coarse
2	carrots, sliced thin
2 cloves	garlic, minced
sm. bunch	celery leaves
2 lg.	tomatoes, peeled, seeded and chopped
to taste	salt and pepper
1 tsp.	sugar
1	lemon, juice of
bunch	parsley, finely chopped

Wash all the fish. Clean and cook the mussels *(see p. 13)*.

In a non-stick pan, sauté the onion in oil until soft. Add carrots and garlic, cook 2 minutes. Add the celery leaves and tomatoes. Season with salt and pepper to taste, sugar and lemon juice. Simmer for a few minutes.

Add the monkfish and simmer for 10 minutes. Then add the red snapper and squid; simmer 4-5 minutes or until just barely done. Cut the monkfish into pieces when it begins to soften. Add the mussels at the last minute so that they are just heated through. Stir in the parsley. Chill. Serve cold.

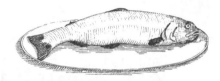

Cook's Note: If you want to use only one kind of fish or seafood, use 2½ pounds fish or squid or 4 pounds mussels. May be served warm or cold.

Nutrient Content Per Serving		**Percent of Calories**	**Fat Breakdown**	
Calories	196.0	54% Protein	Saturated Fat	1.0 g
Protein	26.5 g	22% Carbohydrate	Monounsaturated Fat	1.9 g
Carbohydrates	10.9 g	23% Fat	Polyunsaturated Fat	0.9 g
Fat – Total	5.0 g			
Cholesterol	61.2 mg			
Dietary Fiber	2.2 g			
Sodium	90.4 mg			

GRILLED SNAPPER
Serves 4

2 lbs.   red snapper

Marinade:
1 recipe   Fish marinade *(see p. 555)*
         Make with mint in place of
         of coriander.

Garnish:
         lemon wedges

Marinate red snapper in fish marinade.
Refrigerate 3 hours.

Cook fish over hot coals 5-8 minutes per
side. Baste with marinade when turning.

Garnish with lemon wedges.

Nutrient Content Per Serving

Calories	262.0
Protein	46.7 g
Carbohydrates	1.4 g
Fat – Total	6.6 g
Cholesterol	84.0 mg
Dietary Fiber	0.4 g
Sodium	146.0 mg

Percent of Calories

74% Protein
 2% Carbohydrate
24% Fat

Fat Breakdown

Saturated Fat	1.1 g
Monounsaturated Fat	3.2 g
Polyunsaturated Fat	1.4 g

Cheese Filled Triangles *(page 442)*
Stuffed Grape Leaf *(page 507)*
Cucumber and Tomato Salad *(page 459)*

Lamb Kebabs *(page 484)*
Orange and Olive Salad *(page 463)*

Stuffed Tomato *(page 468)*
Lobster Wrapped with Filo *(page 501)*

Stuffed Greened Peppers *(page 508)*
Fennel and Tomatoes *(page 511)*

LOBSTER WRAPPED WITH FILO
Serves 4

4 6-oz.	lobster tails
½ lb.	scallops
1 Tbl.	shallots, chopped
2 Tbl.	Greek olives (green), rinsed, chopped
½ cup	fresh tomatoes, chopped
¼ cup	feta cheese, chopped
to taste	pepper
10 sheets	filo dough
1 tsp.	olive oil

Lobster steaming liquid:

¼ cup	wine
2 Tbl.	lemon juice
¼ cup	water

Supplies needed:

spray bottle

Steam lobster until shells turn pink. Be careful not to overcook. Cool and remove lobster from shell. Slice on a bias ¼-inch thick.

In a small non-stick frying pan, sauté scallops and shallots in cooking spray. Remove scallops and let cool. Add olives and tomatoes. Cook out most of the moisture. Add feta. Toss several times. Season lightly with pepper to taste. Cool.

To assemble:
Lay out one sheet of filo dough (must work quickly or dough will dry and crack). Spray filo with olive oil. Place a second sheet on top and spray lightly with olive oil. Fold in half (should be long and narrow). Align sautéed vegetables and cheese at one end. Top with slices of lobster. Roll tightly and cut off excess dough at edges. Cut roll into 4 pieces. Place on a cookie sheet prepared with cooking spray and bake at 350° F until golden brown.

Cook's Note: The best method to apply the olive oil is to use a spray bottle. The canned sprays will leave a funny taste in the dish.

Sodium — Above the HM✔ guidelines: This recipe exceeds the HealthMark limits for sodium (800 mg per serving). The excess sodium is coming from the shellfish. If you have hypertension (high blood pressure) and must restrict your sodium intake, this recipe may push your total sodium intake above your desired level for that day. *(Refer to HealthMark dietary goals p. 3.)*

Nutrient Content Per Serving		**Percent of Calories**	**Fat Breakdown**	
Calories	351.0	54% Protein	Saturated Fat	3.1 g
Protein	46.0 g	23% Carbohydrate	Monounsaturated Fat	3.0 g
Carbohydrates	19.3 g	23% Fat	Polyunsaturated Fat	1.6 g
Fat – Total	8.9 g			
Cholesterol	195.0 mg			
Dietary Fiber	0.8 g			
Sodium	1045.0 mg			

SHRIMP AND FETA CASSEROLE
Serves 4

1 lb.	small shrimp, peeled and deveined
1 med.	onion, chopped
1 tsp.	olive oil
1 clove	garlic, minced
3 lg.	firm tomatoes, peeled, seeded and chopped
⅓ cup	white wine
¼ cup	fresh parsley, chopped
to taste	salt and freshly ground black pepper
¼ cup	feta cheese, crumbled

In a non-stick frying pan, prepared with cooking spray, sauté the onions and garlic in oil until soft but not brown. Add tomatoes, white wine, parsley and salt and pepper to taste. Simmer, uncovered for 20 minutes, stirring occasionally. Mixture should not be watery (cook a little longer if it is). Remove from heat and cool.

Stir in shrimp. Spoon into a casserole prepared with cooking spray. Sprinkle top with feta cheese. Bake uncovered at 450° F until cheese is melted and casserole is bubbly (approximately 20 minutes).

Cholesterol — Above the HM✔ guidelines: Occasionally a lowfat recipe is high in cholesterol. In this case the cholesterol stems from the shellfish. The level is moderately high (>150 mg per serving) but may fit into your weekly average of 150 mg per day.

Alcohol Note: The alcohol content was computed prior to cooking. Once the alcohol is heated to the boiling point, the alcohol disappears along with most of the calories from the alcohol.

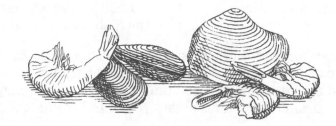

Nutrient Content Per Serving

Calories	209.0
Protein	27.2 g
Carbohydrates	8.1 g
Fat – Total	6.0 g
Cholesterol	235.0 mg
Dietary Fiber	1.9 g
Sodium	437.0 mg

Percent of Calories

52% Protein
16% Carbohydrate
26% Fat
6% Alcohol

Fat Breakdown

Saturated Fat	2.8 g
Monounsaturated Fat	1.9 g
Polyunsaturated Fat	0.8 g

LAMB A LA VERMOUTH
Serves 8

2 lbs.	lamb, leg
½	lemon, juice of
½ tsp.	garlic powder
1 cup	flour
½ tsp.	salt
½ tsp.	black pepper
1 cup	beef stock *(see p. 536)*
1 cup	water
½ cup	dry vermouth
1	onion, chopped
4	carrots, chopped into chunks
4	celery stalks, chopped into chunks

Trim the lamb of all visible fat. Cut into large bite-sized chunks. Squeeze lemon juice over meat. Let stand 10 minutes. In a large plastic bag combine flour and seasonings. Add meat cubes and shake. Lightly brown meat in a non-stick pan prepared with cooking spray. Add liquids. Cook until thick. Add vegetables. Bake at 350° F for 1-1½ hours.

Cook's Note: You may add potatoes for a one-dish meal or serve over rice.

Alcohol Note: The alcohol content was computed prior to cooking. Once the alcohol is heated to the boiling point, the alcohol disappears along with most of the calories from the alcohol.

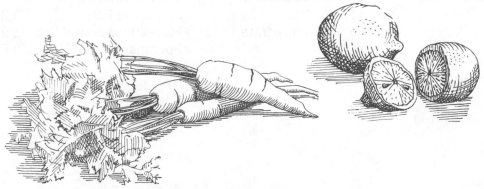

Nutrient Content Per Serving

Calories	322.0
Protein	35.1 g
Carbohydrates	19.0 g
Fat – Total	9.3 g
Cholesterol	101.0 mg
Dietary Fiber	2.2 g
Sodium	253.0 mg

Percent of Calories

45% Protein
24% Carbohydrate
26% Fat
 5% Alcohol

Fat Breakdown

Saturated Fat	3.2 g
Monounsaturated Fat	4.0 g
Polyunsaturated Fat	0.7 g

LAMB MACEDONIAN
Serves 8

2 lbs.	lamb, leg
2 lbs.	potatoes, peeled and sliced
2	onions, sliced
4	tomatoes, cubed
½ tsp.	salt
⅛ tsp.	black pepper
½ cup	fresh parsley, chopped
1 tsp.	garlic powder
¼ cup	fresh mint, chopped

Trim lamb of all visible fat. Cut in small pieces. Layer all ingredients in a baking dish prepared with cooking spray. Cover and bake at 375° F for 1½ hours or until potatoes are done.

Cook's Note: This may be cooked ahead of time. Serve with a green vegetable.

Nutrient Content Per Serving

Calories	351.0
Protein	35.5 g
Carbohydrates	30.8 g
Fat – Total	9.2 g
Cholesterol	101.0 mg
Dietary Fiber	3.3 g
Sodium	226.0 mg

Percent of Calories

41% Protein
35% Carbohydrate
24% Fat

Fat Breakdown

Saturated Fat	3.2 g
Monounsaturated Fat	3.9 g
Polyunsaturated Fat	0.8 g

PASTITSIO
Serves 6

Meat mixture:

1 tsp.	olive oil
1 med.	onion, chopped fine
1 clove	garlic, minced
1 lb.	ground buffalo
15-oz. can	tomatoes, crushed
½ cup	beef stock *(see p. 536)*
½ tsp.	ground cinnamon
pinch	ground cloves
1 tsp.	mint, chopped
to taste	salt and pepper

Pasta:

16-oz. pkg.	ziti
1 tsp.	olive oil
¼ cup	liquid butter replacement
¾ cup	egg substitute
½ cup	parmesan, grated

Sauce:

1 recipe	bechamel sauce *(see p. 554)*
½ cup	parmesan, grated

Meat:
In a large non-stick skillet heat oil. Sauté onion until translucent. Add garlic, cook 1 minute. Add ground buffalo and cook, breaking up into pieces, until almost done. Add remaining ingredients. Cook uncovered 25 minutes. Cook off most of the liquid.

Pasta:
Cook pasta al dente in boiling water. Rinse with cool water. Mix in olive oil, liquid butter replacement, egg substitute and ½ cup grated parmesan cheese.

Sauce:
Prepare 1 recipe of Bechamel sauce. Stir in parmesan cheese until melted.

To assemble and bake:
Prepare a non-stick 9x13-inch pan with cooking spray. Neatly layer half of the pasta in the bottom. Next layer the meat mixture. Top with a neat layer of the remaining pasta. Pour Bechamel sauce over top. Bake at 350° F for 25-30 minutes or until the top is slightly golden.

Cook's Note: May substitute ground turkey breast or ground round for the ground buffalo.

Nutrient Content Per Serving		Percent of Calories	Fat Breakdown	
Calories	488.0	36% Protein	Saturated Fat	5.8 g
Protein	43.4 g	36% Carbohydrate	Monounsaturated Fat	5.1 g
Carbohydrates	43.7 g	27% Fat	Polyunsaturated Fat	2.7 g
Fat – Total	14.7 g			
Cholesterol	81.0 mg			
Dietary Fiber	3.0 g			
Sodium	858.0 mg			

STIFADO
Serves 6

1½ lbs.	lean boneless top round
1 Tbl.	powdered butter replacement
1½ cups	dry red wine
¾ cup	tomato paste
3 cloves	garlic, minced
3 Tbl.	red wine vinegar
2 lg.	bay leaves
1	cinnamon stick, halved
½ tsp.	salt
¼ tsp.	freshly ground black pepper
1 lb.	small white boiling onions
½ cup	crumbled feta cheese
¼ cup	1% cottage cheese

Trim beef of all visible fat. Cut into 1-inch cubes. In a non-stick frying pan, prepared with cooking spray, sauté beef over medium heat until evenly browned, approximately 8-10 minutes.

Add 1 cup water, powdered butter replacement, wine, tomato paste, garlic, vinegar, bay leaves, cinnamon stick, salt and pepper. Bring to boil over medium-high heat. Reduce heat to low. Cover and cook, until beef is almost tender, about 1 hour.

Meanwhile, add onions to 2½ cups boiling water and cook 2 minutes. Transfer to a colander and run under cold water. Peel. Add onions to beef mixture. Cover and continue cooking until beef and onions are tender, about 15 minutes longer.

Discard cinnamon stick and bay leaves. Stir in feta and cottage cheese. Cook, uncovered, until cheese softens, about 2 minutes. Serve hot.

Cook's Note: The cut of beef will determine the fat content of the meal. Buffalo is a good lowfat alternative.

Alcohol Note: The alcohol content was computed prior to cooking. Once the alcohol is heated to the boiling point, the alcohol disappears along with most of the calories from the alcohol.

Nutrient Content Per Serving		Percent of Calories	Fat Breakdown	
Calories	316.0	42% Protein	Saturated Fat	4.6 g
Protein	33.3 g	20% Carbohydrate	Monounsaturated Fat	2.7 g
Carbohydrates	15.9 g	26% Fat	Polyunsaturated Fat	0.5 g
Fat – Total	9.1 g	12% Alcohol		
Cholesterol	90.1 mg			
Dietary Fiber	2.7 g			
Sodium	769.0 mg			

STUFFED GRAPE LEAVES
(DOLMATHES)
Serves 6

½ lb.	extra-lean ground beef
¼ lb.	ground lamb
¾ cup	onion, chopped fine
1 clove	garlic, minced
1 tsp.	olive oil
⅓ cup	long-grain white rice, uncooked
2 Tbl.	fresh parsley, minced
1½ Tbl.	fresh mint, chopped finely (½ tsp. dried)
½ tsp.	dried dill weed
½ tsp.	salt
⅛ tsp.	freshly ground black pepper
1 8-oz. jar	grape leaves, drained (may use fresh — see below)
1½ cups	beef stock *(see p. 536)*
1 tsp.	powdered butter replacement
1 recipe	egg-lemon sauce *(see p. 521)*

Garnish:

lemon wedges

In a large non-stick frying pan sauté meat, onion and garlic in oil until onion is soft. Drain any grease that may appear. Add rice, seasonings and ⅔ cup of water. Reduce heat to low. Cover and simmer 20 minutes or until rice has absorbed all the liquid.

To prepare fresh grape leaves:
Drain and rinse leaves. Bring 2 quarts of water to a boil. Add grape leaves and immediately remove pan from heat. Let stand 1 minute. Transfer leaves to a colander and quickly cool with cold running water. Separate leaves and lay out on paper towels, stem side up. Pat dry. (If using commercial leaves, you need only drain them.)

Lay leaf stem side up. Trim stem to base of leaf. Place 1 level tablespoon of meat and rice mixture in the center of each leaf. Fold edges of leaf over to cover filling completely. Roll up. Arrange filled leaves, folded edges down, in the same large frying pan prepared with cooking spray. Pour stock over rolls and sprinkle with powdered butter replacement. Cover and simmer over low heat until tender, 25-30 minutes. Drain. Serve with egg-lemon sauce *(see p. 521)* and garnish with lemon wedges.

Variation: May also stuff mixture into tomato shells.

Cook's Note: The fat content will depend on the amount of fat in your meat. Over-the-counter ground lamb is not very lean. The best method is to trim a leg of lamb of all visible fat and grind your own. May also substitute ground skinless turkey breast for the ground beef.

Nutrient Content Per Serving		Percent of Calories	Fat Breakdown	
Calories	172.0	46% Protein	Saturated Fat	0.9 g
Protein	19.9 g	37% Carbohydrate	Monounsaturated Fat	1.4 g
Carbohydrates	15.9 g	17% Fat	Polyunsaturated Fat	0.3 g
Fat – Total	3.3 g			
Cholesterol	49.4 mg			
Dietary Fiber	0.5 g			
Sodium	479.0 mg			

STUFFED GREEN PEPPERS
Serves 4

6 lg.	green bell peppers
¼ cup	long-grain white rice
1 sm.	onion, peeled and chopped
1 tsp.	olive oil
1 lb.	ground buffalo
1 Tbl.	fresh parsley, chopped fine
½ tsp.	salt
1¼ tsp.	paprika
⅛ tsp.	freshly ground black pepper
2 med.	tomatoes, peeled, seeded and chopped
1 cup	beef stock (see p. 536)
¼ cup	nonfat sour cream

Cut a thin slice from stem end of each pepper. Leaving pepper intact, discard seeds and thick white membranes. Blanch peppers in the microwave for 5 minutes or until they start to get tender.

Boil ½ cup water. Add rice. Reduce heat to low and simmer 5 minutes. Drain.

In a large non-stick frying pan, sauté onion in oil until soft. Add buffalo and continue cooking, breaking up the meat with a fork until lightly browned, 8-10 minutes. Remove any fat. Add rice, parsley, salt, ¼ tsp. of the paprika and pepper.

Prepare a 5-quart casserole with cooking spray. Spread tomatoes over bottom of casserole. Spoon ½ cup meat mixture into each green pepper. Set peppers on top of tomatoes. Combine stock and remaining paprika. Pour around peppers. Cover and bake at 350° F until peppers are tender, about 45 minutes (or may microwave 15-20 minutes).

Transfer the peppers to a heated serving dish to keep warm. Pour juice into a blender and process until smooth. Return liquid to frying pan and reduce to 1 cup. Remove from heat. Stir in sour cream and pour sauce over peppers. Serve immediately.

Cook's Note: The fat may be removed from the ground buffalo by transferring buffalo to a colander and pouring boiling water over top. The fat content of your meat will determine the final fat content of the dish. Add a loaf of French bread and make a meal.

Nutrient Content Per Serving

Calories	278.0
Protein	36.3 g
Carbohydrates	23.1 g
Fat – Total	4.6 g
Cholesterol	93.2 mg
Dietary Fiber	3.3 g
Sodium	605.0 mg

Percent of Calories

52% Protein
33% Carbohydrate
15% Fat

Fat Breakdown

Saturated Fat	1.4 g
Monounsaturated Fat	2.1 g
Polyunsaturated Fat	0.7 g

ARTICHOKES WITH LEMONY "BUTTER" SAUCE
Serves 4

4	artichokes, fresh
2 cups	water

Sauce:

¼ cup	hot water
¼ cup	fresh lemon juice
2 Tbl.	powdered butter replacement

Remove stem from artichoke so it will sit flat. Remove choke. Trim points off leaves. Steam artichokes until tender.

To prepare sauce:
Mix water and lemon juice. Dissolve butter replacement in water.
Serve with warm lemony "butter."

Nutrient Content Per Serving

Calories	80.2
Protein	4.3 g
Carbohydrates	18.8 g
Fat – Total	0.3 g
Cholesterol	0.1 mg
Dietary Fiber	6.3 g
Sodium	148.0 mg

Percent of Calories
18% Protein
79% Carbohydrate
 2% Fat

Fat Breakdown

Saturated Fat	0.1 g
Monounsaturated Fat	0.0 g
Polyunsaturated Fat	0.1 g

BROCCOLI CHEESE PIE
Serves 8

8 leaves	filo dough
⅔ cup	scallions, sliced thin
4 cups	broccoli, frozen, chopped, patted dry
2 cups	1% cottage cheese, drained
6	egg whites
1 oz.	blue cheese, crumbled
¼ cup	fresh parsley, chopped
3 Tbl.	flour
1 Tbl.	dill weed
1 tsp.	black pepper
1 Tbl.	powdered butter replacement
2 tsp.	butter, melted

Coat a small non-stick frying pan with butter-flavored cooking spray. Over medium-low heat, sauté the scallions.

In a large bowl, combine all ingredients except filo dough.

Coat a springform pan with cooking spray. Lay 4 leaves of filo on bottom. Leaves should come over sides of pan. Press leaves firmly into sides of pan. Spoon broccoli mixture into pan. Fold filo leaves over broccoli. Cut remaining 4 leaves to fit top of pan (9-inch circle). Layer these leaves over top of broccoli. Brush top with melted butter. Score top leaves into 8 wedges. Place springform pan on a cookie sheet (because it might leak). Bake at 350° F for 1 hour or until top is browned and crisp. Let stand 5 minutes before removing from springform pan.

Cook's Note: This recipe just tastes better with the butter. You may substitute olive oil or butter-flavored margarine to decrease the saturated fat. The total fat content will stay the same.

Nutrient Content Per Serving

Calories	151.0
Protein	14.7 g
Carbohydrates	16.5 g
Fat – Total	3.4 g
Cholesterol	7.8 mg
Dietary Fiber	3.3 g
Sodium	417.0 mg

Percent of Calories

38% Protein
42% Carbohydrate
20% Fat

Fat Breakdown

Saturated Fat	1.8 g
Monounsaturated Fat	0.9 g
Polyunsaturated Fat	0.5 g

FENNEL AND TOMATOES
Serves 4

2 lg.	fennel bulbs
2 tsp.	olive oil
1	lemon, juice of
1 Tbl.	fresh marjoram (or ½ Tbl. dry)
1 tsp.	coriander seed, ground
to taste	salt and pepper
8 oz.	canned tomatoes, peeled, chopped, drained

Garnish:

1 Tbl.	fresh parsley, chopped

Clean, trim and quarter fennel. In a non-stick pan, brown fennel in olive oil. Add remaining ingredients. Bring to a boil, reduce heat and simmer, covered for 30 minutes. (Add water or drained tomato juice, if necessary to prevent sticking.) Garnish with parsley before serving.

Nutrient Content Per Serving

Calories	74.7
Protein	2.3 g
Carbohydrates	12.8 g
Fat – Total	2.7 g
Cholesterol	0.0 mg
Dietary Fiber	6.0 g
Sodium	187.0 mg

Percent of Calories

11% Protein
60% Carbohydrate
29% Fat

Fat Breakdown

Saturated Fat	0.2 g
Monounsaturated Fat	0.9 g
Polyunsaturated Fat	0.2 g

GREEN BEANS GRECO
Serves 8

2 lbs.	string beans
1 bunch	scallions, chopped
2 Tbl.	parsley, chopped
1 clove	garlic, minced
1 Tbl.	olive oil
¼ cup	water

Trim ends of beans. Microwave or parboil until barely tender.

In a large non-stick frying pan, sauté green beans, scallions, parsley and garlic in olive oil. Cook until scallions are soft. Add water. Cover and simmer until green beans are tender.

Cook's Note: You may use same recipe for artichoke hearts or zucchini.

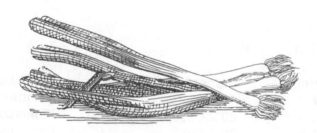

Nutrient Content Per Serving

Calories	53.0
Protein	2.2 g
Carbohydrates	8.7 g
Fat – Total	1.8 g
Cholesterol	0.0 mg
Dietary Fiber	3.7 g
Sodium	8.4 mg

Percent of Calories

15% Protein
58% Carbohydrate
27% Fat

Fat Breakdown

Saturated Fat	0.3 g
Monounsaturated Fat	1.3 g
Polyunsaturated Fat	0.2 g

WHITE LIMA PILAKI
Serves 8

1 lb.	dry white lima beans or 2 15-oz. cans white lima beans
1 med.	onion, chopped fine
2 cloves	garlic, minced
1 stalk	celery, chopped
2 med.	carrots, chopped
½ cup	parsley, chopped
2 Tbl.	olive oil
1 Tbl.	dill weed, dry
1 tsp.	fines herbes
⅓ cup	lemon juice
15-oz. can	tomatoes, chopped
4 cups	chicken stock (see p. 538)
to taste	salt and pepper

Soak beans overnight. Discard soaking liquid. Add fresh water and simmer beans for 30 minutes. Drain again.

In a soup pot, sauté onion, garlic, celery, carrots and parsley in olive oil for 5 minutes. Add dill, fines herbes, lemon juice, tomatoes and chicken stock. Cover and simmer 40 minutes or until beans are tender. Season with salt and pepper to taste.

Cook's Note: Tasty with fish! If using canned white limas, drain well, omit soaking and chicken stock. Reduce cooking time to 20 minutes instead of 40 minutes.

Nutrient Content Per Serving

Calories	255.0
Protein	13.4 g
Carbohydrates	43.4 g
Fat – Total	4.0 g
Cholesterol	0.0 mg
Dietary Fiber	19.2 g
Sodium	111.0 mg

Percent of Calories

20% Protein
66% Carbohydrate
14% Fat

Fat Breakdown

Saturated Fat	0.6 g
Monounsaturated Fat	2.6 g
Polyunsaturated Fat	0.6 g

MIXED VEGETABLES
Serves 6

3 lg.	carrots, cut in sticks
2 lg.	leeks, sliced in rounds
1 sm.	eggplant (about 1 pound), cut in large wedges
2 med.	zucchini, cubed
½ lb.	fresh mushrooms, left whole
13-oz. can	artichoke hearts, drained
⅓ cup	dry white wine
2 Tbl.	fresh lemon juice
1 tsp.	olive oil
4	shallots, chopped
½ tsp.	salt
¼ tsp.	dried thyme, crumbled
⅛ tsp.	freshly ground black pepper

Garnish:

2 Tbl.	fresh parsley, chopped
1 Tbl.	fresh mint, chopped

Combine 1 cup of water, wine, lemon juice, olive oil, shallots, salt, thyme and pepper in a 3-quart saucepan. Bring to a boil. Reduce heat to low. Add carrots and leeks, cook, uncovered, 5 minutes. Add eggplant, cook 5 minutes. Add zucchini, mushrooms and artichokes, cook until all vegetables are crisp-tender, about 5 minutes longer.

Remove vegetables from saucepan with a slotted spoon and transfer to a heated serving bowl. Cover to keep hot. Reduce liquid to ½ cup. Pour over vegetables. Garnish with parsley and mint. Serve hot.

Alcohol Note: The alcohol content was computed prior to cooking. Once the alcohol is heated to the boiling point, the alcohol disappears along with most of the calories from the alcohol.

Nutrient Content Per Serving

Calories	122.0
Protein	4.7 g
Carbohydrates	24.6 g
Fat – Total	1.4 g
Cholesterol	0.0 mg
Dietary Fiber	8.9 g
Sodium	251.0 mg

Percent of Calories

14% Protein
71% Carbohydrate
9% Fat
6% Alcohol

Fat Breakdown

Saturated Fat	0.2 g
Monounsaturated Fat	0.6 g
Polyunsaturated Fat	0.3 g

OKRA WITH TOMATOES
Serves 6

1 lb.	okra, whole pieces
1 sm.	onion, chopped
1	leek, chopped (white portion only)
1 tsp.	olive oil
3 lg.	tomatoes, chopped coarse
1 clove	garlic, minced
2 Tbl.	lemon juice
1 tsp.	sugar
to taste	salt and pepper

Garnish:

¼ cup	parsley, chopped

Remove stems from okra. Wash thoroughly.

In a medium non-stick frying pan sauté onion and leek in olive oil. Add okra and sauté carefully so as not to burn. (Will not cook completely, just start to brown.) Add remaining ingredients, cover and simmer until okra is desired tenderness. Garnish with chopped parsley.

Nutrient Content Per Serving

Calories	68.9
Protein	2.6 g
Carbohydrates	14.3 g
Fat – Total	1.2 g
Cholesterol	0.0 mg
Dietary Fiber	3.4 g
Sodium	15.6 mg

Percent of Calories

13% Protein
73% Carbohydrate
14% Fat

Fat Breakdown

Saturated Fat	0.2 g
Monounsaturated Fat	0.6 g
Polyunsaturated Fat	0.2 g

SPINACH AND CHEESE PIE
Serves 8

Filling:

2 lbs.	spinach (or 3 pkg. frozen)
1 lg.	onion, chopped fine
4	scallions, chopped fine
1½ tsp.	olive oil
4 Tbl.	fresh dill, chopped fine
8	egg whites
4 oz.	feta cheese, crumbled
4 oz.	1% cottage cheese
2 Tbl.	parmesan cheese, grated
pinch	nutmeg
to taste	pepper
½ lb.	filo dough, thawed

Supplies needed:
>   spray bottle

Preheat the oven to 375° F. Squeeze water from the spinach, then shred the leaves. In a large non-stick saucepan gently sauté the onion and scallions in ½ teaspoon of the olive oil. Add the spinach and dill. Stir until the spinach is soft and the liquid has evaporated. Allow to cool.

Lightly beat the egg whites in a bowl. Mash the feta cheese and cottage cheese with a fork and add to the egg whites. Add parmesan cheese, the spinach mixture (drained of its juice), nutmeg and pepper, stir well.

Coat an 11x17-inch pan with cooking spray. Place half the sheets of filo dough at the bottom, one on top of another. Spread the filling evenly on top, fold over the edges of the filo dough and cover with the remaining filo dough, tucking the edges down the sides of the tin. Spray the top with the remaining 1 teaspoon of oil. Cut the top layer of filo into squares or diamonds with a sharp knife, but do not cut through to the bottom or the filling will leak into the pan.

Cover and bake 30 minutes. Uncover and continue baking an additional 15 minutes or until the pie is crisp, golden and puffed up. Cut the squares or diamonds right through to the bottom and serve hot.

Cook's Note: May be prepared ahead and baked when ready to serve. The filo will be more crisp than you are used to, due to the small amount of oil used on the dough.

Nutrient Content Per Serving

Calories	196.0
Protein	13.5 g
Carbohydrates	22.0 g
Fat – Total	6.6 g
Cholesterol	14.5 mg
Dietary Fiber	3.8 g
Sodium	527.0 mg

Percent of Calories

27% Protein
44% Carbohydrate
30% Fat

Fat Breakdown

Saturated Fat	2.9 g
Monounsaturated Fat	1.8 g
Polyunsaturated Fat	1.3 g

SPINACH WITH RICE
Serves 4

1 lb.	spinach, washed, drained, cut rough
1 lg.	onion, chopped
1 tsp.	olive oil
¼ cup	water
1 Tbl.	fresh parsley, chopped
¼ cup	rice

In a non-stick pan, sauté onion in olive oil until golden. Add spinach and water. Bring to a boil. Add parsley and rice. Cover, simmer 20 minutes or until rice is cooked and water is absorbed.

Nutrient Content Per Serving

Calories	87.8
Protein	4.4 g
Carbohydrates	15.6 g
Fat – Total	1.7 g
Cholesterol	0.0 mg
Dietary Fiber	3.6 g
Sodium	91.4 mg

Percent of Calories

19% Protein
66% Carbohydrate
16% Fat

Fat Breakdown

Saturated Fat	0.2 g
Monounsaturated Fat	0.9 g
Polyunsaturated Fat	0.3 g

Zucchini Casserole

Serves 6

2 sm.	zucchini, sliced in thin rounds
1 med.	onion, sliced in thin rings
4 lg.	tomatoes, chopped
1 clove	garlic, minced
1 tsp.	olive oil
1 tsp.	sugar
1 tsp.	oregano
1 tsp.	mint
to taste	salt and pepper
3 oz.	feta cheese, crumbled

Combine tomatoes, garlic, oil, sugar, oregano, mint and salt and pepper to taste. In a baking dish prepared with cooking spray, decoratively layer zucchini with onion slices. Alternate periodically. Top with tomato mixture. Sprinkle top with feta. Bake at 350° F for 30-40 minutes or until zucchini is tender.

Cook's Note: A nice change for zucchini.

% Calories as Fat — Above the HM✔ guidelines: Although this recipe has a high percentage of calories as fat (>30%), the total fat is less than 5 grams per serving. This will easily fit within your allotment of 45 grams per day. This happens most often in low-calorie recipes.

Nutrient Content Per Serving

Calories	70.8
Protein	3.1 g
Carbohydrates	6.5 g
Fat – Total	4.2 g
Cholesterol	12.6 mg
Dietary Fiber	1.5 g
Sodium	167.0 mg

Percent of Calories

16% Protein
34% Carbohydrate
49% Fat

Fat Breakdown

Saturated Fat	2.3 g
Monounsaturated Fat	1.3 g
Polyunsaturated Fat	0.3 g

ZUCCHINI HOT CAKES
Serves 4
Yield: 12 Zucchini Hot Cakes

1 med.	zucchini (8-inch lengthwise), shredded
½ tsp.	salt
2 Tbl.	flour
½ tsp.	fresh mint, minced or ¼ tsp. dried mint (or ½ tsp. basil)
to taste	freshly ground black pepper
1 Tbl.	powdered butter replacement
⅓ cup	feta cheese, crumbled
3	egg whites

Mix zucchini with salt and let stand 1 hour. Squeeze moisture from zucchini with hands, then pat dry with a paper towel.

Toss zucchini with flour to coat. Stir in seasonings and powdered butter replacement. Combine feta and egg whites. Fold into zucchini. Make into patties using 2 tablespoons of batter each.

Spray a non-stick griddle with butter-flavored cooking spray. Heat griddle to medium heat. Brown patties on both sides. Serve hot.

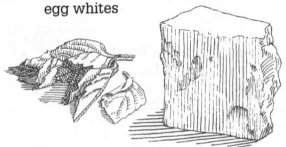

% Calories as Fat — Above the HM✓ guidelines: Although this recipe has a high percentage of calories as fat (>30%), the total fat is less than 5 grams per serving. This will easily fit within your allotment of 45 grams per day. This happens most often in low-calorie recipes.

Nutrient Content Per Serving (3 cakes per serving)

Calories	86.5
Protein	6.2 g
Carbohydrates	5.4 g
Fat – Total	4.4 g
Cholesterol	18.1 mg
Dietary Fiber	0.2 g
Sodium	548.0 mg

Percent of Calories
29% Protein
25% Carbohydrate
46% Fat

Fat Breakdown

Saturated Fat	3.1 g
Monounsaturated Fat	0.9 g
Polyunsaturated Fat	0.2 g

ZUCCHINI WITH CUCUMBER DILL SAUCE
Serves 4

1 lg.	zucchini
	flour
to taste	salt
1 recipe	cucumber dill sauce *(see p. 522)*

Slice zucchini in ¼-inch slices. Let zucchini drain on paper towels for 15 minutes. Dredge in flour. On a broiler pan coated with cooking spray, broil slices until brown. Turn and brown other side.

Serve with Cucumber Dill Sauce.

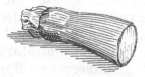 

Nutrient Content Per Serving

Calories	64.3
Protein	4.2 g
Carbohydrates	11.3 g
Fat – Total	0.4 g
Cholesterol	0.8 mg
Dietary Fiber	0.7 g
Sodium	36.6 mg

Percent of Calories

25% Protein
69% Carbohydrate
6% Fat

Fat Breakdown

Saturated Fat	0.1 g
Monounsaturated Fat	0.1 g
Polyunsaturated Fat	0.1 g

Avgolemono Sauce
(Egg-Lemon Sauce)
Serves 6
Yield: 2 cups

3	egg whites	Beat egg whites until stiff. Add flour and beat again. While beating, add egg substitute. Strain the lemon juice to yield a smooth sauce. Pour in lemon juice and stock. Do this very slowly so that the eggs will not curdle. Heat until warm and pour sauce over the food. Serve immediately.
1 Tbl.	flour, sifted	
6 Tbl.	egg substitute	
1	lemon, juice of, squeezed	
1 cup	chicken stock *(see p. 538)*	

Cook's Note: Greek cooks use this on practically everything. May use broth or stock from the dish being prepared. It is very tart so you won't need much! May serve the sauce over steamed vegetables: celery hearts, broccoli, asparagus, leeks or artichokes.

▼ This recipe is used for the following item:
Stuffed Grape Leaves (Dolmathes) (see p. 507)

Nutrient Content Per Serving

Calories	29.6
Protein	3.9 g
Carbohydrates	1.9 g
Fat – Total	0.7 g
Cholesterol	0.3 mg
Dietary Fiber	0.1 g
Sodium	240.0 mg

Percent of Calories

54% Protein
26% Carbohydrate
20% Fat

Fat Breakdown

Saturated Fat	0.1 g
Monounsaturated Fat	0.2 g
Polyunsaturated Fat	0.3 g

Cucumber Dill Sauce

Serves 12
Yield: 3 cups

2 cloves	garlic, minced
½ tsp.	olive oil
2 Tbl.	white wine vinegar
2	cucumbers, peeled, seeded
½ tsp.	dill weed
to taste	salt and pepper
3 cups	plain non-fat yogurt

Combine all ingredients except yogurt in a food processor. Blend. Stir in yogurt. Chill 2-3 hours.

Cook's Note: Serve with vegetables or fish. It will keep one week in the refrigerator.

▼ This recipe is used for the following item:
Zucchini with Cucumber Dill Sauce (see p. 520)

Nutrient Content Per Serving

Calories	43.4
Protein	3.9 g
Carbohydrates	6.4 g
Fat – Total	0.4 g
Cholesterol	1.1 mg
Dietary Fiber	0.5 g
Sodium	48.0 mg

Percent of Calories

35% Protein
58% Carbohydrate
 7% Fat

Fat Breakdown

Saturated Fat	0.1 g
Monounsaturated Fat	0.2 g
Polyunsaturated Fat	0.0 g

APRICOPITA

"Almost HealthMark Dessert"
Serves 12

Apricot filling:

2 lbs.	apricots, fresh or frozen
5 pods	cardamon seeds, crushed
⅓ cup	sugar
½ tsp.	vanilla extract

Meringue filling:

3	egg whites
2 Tbl.	brown sugar
¾ cup	blanched almonds, ground fine

9 sheets	filo dough
2 Tbl.	powdered sugar

Supplies Needed:

spray bottle with 2 tsp. liquid margarine

For apricot filling:
Drop apricots into boiling water for 2 minutes to remove skins. Remove pits. Place apricots in a saucepan with cardamon seeds, sugar and vanilla. Cook until apricots are soft. Transfer mixture to a food processor and purée until smooth.

For meringue filling:
Beat egg whites until stiff. Beat in brown sugar. Fold in almonds.

To assemble:
Prepare a 9x13 baking dish with butter-flavor cooking spray. Place a sheet of filo dough in pan, spray lightly with margarine. Layer 2 more layers. Spread all of apricot mixture on dough. Place 3 more layers of dough, spraying lightly with margarine as you go. Spread meringue mixture on top of the dough. Layer remaining 3 sheets of dough and spray top with remaining margarine. Dust top with powdered sugar. Bake at 375° F for 40-50 minutes or until brown and crisp. Cut into diamond shapes.

Cook's Note: This recipe is as lowfat as we could make it. It's close!

Nutrient Content Per Serving		**Percent of Calories**	**Fat Breakdown**	
Calories	157.0	10% Protein	Saturated Fat	0.6 g
Protein	4.2 g	59% Carbohydrate	Monounsaturated Fat	3.0 g
Carbohydrates	24.3 g	30% Fat	Polyunsaturated Fat	1.6 g
Fat – Total	5.5 g			
Cholesterol	0.0 mg			
Dietary Fiber	2.2 g			
Sodium	82.1 mg			

BAKLAVA
Serves 24
"Almost HealthMark Dessert"
Not quite HealthMark, but very Greek. It's as lowfat as we could make it.

Filling:

1 cup	blanched almonds
1 cup	walnuts
½ cup	unsalted pretzels
¼ cup	brown sugar
1½ tsp.	cinnamon, ground
½ tsp.	nutmeg, fresh grated

Syrup:

½ cup	honey
2 Tbl.	lemon juice, fresh
1 Tbl.	orange-flower water (optional)
8 sheets	filo pastry dough
2 Tbl.	butter, melted

Supplies needed:

1	spray bottle

Filling:
In a food processor, finely chop nuts and pretzels. Add brown sugar, cinnamon and nutmeg.

Syrup:
Heat honey. Add lemon juice and orange flower water. Keep warm enough that the honey will pour, but not watery.

To assemble:
Prepare a 9x13-inch non-stick baking dish with butter-flavored cooking spray. Layer 2 sheets of dough in pan. Spray each with the melted butter. Spread one-third of the nut mixture on dough. Layer 2 more sheets of dough and spray with butter. Repeat until all the nut mixture has been used. Top with final sheets of dough. Spray top with butter. Score top layer into diamond shapes. Bake at 350° F for 20-30 minutes until crisp and golden. Remove from oven. Let cool 10 minutes. Pour syrup over top. Let cool. Cut diamonds all the way through.

Cook's Note: It is crispier than the super-high-fat version, and the layers are apt to shift. But it's just as tasty! Due to the low butter content, the baklava is very crispy. Handle it gently. It still tastes wonderful!

Nutrient Content Per Serving		Percent of Calories	Fat Breakdown	
Calories	140.0	9% Protein	Saturated Fat	1.2 g
Protein	3.4 g	44% Carbohydrate	Monounsaturated Fat	3.2 g
Carbohydrates	16.3 g	47% Fat	Polyunsaturated Fat	3.0 g
Fat – Total	7.7 g			
Cholesterol	2.6 mg			
Dietary Fiber	1.1 g			
Sodium	123.0 mg			

FIGS 'N CREAM
Serves 4

20	figs, dried or fresh
1 Tbl.	powdered sugar
1 Tbl.	strawberry liqueur
½ cup	nonfat sour cream
4 tsp.	almonds, slivered

Soak figs in hot water to plump them. Blend powdered sugar and liqueur into the sour cream. Let stand about 30 minutes to let flavors blend. Put drained figs into a dessert dish and spoon sour cream mixture over top. Garnish with almonds.

Cook's Note: You may chop figs and mix with the sour cream mixture and serve all over nonfat frozen yogurt or angel food cake.

Nutrient Content Per Serving

Calories	288.0
Protein	5.4 g
Carbohydrates	67.4 g
Fat – Total	2.6 g
Cholesterol	0.0 mg
Dietary Fiber	9.0 g
Sodium	30.8 mg

Percent of Calories

7% Protein
85% Carbohydrate
7% Fat

Fat Breakdown

Saturated Fat	0.4 g
Monounsaturated Fat	1.2 g
Polyunsaturated Fat	0.8 g

Fruit and Yogurt
Serves 4

1 cup	nonfat vanilla yogurt
2 Tbl.	honey
1 Tbl.	lemon zest
4 cups	fresh fruit (berries, melon, grapes, etc.)

Garnish:

2 Tbl.	slivered almonds

Mix together yogurt, honey and lemon zest. Arrange fruit in a bowl. Pour yogurt over top. Garnish with almonds.

Nutrient Content Per Serving

Calories	177.0
Protein	5.4 g
Carbohydrates	35.9 g
Fat – Total	2.9 g
Cholesterol	1.1 mg
Dietary Fiber	3.5 g
Sodium	48.2 mg

Percent of Calories

11% Protein
75% Carbohydrate
14% Fat

Fat Breakdown

Saturated Fat	0.4 g
Monounsaturated Fat	1.6 g
Polyunsaturated Fat	0.6 g

ORANGE COMPOTE
Serves 4

4	oranges
½ cup	light corn syrup
4 Tbl.	Grand Marnier (may use Cointreau or Triple Sec)

Garnish:

4 tsp.	sour cream, nonfat
2 tsp.	candied ginger, chopped fine

Peel the oranges. Place the peel in a pan, cover with water and simmer covered until peel is tender. Drain off all but ⅓ cup liquid. Discard the peel. Add the corn syrup and bring to a boil, stirring constantly. Reduce heat and simmer 2 minutes. Remove pan from heat, stir in Grand Marnier. Let the mixture cool.

Cut the oranges crosswise into round slices ½-inch thick. Remove seeds. Cut each slice into quarters. Arrange oranges in a small dessert dish and pour cooled syrup over top. To serve, garnish with sour cream and candied ginger.

Nutrient Content Per Serving

Calories	219.0
Protein	1.6 g
Carbohydrates	52.9 g
Fat – Total	0.2 g
Cholesterol	0.0 mg
Dietary Fiber	3.2 g
Sodium	53.7 mg

Percent of Calories

3% Protein
89% Carbohydrate
1% Fat
7% Alcohol

Fat Breakdown

Saturated Fat	0.0 g
Monounsaturated Fat	0.0 g
Polyunsaturated Fat	0.0 g

ORANGE-FLOWER ORANGES
Serves 4

4   oranges
1 tsp.   orange-flower water
4 Tbl.   dates, chopped
1 tsp.   walnuts, chopped

Garnish:
            fresh mint leaves

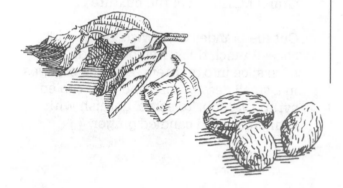

Peel oranges. Cut into sections. (Cut between the membranes, save any juice.) Arrange oranges in a spiral on each serving plate.

Combine orange juice with the orange flower water. Pour over oranges.

Decoratively arrange dates and walnuts over oranges.

Garnish with fresh mint leaves.

Nutrient Content Per Serving
Calories	96.2
Protein	1.6 g
Carbohydrates	23.7 g
Fat – Total	0.6 g
Cholesterol	0.0 mg
Dietary Fiber	4.1 g
Sodium	0.3 mg

Percent of Calories
6% Protein
89% Carbohydrate
5% Fat

Fat Breakdown
Saturated Fat	0.1 g
Monounsaturated Fat	0.1 g
Polyunsaturated Fat	0.3 g

ORANGE YOGURT CAKE
Serves 12

½ cup	egg substitute
1 cup	sugar
½ cup	nonfat dry milk
⅓ cup	canola oil
¼ tsp.	baking soda
1 cup	nonfat plain yogurt
2	lemons, zest of
2½ cups	flour
1 Tbl.	baking powder
4	egg whites

Garnish:

powdered sugar

Prepare a 9-inch round cake pan with butter-flavor cooking spray.

In a bowl beat egg substitute, sugar and nonfat milk powder until smooth. Add oil and baking soda. Beat 1 minute. Beat in yogurt and one-half of the lemon zest. Carefully stir in flour and baking powder.

In a separate bowl, beat egg whites until stiff. Fold into batter.

Pour batter into the prepared pan. Bake at 375° F for 40-50 minutes or until cake tester comes out clean.

Sprinkle top with powdered sugar and decorate with remaining zest.

Cook's Note: It is a plain white cake with orange flavor. May decorate with fresh fruit, serve with a fruit sauce or with nonfat frozen yogurt or fresh fruit. May also prepare as a two-layer cake and fill center with a fruit sauce.

Nutrient Content Per Serving		**Percent of Calories**	**Fat Breakdown**	
Calories	253.0	11% Protein	Saturated Fat	0.7 g
Protein	6.8 g	63% Carbohydrate	Monounsaturated Fat	3.8 g
Carbohydrates	40.0 g	26% Fat	Polyunsaturated Fat	2.5 g
Fat – Total	7.4 g			
Cholesterol	1.2 mg			
Dietary Fiber	0.8 g			
Sodium	112.0 mg			

RICE PUDDING WITH THE ESSENCE OF ROSES
Serves 4

½ cup	short-grain rice
½ cup	water
2½ cups	skim milk
¼	lemon, peel
¼ cup	sugar
2 tsp.	cornstarch
1 Tbl.	egg substitute
1 Tbl.	rosewater

Garnish:

cinnamon, ground
rose petals

Rinse rice. Let soak in water.

In a large saucepan, combine milk and lemon peel. Scald milk. Add sugar, stir until dissolved. Add rice and water. Cover and simmer 30-40 minutes or until most of the liquid has been absorbed.

Dissolve cornstarch in a tablespoon of water. Stir into rice. Cook 2 minutes. Add egg substitute and rosewater and heat 2-3 minutes longer.

Serve garnished with ground cinnamon and fresh rose petals.

Cook's Note: Rosewater may be purchased at specialty stores or health-food stores.

Nutrient Content Per Serving

Calories	146.0
Protein	6.4 g
Carbohydrates	29.4 g
Fat – Total	0.5 g
Cholesterol	2.8 mg
Dietary Fiber	0.4 g
Sodium	86.3 mg

Percent of Calories

17% Protein
80% Carbohydrate
 3% Fat

Fat Breakdown

Saturated Fat	0.2 g
Monounsaturated Fat	0.1 g
Polyunsaturated Fat	0.1 g

STANDARD PREPARATIONS

In this section you will find a variety of standard preparations that are used throughout the book. These have been included to provide the accomplished cook a gourmet setup. Gourmet cooks use a variety of standard preparations in their meals from stocks to relishes. These items are simple to prepare and lend a wonderful flavor to your dishes.

Take a few moments on a cold, rainy (or snowy) day and cook up a batch of chicken or beef stock. Enjoy the wonderful aroma as it simmers half of the day. Let the stock cool, then freeze it in one-cup containers. Unmold the frozen stock and place in plastic freezer bags. Now you will have a supply of delicious, lowfat, low-sodium chicken or beef stock to use in many recipes. Of course, you do not have to prepare our stock in order to cook the recipes that call for stock. There are stock bases available in the supermarket. You may substitute any of these that you like. Be sure to use a stock and not a bouillon or a broth. Bouillons contain large quantities of sodium,

and broths have both sodium and fat. If you have sensitivities to MSG, read the stock labels carefully.

Fish stock takes a little more care to prepare. I prefer to prepare fish stock on a warm day so the windows can be opened. When the stock cools, freeze it in one-cup paper cups, then seal them in a plastic freezer bag. (If you freeze the fish stock in reusable plastic containers, it will leave a fishy taste on the plastic.) The fish stock is an important addition to fish soups and to sauces used for fish. If you do not have fish stock, you may substitute chicken stock or vegetable stock.

In addition to the stocks, you will find some relishes, chutneys and sauces in this section. Items such as Grenadine Onions *(see p. 533)* or Tomato Relish *(see p. 550)* may be used on a variety of dishes. Many of these items can be prepared ahead and be used on other foods as well. Read the cook's notes for suggestions.

The key is to use your imagination. Chances are you won't go wrong!

TABLE OF CONTENTS

MOST COMMONLY USED ITEMS FOR BASIC RECIPES

▼ FRESH INGREDIENTS
Onions
Lemons
Carrots
Celery
Wine
Garlic
Mushrooms
Tomatoes
Basil
Rice vinegar
Shallots

▼ PANTRY SUPPLIES
Garlic powder
Bay leaves
Peppercorns
Thyme
Rosemary
Dry mustard
Olive oil
Honey
Paprika

GRENADINE ONIONS
Serves 10

2 med.	yellow onions, julienne
¼ cup	grenadine syrup

In a small saucepan, combine ingredients and cook until onions are tender. Use as a garnish for meat or salads.

▼ This recipe is used for the following items:
Charred Buffalo Carpaccio (see p. 109)
Grilled Vegetable Salad (see p. 320)
Orange and Olive Salad (see p. 463)

Nutrient Content Per Serving

Calories	22.6
Protein	0.4 g
Carbohydrates	5.4 g
Fat – Total	0.1 g
Cholesterol	0.0 mg
Dietary Fiber	0.5 g
Sodium	1.3 mg

Percent of Calories

6% Protein
92% Carbohydrate
2% Fat

Fat Breakdown

Saturated Fat	0.0 g
Monounsaturated Fat	0.0 g
Polyunsaturated Fat	0.0 g

PAPRIKA-SEASONED CROUTONS
Serves 8

Croutons:
½ loaf   white bread

Paprika Seasoning Mix:
1 Tbl.   olive oil
3 Tbl.   paprika
1 Tbl.   garlic powder
2 Tbl.   lemon juice

Remove crusts from bread. Slice bread into small cubes. Toss with paprika seasoning mix. Spread cubes in a single layer on a baking sheet. Bake at 375° F until crispy brown. (Approximately 5 to 8 minutes.)

Cook's Note: Use the croutons with soups, caesar salads or tossed salads.

▼ This recipe is used for the following items:
Alsatian Onion Soup (see p. 164)
Caesar Salad (see p. 310)
Soup of the Sea (see p. 456)

Nutrient Content Per Serving

Calories	98.1
Protein	2.8 g
Carbohydrates	15.8 g
Fat – Total	2.8 g
Cholesterol	0.8 mg
Dietary Fiber	1.3 g
Sodium	144.0 mg

Percent of Calories

11% Protein
63% Carbohydrate
26% Fat

Fat Breakdown

Saturated Fat	0.5 g
Monounsaturated Fat	1.7 g
Polyunsaturated Fat	0.6 g

ARTICHOKE STOCK
Serves 6

1 tsp.	caraway seeds
1	bay leaf
1 tsp.	whole black peppercorns
2 qts.	water
1	whole lemon, cut in half
2 Tbl.	sugar
to taste	salt

Wrap caraway, bay leaf and peppercorns in cheesecloth. Combine all ingredients and bring to a boil. Simmer for 15 minutes to bring out full flavor. Strain and set aside until ready to use.

To use:
Place the stock in the bottom of a steamer when steaming artichokes. May also be used for artichoke soup.

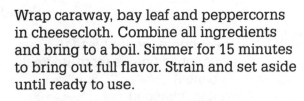

Nutrient Content Per Serving

Calories	20.2	
Protein	0.2 g	
Carbohydrates	5.2 g	
Fat – Total	0.1 g	
Cholesterol	0.0 mg	
Dietary Fiber	0.3 g	
Sodium	0.3 mg	

Percent of Calories
3% Protein
93% Carbohydrate
3% Fat

Fat Breakdown

Saturated Fat	0.0 g
Monounsaturated Fat	0.0 g
Polyunsaturated Fat	0.0 g

BEEF/VEAL STOCK

Serves 20

Yield: 2 quarts

6 lbs.	beef bones, walnut sized, chopped (may substitute veal bones)
1	onion, chopped
1	carrot, chopped
2	celery stalks, chopped
2 cloves	garlic, halved
1 tsp.	peppercorns
½	leek, chopped
¼ cup	tomato paste
1 qt.	burgundy wine
8 qts.	water
1 tsp.	thyme
1 tsp.	rosemary
1	bay leaf
to taste	salt and pepper

Preheat oven to 400° F. Place bones in a large roasting pan, and bake until the veal bones begin to brown. When golden brown, add the onion, carrot, celery, garlic, peppercorns and leek. Brown them. Add the tomato paste, mixing into the bones. Let them sweat.

Remove the roasting pan from the oven and place on stove over medium heat. Add the wine and simmer, covered, for 15 minutes. Add the water, thyme, rosemary, bay leaf and salt and pepper if desired. Slowly simmer, partially covered, for 3-4 hours. Periodically remove the built-up foam.

Strain through a sieve and chill quickly by placing the pan of stock in a pan of ice water. Remove any fat that has hardened on the top. Freeze in 1-cup containers for future use.

Cook's Note: Veal bones can be obtained from your butcher.

Alcohol Note: The alcohol content was computed prior to cooking. Once the alcohol is heated to the boiling point, the alcohol disappears along with most of the calories from the alcohol.

▼ This recipe is used for the following items:
Escargots with Herbed Plum Tomatoes (see p. 42)
Beef with Plums (see p. 108)
Sautéed Elk Medallions (see p. 237)
Pork a l'Orange (see p. 238)
Autumn Soup (see p. 299)

(continued)

BEEF/VEAL STOCK *(CONTINUED)*
Serves 20
Yield: 2 quarts

Autumn Soup (see p. 299)
Seared Chicken Breast (see p. 359)
Veal Medallions with Port Wine Sauce and Artichokes (see p. 388)
Tomato Pilaf (see p. 479)
Lamb a la Vermouth (see p. 503)
Pastitsio (see p. 505)
Stuffed Grape Leaves (Dolmathes) (see p. 507)
Stuffed Green Peppers (see p. 508)

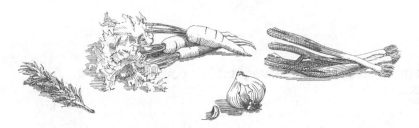

Nutrient Content Per Cup		**Percent of Calories**	**Fat Breakdown**	
Calories	50.0	5% Protein	Saturated Fat	0.0 g
Protein	0.6 g	34% Carbohydrate	Monounsaturated Fat	0.0 g
Carbohydrates	4.5 g	2% Fat	Polyunsaturated Fat	0.0 g
Fat – Total	0.1 g	59% Alcohol		
Cholesterol	0.0 mg			
Dietary Fiber	0.9 g			
Sodium	36.3 mg			

CHICKEN STOCK
Serves 20
Yield: 20 cups

6 lbs.	chicken bones
7 qts.	water
1	yellow onion, chunks
1	carrot, chunks
2 stalks	celery, chunks
2 cloves	garlic, whole
1 tsp.	crushed peppercorns
½	leek, chunks
to taste	salt

Place chicken bones in a pot filled with 7 quarts of water and slowly bring to a boil. Constantly remove the built-up foam so the stock doesn't get cloudy. Add remaining ingredients. Let simmer for about 3-4 hours. Strain through a sieve and chill.

Cook's Note: A great stock for soups, vegetables, poultry and all kinds of ragouts.

▼ This recipe is used for the following items:

Butternut Squash Soup with Apples (see p. 53)
Garlic Soup (see p. 55)
Onion Soup España (see p. 59)
Cream of Pea Soup with Shrimp (see p. 60)
Radish Soup (see p. 61)
Rice and Vegetable Soup (see p. 63)
White Bean Soup (see p. 65)
Vegetable Soup (see p. 66)
Zucchini Soup (see p. 67)
Garbanzos a la Catalana (see p. 79)
Spiced Tomato Sauce (see p. 123)
Rice with Sherry (see p. 80)
Spinach with Rice (see p. 81)
Saffron Rice with All the Trimmings (see p. 83)
Black Beans (see p. 84)
Crab in a Sherry and Brandy Sauce (see p. 91)

Tequila Prawns (see p. 96)
Swordfish with Tomatillo Sauce (see p. 98)
Braised Chicken with Almonds (see p. 103)
Chicken with Garlic (see p. 104)
Chicken with Saffron Rice (see p. 105)
Fricando (see p. 110)
Tomatoes Stuffed with Rice (see p. 155)
Chestnut Soup (see p. 160)
Creamy Carrot Soup (see p. 162)
Alsatian Onion Soup (see p. 164)
Split Pea Soup (see p. 165)
Snow Pea Zucchini Soup (see p. 168)
Tomato Consommé (see p. 169)
Cream of Watercress Soup (see p. 170)
Lentil Salad (see p. 176)
Octopus Salad (see p. 178)
Vegetables with Roasted Peppers, Mushroom and Basil Vinaigrette (see p. 188)
Rice Timbale with Artichokes (see p. 195)

(continued)

CHICKEN STOCK *(CONTINUED)*
Serves 20
Yield: 20 cups

Rice Confetti *(see p. 196)*
Lemon Herbed Rice *(see p. 197)*
Risi Bisi Rice *(see p. 198)*
Chicken Fricassée *(see p. 213)*
Chicken with Spring Vegetables
   (see p. 215)
Pork a l'Orange *(see p. 238)*
Broccoli au Gratin Crepes *(see p. 242)*
Glazed Carrots *(see p. 245)*
Carrots with "Cream" *(see p. 247)*
Château Potatoes *(see p. 253)*
Snow Peas and Shallots *(see p. 257)*
Zucchini and Potato Gratin *(see p. 262)*
Creamy Broccoli-Leek Soup *(see p. 300)*
Googoots (Italian Stew) *(see p. 303)*
Creamy Pepper Soup *(see p. 307)*
Tomato Soup *(see p. 308)*
Zuppa Pizzialo *(see p. 309)*
Mushroom Risotto *(see p. 329)*
Spinach-Herb Risotto *(see p. 330)*
Cacciatore Risotto *(see p. 332)*
Fennel Risotto *(see p. 333)*
Peppered Corn Risotto *(see p. 334)*
Whole Wheat Pasta with Vegetables
   (see p. 346)

Ricotta Cheese Tortellini with Sun-Dried
   Tomato Sauce *(see p. 350)*
Turkey, Gorgonzola Ravioli with Red
   Pepper Sauce *(see p. 351)*
Linguini with Calamari *(see p. 354)*
Chicken Cacciamani *(see p. 360)*
Chicken Marsala *(see p. 371)*
Chicken Modena Style *(see p. 372)*
Lemon Chicken Scallopini *(see p. 375)*
Cioppino *(see p. 378)*
Poached Lobster over Red Linguini
   (see p. 379)
Baked Fennel *(see p. 393)*
Marinated Vegetables *(see p. 449)*
Chicken and Lemon Soup *(see p. 451)*
Egg-Lemon Soup *(see p. 452)*
Cream of Spinach Soup *(see p. 453)*
Olive Soup *(see p. 455)*
Pilaf *(see p. 477)*
Pilaf al Greco *(see p. 482)*
Spicy Risotto with Vegetables *(see p. 483)*
White Lima Pilaki *(see p. 513)*
Avgolemono Sauce (Egg-Lemon Sauce)
   (see p. 521)

Nutrient Content Per Cup

Calories	5.7
Protein	0.2 g
Carbohydrates	1.3 g
Fat – Total	0.0 g
Cholesterol	0.0 mg
Dietary Fiber	0.3 g
Sodium	112.0 mg

Percent of Calories

11% Protein
85% Carbohydrate
 4% Fat

Fat Breakdown

Saturated Fat	0.0 g
Monounsaturated Fat	0.0 g
Polyunsaturated Fat	0.0 g

FISH STOCK
Yield: 5 quarts

6 lbs.	fish heads (any type)
7 qts.	water
1½ cups	yellow onions, cubed
2½ cups	leeks, sliced
2 cups	celery, cubed
1½ cups	mushrooms, sliced
2 cups	white wine
to taste	salt and pepper

In a large cooking pot, add water and fish heads. Bring to a boil. Remove the built-up foam as it rises to the top. Add the remaining ingredients. Cover and simmer for 3-4 hours. Strain through a sieve and chill.

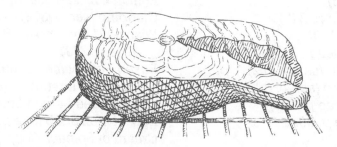

Cook's Note: This stock is a good basic foundation for many seafood dishes. Prepare ahead and freeze in small amounts. Use it in recipes throughout the year. Fish heads can be obtained from your supermarket fish counter. Just call ahead and ask to have them saved for you. This can usually be done at no cost. Salmon heads make a very flavorful stock.

Alcohol Note: The alcohol content was computed prior to cooking. Once the alcohol is heated to the boiling point, the alcohol disappears along with most of the calories from the alcohol.

FISH STOCK *(CONTINUED)*
Yield: 5 quarts

▼ This recipe is used for the following items:
Clams in a Garlic Vegetable Broth (see p. 41)
Steamed Mussels with Balsamic-Ginger Vinaigrette (see p. 45)
Spanish Prawn Cocktail (see p. 47)
Sautéed Prawns with a Spiced Tomato Marmalade (see p. 48)
Mussel Soup (see p. 58)
Cream Mussel Soup (see p. 163)
Shrimp Bisque (see p. 167)
Gratin of Seafood (see p. 223)
Baby Clam Soup (see p. 301)
Shrimp Risotto (see p. 335)
Cioppino (see p. 378)
Sherried Scallops (see p. 381)
Soup of the Sea (see p. 456)
Mussel Pilaf (see p. 480)

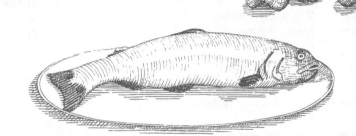

Nutrient Content Per Cup

Calories	43.6
Protein	0.6 g
Carbohydrates	3.7 g
Fat – Total	1.5 g
Cholesterol	0.0 mg
Dietary Fiber	0.8 g
Sodium	14.6 mg

Percent of Calories

5% Protein
33% Carbohydrate
29% Fat
34% Alcohol

Fat Breakdown

Saturated Fat	0.1 g
Monounsaturated Fat	0.8 g
Polyunsaturated Fat	0.4 g

VEGETABLE STOCK
Serves 20

5 Tbl.	vegetable oil
1	yellow onion, chopped
1 med.	carrot, peeled, chopped
2 stalks	celery, chopped
2 cloves	garlic, peeled
1 tsp.	crushed peppercorns
½	leek, cut into small chunks
4 cups	dry white wine
½ cup	fresh fennel, chopped
1	bay leaf
1 clove	garlic
3 lg.	tomatoes, chopped
¼ bunch	fresh basil, chopped
6 qts.	water
to taste	salt and pepper

In a large skillet, heat the oil over medium heat. Cook the onion, carrots, celery, garlic, crushed peppercorns and leek until slightly brown. Add the wine and reduce for 15-25 minutes. Add the fennel, bay leaf, garlic, tomatoes, basil and water. Simmer partially covered for 3-4 hours. Season with salt and pepper to taste. Strain through sieve and chill.

Cook's Note: A good stock for vegetarian dishes as well as seafood dishes.

% Calories as Fat — Above the HM✔ guidelines: Although this recipe has a high percentage of calories as fat (>30%), the total fat is less than 5 grams per serving. This will easily fit within your allotment of 45 grams per day. This happens most often in low-calorie recipes.

Alcohol Note: The alcohol content was computed prior to cooking. Once the alcohol is heated to the boiling point, the alcohol disappears along with most of the calories from the alcohol.

▼ This recipe is used for the following items:

Thyme Soup (see p. 64)
Garbanzos a la Catalana (see p. 79)
Swordfish with Tomatillo Sauce (see p. 98)
Fresh Tuna-Potato Stew (see p. 99)

Paella (see p. 106)
Vegetable Risotto (see p. 331)
Fennel Risotto (see p. 333)
Whole-Wheat Pasta with Vegetables (see p. 346)

Nutrient Content Per Cup

Calories	74.2
Protein	0.5 g
Carbohydrates	2.8 g
Fat – Total	3.7 g
Cholesterol	0.0 mg
Dietary Fiber	0.8 g
Sodium	5.9 mg

Percent of Calories

2%	Protein
15%	Carbohydrate
43%	Fat
40%	Alcohol

Fat Breakdown

Saturated Fat	0.5 g
Monounsaturated Fat	0.9 g
Polyunsaturated Fat	2.1 g

SAGE WINE REDUCTION
Serves 6

1 cup	vegetables, chopped
2 Tbl.	canola oil
2 Tbl.	sage
1 Tbl.	garlic, roasted
1 tsp.	tomato paste
1 cup	port wine
12 cups	veal stock *(see p. 538)*
1 Tbl.	fresh lemon juice

In a saucepan, heat the oil and sauté the vegetables and garlic. Add remaining ingredients and simmer 40-60 minutes until sauce starts to thicken. Remove and strain.

Cook's Note: This sauce can be made ahead and even frozen in ice cube trays for better portioning. Choose any vegetables you have available such as carrots, onions, celery, etc. This is especially good for roasted duck, chicken, veal and even lean pork.

Alcohol Note: The alcohol content was computed prior to cooking. Once the alcohol is heated to the boiling point, the alcohol disappears along with most of the calories from the alcohol.

▼ This recipe is used for the following item:
Chicken with Apricot Chutney (see p. 208)

Nutrient Content Per ¼ Cup

Calories	120.0
Protein	1.2 g
Carbohydrates	7.2 g
Fat – Total	5.1 g
Cholesterol	0.0 mg
Dietary Fiber	1.6 g
Sodium	10.1 mg

Percent of Calories

4% Protein
24% Carbohydrate
37% Fat
35% Alcohol

Fat Breakdown

Saturated Fat	0.5 g
Monounsaturated Fat	2.0 g
Polyunsaturated Fat	2.3 g

APPLE CHUTNEY
Serves 30

8 med.	granny smith apples, peeled, seeded, cubed
2	yellow onions, diced
1½ cups	raisins
1 cup	rice vinegar
1 cup	brown sugar
2 tsp.	salt
1 Tbl.	prepared mustard
1 cup	white wine
dash	cayenne pepper
1 tsp.	turmeric

In a large pot, combine all ingredients except cayenne pepper and turmeric. Simmer over medium heat for 30 minutes or until it becomes very sticky. Add the cayenne pepper and turmeric. Chill.

Cook's Note: It may be refrigerated for 2-3 weeks. A wonderful accompaniment to barbecued meats such as pork, chicken and even lamb.

Alcohol Note: The alcohol content was computed prior to cooking. Once the alcohol is heated to the boiling point, the alcohol disappears along with most of the calories from the alcohol.

Nutrient Content Per Tablespoon

Calories	74.7
Protein	0.5 g
Carbohydrates	18.1 g
Fat – Total	0.2 g
Cholesterol	0.0 mg
Dietary Fiber	1.4 g
Sodium	152.0 mg

Percent of Calories

2% Protein
89% Carbohydrate
2% Fat
6% Alcohol

Fat Breakdown

Saturated Fat	0.0 g
Monounsaturated Fat	0.0 g
Polyunsaturated Fat	0.1 g

APRICOT CHUTNEY
Serves 20

1 lb.	dried apricots, sliced
¼ lb.	red peppers, roasted, diced *(see p. 13)*
¼ lb.	onion, diced fine
½ cup	rice vinegar
2 Tbl.	brown sugar
½ tsp.	turmeric
¼ tsp.	cajun pepper
½ tsp.	mustard
dash	salt
1 cup	white wine

In a saucepan, combine all ingredients. Cook slowly until it becomes sticky. Chill and refrigerate.

Cook's Note: A great accompaniment for lamb, poultry, turkey or game dishes, or on toasted French bread.

Alcohol Note: The alcohol content was computed prior to cooking. Once the alcohol is heated to the boiling point, the alcohol disappears along with most of the calories from the alcohol.

▼ This recipe is used for the following item:
Chicken with Apricot Chutney (see p. 208)

Nutrient Content Per 1½ Tablespoons

		Percent of Calories	**Fat Breakdown**	
Calories	70.0	5% Protein	Saturated Fat	0.0 g
Protein	1.0 g	84% Carbohydrate	Monounsaturated Fat	0.0 g
Carbohydrates	16.2 g	2% Fat	Polyunsaturated Fat	0.0 g
Fat – Total	0.1 g	9% Alcohol		
Cholesterol	0.0 mg			
Dietary Fiber	2.0 g			
Sodium	9.9 mg			

CORN AND PEPPER CHUTNEY
Serves 8

3 cups	corn, fresh or frozen
1½ cups	sweet red peppers, seeded, diced
½ med.	yellow onion, diced
2 Tbl.	olive oil
½ cup	tomatoes, peeled, seeded, diced
½ cup	sugar
¼ cup	mustard seed, ground for better flavor
½ cup	rice vinegar
2 Tbl.	turmeric
to taste	salt and pepper

In a medium non-stick pot, sauté the onion in the olive oil over medium heat. Glaze the onions, but do not let them brown. Add the corn, pepper, tomatoes, sugar and mustard seeds. Cook for 3-5 minutes stirring constantly. Add the rice vinegar and turmeric, stir well. Cook for 5-10 minutes until it becomes a thick ragout (stew-like). Season with salt and pepper to taste. Chill.

Serve as a garnish.

Cook's Note: Makes 1 quart. It may be stored in the refrigerator for up to 1 week. It is great with barbecued chicken, grilled beef and seafood.

Nutrient Content Per Serving

Calories	190.0
Protein	4.0 g
Carbohydrates	34.4 g
Fat – Total	6.0 g
Cholesterol	0.0 mg
Dietary Fiber	4.6 g
Sodium	13.3 mg

Percent of Calories

8% Protein
66% Carbohydrate
26% Fat

Fat Breakdown

Saturated Fat	0.7 g
Monounsaturated Fat	3.8 g
Polyunsaturated Fat	1.0 g

CRANBERRY CHUTNEY
Serves 30

2 lbs.	fresh cranberries
2 cups	light brown sugar
2 cups	fresh orange juice
1 cup	white wine
2	lemons, zest of
2	oranges, zest of
2 tsp.	dry mustard

In a saucepan, combine all ingredients and cook slowly over medium heat. Stir constantly until sticky.

Cook's Note: Excellent for the holidays. It goes well with roasted turkey and wild game, patés and terrines. It may be refrigerated for 2 weeks.

Alcohol Note: The alcohol content was computed prior to cooking. Once the alcohol is heated to the boiling point, the alcohol disappears along with most of the calories from the alcohol.

Nutrient Content Per Serving

Calories	63.8
Protein	0.2 g
Carbohydrates	15.0 g
Fat – Total	0.1 g
Cholesterol	0.0 mg
Dietary Fiber	1.3 g
Sodium	4.6 mg

Percent of Calories

1% Protein
90% Carbohydrate
1% Fat
8% Alcohol

Fat Breakdown

Saturated Fat	0.0 g
Monounsaturated Fat	0.0 g
Polyunsaturated Fat	0.0 g

MINT CHUTNEY
Serves 10

35 sprigs	fresh mint
2	green chili peppers, seeded
1 tsp.	fresh gingerroot, chopped
2	scallions, sliced fine
1 clove	garlic, minced
2	limes, juice of

Combine all ingredients in a food processor. Pulse to desired consistency.

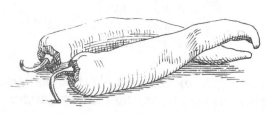

Cook's Note: Makes 1½ cups. A great enhancement to lamb.

Nutrient Content Per Serving

Calories	5.3
Protein	0.2 g
Carbohydrates	1.3 g
Fat – Total	0.0 g
Cholesterol	0.0 mg
Dietary Fiber	0.2 g
Sodium	0.9 mg

Percent of Calories

15% Protein
82% Carbohydrate
3% Fat

Fat Breakdown

Saturated Fat	0.0 g
Monounsaturated Fat	0.0 g
Polyunsaturated Fat	0.0 g

TOMATO MARMALADE
Serves 20

1 Tbl.	olive oil
6 Tbl.	shallots, chopped fine
18 cloves	garlic, chopped fine
2 cups	tomatoes, peeled, seeded, diced
¼ cup	capers, rinsed, drained
½ cup	white wine
¼ oz.	fresh cilantro, chopped
2 Tbl.	old-fashioned balsamic dressing *(see p. 409)*
1 Tbl.	honey
1½ tsp.	flaked peppers

Heat oil in a large non-stick skillet over medium heat. Sauté shallots and garlic until fragrant. Add tomatoes, capers and white wine. Simmer 15-20 minutes or until the tomatoes start to get sticky and thick. Remove from stove and add remaining ingredients. Cool.

Cook's Note: It may be stored in the refrigerator for 1-2 weeks. This is delicious on toasted french bread as an appetizer. It is also a great accompaniment to grilled meat or seafood.

Alcohol Note: The alcohol content was computed prior to cooking. Once the alcohol is heated to the boiling point, the alcohol disappears along with most of the calories from the alcohol.

▼ This recipe is used for the following item:
Sautéed Prawns with a Spiced Tomato Marmalade (see p. 48)

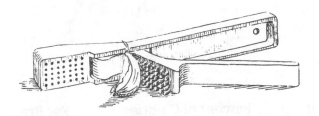

Nutrient Content Per Serving

Calories	28.6
Protein	0.4 g
Carbohydrates	4.2 g
Fat – Total	0.9 g
Cholesterol	0.0 mg
Dietary Fiber	0.5 g
Sodium	24.6 mg

Percent of Calories

6% Protein
55% Carbohydrate
26% Fat
13% Alcohol

Fat Breakdown

Saturated Fat	0.9 g
Monounsaturated Fat	0.6 g
Polyunsaturated Fat	0.1 g

TOMATO RELISH
Serves 6
Yield: 2½ cups

2 cups	tomatoes, peeled, seeded	
¼ cup	yellow onion	
1	jalapeño pepper	
2 Tbl.	red wine vinegar	
2 tsp.	fresh cilantro	

Combine all ingredients in a food processor. Pulse until you obtain a relish consistency. Chill.

Cook's Note: This may be stored in the refrigerator for 2 days only. It goes well with grilled items like poultry, seafood and veal steaks and can be used with Mexican dishes as well.

▼ This recipe is used for the following items:
Grilled Swordfish Steak (see p. 97)
Grilled Swordfish Steak Sandwich (see p. 218)
Tomato and Roasted Pepper Crostini (see p. 293)

Nutrient Content Per Serving

Calories	15.5
Protein	0.6 g
Carbohydrates	3.6 g
Fat – Total	0.2 g
Cholesterol	0.0 mg
Dietary Fiber	0.9 g
Sodium	26.3 mg

Percent of Calories
13% Protein
77% Carbohydrate
10% Fat

Fat Breakdown

Saturated Fat	0.0 g
Monounsaturated Fat	0.0 g
Polyunsaturated Fat	0.1 g

RADISH RELISH
Serves 15

1 cup	radishes, diced
1 cup	zucchini, diced
1½ cups	tomatoes, peeled, seeded, diced
1 Tbl.	lime juice
1 Tbl.	rice vinegar
½ cup	chives
¼ cup	red onion, diced
to taste	salt and pepper

Combine all ingredients and marinate for 30 minutes.

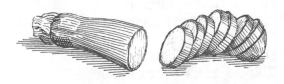

Cook's Note: This has a very strong flavor. It is so tasty it can be eaten alone or with grilled seafood such as swordfish, salmon and snapper. It can also enhance other salads. Try making this in your food processor using a pulsing technique.

Nutrient Content Per Serving

Calories	7.4
Protein	0.3 g
Carbohydrates	1.6 g
Fat – Total	0.1 g
Cholesterol	0.0 mg
Dietary Fiber	0.4 g
Sodium	3.2 mg

Percent of Calories

14% Protein	
75% Carbohydrate	
12% Fat	

Fat Breakdown

Saturated Fat	0.0 g
Monounsaturated Fat	0.0 g
Polyunsaturated Fat	0.0 g

TOMATO RAGOUT

Serves 10

15 oz.	canned tomatoes, peeled, drained, chopped, reserve juice
4 cloves	garlic, minced
2	shallots, chopped
1 Tbl.	olive oil
12 cups	V-8 juice, low-sodium
2 Tbl.	black olives, chopped
¼ cup	fresh basil, sliced thinly
10	fresh tomatoes, seeded, peeled, chopped
to taste	salt and pepper

In a large non-stick frying pan, sauté garlic and shallots in oil. Add tomato juice reserved from canned tomatoes, V-8 juice, shallots and garlic. Reduce liquid over medium heat, until it thickens. Remove from heat and chill. When chilled, add remaining ingredients. Season with salt and pepper to taste. Refrigerate for 2 hours to allow flavors to blend. Heat through before serving.

Variation:

■ Add 4 cups sliced mushrooms for a mushroom ragout.

Cook's Note: It may be served with pasta, seafood and poultry dishes. The completed Ragout may be frozen and kept up to 3 months.

▼ This recipe is used for the following items:
Grilled Shrimp with Spiced Tomato Sauce (see p. 95)
Cacciatore Risotto (see p. 332)
Fancy Polenta (see p. 337)
Angel-Hair Pasta with Fresh Basil Tomato Sauce (see p. 344)
Manicotti or Stuffed Shells (see p. 348)
Angel-Hair Pasta with Seared Scallops and Prawns (see p. 357)
Sausage and Pepper Sandwich (see p. 385)

Nutrient Content Per ½ Cup Serving		**Percent of Calories**	**Fat Breakdown**	
Calories	107.0	11% Protein	Saturated Fat	0.3 g
Protein	3.4 g	71% Carbohydrate	Monounsaturated Fat	1.3
Carbohydrates	21.7 g	17% Fat	Polyunsaturated Fat	0.5 g
Fat – Total	2.4 g			
Cholesterol	0.0 mg			
Dietary Fiber	4.1 g			
Sodium	98.1 mg			

WHOLE-GRAIN MUSTARD SAUCE
Serves 6

¼ cup	whole-grain mustard
¼ cup	Sauterne wine
¼ cup	lemon thyme
dash	red pepper flakes
½ cup	mayonnaise, fat-free
to taste	salt and pepper
¼ cup	nonfat plain yogurt, drained

Simmer Sauterne with fresh thyme, whole-grain mustard and red pepper flakes for about 10 minutes over medium heat. Remove from heat and chill. Blend with remaining ingredients. Season with salt and pepper if desired.

Cook's Note: Lemon thyme is a fresh herb found in specialty markets. You may substitute plain thyme. This is very good with smoked and cured seafood.

Alcohol Note: The alcohol content was computed prior to cooking. Once the alcohol is heated to the boiling point, the alcohol disappears along with most of the calories from the alcohol.

▼ This recipe is used for the following items:
Charred Buffalo Carpaccio (see p. 113)
Chilled Barbecued Prawns with Whole-Grain Mustard Sauce (see p. 157)

Nutrient Content Per Serving

Calories	34.3
Protein	1.1 g
Carbohydrates	5.1 g
Fat – Total	0.5 g
Cholesterol	0.2 mg
Dietary Fiber	0.3 g
Sodium	364.0 mg

Percent of Calories

12% Protein
57% Carbohydrate
13% Fat
18% Alcohol

Fat Breakdown

Saturated Fat	0.0 g
Monounsaturated Fat	0.4 g
Polyunsaturated Fat	0.0 g

BECHAMEL SAUCE

Yield: 3 cups

1½ Tbl.	liquid margarine
2 Tbl.	white flour
3 cups	skim milk
3 Tbl.	cornstarch
¼ cup	parmesan cheese, grated
¼ tsp.	nutmeg, fresh grated
¼ tsp.	white pepper

In a saucepan, melt margarine. Add flour, mix well and cook over low heat for 3 minutes. Whisk in milk. Cook 5 minutes. Dissolve 3 tablespoons cornstarch in 3 tablespoons of water, whisk into milk. Cook until mixture thickens, stirring constantly with a wire whisk. Add parmesan, nutmeg and pepper.

Cook's Note: It may be served over pasta, rice or vegetables.

% Calories as Fat — Above the HM✔ guidelines: Although this recipe has a high percentage of calories as fat (>30%), the total fat is less than 5 grams per serving. This will easily fit within your allotment of 45 grams per day. This happens most often in low-calorie recipes.

▼ This recipe is used for the following items:
Vegetable Canalon (see p. 87)
Canalon with Seafood (see p. 88)
Velvet Seafood Platter (see p. 100)
Broccoli with Bechamel Sauce (see p. 113)
Rice Timbale with Artichokes (see p. 195)
Zuppa Pizzialo (see p. 309)
Broccoli-Spinach Lasagna (see p. 353)
Pastitsio (see p. 505)

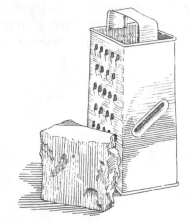

Nutrient Content Per ½ Cup

Calories	112.0
Protein	6.3 g
Carbohydrates	11.7 g
Fat – Total	4.4 g
Cholesterol	5.5 mg
Dietary Fiber	0.1 g
Sodium	168.0 mg

Percent of Calories

23% Protein
42% Carbohydrate
35% Fat

Fat Breakdown

Saturated Fat	1.4 g
Monounsaturated Fat	1.4 g
Polyunsaturated Fat	1.3 g

CORIANDER FISH MARINADE

2 Tbl.	lemon juice
1 Tbl.	olive oil
1 Tbl.	coriander

Combine all ingredients in a bowl. Use to marinate fish.

Cook's Note: When you marinate the fish, some of the fat is transferred to the fish. You have the option of omitting the olive oil.

% Calories as Fat — Above the HM✔ guidelines: Although this recipe has a high percentage of calories as fat (>30%), the total fat is less than 5 grams per serving. This will easily fit within your allotment of 45 grams per day. This happens most often in low-calorie recipes.

▼ This recipe is used for the following items:
Chilled Barbecued Prawns with Whole-Grain Mustard Sauce (see p. 157)
Grilled Swordfish Steak Sandwich (see p. 218)
Fresh Grilled Swordfish Salad (see p. 319)
Grilled Snapper (see p. 496)

Nutrient Content Per Recipe (Recipe is for 4 servings)

Calories	35.5
Protein	0.2 g
Carbohydrates	1.4 g
Fat – Total	3.6 g
Cholesterol	0.0 mg
Dietary Fiber	0.4 g
Sodium	0.5 mg

Percent of Calories

2% Protein
14% Carbohydrate
84% Fat

Fat Breakdown

Saturated Fat	0.8 g
Monounsaturated Fat	2.7 g
Polyunsaturated Fat	0.3 g

PAPRIKA FISH MARINADE

2 Tbl.	lemon juice, fresh
2 Tbl.	lime juice, fresh
1 Tbl.	olive oil
1 tsp.	paprika

Combine all ingredients in a bowl. Use to marinate fish.

Cook's Note: When you marinate the fish, some of the fat is transferred to the fish. You have the option of omitting the olive oil.

% Calories as Fat — Above the HM✔ guidelines: Although this recipe has a high percentage of calories as fat (>30%), the total fat is less than 5 grams per serving. This will easily fit within your allotment of 45 grams per day. This happens most often in low-calorie recipes.

▼ This recipe is used for the following items:
Chilled Barbecued Prawns with Whole-Grain Mustard Sauce (see p. 157)
Grilled Italian Fish Sandwich (see p. 377)

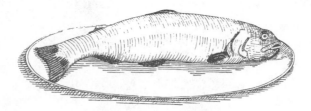

Nutrient Content Per Recipe
(Recipe is for 4 servings)

Calories	35.5
Protein	0.1 g
Carbohydrates	1.7 g
Fat – Total	3.5 g
Cholesterol	0.0 mg
Dietary Fiber	0.3 g
Sodium	0.3 mg

Percent of Calories

2% Protein
17% Carbohydrate
81% Fat

Fat Breakdown

Saturated Fat	0.5 g
Monounsaturated Fat	2.5 g
Polyunsaturated Fat	0.3 g

CREAMY CUCUMBER DRESSING
Serves 15

1	cucumber, with peel, seeded, cut in chunks
1 cup	cottage cheese, nonfat
¼ cup	yogurt, nonfat
1 Tbl.	horseradish
1 Tbl.	honey
1 tsp.	dill weed, fresh or dried
¼ cup	rice vinegar

Combine all ingredients in a food processor. Process until smooth. Let sit in refrigerator 1 hour before serving.

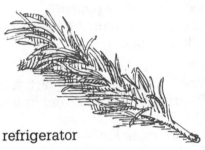

Cook's Note: A cool and light dressing. It may be stored in the refrigerator up to 1 week. It is good on pasta salad, too.

Nutrient Content Per 2-Tablespoon Serving

Calories	19.5
Protein	2.4 g
Carbohydrates	2.8 g
Fat – Total	0.0 g
Cholesterol	0.7 mg
Dietary Fiber	0.2 g
Sodium	60.8 mg

Percent of Calories

46% Protein
53% Carbohydrate
 2% Fat

Fat Breakdown

Saturated Fat	0.0 g
Monounsaturated Fat	0.0 g
Polyunsaturated Fat	0.0 g

RASPBERRY DRESSING
Serves 30
Yield: 4 cups

2 cups	raspberry vinegar
½ cup	canola oil
1 Tbl.	salt
dash	white pepper
1½ cups	raspberries, fresh or frozen
1 Tbl.	sugar

Combine all ingredients in a blender and mix well.

Cook's Note: Makes 1 quart. It may be stored in the refrigerator for 2-3 weeks. It compliments all varieties of lettuce and grilled, as well as steamed and poached seafood and poultry.

% Calories as Fat — Above the HM✓ guidelines: Although this recipe has a high percentage of calories as fat (>30%), the total fat is less than 5 grams per serving. This will easily fit within your allotment of 45 grams per day. This happens most often in low-calorie recipes.

Nutrient Content Per 2-Tablespoon Serving

Calories	39.0
Protein	0.1 g
Carbohydrates	2.1 g
Fat – Total	3.7 g
Cholesterol	0.0 mg
Dietary Fiber	0.3 g
Sodium	213.0 mg

Percent of Calories

1% Protein
20% Carbohydrate
79% Fat

Fat Breakdown

Saturated Fat	0.5 g
Monounsaturated Fat	0.9 g
Polyunsaturated Fa	2.1 g

GINGER BALSAMIC VINAIGRETTE
Serves 30

2 cups	balsamic vinegar
⅔ cup	canola oil
¼ cup	shallots, chopped
to taste	freshly ground black pepper
1 bunch	fresh basil, chopped
¼ bunch	fresh thyme, chopped
½ cup	fresh ginger, peeled, chopped

Combine all ingredients in a blender or food processor. Process until smooth.

Cook's Note: Very good for marinating poultry, lamb, seafood and vegetables for salads. It may be refrigerated for 2-3 weeks.

▼ This recipe is used for the following items:
Steamed Mussels with Balsamic-Ginger Vinaigrette (see p. 45)
Grilled Vegetarian Sandwich (see p. 343)

Nutrient Content Per 2-Tablespoon Serving

Calories	47.0
Protein	0.1 g
Carbohydrates	1.5 g
Fat – Total	4.8 g
Cholesterol	0.0 mg
Dietary Fiber	0.1 g
Sodium	0.6 mg

Percent of Calories

1% Protein
12% Carbohydrate
87% Fat

Fat Breakdown

Saturated Fat	0.3 g
Monounsaturated Fat	2.8 g
Polyunsaturated Fat	1.4 g

ROASTED SHALLOT-HONEY VINAIGRETTE
Serves 12

6 lg.	shallots, left whole
¼ cup	olive oil
¾ cup	sherry wine vinegar
½ cup	honey
1½ Tbl.	dijon mustard
1½ tsp.	garlic, minced
to taste	salt and pepper

Place shallots on a baking sheet. Drizzle a few drops of olive oil over shallots. Bake in a preheated 350° F oven, until golden. Peel and cool.

Combine shallots and remaining ingredients in a blender and mix until smooth. Add salt and pepper to taste.

Cook's Note: This dressing will last 2-3 weeks in the refrigerator. If you measure the olive oil in your measuring cup first and the honey second, the honey will just slide out. Serve with your favorite tossed salads and fruit salads. Makes a great marinade for chicken.

% Calories as Fat — Above the HM✔ guidelines: Although this recipe has a high percentage of calories as fat (>30%), the total fat is less than 5 grams per serving. This will easily fit within your allotment of 45 grams per day. This happens most often in low-calorie recipes.

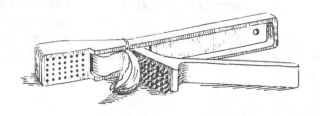

**Nutrient Content Per
2-Tablespoon Serving**

Calories	88.0
Protein	0.2 g
Carbohydrates	13.0 g
Fat – Total	4.6 g
Cholesterol	0.0 mg
Dietary Fiber	0.1 g
Sodium	25.4 mg

Percent of Calories

1% Protein
55% Carbohydrate
44% Fat

Fat Breakdown

Saturated Fat	0.6 g
Monounsaturated Fat	3.4 g
Polyunsaturated Fat	0.4 g

TARRAGON VINAIGRETTE
Serves 12

½ cup   apple juice
½ cup   lemon juice
3 Tbl.   dijon mustard
2 tsp.   tarragon leaves, dry or fresh,
              chopped
¾ tsp.   sugar
⅓ cup   canola oil

Combine all ingredients except oil. Mix well. Slowly whisk in oil.

Cook's Note: A good overall salad dressing. May refrigerate the dressing for 2-3 weeks.

Nutrient Content Per 2-Tablespoon Serving		**Percent of Calories**	**Fat Breakdown**	
Calories	63.9	1% Protein	Saturated Fat	0.4 g
Protein	0.2 g	14% Carbohydrate	Monounsaturated Fat	3.7 g
Carbohydrates	2.4 g	82% Fat	Polyunsaturated Fat	1.8 g
Fat – Total	6.2 g			
Cholesterol	0.0 mg			
Dietary Fiber	0.1 g			
Sodium	51.4 mg			

BASIL MUSTARD-SEED OIL
Yield: ¾ cup

2 cups	apple juice
¼ cup	sweet port wine
1 bunch	fresh basil
2	shallots
2 cloves	garlic
¼ cup	whole-grain dijon-type mustard
¼ cup	olive oil
¼ cup	balsamic vinegar
to taste	salt and pepper

In a saucepan, reduce the apple juice and wine to ½ cup. Then cool.

Transfer the mixture to a blender. Add the basil, shallots, garlic and mustard. Start blending and slowly add the oil and vinegar. When blended, season with salt and pepper to taste.

Cook's Note: This is good for smoked seafoods like salmon or smoked or roasted meats. Makes a nice spread for sandwiches.

% Calories as Fat — Above the HM✔ guidelines: Although this recipe has a high percentage of calories as fat (>30%), the total fat is less than 5 grams per serving. This will easily fit within your allotment of 45 grams per day. This happens most often in low-calorie recipes.

Alcohol Note: The alcohol content was computed prior to cooking. Once the alcohol is heated to the boiling point, the alcohol disappears along with most of the calories from the alcohol.

▼ This recipe is used for the following item:
Charred Buffalo Carpaccio (see p. 113)

Nutrient Content Per	1 Tablespoon	Percent of Calories		Fat Breakdown	
Calories	68.8	2% Protein		Saturated Fat	0.6 g
Protein	0.3 g	33% Carbohydrate		Monounsaturated Fat	3.5 g
Carbohydrates	5.9 g	60% Fat		Polyunsaturated Fat	0.4 g
Fat – Total	4.8 g	5% Alcohol			
Cholesterol	0.0 mg				
Dietary Fiber	0.2 g				
Sodium	67.0 mg				

VANILLA OIL
Serves 96

2 cups	olive oil
3	vanilla beans, split open

Put the vanilla beans into the oil. Let sit at room temperature about 48 hours. Smell the aroma — unbelievable!

Cook's Note: Use the oil in salad dressings and desserts. Keep it refrigerated until ready to use. This recipe is purely a fat because it is oil. Therefore, all the calories come from fat. When you use the vanilla oil, you will be using small quantities.

▼ This recipe is used for the following items:
Mango Vanilla Dressing (see p. 125)
Poached Lobster over Red Linguini (see p. 379)

**Nutrient Content Per
1-Teaspoon Serving**

Calories	39.8
Protein	0.0 g
Carbohydrates	0.0 g
Fat – Total	4.5 g
Cholesterol	0.0 mg
Dietary Fiber	0.0 g
Sodium	0.0 mg

Percent of Calories
0% Protein
0% Carbohydrate
100% Fat

Fat Breakdown

Saturated Fat	0.6 g
Monounsaturated Fat	3.3 g
Polyunsaturated Fat	0.4 g

SWEET COFFEE "CREAM"
Serves 8

1 cup	skim milk
⅓ cup	non-fat dry milk powder
1 tsp.	lite corn syrup
½ tsp.	vanilla (use white vanilla if you have it)

In a saucepan, combine all ingredients and heat until powdered milk and corn syrup are dissolved. Chill. Serve with coffee or espresso.

Cook's Note: May flavor with amaretto or cherry brandy.

Nutrient Content Per Serving

Calories	32.1
Protein	2.9 g
Carbohydrates	4.8 g
Fat – Total	0.1 g
Cholesterol	1.5 mg
Dietary Fiber	0.0 g
Sodium	43.5 mg

Percent of Calories

36% Protein
61% Carbohydrate
3% Fat

Fat Breakdown

Saturated Fat	0.1 g
Monounsaturated Fat	0.0 g
Polyunsaturated Fat	0.0 g

Pears with Ricotta Cheese Topping *(page 427)*
Sicilian Cassata with
Semi-Sweet Chocolate Frosting *(page 419)*

ITALIAN DESSERTS

Baklava *(page 524)*
Figs 'n Cream *(page 525)*
Orange Yogurt Cake *(page 529)*

GREEK DESSERTS

Cherry Souffle *(page 275)*

**FRENCH
DESSERT**

Sponge Cake Roll *(page 140)*
Caramel Custard *(page 134)*

SPANISH DESSERTS

ORDER FORM

Send to: HealthMark Centers, Inc., 5889 Greenwood Plaza Blvd., Suite 200
Englewood, CO 80111; (303) 694-5060

NAME _____ TELEPHONE _____ (day) _____ (eve)

STREET ADDRESS _____

CITY/STATE/ZIP _____

	Quantity	Price	Tax*	Total
Viva La Mediterranean *A Cultural Feast from HealthMark*	_____	$21.95	$.83 per book	_____
Delitefully HealthMark	_____	$10.00	$.38 per book	_____
The HealthMark Program for Life	_____	$15.00	$.57 per book	_____

Plus $4.00 shipping and handling for first copy, $2.00 for each additional _____

TOTAL ENCLOSED _____

Please make checks payable to: HealthMark Centers, Inc. Please do not send cash. Sorry, no COD's.
*Colorado Residents only

✂ -

ORDER FORM

Send to: HealthMark Centers, Inc., 5889 Greenwood Plaza Blvd., Suite 200
Englewood, CO 80111; (303) 694-5060

NAME _____ TELEPHONE _____ (day) _____ (eve)

STREET ADDRESS _____

CITY/STATE/ZIP _____

	Quantity	Price	Tax*	Total
Viva La Mediterranean *A Cultural Feast from HealthMark*	_____	$21.95	$.83 per book	_____
Delitefully HealthMark	_____	$10.00	$.38 per book	_____
The HealthMark Program for Life	_____	$15.00	$.57 per book	_____

Plus $4.00 shipping and handling for first copy, $2.00 for each additional _____

TOTAL ENCLOSED _____

Please make checks payable to: HealthMark Centers, Inc. Please do not send cash. Sorry, no COD's.
*Colorado Residents only